METHUEN'S
HANDBOOKS OF ARCHAEOLOGY

West Africa before
the Europeans

West Africa before the Europeans

ARCHAEOLOGY & PREHISTORY

Oliver Davies

METHUEN & CO LTD

11 New Fetter Lane London EC4

First published in 1967 by
Methuen & Co. Ltd,
11 New Fetter Lane, London EC4
© O. Davies 1967
Printed and bound in Great Britain by
The Camelot Press Ltd,
Southampton

Distributed in the U.S.A. by
Barnes & Noble, Inc.

IN MEMORIAM
CANON ISAAC TAYLOR
HAROLD PEAKE

CONTENTS

ABBREVIATIONS

ARGS   *Geological Survey of the Gold Coast (Ghana), Annual Report* (Accra)

Asequa   *Association sénégalaise pour l'Etude du Quaternaire de l'Ouest Africain, Bulletin de Liaison* (Dakar)

CEHSAOF *Comité d'Etudes historiques et scientifiques de l'A.O.F., Bulletin* (Dakar)

CIAO   *Conférence int. des Africanistes de l'Ouest, Comptes rendus*

CISPP   *Congrès int. des Sciences préhistoriques et protohistoriques, Comptes rendus*

CPF   *Congrès préhistoriques de France, Comptes rendus* (Paris)

CRAS   *Académie des Sciences, Comptes rendus* (Paris)

ESén   *Etudes sénégalaises* (Dakar)

GJS   *Ghana Journal of Science* (Accra)

GSFNB   *Geological Survey of the Gold Coast (Ghana), Field note-books*

IEC   *Institut d'Etudes centrafricaines, Bulletin* (Brazzaville)

IFAN   *Institut français d'Afrique noire, Bulletin* (Dakar); also *IFAN Mémoires*

Inqua   *International Quaternary Association, Reports*

IRS   *Institut de Recherches sahariennes, Mémoires et Travaux* (Algiers)

LAPE   *Libyca, Anthropologie—Archéologie préhistoriques* (and similar titles), Algiers

NA   *Notes africaines* (Dakar)

RGD   *Revue de Géomorphologie dynamique* (Paris)

RGPGD   *Revue de Géographie physique et de Géologie dynamique* (Paris)

SAAB   *South African Archaeological Bulletin* (Claremont)

SAfr   *Société des Africanistes, Journal* (Paris)

SAP   *Société d'Anthropologie de Paris, Bulletin et Mémoires*

SGFB   *Société géologique de France, Bulletin* (Paris)

SGFCR   *Société géologique de France, Comptes rendus des Séances*

SHNAN	*Société d'Histoire naturelle de l'Afrique du Nord, Bulletin* (Algiers)
SPF	*Société préhistorique française, Bulletin* (Paris)
SPF CR	*Société préhistorique française, Comptes rendus* (from 1964)
WASA	*West African Science Association, Journal* (London)

PREFACE

At the end of 1964 I published a book entitled *The Quaternary in the Coastlands of Guinea*. The text had been completed at the end of 1960. It was intended to be a detailed account of the quaternary geological record and the Stone Age in West Africa; and in fact, a large part of it is based on my own field-work, because extremely little had been known about the prehistory of most West African territories. A slight attempt had been made by that time to explore Nigeria. The efforts of French scholars, apart from observations in the neighbourhood of the cities of Dakar and Bamako, where prehistorians were stationed, had been directed principally to the southern Sahara. This region I consider to be outside my own studies, and I have been little interested in it, because it appears that almost everywhere artefacts of all periods lie on the surface, without stratification. Being stationed in Ghana, I devoted myself to the coast, forest and wooded savannah, where quaternary geology determines stratification and prehistory provides the zone-fossils.

Being a record of field-work, my previous book paid attention to topography and other details which must be recorded but are not of general interest. It was not anticipated that it would be widely purchased except by libraries. The present book treats roughly the same field from a different angle. There is less detail and more general discussion. This book is intended rather for educated readers and for university students. It also has much to add to the previous one, the results of five years' further field-work at a time when the tempo of research is quickening, and a chapter on the early Iron Age down to the fifteenth century. I have referred frequently to my previous book and have borrowed some illustrations from it, where they are the best at present available; but the present book contributes much that is new; and where possible, I have used new illustrations, as there is much material lying unpublished.

We are reaching the stage when the prehistory of West Africa will break up locally, each section directed by the authority of a separate government. Several African governments are conscious of the need to foster archaeological research, and there are in some centres groups of prehistorians who are ready to contribute. The old Institut français d'Afrique noire has been dismembered; in fact, only a small part of its effort was devoted to prehistory, and its excellent publications continue to be issued from Dakar. But we would congratulate a number of local institutions which have arisen, the Association sénégalaise pour l'Etude du Quaternaire in Dakar, the Centre tchadien pour les Sciences humaines at Fort Lamy, the Institut des Recherches du Mali at Bamako, and the Société préhistorique gabonaise at Libreville. The Historical Societies of Ghana and Nigeria are showing more interest in archaeology and giving it a good deal of their publication space. In ten years we are likely to see an archaeological organization and probably a periodical in nearly every West African state.

There is a danger that political rivalries, unconnected with scientific work, may increase difficulties of communication between African territories. It is now not easy to cross many land frontiers. Hence the great importance of international congresses, especially the Panafrican Congress on Prehistory, at which we can meet our opposite numbers. It is to be hoped that scientific work will not be impeded by unsympathetic secret police or immigration officials; that, in accordance with the recommendations of Unesco, difficulties will not be put in the way of congress delegates, and that the Panafrican Congress will continue from strength to strength, across frontiers which to us are ephemeral, and devoting itself to pure science without the mud of political propaganda.

It is by now possible to give a framework for West African prehistory and at least for the later Quaternary, without forcibly adapting the somewhat suspect frame of East Africa. This has been aided by coastal studies, which until fifteen years ago had been neglected everywhere south of the Sahara. Our evidence is still scanty for formations earlier than 50,000 ± years ago. Previously human occupation had perhaps been patchy. West Africa being in large part a shield, sediments earlier than the Late Quaternary have seldom survived. The major basins of sedimentation had sunk too rapidly for their older phases to be accessible; and the west coast also seems to have foundered.

Yet even within the Late Quaternary the gaps in our knowledge are still enormous. Regions the size of a major European state remain totally unexplored. I am a believer in a thorough surface survey before launching out on excavation. With the West African climate, poor communications and difficulties of living conditions it would take fifty archaeologists at least five years to carry through an adequate surface coverage of the sub-continent. At the same time, urgent rescue work would provide a good provisional picture of the stratification. At present there is no one to watch public works or to keep a record of observations in the large centres. It has not even been possible to watch building in Accra and Kumasi, let alone the many other cities of West Africa. At best, we have a fairly comprehensive record of the university site at Legon. Despite the gaps, however, and despite the risk of mistakes, I think it worth while to put out this book as a foundation for future knowledge and a stimulus to future archaeologists to point out where it is wrong.

I have alluded not infrequently to work in Nigeria. But I consider that Nigeria falls outside the scope of this book, because its own Antiquities Service is rapidly collecting the material to describe its prehistory. There is still much to learn there. But as I hope that in five years a comprehensive 'Prehistory of Nigeria' may come from the printer, it is presumptuous at this moment to do more than mention Nigerian antiquities by way of comparison with lands to the west. Moreover, it is almost certain that Nigeria has special problems. Its position on the angle of the Gulf of Guinea, where prehistoric people coming from the north turned either to the right or to the left, or coming from the south first rounded the corner and reached West Africa; its role as the terminal for routes from the Nile in the neolithic and Iron Age; all these must have complicated its archaeological record. There are in Nigeria many problems of interest, and the local archaeologists are competent to tackle them.

Almost all effort in Ghana for the last two years has been concentrated on the area being flooded by the Volta Lake and by other projected dams. The area of Lake Volta is very large and much of it was extremely inaccessible; it has not been possible to cover it completely, but about 1,500 sites have been registered, the majority not earlier than the sixteenth century. The appointment of two research fellows has enabled the excavation of many of the more important places. A few results of the survey are incorporated in this book, but I have mentioned only work which I have done, and say nothing about that of my colleagues.

The generosity of the Ghana Government in providing all the money which with our resources we could spend in the Volta Basin should be mentioned with particular praise. We had on the Volta no international teams sent by Unesco; attempts to obtain help from abroad were fruitless. So the whole rescue work has been done by Ghana herself, from her own resources.

There is mention of a survey having been carried out in the area of the

Kainji Dam in Nigeria. Large public works, especially hydroelectric and irrigation reservoirs, will doubtless be executed in many West African states in the next few years. It is unlikely that much international aid for archaeological rescue work will be forthcoming. Foreign parties can be attracted by the glamour of the Nile Valley and the comparative comfort of life there; they will be less anxious to live in a swamp, with violent rainstorms and uncertain communications. Thus we hope that governments planning public works will be alive to the need of devoting what are comparatively small sums to record the archaeology which will be destroyed, and we would recommend countries giving technical assistance to remind their hosts of this aspect of the tasks to be carried out.

There is still difficulty about archaeological publication in West Africa. It is easy to place general articles abroad, and there is room to publish fairly short accounts of small excavations. But large excavations require series of monographs, such as the Mémoires of the Institut français d'Afrique noire. It is to be hoped that other countries will find money for such monographs, and contributions from developed countries could profitably form a small but significant part of their technical aid.

There is fairly good map coverage for much of West Africa. Southern Ghana is mapped at 1/62500, and this series is being extended north-wards. A special series was issued at 1/50000 for the Volta Basin. These good maps have greatly assisted field exploration. Most of former French West Africa is covered at 1/200000 and there are for some areas maps at 1/50000, which, however, add no significant detail. Some of the former British territories were well mapped, Nigeria less so. There are a few black spots, for which there is nothing but the inaccurate and out-of-date series at 1/1000000. These maps may not be easily obtainable overseas. So not wishing to fill the text with detail, I have given accurate co-ordinates of latitude and longitude, wherever possible, in the Topographical Index.

Many of the drawings in this book were prepared by Mr J. A. Quansah of the Department of Archaeology at the University of Ghana, who has worked devotedly for a number of years. Other members of the Department have assisted me on excavations, and further tech-nicians were recruited for the work in the Volta Basin. But all our field-work has had to be on a fairly small scale, through lack of pro-fessional personnel; and nearly all the field-survey I have carried out alone. I have received much assistance from other departments of the

University of Ghana, especially from Geology, and from various government institutions, above all from the Geological Survey, many of whose records were placed at my disposal.

I wish also to thank the Institut français d'Afrique noire at Dakar and especially its prehistory-director, Monsieur H. J. Hugot, for hospitality and assistance. Monsieur R. Mauny left Dakar a few years ago; while he was there, he also put all facilities at my disposal, and I have been able to go right through the archaeological collections. I have not recently visited other West African countries. A few years ago I was received at many of the branches of I.F.A.N., and I went to Nigeria. To all those who assisted me in these countries I express my thanks.

Legon, August 31, 1965

West Africa before
the Europeans

CHAPTER ONE

The Geographical Background

Introductory

West Africa is the territory which bounds the Gulf of Guinea on the north. From east to west it extends roughly 2,700 kilometres, from Cap Vert to the Cameroons Mountains. Its north–south width is less, at a maximum 1,350 kilometres, because it is rightly considered to cease at the River Niger and the edge of the Sahara. The Sahara itself is not properly a part of West Africa, although colonial frontiers by chance included large blocks of it in the West African territories, Mauritania and Niger which are almost wholly Saharan, and a big wedge north of the Niger bend which was attached to the French Sudan. But the ecology and human geography of the desert is entirely different from that of the cultivated savannah and forest; and there is evidence that in pluvial times, when the Sahara was more densely populated by animals and plants as well as by man, it enjoyed on the whole a winter rainfall and so formed a projection of the Mediterranean Maghreb rather than of the West African tropics.

This book will discuss mainly the western and central parts of West Africa, with no more than occasional reference to its eastern quarter, now Nigeria. It is not thereby implied that Nigeria does not resemble the rest of West Africa. It has its own problems; there is no parallel farther west to the great embayment filled with soft tertiary deposits and now occupied by the delta of the Niger. The reason for omitting a detailed description of Nigeria is practical. The Nigerian archaeological survey, and now several of the Nigerian universities are devoting close attention to the prehistory of their country. Within the next ten years it is expected that a mass of information will be collected in Nigeria, and then it will be for the local scholars to write it up. At present the record is patchy, and anything written now about Nigeria will rapidly be out of date. For the rest of West Africa, however, educational and scientific prospects are very different. Some countries, such as Ghana and a few of the territories served by the Institut français d'Afrique noire (I.F.A.N.), especially the Dakar area and the Niger Valley between Bamako and Timbuktu, are well explored archaeologically; for these this book may form a useful summary of our present knowledge and a foundation for future work, as we have reached the critical stage where little more surface surveying can profitably be carried out and where excavation must be planned to solve specific problems. In many other areas hardly any surface work has been done, and there seems little likelihood of any being done for many years. There are no local scholars, and the political fragmentation of West Africa makes it more and more difficult for exploration to be conducted from neighbouring states. For these territories this book will rather consolidate our ignorance than form a foundation for future knowledge, and I can do no more than refer to any scraps of information which seem to be relevant to the general picture. Liberia is the worst; we know nothing at all about its archaeology. Sierra Leone and Portuguese Guinea are nearly as bad. About the remaining territories we know something, but not enough to piece together the archaeological record of any one of them. Some are at present in nearly the same state as Nigeria, but without the hope that Nigeria has of great advance within the next few years.

Physical Geography, Rainfall, Vegetation

The physical geography of West Africa is rather dull. Violent pre-Cambrian distortion followed by peneplanation left a stable plateau whence protrude ridges of resistant quartzite. On it accumulated deposits from palaeozoic seas, and round its margins there have been transgressions of the ocean, which have not extended very far except in Senegal. Some of the Late pre-Cambrian peneplain may never have been submerged. Between the Mamelles at Dakar and the Cameroons fault there has been slow epeirogeny, but few signs of tectonic movement or vulcanism; on the north too the last areas of tectonic activity are the Hoggar, the Aïr and Tibesti.

The axis of West Africa is the summit of the pre-Cambrian peneplain which runs parallel to the south coast and, except through the Ivory Coast, not more than 300 kms. inland, from Sierra Leone to Nigeria. This plateau consists of granites and of folded sedimentary rocks, which generally strike north-north-east. Catching the rain from the south-west, it is covered by forest. In general, its summit is not much more than 300 m. S.L.; but there stand out from it ridges of harder rock like the Togo quartzites (above 600 m.) and Mt. Nimba (summit

over 1,600 m.). The forest only just extends north of it, for in its rain-
shadow the rainfall drops rapidly, the dry season lengthens and orchard
bush begins. This plateau is in general a watershed, drained to the
south by numerous short and turbulent rivers; but in the Ivory Coast
the watershed bends to the north, and the Comoe has cut back through
it to rise in the palaeozoic Banfora massif 560 kms. from the coast. In
general, however, the drainage from the northern slopes of this watershed flows northward into the wide level basin of the western Sudan.
At the western end the Gambia and some of the tributaries of the
Senegal turn westward, down the westward slope of the basin, into the
Atlantic. The streams behind Sierra Leone, Liberia and the north-
western Ivory Coast flow into the great swamps of the Upper Niger,
whence on occasions they drained westward, more recently have formed
vast lakes in the southern Sahara, and in very recent times have overflowed and cut a passage into the Lower Niger near Bourem.[1] The east-
central region is the basin of the Volta, which breaks through a gorge
formed by faulting into the Gulf of Guinea. Behind and east of it is the
interior basin of the Lower Niger, which again has cut its way through
several hard ridges into the delta zone of subsidence.

The palaeozoic sandstones and shales, generally horizontally bedded,
must formerly have covered large parts of West Africa, and have been
fragmented by erosion. Tropical weathering is prone to cause scarp
retreat, and fallen rock fragments disintegrate and are removed on the
moister valley floors. Prominent precipices bound the surviving blocks
of sandstone, like those round the Volta sandstones in Ghana or the
Falaise de Banfora (Upper Volta); they also confine valleys draining the
massifs. Weaker beds in the rock may be hollowed by wind or underground streams, and caves are formed [pl. 1], which have been used for
habitation or ritual. But scarp retreat is so rapid that none of these
caves is very ancient. The oldest yield neolithic remains (Bosumpra
near Abetifi, Ghana; and some of the caves in F. Guinea) or paintings
which are believed to be Iron Age (especially in the Bamako region[2],
a very few are known in Ghana) [fig. 112].

But widespread uniformity of relief, with well-developed ancient
land surfaces, does not imply uniformity of ecology. The vegetation
changes rapidly as one travels inland from the coast. The coastal hills
trap rain-bearing winds, and West Africa lies at a critical latitude
where rainfall declines from degree to degree. Below 8° N there is usually
dense equatorial forest [pl. 2]. The extent of this must have varied in
the past, but it cannot within geologically recent times have entirely

disappeared, as it would have been unable to recolonize. In places there is a strip of savannah, humid but with low rainfall, between the forest and the shore. North of Sierra Leone the forest disappears, and all along its northern margin it is fringed with orchard bush, trees about 10 m. high able to resist spells of drought, and much tall grass. As one proceeds north, the grass becomes less luxuriant; trees are smaller and give way to thorn bush and scrub; and these ultimately to desert. The vegetational zones[3] are not strictly parallel, but run fairly closely along lines of latitude; they are determined entirely by the length of the dry season and also by the depth of soil able to store moisture. Patches of forest in orchard bush [pl. 3] often mark old sites where the earth is richer and deeper. Lines of gallery forest [pl. 4] extend far up the rivers into the savannah, not only along the banks but over the deep silts which fill pleistocene valleys much wider than the modern.

As West Africa lies within the tropical belt, almost all its rainfall is in the form of heavy showers, usually short, though at the peak of the rainy season they may last many hours, and several inches of rain within one day are not uncommon. The storms follow the progress of the sun. Near the coast, where the sun crosses the zenith in April and September, there are two peaks of rainfall, in June and October, and usually a minor peak in April or May. Further inland there is a single peak, in July or August. At the height of summer, parts of the coast come within the south-east trade-winds, and there are sometimes in June days of wet cold mist without storms, blown in from the Gulf of Guinea; July is often cold and dry, with little sun. In mid-winter the dry north-east trade winds blow down to the edge of the forest, and sometimes break through for a few days to the coast, causing humidity to drop sharply.

Seasonal rainfall controls the behaviour of West African rivers. The coastal streams are short and turbulent, at all seasons carrying a good deal of water because there is never a true dry season in the forest, but with rock-barriers which hinder navigation. Owing to fluctuations of pleistocene base-level they are all young, and have not had time to grade their beds to a mature stage. The whole of the interior is drained by few very large rivers which cut their ways through the watershed to the coast; and the re-entrant of the watershed in the Ivory Coast produces much longer and wider coastal streams.

Heavy seasonal rains in the southern savannah and the northern edge of the forest provide a great deal of water which must be drained away, so that the large rivers rise eight or ten metres towards the end of the rainy season. They are navigable for small boats even against the strong current. In the dry season the Volta and Comoe are very low, there are many rocks in the bed, and they are navigable only with caution by canoes. Between dangerous rapids and sandbanks there are deep stretches in which fish and crocodiles take refuge. The Niger is so long and traverses such different climates that it carries a good deal of water at all seasons, and navigation is possible except through the rock-barriers [pl. 5]. At Bamako, near its source, it falls in the winter and exposes the bar of Sotuba; but at Niamey last summer's floodwater from the head-waters arrives only in the middle of the dry season, while the river is fed in the wet season by local savannah rains. Shorter rivers, like the Senegal and Benue, are navigable only for a limited period in the wet season.

There are small areas of swamp in the forest, and especially along the drowned coast from Sierra Leone to north of the River Gambia, where mangroves fringe sluggish channels and delimit sandy islands. The savannah is too parched in the dry season for permanent swamps [pl. 6], though numerous pans north of the Niger become very wet during the rains, the plateau being too level for proper drainage. Only in the old delta of the Niger, between Mopti and Timbuktu, are there large swamps, which formerly drained into lakes in the Sahara, but since the eastward diversion of the upper Niger are retained by the rock-sill at Taoussa (Tosaye), which has not yet been incised sufficiently to carry off the water ponded above it. Some coastal lagoons too have silted so as to become swamps.

From the ecological point of view, the important factor of the rainfall is not so much the annual amount as the distribution. Only hardy plants can resist the long dry season of the Niger Valley, and certain specialized trees like the baobab store moisture in their huge trunks and so are dominant in Senegal. In the forest zone there is a very short dry season, during which moisture remains in the soil and vegetation, so that humidity is always high. To the coast regular south-west winds bring moisture even when rainfall is low; on the Accra Plains green grass and low herbs are abundant, though it is too dry for forest trees, and under normal tropical conditions there would be semi-desert. It is likely that the variations in rainfall during the pleistocene, which produced considerable geological effects probably dependent on the vegetation cover, were as much a matter of altered distribution as of absolute quantity. At least during Sub-pluvial II (neolithic), for which we have good evidence as the sediments are preserved, there seems to have been well-distributed rain in the southern savannah without violent storms, leading to sedimentation in swamps rather than incision of river channels; and at the same time there was heavy rain, probably stormy, in the southern Sahara,[4] which filled lakes and watercourses and encouraged fish and aquatic animals in places where now is desert.

Along much of West Africa below 8° N the coast faces south or south-west, so that the long-shore equatorial current from the west-south-west brings monsoon winds and heavy precipitation, with forest to the water's edge [pl. 7]. At the same time, the current induces sedimentation in any embayment along this coast; this started in the cretaceous and the eocene, and has been active during the pleistocene. Soft sediments build out the shore, leaving behind them strip-lagoons parallel to the sea-margin. This process was assisted by pleistocene fluctuations of ocean-level. Such lagoons are best developed in the Ivory Coast and Dahomey. West of the boundary of the forest, in northern Sierra Leone and F. Guinea, the old continental surface, with a lateritic crust characteristic of the savannah, passes beneath present sea-level and must have developed its present profile during the eustatic lows of the pleistocene. Farther north, in Portuguese Guinea and southern Senegal, lie the flooded deltas of the 'Rivières du Sud', again a product of the interaction of high and low pleistocene sea-levels; along the coast is mangrove-swamp with abundant molluscs, but little else, to eat.[5] North of Joal are low, very recent dunes with scrub and grass, resting on a cretaceous-tertiary platform and passing more and more into desert as one approaches the River Senegal. In this region the prevailing current is cool from the north, and it brings no rain. The molluscs are not now Guinean, though it must have been along this coast that the Strombus-fauna reached the Mediterranean in the last interglacial; so at times the Canaries Current must have been weaker than today.

In central Guinea, on stretches where the coast faces not south but south-south-east, in the western Ivory Coast and east of Cape Three Points in Ghana, there has been no long-shore sedimentation, but the land breaks away in cliffs of ancient crystalline rock, which in Ghana preserve an admirable set of raised beaches [pl. 8]. In the Ivory Coast this change of direction has not sufficiently affected the rainfall to destroy the forest. In Ghana, east of Takoradi, there is a strip of savannah along the coast, not more than one kilometre wide at the west end and broadening to fifty kilometres in the Accra Plains. It seems that under natural conditions there were some trees on this strip; but since they were cut in recent times, they have been unable to regenerate. This is not surprising, as along the coast east of Accra the annual rainfall is below 750 mms. Along this stretch, lagoons are perpendicular to the coast, being flooded valleys which were incised during eustatic lows; in one or two places mesozoic sediments have filled much older similar valleys.

East of the Volta the coast turns to face south, but as far as the Nigerian border there is no true forest, only tall grass with borassis-palms behind the strip-lagoons. The strike of the hills just west of Accra carries most of the rain inland, leaving an open corridor along and east of the Volta Valley. Apparently the south-east trade winds bring the cold Benguela Current to the surface on the Ghana coast at the peak of the rainy season, whereby the monsoons are deflected northward and the coast itself remains comparatively dry. The sea near Accra is chilly and stormy in June and July.

Behind the coastal savannah begins the true Guinea forest. The wettest areas are isohyetic islands near the coast with over 2,000 mms. of rain. Dense tree cover, with a few giants overtopping a regular canopy about forty metres high, and matted lianes wherever a ray of sunlight can penetrate to the ground, make access and human settlement difficult. In the past it was almost impossible, as man did not have the tools to master the forest; there is little food within reach, and most of what is edible, fruits and the mammals which live on them, are at the tops of the trees. So far as we know, this wet forest has not been settled until neolithic times, save along river-banks, which offered avenues of penetration. Much of the soil is swampy. No sites have been found of any period in western Ghana, west of the lower Ankobra. Even today the villages of this area are small and poor, the only industry is the exploitation of timber, and the forest grows too fast for man to master it.

Between and behind the islands of wet forest is drier forest with 1,200–2,000 mms. rainfall. As one goes north and the dry season lengthens, the trees become smaller with some deciduous and drought-resisting species. The borassis-palm, of varying uses in many parts of the world, is characteristic of the northern edge of the forest. In this country, the forest can be cut and mastered by co-operative effort; the soil is fertile, especially for plants which have been imported from the New World. The population is dense, and the suitability for cash-crops makes it wealthy. Before the Iron Age the population was apparently thin, probably owing to lack of tools to master the forest; where I have found palaeoliths, I have normally taken this to be evidence that owing to climatic fluctuations the forest at times did not cover these regions.

Even in the early Iron Age there seem to have been no more than a few extensive clearings, several miles across, over which the forest was kept down by rotation of tillage and settlement; Kumasi, for example, seems to have been a cleared area since the neolithic. That more of the forest was not cleared may have been due to lack of suitable indigenous food crops. The African yam is small,[6] and it was cassava from America which multiplied the population. The forest is also unhealthy, and was not easy to settle until the colonial powers improved sanitary conditions.

The northern edge of the forest, for instance the Afram Plains in Ghana, is poorly populated today and has yielded few signs of ancient settlement. The land is less fertile and attractive than the true forest, and when abandoned it becomes rapidly overgrown with dense low bush, which is not easy to clear.

Farther north there are traces of early settlement in the orchard bush, where yams can be satisfactorily cultivated, as can sorghum and millet, probably indigenous farther north. The orchard bush is too disease ridden for cattle on more than a very small scale; they do not flourish south of 10° N. At the same time, water is scarce enough to make settlement rather difficult, while along the rivers there is sleepy sickness and fly-blindness. Even at 11° N swampy valleys like the Sissili and Bougouriba are among the most unhealthy in West Africa.

Instead of tall grass and trees, about 11° N begin thorn bush and low, wiry grass [pl. 10]; on particularly poor soil patches of thorn bush occur much farther south, for instance on the old silts of the Volta [pl. 11]. If land is cleared for cultivation, it becomes more and more liable to erosion as one goes north. From 9° N signs of former erosion become common, and one sees laterite nodules peeping through the thin soil. Any cleared slope will almost certainly be eroded before the natural vegetation can re-establish itself; and regular bush-fires further the process. Cultivation can be carried out safely only on tablelands, and even there the dry winds of winter blow away the soil. Thus tillage becomes more and more confined to small favoured patches; villages are widely spaced owing to lack of water. Here and there are herds of cattle or sheep; but in general the savannah is thinly populated and only a small part of it can be utilized to produce food. In the northern savannah food crops are practically impossible save with irrigation in large valleys, like the middle Niger and the Senegal.

The savannah was further cursed with slave raiding. Smaller tribes were first driven out of the more favoured areas, and then systematically exploited, save where they could take refuge in mountains difficult of access, in the Cameroons and parts of northern Ghana and Nigeria. One of the most desolated areas is Gonja; a few poor villages survive far apart in a land where archaeology indicates abundant habitation two or three centuries ago.

Animal Life

West Africa harboured most of the tropical mammalian fauna except the rhinoceros, which occurs on rock engravings rarely west of the Hoggar and hardly ever south of it;[7] it seems therefore to have been retreating south-east in early Sub-pluvial II. There were elephant, hippopotamus, giraffe and many types of antelope [fig. 46]. Post-pluvial III aridity drove nearly all animals south from the Sahara. Pressure of population and acquisition of fire-arms has greatly reduced them in the savannah, and in some areas they are practically extinct. In neolithic times game was almost as abundant for food as on the high plains of South Africa.

Practically none of the African fauna has been domesticated, and none from the forest and savannah zones. The negro peoples seem to have been psychologically agriculturalists; almost all the herdsmen today are of partly Hamitic origin, and their racial distinctiveness is evident in their cast of countenance. They have been probably forced out of the Sahara by increasing aridity. The donkey seems to be of North African origin.[8] The camel existed in Africa until the neolithic and the Egyptian predynastic,[9] when it may have been domesticated; but it apparently became extinct and was reintroduced to Egypt by the Assyrians or the Persians in the first millennium B.C.[10] The Old Kingdom Egyptians experimented in domesticating gazelles,[11] but seem not to have gone further than to herd them semi-wild in enclosed parks. That proper handling might have brought about domestication is shown by the use made of the African elephant in war. Both the Ptolemies and Carthage used African elephants as they had no access to supplies from India;[12] but they may at first have had to introduce Indian mahouts to drive them.

The common Eurasiatic domestic animals arrived at an early date in Africa. Large herds of oxen appear in Saharan rock paintings, and give their name to the 'Bovidian' period, extending from early in the neolithic to the introduction of horses. The mouflon, which is common in north Saharan art, seems to have been a sacred animal but was perhaps not domesticated;[13] sheep and goats reached Egypt in predynastic times. The domestic pig was introduced to Egypt in Tasian times, but it could not have crossed the Sahara even under conditions more favourable than the present, and it must have reached equatorial Africa by devious routes or perhaps direct by sea from the east, and there it probably crossed with African wild pigs. The dog had reached Egypt in predynastic times, and several breeds had developed; but its capabilities, so valuable in other parts of the Old World, have not been fully utilized, and in the tropics it has often become a scavenger or a food-animal.[14] The horse reached Egypt with the Hyksos,[15] and by the beginning of first millennium B.C. was widely used by steppe and desert tribes for riding and driving.[16] The camel was replacing it in the desert by the fourth century A.D.,[17] but did not become dominant in the Sahara until the Arab invasions.

Cattle and above all horses cannot be used south of 10° N, because they are allergic to trypanosomiasis, carried by tsetse from the gallery forest. Dwarf short-horn cattle are more resistant and are found in some parts of the forest. The large Bos Africanus and the zebu cannot be bred to the south, though they can be walked through the forest for immediate slaughter. Horses, as prestige symbols of chiefs, may occasionally be kept as far south as 9° N. There are small numbers of dwarf sheep in the forest.

Human Activity in Modifying the Landscape

Human activity has in recent centuries greatly modified the West African landscape. The iniquitous goat, which has ruined the forests of the Mediterranean, is rare in West Africa; and the negro population is little given to pasturage and in the past was less so, for pastoralists have been pressing down from the Saharan fringe for the last 2,000 years. Yet other bad habits have become endemic. Tillage, whether of cereals or tubers, is unlikely to have ruined the soil; for the plough has been unknown until introduced, usually in mechanical form, in very recent years; and the hoe did no more than clear small patches for planting. Where the climate was damp enough for crops, it would also favour weeds; so the ground remained relatively protected after the harvest and even during the growing season. Wind erosion has been slow; and with a proper rotation in the savannah of ten to twenty years fallow after three years cropping, it would have been negligible.

What has caused serious harm has been the practice of burning in the orchard bush. Probably in both Europe and Africa this goes back to the palaeolithic age, and was a recognized if wasteful means of hunting. Even today, towards the end of the dry season when the vegetation burns most fiercely and the greatest harm is done, unemployed youths recklessly kindle the countryside to drive into the open the last remaining game. No one seems to care if houses or useful trees are burned. If questioned, the people will say that burning destroys noxious creatures like snakes.

Apart from damage to personal property, burning destroys young savannah trees, and areas which are regularly burned have only old trees whose bark has become fire resistant. Trees are replaced by tall indigestible grasses, and the whole countryside will ultimately become deforested. Burning kills soil bacteria and reduces fertility. It encourages wind erosion and run-off on the baked surfaces. West African soils are very fragile. In Europe soft glacial and periglacial clays act as soil reservoirs and easily replace soil which has been removed; in Africa there is seldom more than three feet of loam above a surface of laterite nodules or rubble which marks the Post-pluvial III horizon; and in many places earlier erosion has destroyed the older soil of Sub-pluvial II, so that a hard ferruginous crust is exposed on which practically nothing will grow.[18] Thus by burning man is rapidly spreading the desert, and this process is the more severe because of the natural increase of population. The forest, fortunately, even when cleared is too damp to burn; it is the orchard bush, providing abundant fuel from its tall dry grasses, which is suffering most intensely.

Soil-erosion is now more serious than ever before. But at least since the rise of organized states it has occurred patchily, near the political centres where population was dense. It is likely that each Sudanic empire fell as much owing to soil-exhaustion as to political and military weakness. Under present climatic conditions West Africa cannot carry more than a limited human population per square kilometre, and any attempt to increase the density must lead to disaster.

Climatic Shifts in the Past and their Influence on Human Habitation

Throughout the world there have been sharp fluctuations of climate during the pleistocene, both in temperature and in precipitation. For this recent period the geological record is far more accurately preserved than for earlier ages, so our evidence for climatic change is fuller; but it does appear that in the pleistocene the changes have been more rapid and more violent than in almost all previous periods. The switch from glacial to interglacial conditions in cycles of less than 100,000 years does not seem paralleled in early glacial epochs; the Permian Ice Age apparently underwent roughly the same number of fluctuations in many million years as the pleistocene has in one million. In non-glacial periods there may have been cycles of change,[19] but they have been of small magnitude because it is only when temperature reaches the critical freezing-point that a chain-reaction of great intensity occurs. Ice generates more ice by reason of albedo and the high air-pressure over an ice-field, so that incoming solar radiation is reflected and cold air spreads outwards. An ice sheet therefore grows rapidly, once the summer temperature is too low to clear away the snow each year. Its natural limits depend on geographical conditions; it appears from the course of pleistocene events that it will easily reach a diameter of $30°$ of latitude; but above that size it cannot grow, probably because of low precipitation and ice starvation.

It is in the northern hemisphere that our knowledge of pleistocene climatic changes is fullest, because over the large land masses we can investigate glacial and periglacial deposits. In the Arctic and temperate regions of this hemisphere are several mountain masses, Scandinavia, Spitzbergen, Scotland, Ulster, the Alps, the Canadian Shield and parts of Siberia, well placed to attract precipitation in chilly damp periods, such as the early part of the Würm glaciation seems to have been. The temperature need not have been exceedingly low. But if enough snow fell each winter not to melt in summer, mountain ice-sheets would rapidly start and grow of their own momentum, and in due course would become sufficiently thick to spread to the surrounding plains and even over shallow seas.

The southern hemisphere is mainly sea except for Antarctica. On this continent ice has probably been building up throughout the pleistocene. On well-situated mountains in Tasmania, New Zealand and South America there have been glaciations. Their number is not certain, and as we shall see, their contemporaneity with those of the northern hemisphere is unsatisfactory.

In sub-tropical and tropical regions the main evidence is for variation in precipitation. During the last northern glaciation there were cooler temperatures in tropical Central and East Africa[20] and in Columbia.[21] There is also evidence on the high mountains of East Africa for small glaciations more extensive than the present;[22] but when these occurred we cannot do more than guess.

It has been frequently assumed that glaciations in both hemispheres have been contemporary, and that tropical pluvials were contemporary with them. The first of these assumptions is unproven,[23] because no agreement has been reached on the cause of glaciations. It is likely anyhow that large ice-caps in one hemisphere will have a slight cooling effect on the whole world; but this cooling will be most marked at the end of a glaciation, when ice-calving and large rivers of melt-water bring much cold water into the extra-glacial oceans. It will thus rather delay the temperature amelioration than induce the deterioration. At the same time, while temperature may have been lower at any particular present-day altitude above sea-level in the tropics, this lowering would be counterbalanced by the greatly lowered eustatic sea-level of glacial periods; so the contour under discussion would have been roughly 120 metres higher[24] during the peak of the Würm glaciation than it is today. Botanists have tried to calculate the general lowering of temperature during the last glaciation. While in exposed areas, like the Central European corridor between the Scandinavian and Alpine glaciers, it may have been up to 12° C, some agreement has been reached that in most extra-glacial temperate zones it was of the order of 5–6° C.[25] At Kalambo Falls (Zambia), however, it is reckoned to have been about 3–5° C, on the Kenya highlands 5°, in Lunda (north-east Angola) 3°; so the profiles constructed of a lowered snow-line exactly concentric with the present[26] are not accurate. From these figures must be subtracted 1° to allow for the relative emergence of the land. That on sea-level tropical temperatures cannot have been markedly lower than today is shown by the survival of highly sensitive flora, at least in refuges.[27]

Many theories have been advanced about the causes of glaciations. These are complicated by the superposition of two cycles. A long-term cycle seems to have lowered the temperature of the earth to a critical point about every 250,000,000 years; a short-term cycle, which may well have been operating in non-glacial epochs as well, has produced fluctuations of the order of 100,000 years, and smaller fluctuations (glacial stadials) at more frequent intervals. The short-term cycle may itself be multiple; and the causes of these several cycles are almost certainly different. Nor may the geographical background be neglected; glaciers can form only with suitable distribution of land and sea, on mountains well sited to attract moist winds. Over a low-lying and largely oceanic earth a very great drop in temperature would be required to induce glaciation. Recent orogeny in the Andes and the Alpine–Himalaya chain has undoubtedly assisted pleistocene glaciation, though it is unlikely to be its cause.

In a discussion of pleistocene conditions the long-term cycle of

c

glacial epochs is irrelevant. We may accept that the pleistocene is one of these epochs. The theories which have been propounded to explain the short-term fluctuations are of two main types: either their cause was extra-terrestrial, in solar radiation, and they will have affected both hemispheres simultaneously; or it was concerned with the earth's rotation, so that glaciations are out of phase in the two hemispheres. It is a vicious argument to assume that glaciations were contemporary in both hemispheres, for which the evidence is scanty, and therefore theories of the second type are ruled out. The disproof of any theory must depend on the unreasonableness or invalidity of any of the arguments put forward in support.

A good many of the causes suggested over the last hundred years have been shown to be unacceptable, and those which hold the field at present are as follows. The extra-terrestrial cause, which would affect the whole earth simultaneously, must be variable solar radiation. Suggested variations either in the opacity of interstellar matter or in the amount of carbon dioxide or volcanic dust in the earth's atmosphere[28] seem too casual to have induced glacial epochs or fluctuations, and should have been operative much more frequently in geological time than the glaciation record. Simpson[29] has constructed a meteorological scheme of glacials and pluvials to fit dubious geological evidence, and has adapted his scheme as the geological theories altered; the mechanism is based on unexplained cycles of solar radiation, and glaciations are alleged to occur when greater warmth increases evaporation and cloud-cover, though one would expect the precipitation in warm periods to be in the form of rain rather than snow. Fairbridge's variations in the sunspot-cycle[30] are equally unexplained, and there seems little correspondence between the secular build-up of even so minor a fluctuation as the Little Ice Age and the annual number of sun-spots. Öpik has attempted to work out an astrophysical theory of solar variations on a long-term cycle with short-term fluctuations.[31] His theory is better reasoned than most others which presuppose contemporary glaciation in both hemispheres; but it seems to explain the long-term glacial epochs rather than the short-term fluctuations, and though based on the assumption that sun and earth are becoming hotter, it fails to produce evidence for very cold conditions in early pre-Cambrian times.

A cause within the earth itself may affect both hemispheres independently. The best-known theory of this type is the insolation-curve of Milankovich,[32] recalculated by van Woerkom.[33] According to this curve, which is constructed on the variability of three elements in the earth's rotation, insolation minima occur independently in the two hemispheres, but tend to occur in pairs.[34] Strong opposition has been elicited from scientists of several different disciplines, much of it on theoretical grounds or on the basis of dubious facts. The objection that the orbital elements have varied throughout time, but glaciations started only in the quaternary, is countered by the demonstration of similar pliocene fluctuations, without sufficient drop in temperature to produce ice.[35] Even the telling argument that the insolation-curve fits very badly the known radiocarbon dates of the Late Pleistocene now loses force, since the whole of the Central European sequence has been thrown into the melting-pot. It is fairly certain that there would be a time-lag between an insolation minimum and a glacial maximum; and the curve as calculated is independent of the interpretations put upon it regarding glaciations and stadials.

A recent theory by Ewing and Donn[36] follows a pattern of purely geographical causation, which otherwise has been abandoned. Other solely geographical causes, like late tertiary orogeny,[37] are regarded as contributory but unfit to account by themselves for pleistocene glaciations. The authors suggest that an ice-free Arctic would induce precipitation in the form of snow on circumpolar mountains, which would become foci of glaciations able to expand under purely meteorological conditions. Eustatic lowering of the oceans would make so shallow the Whyville–Thomson ridge between Greenland, Iceland and Norway that little warm Atlantic water could pass into the Arctic Ocean, which would therefore freeze; and owing to Arctic water no longer reaching the Atlantic, this ocean would become warmer and would melt the continental glaciers. This becomes a continuous cycle, which in fact can arise and be broken only by a radical change of temperature due to extra-terrestrial causes. Northern glaciations have no effect on the southern hemisphere, except in so far as they induce a general cooling of the atmosphere.

Arguments put forward in a more recent article[38] imply that the authors themselves have abandoned this theory. It is certainly untenable. It implies rapid polar wandering, as a glacial epoch must occur when one pole is trapped in a landlocked ocean;[39] so the North Pole can have reached the Arctic Ocean only at the beginning of the pleistocene. There is no evidence that throughout the tertiary the poles have been somewhere in modern temperate or tropical latitudes. Moreover, beneath the Arctic Ocean there are great depths of fine sediment, indicating that there has been no open water with icebergs for a very long time;[40]

and the two periods without Atlantic foraminifera in the Arctic basin during the last 50,000 years[41] suggest a rhythm of freezing in the North Atlantic which does not correspond to the course of the Würm glaciation. Foraminifera were abundant in the Arctic about 9300 ± 180 B.P.,[42] at a date when *ex hypothesi* Ewing and Donn this ocean should have been frozen for some 10,000 years and have continued frozen until nearly the present day. Dated pollen-bearing strata in Alaska show that in the last glaciation the Arctic Ocean was cold and not warm.[43]

A rather similar automatic mechanism for glaciations, based on the varying width of the Antarctic ice-shelf[44] has recently been propounded. It also implies tertiary polar wandering, as it works only if Antarctica is symmetrical about the pole; and it is no more convincing than the theory of Ewing and Donn.

It is impossible at present to give a satisfactory explanation of the pleistocene glaciations. Öpik's theory fails to explain the short-term fluctuations; the variation of the orbital elements is admitted to have had some effect on insolation and climate, but whether sufficient to produce the crises of quaternary temperature is uncertain. Glaciations must have started with heavy precipitation in high latitudes; but no one has demonstrated whether this is to be correlated with African pluvials. Possibly Bernard's calculations[45] on the shifts of the caloric equator may provide an answer on this line. It seems certain that once a predisposition to glaciation has been established, whether from diminished solar radiation or from orogeny, ice-sheets can spread rapidly and last long after the occasion which triggered them; while their ablation is much less simple and requires a major climatic change.

The cause of pleistocene glaciations is of minor importance for West African prehistory, except in so far as there is likely to have been a slight cooling of the atmosphere (less than $5°$ C) and a cooling of the ocean water off the West African coasts, which might well affect the rainfall. The western coast of West Africa is bathed by the Canaries Current, which is unlikely to have been much colder during the onset or peak of a glaciation, but will probably have been colder during its waning,[46] when icebergs will have been calving as far south as Ireland and abundant melt-water will have been replenishing the North Sea, the Mediterranean and most of the North Atlantic. Bergs floated as far south as Galicia and perhaps as the Azores [47] The enormous quantities of melt-water reaching the Gulf of Mexico via the Mississippi and much later coming down the St Lawrence River must have cooled the whole North Atlantic. On the southern side of West Africa, the Gulf of Guinea is a trap for cold Antarctic water flowing up the west coast of South Africa and Angola as the Benguela Current; and in Antarctica either greater precipitation, activating the glaciers which are at present sluggish, or warmer periglacial conditions would greatly increase calving from the ice-shelf. Icebergs have recently been sighted as far north as 35° S, and very rarely up to 27° S, which is north of the Orange River; but under favourable conditions they could have reached the tropic.

Some scholars have happily assumed that glaciations (only in the northern hemisphere) have induced pluvial conditions in tropical Africa, on both sides of the equator.[48] This assumption, in its crudest form, misunderstands the meteorological mechanism of a glaciation: wetter conditions with cooler summers start in high latitudes at the peak of an interglacial, and continue, doubtless with stadial fluctuations, until near the peak of a glaciation; then drier conditions supervene over the glaciers and higher temperatures, probably much higher, occur in extra-glacial regions, probably along with lower rainfall, during the whole of later glacial times until the peak of the interglacial.[49] Consequently, assuming that rainfall varies concurrently in the tropics and in higher latitudes, tropical pluvials cannot be in phase with glaciations, but must have occurred earlier in each cycle.

Others have assumed[50] that glaciations in Europe have shifted southward all the meteorological zones, so that the Saharan desert belt would have approached the equator. This would imply that northern glaciations are contemporary with tropical interpluvials, at least north of the equator. This mechanism also seems too simple; it is just as likely that the tropical zone of high pressure has contracted from one or perhaps from both sides.[51] There is no evidence that it must maintain a constant width, though it seems improbable that it can entirely disappear.[52]

In fact, tropical pluvials may have been due to several causes; that some at any rate were not contemporary with northern glaciations can be proved chronologically The evidence will be set out in detail later; I need here only to summarize results:

(1) The beginnings of the Sangoan culture, both north and south of the equator, fall in the last tropical interpluvial (Kanjeran–Gamblian in East Africa, Kamasian II–Gamblian in West Africa; often unsatisfactorily called the First Intermediate); a date from Kalambo Falls shows that the Sangoan cannot have started before 55000 B.P., and

the advanced Sangoan (Early Lupemban) was developing by 40000 B.P.[53] This interpluvial must therefore coincide with a fluctuating interstadial before the peak of the Würm glaciation,[54] and not with the last or Eem interglacial,[55] which had ended by 70000 B.P. and had reached its maximum probably before 90000.

(2) Sub-pluvial II or Makalian, wetter in the Near East,[56] East Africa and West Africa, as indicated by the inner silt-terraces of the rivers and the Saharan lakes, is dated in the Sahara to the fifth and fourth millennia B.C.[57] It therefore corresponds to the Atlantic period in northern Europe, a period of warmth and fairly high precipitation, dated about 5500–3000 B.C.[58] The Atlantic period is not a glaciation but the peak of an interglacial.

(3) The oldest marine transgression recorded in the Senegal delta, probably Beach V, was accompanied by wetter conditions than the regressions preceding and succeeding it.[59]

We need to define what we mean by a tropical pluvial. Pluvial conditions may imply greater or better distributed annual rainfall; in both cases, the geological evidence is likely to be similar, thicker vegetation will help to build up soils and resist erosion. The formation of lateritic or calcareous crusts is due to ill-distributed rainfall and sharp seasonal contrasts; erosion will be due to reduced protection from vegetation cover, either from lower annual rainfall or from bad distribution. For this reason, in place of the simple contrast pluvial–interpluvial, Bernard[45] has introduced the notion of three stages, isopluvial–displuvial–interpluvial: an isopluvial is a period of well distributed and probably high rainfall, though the total annual amount need not exceed that of a displuvial; a displuvial is a period with heavy rainfall for part of the year and sharp seasonal contrast; an interpluvial is a period with diminished rainfall and normally seasonal contrast.

Bernard begins his argument with the notion of the caloric equator, the latitude at which the insolation of summer and winter is equal. This line is at present at 3° N, but has shifted during the pleistocene between 10° 45' N and S, with a cycle of just over 20,000 years, being controlled by the orbital elements of Milankovich. As isopluvial conditions develop near the caloric equator and displuvial at greater distance, its cyclic movement will in the past, with due reference to local geographical conditions such as distribution of land and sea, have caused fluctuations between heavy pluviosity and great aridity in every part of the tropics. Our knowledge of African chronology is still too limited to decide whether the pluvial shifts do follow Bernard's theoretical curve; and the latter certainly cannot be used as a calendar to date geologically observed pluvials and interpluvials.

Food

As explained, variations in rainfall control the vegetation belts, and thereby the distribution of human habitat. Primitive hominids were probably as omnivorous as is man today; before the neolithic revolution men lived on such fruits, leaves and tubers as they could find – the latter hardly before the mastery of fire enabled them to cook – also on game they could kill and carrion from the kills of stronger animals. Perhaps even the earliest tool-using hominids could kill animals of their own size with clubs of bone or wood.[60] By Late Acheulian times certain forms of trap may have been developed, by which men could kill animals much larger than themselves;[61] and the development of the spear in the early Middle Stone Age (Lupemban, Stillbay) and the bow perhaps as early as the Aterian and Tsitolian cultures equipped them to provide themselves with meat.

It is in general likely that primitive man could not survive in the equatorial forest [pl. 2]. The thick bush round the edge made it difficult of access save along rivers, whither large animals might make paths to drinking water, on which they could be ambushed. The rivers also contained fish. In thick forest movement is not difficult between the trunks, but there is no food save on the tree-trops, and the only game also is far above the ground. The forest will not burn, and could not be cleared until man acquired efficient tools to cut the trees and organized societies to co-operate against nature. When cleared, it is for a time recolonized by impenetrable bush [pl. 12]. One finds in the forest small patches of microliths, perhaps the relics of one or two refugees or adventurous hunters; in general, penetration into the West African forest and the clearing of large areas is not older than the neolithic. I have assumed that where palaeolithic tools occur, the forest at that time was not there. It probably shrank considerably in marginal areas of Ghana during some interpluvials. At other times, during isopluvials, the forest may have extended much farther north than at present, Urvoy suggests from the evidence of fossil soils even to 14° N;[62] at least the absence of Kalinian (Early Lupemban) remains from Ghana suggests that it extended to 11° N during the Gamblian pluvial. It is remarkable that those palaeolithic cultures which flourished in the Sahara and near the desert margin are unrepresented in Ghana and vice versa. With increase in rainfall man and the game he followed were chased north by the expanding forest; during interpluvials, the forest contracted and the desert spread; man and the animals had to migrate southward.

The stretches of savannah coast, especially in Ghana [pl. 9], may always have been open and attractive for human settlement. Especially near the mouth of the Volta the modern rainfall is so low that a general increase of 500 mms. would not bring the coast within the forest zone. Today there are patches of thorn bush and low grass near the coast, suitable for smaller mammals like duiker, for crustacea and other edible creatures. Near the hills on deeper soils the bush can grow very thick and impenetrable. In parts of the Accra Plains the baobab, a valuable food-tree yielding vitamin C, seems indigenous. There is also sea-food where the shore is rocky; and since palaeolithic times the coast has been straightened, so that formerly there were larger lagoons where oysters would thrive. During eustatic low sea-levels the coast may have been similar to today, farther out on the continental shelf, indented by rapidly flowing streams which had not had time to form lagoons at their mouths, for the lagoons are valleys drowned by the rising inter-glacial ocean. Men who reached the coast during the last interpluvial (Kamasian II–Gamblian) down the fairly open Volta Corridor seem to have been cut off there by the spread of the Gamblian forests, and for a long period eked out an isolated existence, developing a Late Sangoan culture of different type from the Lupemban of the savannah. It is not impossible that they survived until drier post-Gamblian conditions re-established communications with the interior, as there seems to be a Late Sangoan element in the indeterminate coastal M.S.A. If they did not, it will have been interbreeding rather than starvation which exterminated them.

North of the forest the wooded savannah or orchard bush was suitable for primitive human occupation. Food is provided by valuable fruit-trees, like the shea-butter, and tubers such as wild yams. Above all, this region must have contained abundant game. The chief danger for man was to be lost in tall trackless grass; and he lived principally near the rivers.

The yam requires a heavy rainfall in the growing season and does not do well north of 9° N. From this latitude, in a zone which is still heavily grassed with abundant trees, the staple crop is millet and sorghum, or in the west rice. All these grains are of African origin, and some species seem to be native to West Africa. From them is made fermented drink as well as food. Winter-rain cereals, widely sown round the Mediterranean, cannot be cultivated in West Africa owing to their susceptibility to rust.

Farther north is the zone of thorn bush and low grass, today south of the Niger, but during pluvials extending far into the Sahara, where at least in the Gamblian and Sub-pluvial II there were reedy lakes.[63] Many of these lakes existed also in the Kamasian. They harboured large aquatic animals; and game, which fed on the steppe, had to come to water and there could be trapped. There is not much vegetable food; in some areas wild millet probably grew; and other plants, today despised, could be eaten. So this zone too, as far as the fluctuating edge of the desert, was hospitable to primitive man.

The south-western Sahara, though in the past fertile, is today covered with longitudinal dunes following the line of the trade-winds from the north-north-east [pl. 15]. During pleistocene interpluvials these extended much farther south, even to the Gambia River and south of the Niger to the latitude of Niamey; they have become fossilized and grass-covered in the northern savannah.[64] It has not been possible to establish their date. During very wet periods, like the Kamasian, fossil dunes may have been almost entirely washed away; but recent less important pluvials they have survived. The minor dry phase of Post-pluvial III caused no more than some redistribution of dune-sand, especially round Dakar. Even under present conditions in the central Sahara blowing sand causes much damage by choking lakes and water-holes; it is a more potent factor in desertification than reduced rainfall. In drier periods it seriously interfered with the drainage, and brought about the fragmentation of some of the lakes around Goundam.

Disease

It was not only food and water that man needed. Today he is the prey of diseases which are particularly dangerous close to the savannah-rivers. The vectors, mosquito tsetse and semulium, have probably long been indigenous; but so long as there were very few human hosts, the parasites could not easily complete their life-cycles.[65] It is not known when malaria, sleepy-sickness (trypanosomiasis) and fly-blindness (onchocerciasis) became endemic in West Africa. It is likely that until recent times they existed only in limited areas; the malaria mosquito would have difficulty in breeding in unbroken forest, tsetse and semulium like gallery forest in the savannah. Today most villages lie far from rivers and gallery forests; on the river bank are only a few temporary fishing hamlets. On the Volta, near Kete Krachi and further upstream,

we have found many old villages, either on the river bank or concealed
in the gallery forest. The most recent belong to the eighteenth century,
the older go far back into the middle ages.[66] Patches of sherds, not very
old, towards the White Volta below Kugri show that there too the
river-valley has been recently evacuated. It appears therefore that at
least in the Volta Valley riverine diseases are of very recent introduction;
with adequate hosts they have been able to establish themselves.

Vegetable Products

I have made mention of the food resources available in the various
zones. There were other vegetable products, especially for tools and
clothes. A great variety of timbers would serve all needs for tools and
building, the main difficulty in early days being to fell them with
primitive tools, even with the help of ringing and burning. Lighter
vegetable substances were readily available, grass for thatching in the
savannah, palm-fronds for roofs and as frames for mud houses, and
bark cloth which was probably the principal material for clothes in the
forest before the import of European textiles. Bark cloth was usually
beaten with mallets; stone hammers scored on the face and believed
to have been used for this purpose have been found at Fénaria in the
Soguinex diggings (F. Guinea).[67] Wool was not available as West
African sheep are hairy; nor was linen, so much appreciated in Egypt.
The wearing of leather was probably confined to North Africa.[68]
Certain species of cotton are indigenous; this was known but not widely
used in ancient Egypt, and its exploitation in the West African savannah
was probably introduced by the Arabs. Dyeing with indigo or similar
indigenous plants is likely to be an ancient practice. In fact, before
Islam the West African probably wore very little save on ceremonial
occasions, and some relict tribes still often go naked. The pigment and
abundant sweat glands in negro skin are adequate protection against
the sun.

Minerals

In describing the stone industries of West Africa, I will discuss in more
detail the stones available for tools. Though here and there there were
good stones, in many areas primitive man was forced to use refractory
materials, hard to flake and even harder to trim to the exact form
required. Commonest among these is quartz, which in many regions
had to be used both for the large rough tools of the Old Stone Age
(especially the Sangoan) and for the microliths of the Neolithic. Equally

refractory are the lavas phthanites and dolerites, used especially in the Lupemban industries of Bamako, Dakar and Mauritania. The Buem cherts of the Chellean of Ghana again were excessively difficult to flake. On the other hand, in some areas fine-grained stones were available for the small tools of the mesolithic, and very delicate trimming may be found. There is flint around Dakar and in the southern Sahara; on a few sites in Ghana chalcedony partly replaced quartz, but it seems to have been rare, and often it appears that only a few stray pebbles had been available, presumably the relics of ancient siliceous crusts formed under a different climate. Good quartzites were to hand in some areas, especially along the Akwapim–Atacora range; this stone is not easy to flake, but can be made into well shaped, serviceable large tools. For polished axes there were especially the greenstones of Ghana, which can be sharpened easily and give a keen blade, now difficult to appreciate because the stone patinates rapidly; in the Ténéré there was a green jasper of extremely good quality, yielding lovely tools.

Semi-precious stones were available in some areas, and were probably exported widely. One of the most desired was amazonite, principally from Eguei Zouma.[69] Though common bracelets may have been made in many regions, the use of hard, coloured stones was a specialized art, and such objects were exported, for instance grey veined marble from Hombori and bituminous shale from Aïr.[70] Even bracelets of indurated sandstone seem to have been manufactured industrially in the Oueyanko Valley (Bamako). Near Gao, on the Gadaoui dunes, were made beads of quartz, some of a delicate pink colour.[71] Quartz was probably made into beads in many other regions, as quartz beads are widespread, and it is unlikely that under the primitive isolationism of the neolithic they were all imported from a few centres. But the difficult techniques of boring and polishing seem to have been diffused from the Niger Valley. Occasionally are found very crude beads, evidently unskilled attempts at imitation. In southern Togoland were made irregular quartz beads.[72] In Ghana and Ivory Coast large beads were made of speckled pink and black rocks of the hornblende-porphyry group, which probably out-crops and was worked at several places. There is no evidence for the use of precious stones like diamonds; most West African diamonds are unattractive industrial stones, and it does not appear that the Portuguese found diamonds worn on the Guinea coast.

There has recently been an important glass industry at Bida (Nigeria),[73] particularly for the manufacture of beads. There is no evidence on its antiquity, but it may well have been founded by Arabs from across the Sahara, as Egypt is a very ancient centre for glass. In general, glass was diffused in West Africa by European imports, especially of beads from Venice. It is not proved that the old blue cane-glass beads (probably the famous Aggrey beads) which have been dug up in native cemeteries[74] are in fact pre-European. Local artisans have recently ground up imported glass beads and made their own beads from the partly fused frit; but older African beads seem to have been of stone and sometimes of terracotta or a sort of faience.

Metals

Certain metals occur abundantly in the ancient rocks of West Africa. I will deal later in detail with the metal industry, which is of importance for the archaeology and history of the Iron Age, and will here summarize the natural resources.

Gold has always been the most valuable West African product. Derived mainly from the pre-Cambrian hills which separate the coastal belt from the interior basins of the Niger and Volta, it occurs widely in placers, often as visible nuggets, whence it may be recovered by no more than washing. There are also valuable lodes, especially in Ghana. but these require scientific mining, an art which was probably introduced by the Portuguese, and greatly developed by European engineers within the last century. There are two types of placer. Mostly in the larger valleys near Kankan, in Lobi territory (Upper Volta), on the upper Birim and Ofin and on the Falémé,[75] deep-level late tertiary gravels are covered by 6–10 metres of overburden. These gravels are rich and extensive; but their exploitation by pitting through the overlying sands is a skilled profession, not beyond the techniques of trained African miners,[76] but not for the amateur. In the streams of Ashanti are small pockets of auriferous sand. They can be dug and washed by any local peasant; sometimes they will have yielded a nugget or a good return of dust, but their content is very uncertain and often a day's labour would be fruitless.

Vague notices in classical authors indicate that a little gold was reaching the west coast and North Africa overland by the fifth century B.C.[77] This gold will almost certainly have come from the placers either of Wangara (upper Niger) or of the Falémé; but no archaeological remains have been found in these areas to suggest either exploitation or long-distance commerce at so early a date. However, soon after the Muslim invasions gold was reaching the Middle Niger and thence the Mediterranean,[78] and the gold trade was the mainstay of the Sudanic empires, from Ghana in the Dark Ages right through the Middle Ages. The Wangara gold-fields cannot have been opened suddenly, and we know nothing of Arab prospectors who wandered south into darkest Africa to discover them; so we must assume that a native industry had been developed over a long period, probably since before our era, and became important when political stability to the north and the opening of the Saharan routes, with the growing importance of the camel, encouraged commerce on a large scale.

Probably not much before the end of the Middle Ages, merchants and prospectors pushed south-eastwards to open up the goldfields of Ashanti.[79] In this area the forest-people may have found small quantities of gold for a long time; but they were too remote to barter it away, and the exploitation remained primitive. It was at the mouth of the River Pra that the Portuguese first found Africans wearing gold ornaments; and it was on the Gold Coast that they established their first fortified settlements, to open up the gold trade with Europe by sea.

Iron was widely worked on a peasant-scale in West Africa. It is unlikely that until recently it was traded very far, and small quantities could be produced in many areas. I will discuss later the distribution of iron slag-heaps so far as we know them [fig. 79]; but in view of the inadequate exploration of most of West Africa, almost certainly many centres of local production remain to be located. There are a few large deposits of iron-ore. These would require mining, at least opencast, and may not have been worked at an early date. It is likely that use was normally made of the ubiquitous lateritic crusts, both of redeposited iron-salts on the rock-surface and of altered rock whence most of the silica had been leached and stringers of nearly pure hematite occur.[80] Much of the laterite contains little iron; but hand sorting in an age when time and labour were of slight value and the climate permitted only limited seasons for agriculture yielded enough for small furnace-charges, with the production of blooms adequate for limited local needs, like hoes. The better weapons which some of the Sudanic kingdoms possessed may have been imported or made in industrial centres where good ore was available, like Koro Toro,[81] which was probably worked for the kings of Kanem.

Silver and lead occur rarely in West Africa, and there is no evidence for their ancient exploitation. There was copper at Akjoujt,[82] Takedda[85] and Marandet;[84] the first was worked in a copper age which may have been retarded but certainly derived its techniques from the chalcolithic of Spain.[85] Farther south, in the savannah and forest, no copper was found, and West Africa passed directly from the neolithic to the Iron Age. Except for Egypt, the African continent nowhere developed a true Bronze Age; even the Maghreb, facing the Mediterranean, has yielded very few copper and bronze objects[86] and apparently passed from a belated Stone Age to the use of iron. Tin was available on the Jos Plateau (Nigeria), and was smelted in small quantities by the Nok-people at the beginning of the Iron Age; but only for the production of beads. The manufacture of bronze by the alloying of copper with Nigerian tin started presumably under Arab direction.[87] The school of Ife used not bronze but imported brass.[88] It must be older than Benin, which itself is older than the arrival of the Portuguese and traditionally started in the late fourteenth century.

NOTES

1. Furon, R., 1929; Palausi, *RGD* v (1955), p. 217; Clos-Arceduc, *Tropiques* 371 (Mar. 1955), p. 36.
2. Furon R., 1932; Griaule M., 1934; Rouch J., 1953, p. 154, pl. IV and V.
3. See *Vegetation Map of Africa* (1959), ed. Keay.
4. The terraces in the Sahara are irregular, implying torrential rainfall; see Balout, *CISPP* iii (1950), p. 163; Rognon, *IRS Travaux* xxi (1962), p. 57.
5. Cp. the shell-middens of the Joal area: Corre, *Revue d'Ethnographie* ii (1883), p. 18; Mauny R., 1961 (1), pp. 157–8.
6. 15–40 cms. long and 2 cms. in diameter; see Chevalier, *Revue de Botanique appliquée* xxix (1949), p. 609.
7. Mauny R., 1956; Huard, *Notre Sahara* vii (1959), p. 33.
8. Boettger C. R., 1958.
9. Murray, *Institut Fouad I du Désert Bulletin*, II i (1952), p. 105.
10. It is not proved that predynastic camels were domestic, and there is no good evidence for camels in Egypt or Africa in the third or second millennia B.C., despite the plea of Demougeot, *Annales* xv (1960), p. 208; cp. Courtois, *Les Vandales et l'Afrique*, pp. 98–104. The first mention of them in the Maghreb is Caesar, *B. Africum* 68, but they may possibly be mentioned in Massinissa's inscription at Dougga.
11. Dechambre, *Société de Biogéographie*, *C. R. Séances* (1950), p. 147.
12. Agatharcides, in *Geographi Graeci Minores* i, p. 111; Polybius 5 84. Both Carthage and the Numidian kings must have tamed African elephants, as they had no access to Indian; cp. Aurigemma, *Africa italiana* vii (1940), p. 67.
13. Espérandieu, *Société de Zootechnie d'Algérie Bulletin* ii (1954), p. 23.
14. Chalumeau, *Bulletin de Liaison saharienne* xvii (1954), p. 77 and xxx (1958), p. 106; also other articles in this journal.
15. Emery (*Kush* viii (1960), p. 7) claims a pre-Hyksos horse from the brick

pavement of the Middle Kingdom fort at Buhen (Sudan) on unconvincing evidence. The skeleton was found ½ metre below the burnt sacklayer which was dated 1675 ± 150 B.C.; the Hyksos dynasty is now dated 1674–1567 B.C. Assuming that the horse lay where it fell and was not buried in a pit, the pavement is likely to have been kept clean until the attack, and the beast could easily have belonged to the attackers who were probably Hyksos. Espérandieu considers that the African Equus Mauritanicus was not domesticated.

16. The recent plausible suggestion (Picard, *C. R. Académie des Inscriptions* (1958), p. 44) that the 'flying gallop' in Saharan rock art does not represent the exploits of the Garamantes in the fifth century B.C., but is a copy of Roman mosaics of the circus, somewhat diminishes the evidence for the horse in the Sahara; but there is little doubt that it was sometimes used in regions where water may have been more abundant than today.

17. Ammian 28 6 5. There is no evidence that the nomads had the camel before the sixth century A.D.; but if Roman troops had it, nomads will almost certainly have stolen or procured some.

18. Maignien R., 1958; Chételat, *RGPGD* xi (1938), p. 5. There are small similar patches in north-western Ashanti.

19. Altehenger, *Eiszeitalter und Gegenwart* ix (1958), p. 104.

20. Clark and van Zinderen Bakker, *Nature* 4923 (1964), p. 971; eid., *ibid.*, 4855 (1962), p. 639; van Zinderen Bakker, *Geologie en Mijnbouw* xliii (1964), p. 123.

21. Van der Hammen and Gonzalez, *Geologie en Mijnbouw* xxii (1960), p. 737.

22. Gregory, *Q.J. Geological Society* 1 (1894), p. 515; de Heinzelin de Braucourt, 'Les stades de Récession du Glacier Stanley Occidental', in *Exploration du Parc national Albert* II, fasc. 1; Nilsson, *Geografiska Annaler* xiii (1931), p. 249 and xxii (1940), p. 1. Cp. *Radiocarbon* v, p. 62, date for probably the beginning of the ice-retreat on Ruwenzori: 1–556, 14700 ± 290.

23. Ice-accumulation must have taken place on Antarctica during northern glaciations, because eustatic lowering of the oceans would expose more of the domed continental surface. The area of sea-ice may or may not have been reduced thereby, as there is no evidence for or against greater snowfall or lower temperatures in Antarctica. Nor would accumulation on the Antarctic continent necessarily affect the mountains in the temperate zone of the southern hemisphere. See Hollin, *Journal of Glaciology* xxxii (1962), p. 173. For general criticism of the assumption of contemporaneity see Heusser, *New York Acad. Sciences Annals* 95 i (1961), p. 642.

24. A shelf at about – 120 m., which may mark the minimum of one of the glaciations, has been observed off the River Orinoco. In other parts of the world a sharp break of slope occurs about – 100–– 130 m., formed by abrasion which can take place only within the depth of wave-action, and so indicating actual sea-level at – 110–– 120 m., see Dietz and Menard, *American Association of Petroleum Geologists Bull.* xxxv (1951), p. 1994; also Donn, Farrand and Ewing, *Journal of Geology* lxx (1962),

p. 206. The dated depths in the Mississippi delta (McFarlan, *Geological Society of America Bull.* lxxii (1961), p. 129; Fisk and McFarlan in Poldervaart, 'The Crust of the Earth', *Geol. Soc. America, special paper* 62) cannot be used owing to tectonic instability of the area and compaction of loose sediments. The conventional eustatic drop to −90−−95 m. has been disproved by evidence for thicker ice than had been calculated, see Ewing, Donn and Farrand, *Geol. Soc. America Bull.* lxxi (1960), p. 1861.

25. Viet, *Zeitschrift für Meteorologie* iii (1949), p. 65. See also Frenzel, 'Die Vegetations- und Landschaftszonen Nord-Eurasiens während der letzten Eiszeit' (*Akademie der Wissenschaften in Mainz, Abhandlungen d. math.-naturw. Kl.* (1959), no. 13 and (1960), no. 6.

26. E.g. by Büdel, *Naturwissenschaften* xxxvi (1949), pp. 105, 133; *Eiszeitalter und Gegenwart* i (1951), p. 16; *Erdkunde* vi (1952), p. 104.

27. Cp. Leroi-Gourhan, *SGFB* VII v (1963), p. 414.

28. Plass, *American Journal of Physics* xxxiv (1956), p. 376; Menzel, in Shapley, *Climatic Change*, ch. 7. Plass (*American Scientist* xliv (1956), p. 302) suggests that orogeny induced intense weathering of fresh rock, and so withdrew much carbon dioxide from the atmosphere.

29. *Linnaean Society Proc.* 152 (1939–40), p. 190; *Q.J. Royal Meteorological Society* lxxxv (1959), p. 332.

30. *RGPGD* iv (1961), p. 2.

31. 'Climatological and Astronomical Interpretation of the Ice Ages' (*Armagh Observatory Contributions* 9); *Irish Astronomical Journal* v (1958), p. 97.

32. *Mathematische Klimalehre.*

33. Shapley, *Climatic Change*, ch. 11.

34. Wundt, *Quartär* 10–11 (1958–9), p. 15.

35. Remy, *Eiszeitalter und Gegenwart* ix (1958), p. 83; Altehenger, *ibid.*, p. 104.

36. *Science* 123 (1956), p. 1061.

37. Tertiary orogeny was succeeded by glaciation only after a long interval, and earlier orogeny has led to no glaciation; see Schwarzbach, *Das Klima der Vorzeit*, ch. VI A 2.

38. Ewing, Donn and Farrand, *Geological Society of America Bull.* lxxi (1960), p. 1861.

39. Donn, *New York Academy of Sciences Trans.* II xxii (1960), p. 491.

40. Andree, *Geologie des Meeresbodens* II.

41. Saks *et al.*, *Priroda* vii (1955), p. 13.

42. Hunkins, *American Geophysical Union Trans.* xl (1959), p. 159.

43. Colinvaux, *Dissertation Abstracts* xxiii (1962–3), p. 4311.

44. Wilson, *Nature* 4915 (1964), p. 147.

45. Bernard E. A., 1962.

46. Lecointre (*Inqua V Résumés*, p. 104) remarks on the cool fauna in the Mauritanian Gulf at the time of Beach V, and suggests that during the transgression icebergs floated far to the south. However, it has been shown that species-distribution of molluscs is unreliable evidence for ocean temperature, and that marked variation may have occurred even

during a eustatic high level, see Valentine and Meade, *University of California Publ. in Geological Sciences* XL i (1961), p. 1. I suspect that the warm period at 0·4–0·45 m. in Albatross core 22 from near Madeira (Schott, *Göteborgs K. Vetenskaps- och Vitterhets-Samhälles Handlingar* VI B 6 no. 2 (1952) = *Oceanografiska Institutet i Göteborg Medd.* 18) is really early post-glacial (or European Late Glacial), as the temperature curve is unlike that generally determined for the Eem glaciation; and it was succeeded by a very sharp cold spell, which I think was due not to a glaciation but to melt-water pouring into the North Atlantic in a more advanced post-glacial stage.

47. Phleger, *Geological Society of America Bull*, lx (1949), p. 1457.

48. The assumption that African pluvials are the tropical equivalent of European glaciations was natural when the African sequence was first investigated; it is the detailed work in many districts and along many lines of evidence which has revealed discrepancies and complications. Mention may be made of a recent attempt to prove that Kageran = Günz and Kamasian = Mindel by comparing the proportion of extant mammals from australopithecine sites in South Africa of the Kageran–Kamasian interpluvial and of the Kamasian with that in the claimed European stages (Kurten, *Stockholm Contributions to Geology* vi (1960), p. 9); only because it illustrates the fallacy of ill-considered biological arguments. In fact, no comparison can be made because the African collections are small and all but one from the Transvaal; mammals form a very small part of the whole biological world; and one may not compare evolution under fairly stable African climatic conditions with that under the violent changes which Europe has undergone. Cp. the note of warning about such arguments by Ewer, *South African Journal of Science* lix (1963), p. 340).

49. For warm temperatures in the Alleröd as far as 45° N, see Tricart, *SGFCR* (1959), p. 132. Temperatures close to glaciated areas remained low in the Alleröd, cp. Manley, *Liverpool and Manchester Geological Journal* II ii (1959), p. 188.

50. Balout, *IRS Trav.* viii (1952), p. 9.

51. Cp. Conrad, *CRAS* 257 (1963), p. 2506.

52. N.B. the desert-dust in all deep-sea sediments of glacial age off Cape Verd Islands: Radczewski in Trask, *Recent Marine Sediments*, p. 496; Goldberg in *Physics and Chemistry of the Earth* IV, p. 281.

53. L-399C; cp. Clark and van Zinderen Bakker, *Nature* 201 (1964), p. 971. See also the dates from Pomongwe cave, Rhodesia) SR 7-8, Cooke, SAAB 18 (1963), pp. 146–50.

54. It is difficult at present to obtain a satisfactory correlation with Europe, because the chronology and stratification of the Würm glaciation is in the melting-pot, apparently because of the difficulty of correlating the fossil soils in the Central European löss with each other and with other geological phenomena, doubts about the accuracy of the recorded stratification and the suitability of samples taken for radiocarbon dating, and perhaps about the oldest radiocarbon dates themselves owing to the

D

possibility of considerable errors where activity is very weak. The previously accepted dates for the main Würm interstadial 42300–29000 B.P. (Gross, *Eiszeitalter und Gegenwart* ix (1958), p. 155) seem untenable, and cold conditions were prevailing in England back to 41900 B.P. (GRO 1245; Godwin, *Proc. Royal Society* 153B (1960), p. 287; but about the same time there was some amelioration in Austria (GRO 1740; de Vries, *K. Nederlandse Akademie van Wetenschappen* 42B (1959), p. 84), succeeding the main Würm interstadial soil, perhaps unconformably. Fink throws the whole of the Göttweig interstadial back into the last interglacial (*Geologische Gesellschaft in Wien Mitt.* liv. (1961), p. 1). But there is good evidence in north-western Europe for the Brörup interstadial, for which dates round about 58000 have been obtained (GRO 1292, 1470, 1729); and it may have lasted later than this. Unfortunately where the highest dates are open to suspicion, very little cultural material has been found associated with the fossil soils. It does appear that there was an interstadial before or perhaps just after (Gross, *Forschungen und Fortschritte* xxxiv (1960), p. 297) 50000 B.P.: whether and how far it contributed by its warmth and dryness (cp. Ložek and Kukla, *Eiszeitalter und Gegenwart* x (1959), p. 81) to the eustatic rise of the ocean of Beach V, with which the development of the Sangoan culture is closely associated, cannot be determined so long as we lack evidence about conditions in Antarctica at that time.

55. Cp. the core A 240–M 1, Rosholt, Geiss, Koczy and Wangersky, *Journal of Geology* lxix (1961), p. 167; and discussion of Eem-chronology, Davies, *GJS* iii (1963), p. 104.

56. Butzer K. W., 1958.

57. Butzer starts Sub-pluvial II about 5500 B.C. in north-east Africa. This figure is reasonable, compared with W-98, 6800 ± 350 B.P. for the start of the neolithic at Haua Fteah (Cyrenaica). Dates of the neolithic from the central Sahara, during a wetter phase than the present, are Beni Abbes 6160 ± 320, Conrad, *CRAS* 257 (1963), p. 2506; Meniet (Hoggar) 5410 ± 300, Delibrias, Hugot and Quezel, *LAPE* v (1957), p. 267, Sa-59; Taessa (Hoggar), Sa-55 4680 ± 300, believed to be the very end of Sub-pluvial II.

58. Godwin, *Proc. Royal Society* 153B (1960–1), p. 287.

59. Tricart, *Association de Géographes français Bull.* (1955), p. 109; Tricart and Brocker, *RGD* vi (1955), p. 145; Tricart, *SGFCR* (1956), p. 164; Brigaud F., 1960, pp. 53–56.

60. Cp. Dart, *American Journal of Physical Anthropology* vii (1949), p. 1. Leakey's land surfaces in Bed I at Olduvai are littered with bones.

61. The very large Acheulian bifaces found here and there throughout Africa could hardly be wielded by a man of present-day strength, and are likely to have been the armature of fall-traps.

62. 'Les Bassins du Niger', *IFAN Mémoires* 4.

63. Cp. the sites near Bouraya (19° 15' N, 3° 40' W) and south of Guir (18° 49' N, 2° 51' W) with bones of hippo, cane-rat, crocodile and fish:

Roman, *Ass. régionale de Paléontologie et de Préhistoire de Lyon Bull.* v (1935); there are many other such sites.

64. Tricart and Brocker, *RGD* vi (1955), p. 145.
65. Cp. Livingstone, *American Anthropologist* lx (1958), p. 553.
66. Davies O., 1964 (1).
67. Mauny R., 1954 (1).
68. Camps, *LAPE* xi (1963), p. 169.
69. See Dalloni and Monod, *Mémoires des Missions scientifiques au Fezzan VI, Géologie et Préhistoire* (Institut de Recherches sahariennes); Mauny, *IFAN* 18B (1956), p. 140; Mauny R., 1961 (1), p. 316–18
70. de Zeltner, *SAP* VI iii (1912), p. 394; Lhote, *IFAN* xii (1950), p. 456.
71. Lhote, *SPF* xxxix (1942), p. 277; id., *CPF* xiii (1950), p. 446; Amblard-Rambert, *NA* 81 (1959), p. 1.
72. Davies O , 1960.
73. For description fifty years ago see Frobenius, *Voice of Africa* ii, ch. 20.
74. Comé (Dahomey), Mauny, *Encyclopédie maritime et coloniale A.O.F., Protohistoire*, p. 37, fig. 5; Gogoro Ouessé and Sé (Dahomey), Mauny R., 1961 (1), p. 179; Gourounsi territory in north-western Ghana, Delafosse, *Anthropologie* xiii (1902), p. 480.
75. Mathelin de Papigny, *Congr. int. d'Anthropologie et d'Archéologie préhistoriques* xv (1931), p. 320.
76. The Falémé gravels have yielded Iron Age remains, kwes and stone balls; for the other rivers there is no material evidence.
77. Herodotus iv, 195–6.
78. Mauny R., 1952 (1); Mauny R., 1961 (1), pp. 293–306.
79. Cp. Wilks, *The Northern Factor in Ashanti History*; Joseph, *SAP* VI iv (1913), no. 3.
80. Brückner W., 1955.
81. Seliquer, *SAP* IX ii (1941), p. 112; id., *IFAN* vii (1945), p. 195. The slag is said to be associated with painted pottery of Christian Nubian type, Mauny R., 1963.
82. Mauny, *IFAN* xiii (1951), p. 168; Mauny R., 1952 (1); Bessac, *IFAN* 20B (1958), p. 352.
83. Probably modern Azelik, Mauny, *NA* 62 (1954), p. 33.
84. Mauny, *NA* 58 (1953), p. 33.
85. Cp. Martin, *Cuadernos de Historia primitiva* iv (1949), p. 111.
86. Camps and Giot, *LAPE* viii (1960), p. 263; Camps, *Revue africaine* 104 (1960), p. 31.
87. The Ife heads are of brass; the account by Fagg and Willett (*IV Panafrican Congress* ii, p. 357) uses the two terms synonymously, in a most unscientific manner. Anything made later than A.D. 1500 is likely to be of brass, metal imported by the Portuguese from Aachen. Bronze earlier than the arrival of the Portuguese could have been alloyed in West Africa from Saharan copper and Nigerian tin; but brass is likely to have been imported as alloy from the Near East, as its manufacture was difficult and confined to a few centres, and the necessary calamine is not known to occur in West Africa.
88. Barker, *Man* lxv (1965), no. 8.

CHAPTER TWO

Chronology

Introductory

The establishment of a relative and absolute chronology provides the only sound basis for all forms of historical investigation. Dates may be soulless and mechanical; without the frame which they give it is impossible to understand the development and interrelations of human cultures. Until very recently absolute chronologies could be established only for literate cultures, and by trade-relations for their illiterate neighbours. The extant historical records of Greece and Israel went back into the first millenium B.C.; behind that were several centuries of oral tradition, lovingly preserved by ancient authors of nationalistic outlook but liable to factual distortion and to contamination by myth and ritual, and so usable only with the greatest caution. The decipherment of hieroglyphs and cuneiform began to provide historical documents back to the third millennium B.C.; but the continual excavation of new documents, better study of the texts, and the decipherment of other Near Eastern languages have entailed several rather drastic revisions of the precise chronology which had been worked out. At the present time the literary chronology of the Near East can be pushed back in some countries to the third millennium B.C., and a less certain frame has been built for neighbouring countries, principally by means of imports.

For barbarian Europe and to a much less certain extent for barbarian Africa some relative chronology has been available. Prehistoric cultural development in Europe has not been stagnant, and indications apparently of important invasions and of political events of far-reaching consequence provided chronological landmarks. In Africa culture seems to be more static; there have been no big states and no important wars before the coming of Islam, and hardly any information filtered across the Saharan barrier to Greco-Roman geographers.

Astronomical, Biological and Isotopic Chronologies

Since the second quarter of this century the natural sciences have provided methods by which absolute chronology can be evaluated, not merely in one sub-continent but throughout the world, which can thus be linked within a single chronological frame. One of the earliest attempts was Milankovich' orbital elements, which has been discussed in Chapter 1. This purports to provide absolute dates, on a wide-reaching scale, for climatic shifts which have been interpolated into the geological and cultural record. But little agreement exists whether the perturbations of the earth's rotation can have had the postulated effects, or whether the chronological interpretation of Milankovich' curves is correct. For instance, he accepted the current theory that there had been three peaks of the last glaciation, and equated them with his three last minima of radiation, thus pushing back the beginning of Würm to about 150000 B.P. Now that it seems more likely that there were two peaks, the last interglacial would have to be brought forward to about 100000–75000 B.P., and all the equivalences with earlier glaciations adjusted accordingly. Milankovich' curves have been used and misused by people who had little knowledge of pleistocene geology and related sciences. It cannot be used as a chronological yardstick.

Nor can Bernard's frame of tropical African climatology, also based on the orbital elements, be used to date the climatic shifts which are still a matter of geological interpretation rather than of proof. Even did these astronomical theories command much wider agreement than they do, the climatological time-lag, which cannot be determined, renders their absolute chronology so vague that it becomes useless.

The postulation of polar wandering at a calculable rate,[1] which can be applied to climatic shifts, is no longer accepted. During the pleistocene the poles seem to have remained nearly stationary.

In Europe limited success has been achieved by measuring the remanent magnetism of fixed objects, and comparing it with the movements of the magnetic pole.[2] This has not been tried in sub-Saharan Africa.

Fairly accurate chronological scales have been obtained for periglacial areas by the counting of varves, which are layers of clay or silt distinguishable by their coarseness or colour. It is reasonable to suppose that in an area subjected to heavy winter frosts finer sedimentation in pools will take place in autumn and winter when streams are frozen or flowing low, and the coarser material will be deposited during the melting season in spring or summer. Theoretically, varves should exist and be countable in African sediments where there are marked annual dry and wet seasons. But heavy rain is not sufficiently regular to provide a time-scale, and some years may experience more than one flood or no flood at all. Examination of the outer silt terraces of the Volta, which consist of sediments deposited by floods in the last few centuries, has revealed lighter and darker bands, which probably indicate deposition and static conditions with vegetation; but the régime seems rather to have been a long-term cycle of higher and lower floods.

Dendrochronology has yielded satisfactory results in regions where there are long-lived trees with annual growth-rings. Though some African trees have growth-rings, it is not known if they are annual; and many of the longest-lived trees, like the baobab,[3] lack them.

Biological development has given in Europe a fairly accurate time-scale, because pleistocene climatic fluctuations have been so violent that comparison of the biotope of one site with another not too far removed and of known relative or absolute date is permissible. In particular, the presence or absence of a known cold or warm fauna gives limiting dates. Mammals, with greater tolerance of extreme conditions, are less satisfactory than, for instance, molluscs. Biological dating has been most acceptably carried out with pollen preserved in peat or clay, provided that allowance be made for stray grains which may have travelled great distances; for regression, especially of trees, and recolonization of periglacial zones has taken place at rates which, at least for the early holocene, are fairly well known.

For Africa biological dating seems to be much less promising. Fairly large faunal assemblages can vaguely be classed as Early Middle or Late Pleistocene; but always with the reservation that in outlying areas relict fauna may have lingered. Climatic fluctuations have created and destroyed so many barriers that rates of development may be guessed only with local study far more accurate than is ever likely to be possible in a continent where sedimentation is scanty and soils are acid. To consider only the genus Homo: Neanderthalensis was living in North Africa[4] at a date roughly comparable with his last appearance in Europe. The Mousterian culture which he practised developed into the Aterian, which lasted very late in the Sahara;[5] and the last offshoots of the Mousterian on the Guinea coast are subsequent to the Flandrian transgression (about 3500–2700 B.C.). We do not know what type of man carried these Ultimate Middle Stone Age cultures; it is a reasonable guess that they were relict descendants of Neanderthalensis, who were not replaced in West Africa, behind the barriers of the Sahara and the Guinea forest, until the neolithic invasions.

Palynology does not promise an accurate chronology in West Africa. Climatic changes have been far too weak. Extremely interesting results have been obtained, especially from marginal regions like the Sahara.

But suitable deposits are few, and we can trace no regular process of recolonization.

Climatic change is mirrored also in deep-ocean sediments, in which temperature can be estimated either biologically or from quantity of calcium carbonate or from oxygen-18.[6] Absolute dates of certain points in the cores are determined by radiocarbon or by ratio of the disintegration products of uranium, present in sea-water. Even in cores believed to be undisturbed by slumping, a large margin of error is involved because of the slowness of sedimentation and mixing by bottom-feeders. Nevertheless, fairly consistent results have been obtained for the rise of temperature at the end of the last glaciation, less consistent for earlier events. The advantage of this study is that it gives hope of fixing a skeleton-chronology well behind the limits of radiocarbon, probably to nearly 400,000 years. The determination of dates by ionium-230: radium-226 has proved unreliable; but a method is being evolved based on ionium-230: protactinium-231,[7] which seems to be more promising. Dates of only three long cores have so far been published: 100000–70000 B.P. seems reasonable for the Eem interglacial, and behind it are perhaps indicated a long Warthe glaciation and a short Riss–Warthe interglacial. But the reliability of this method is unproven until we are able to compare the consistency of results from a number of cores. Moreover, no long cores have been raised in the Gulf of Guinea, where it should be possible to obtain exceptionally interesting results at the meeting of the cold Benguela and warm equatorial currents. The interaction of warm and cold water probably has had great effect on West African climatic fluctuations.

Dating by estimating the decay of potassium-40 to argon-40 is not at present satisfactory for pleistocene events, owing to the extremely long half-life of the former isotope. The first dates published[8] appeared reasonable; but the divergent dates of Olduvai I from two different laboratories have brought the method into disrepute.[9]

For fairly recent dating the most satisfactory isotopic method is radiocarbon, with a half-life standardized at 5,570 years,[10] and an absolute limit of 70,000 years.[11] It is to be hoped that one day study of other nuclear disintegrations will be developed, to check radiocarbon. In the meantime, frequent cross-checking and discussion by radiocarbon laboratories are ironing out many difficulties. Agreement is being reached as to what materials are unsuitable for radiocarbon dating, and the increasing number of consistent dates is silencing the earlier critics. There are still difficulties, many due to careless collecting of samples by archaeologists. There are a few freak results, and the statistical method of calculating dates admits that an occasional date may be aberrant. There may be grave errors of interpretation by the archaeologist. It is not understood why dates from certain regions are regularly too low, like the lower Nile Valley.[12]

I give at the end of the chapter a table of dates important for West Africa, after I have outlined the geological and cultural framework into which they are to be fitted. They would be misleading before the sequence of events to which they refer is understood.

The Geological Sequence: Raised Beaches

Raised beaches mark former high ocean levels. Whereas in geologic periods the distribution of land and sea and the contours of the crust-surface have varied greatly, during the fairly short and well-known Pleistocene only two factors are involved, small tectonic movements of several types and the variation of the absolute water-content of the oceans. As during the Pleistocene there have probably been but negligible variations in the total surface-water of the earth, the only factor which will have caused the water-content of the oceans to vary will have been withdrawal of surface-water by ice-accumulation on the continents. Consequently, if the eustatic variations of the oceans can be isolated from those caused by tectonic movements, and provided that there has been no shift in the earth's centre of gravity, the absolute height of the oceans or the eustatic constant at any particular moment in the past should be determinable and applicable to all coasts of the world.

Variation in the eustatic constant ought further to provide a rough chronological frame, because it should theoretically be possible to associate each glacial or interglacial with geological landmarks in the unglaciated continents, and these with each other. Unfortunately, the solution is not quite so simple. Even regions which are regarded as extremely stable have undergone crustal warping which upsets the small range of pleistocene eustatic constants (from a figure now regarded as rather more than $+55$ m. to roughly -120 m.) and has caused deformation of ancient beach-lines.

Something is known of orogenic and epeirogenic movements, nearly all of which originated before the Pleistocene and so can be traced in the geologic record into the tertiary. But practically nothing is known of the rate of such movements, which need not have been constant, save what can be deduced from raised beaches; so they cannot be allowed for in reckoning eustatic constants. A special type of tectonic movement is isostatic adjustment of the crust to overloading. Even where the load has been very great, the sub-crustal compression seems to have been nearly vertical, and there is no geological evidence in warped river terraces for magma having been squeezed out from beneath the load and caused a swelling of the surrounding land at considerable distances. Isostatic adjustment is very slow; it appears that Fennoscandia has undergone not much more than half its total recovery since the removal of the last ice-sheets; the earliest stages were the most rapid.[13]

Some types of load have been more or less universal, so have little affected the calculation of the relative eustatic constant. For instance, increase of water in the oceans will have depressed all coast-lands simultaneously; and progressive continental erosion should have proceeded at roughly the same rate all over the earth. Other loads are local. The filling of tectonic troughs with sediment will have slightly depressed these troughs. Much more important has been the weight of ice-sheets. It seems possible that the great accumulation of ice in Antarctica may have sufficiently shifted the earth's centre of gravity to invalidate the calculation of the eustatic constant at some latitudes.

Africa has not during the Pleistocene seen important local isostatic adjustments. Its glaciers have been very small; its troughs, like the Niger delta, limited in size. Moreover, many regions are remarkably stable. So it seems to be a continent where the eustatic constants of the Pleistocene are calculable with some precision; and in fact a few regions, like Morocco and to a rather lesser degree Ghana, have yielded satisfactory figures.

Raised beaches represent interglacial peaks; for in fact we know practically nothing about low stands at glacial maxima, and beaches formed during a transgression or regression are meaningless unless it is possible to determine the exact stage to which they belong. Throughout the world absolute ocean-levels have diminished progressively since the Calabrian (the earliest pleistocene beach); and on this fall of the eustatic constant have been superposed the fluctuations of the northern glaciations. The continued drop of the ocean does not seem explicable by progressive climatic deterioration, as northern interglacials have been warm and have melted the ice. Recent work of the I.G.Y. in Antarctica has revealed enormous masses of ice, which appear to have been steadily accumulating throughout the Pleistocene, though doubtless with fluctuations, and to have withdrawn progressively more water from the oceans.

Raised beaches were first studied on the Mediterranean, and Medi-

terranean names were given to them.[14] Unfortunately, the whole of the
Mediterranean young mountain zone has undergone tectonic movement during the Pleistocene, and some of the names first given refer to
places where it has been found that there is no independent beach.
Attempts to adapt names to beaches other than those to which they
first referred[15] have increased the confusion, and it has been essential
to discard the old names. The Moroccan names[16] might be used, as
most of Morocco has been fairly stable; but they have been badly worked
out, the term Anfatian has been applied to two different beaches, and
Uljian seems to be used by some French authors for several beaches
other than the one which it first signified. So I have found it necessary
to reject all the current beach-names and to use numbers, each of which
can be subdivided if it is proved that it refers to more than one ocean
maximum. In fact, Beach I (pre-Günz) almost certainly had more than
one stage, and Beach VI (holocene) a number of minor fluctuations
described in great detail by Fairbridge.[17]

It is not possible to tabulate all the names given by authors to the
beaches. The following table refers to some of the principal systems:

	NORTH SEA (Woldstedt)	MEDITERRANEAN (Zeuner)	MOROCCO (Biberson)	MOROCCO (Gigout)
I	Tegelen and Waal	Sicilian	Messaoud	Calabrian
II	Cromer	Milazzian	Maarif	Sicilian
III	Holstein (Neede)	Tyrrhenian	Anfatian	Anfatian I
IV	Eem	Monastirian I (or Main Mon.)	Harounian	Anfatian II
V	unidentified	Monastirian II (or Late Mon.)	Uljian	Uljian
VI	Flandrian		Mellah	Flandrian

For all these beaches an approximate eustatic constant has been
calculated from data derived from all parts of the world. Altitudes,
however, can never be exact owing to probable slight fluctuations during
high ocean-levels; and identification of beaches by altitude is a hazardous
procedure:

Beach I	roughly +100 m. with an isostatic component
II	apparently about +50–60 m.
III	+30 m.
IV	+17 m.
V	+8 m.
VI	+3 m.

Beach VI is post-glacial. The ocean rose rapidly from the very low levels of the Würm glaciation at an average rate of about 9 mms. per year, with fluctuations corresponding to the glacial retreats and re-advances which have been traced in detail in Europe and North America. The rise slowed down in the Atlantic period, which seems to have been the warmest period in post-glacial time, about 6200 B.P.; the sea reached modern ocean-level on stable coasts about 5500 B.P.[18] It rose further to + 2–3 m.; the regression began about 2650 B.C. Since that time there have been slight fluctuations; but I regard the whole holocene complex as sub-divisions of a single beach.

Beach I is pre-glacial, or probably pre-Günz. In Europe evidence is accumulating for a Donau glaciation,[19] though traces of it do not yet seem to have been noticed in North America; and in Holland there are signs of a short but sharp cold period, the pre-Tiglian, at the very beginning of the Pleistocene. Beach I seems to cover both the Donau–Günz and the pre-Donau interglacials, and it has not been possible in most regions to subdivide it. In Morocco, despite its extremely clear record, only a single transgression seems distinguishable, the Messaoud stage.[20] At Alexandria Beach I corresponds to four coastal bars and two Nile terraces.[21] At Alexander Bay (South Africa) there is a cliff about 12 m. below the top of the regression-beach,[22] which should indicate a transgression; rolled pebble-tools were found only on the lower part of the beach. Behind the Pleistocene there is no connected series of beaches, and we are driven back on the much vaguer evidence of land-surfaces, which are likely to have been formed by epeirogenic rather than eustatic movements. At least the last two surfaces, the mid-tertiary and the end-tertiary, are distinguishable in the stable parts of Africa. A more detailed sequence has been proposed at the mouth of the Congo.[23]

The end-tertiary surface is associated in Ghana with Beach I, and the profile behind Accra is particularly informative. Beach I appears in situ north-east of Abubiasi and east of Odorkor, rather above 50 m. S.L. and about six kilometres from the present coast. The peneplain can be traced from the airport to north-east of Legon, from 65 to 80 m. S.L. 8–13 kms. from the coast. At Legon there rises to a height of about 20 m. above it a heavily lateritized inselberg, which is the remnant of an older surface.

Beach II has been identified, in Natal with rolled pebble-tools[24] and with perhaps initial Chellean in Morocco (Maarif stage).[20] It must be the beach of the Cromer interglacial, which in Europe is associated with the beginnings of the Chellean culture.[25] It is seldom exposed in Africa.

Beach III has been identified in many places. Both in Western Europe and in Africa it and its associated river gravels carry rolled Late Chellean or Early Acheulian tools. It is the beach of the Swanscombe gravels, and it has been traced also on the River Somme. It certainly belongs to the Holstein or Mindel–Riss interglacial. This is believed to have been of long duration (though there are no absolute dates); pollen diagrams, though not very clear, suggest two warm maxima.[26] There seems to be only one Beach III in Morocco (Sidi Abderrahman J-O, though Biberson considers that it is superposed on a regressive Beach II) and in Ghana, with a slight fluctuation at Senya Beraku; in both regions the industry conforms to type. In the southern Cape and Natal, Beach III was a period of rapid epeirogenic emergence, normally the Major Emergence of Krige,[27] so that as many as five beaches are reckoned to this stage and contain the same industry.[28] In the western Cape the beach is not found and must be below modern ocean-level.

About Beaches IV and V there is doubt. The two beaches are clearly distinct and not parts of a single regression, so after Beach IV there must have been a regression below the level of Beach V, though not necessarily very much below, followed by a transgression. Near the mouth of the Oliphants River below Vredendal there are three terrace gravels.[22] The uppermost is a thick gravel on a rock terrace about 22 m. above the plain; it may have been deposited in a calm estuary, as the pebbles are poorly bedded and sub-angular. It contains rolled Chellean or Early Acheulian tools, and on it is some unrolled Late Acheulian or Sangoan. The upper part of the gravel is better bedded, probably because the current increased as incision started. This could be the equivalent of either Beach III or IV, probably the latter. Below it a gravel dips fairly sharply to the valley floor and disappears; on it is rolled Acheulian and unrolled Sangoan material. The third gravel is about 10 m. above the present river and contains slightly rolled Sangoan tools; rolled Sangoan is never found on Beach IV, so this gravel must be associated with Beach V. No borings have been made in the Oliphants Valley, so there is no evidence for the depth of the second gravel or the form of the incised valley to which it belongs; indeed, such evidence is likely to have been destroyed by the more prolonged incision after Beach V, corresponding to the Würm glaciation. If the upper gravel belongs to Beach IV, there was a regression at least to modern S.L. between IV and V. At the Wilderness (Cape Prov.) there was a regression to at least − 30 m. between two transgressions, which may be Beaches IV and V;[29] but the identification of the beaches there is speculative. There was a regression to at least −5 m. in Majorca between what are called Tyrrhenian II and III;[30] these may be Beaches IV and V in my terminology, but again identification is uncertain.

Beaches IV and V have been identified in Angola and Ghana. The former normally contains rolled Acheulian[31] and never rolled Sangoan [fig. 1]; it must belong to near the end of the Acheulian period. Beach V usually has unrolled or slightly rolled Sangoan and unrolled M.S.A.; so it is near the beginning of the Sangoan period. In Morocco, Sidi Abderrahman G at +24 m., with slightly rolled tools regarded as fairly advanced Acheulian, must be Beach IV.[32] The Uljian Beach, with cliff at +6–8 m., must be Beach V; immediately overlying it in Algeria are red dune sands, and Aterian tools were left on it while still unconsolidated.[33] Aterio-Mousterian is common in the dune sands which accumulated during the regression from Beach V.[34] It may be noted that the term Uljian has been applied by some French workers in different regions of Africa in an imprecise way; it may refer to a beach which must be IV rather than V. Both beaches are identifiable at Gibraltar, probably at Cadiz,[35] and near Lisbon.[36] Tectonic movements in many parts of the Mediterranean make it less easy to be certain of them.[37]

It is generally agreed that Beach IV belongs to the Eem interglacial; for though in North Germany the Ohe interstadial (Saale–Warthe) has been recognized, there is no evidence for a eustatic rise above modern sea-level at that time. European workers, unable to find that their climate ameliorated sufficiently at any time during the Würm glaciation to cause a eustatic rise to about +8 m., assume that Beach V also is part of Eem; they forget that eustatic sea-levels are world-wide phenomena, and that Europe is not the only continent, nor the northern the only hemisphere. Zeuner goes so far as to place Beaches IV and V in Eem, but to produce not very satisfactory evidence of a third stage at about +2–3 m., which he calls Epimonastirian.[38]

However, most of the Eem pollen diagrams from Europe indicate a single interglacial peak and not the kind of fluctuation which the beach sequence would demand. In a few diagrams from Western Europe there may be a fluctuation,[39] but some of them are disputed. There is evidence for a warm damp period in Provence after the Eem interglacial.[40] At Weimar-Ehringsdorf the upper travertine with warm fauna lies between two colder stages;[41] it has, however, been suggested that the Pariser clay between the two travertines is indicative of drought rather than lowered temperature.

Radiocarbon dates from Africa indicate more clearly that Beach V is subsequent to the Eem interglacial and belongs to a Würm interstadial. Shells from a 4-metre beach at Sedgefield near Knysna (Cape) gave a date 37700±2000.[42] This is far older than the marine level of about −3 m. at Groenvlei (6870±160),[43] and the older beach was capped by a sandy plain with a fossil soil. Dates from coral of a sea-level of about +4 m. in Western Australia are 35000±3700 and >37000.[44] In Louisiana there was a fairly high sea-level, apparently about 30000 B.P.[45] I lay less stress on dates of about 30000 B.P. from Hawaii (LJ 205 and 253–4), as this island has probably been unstable.

At Kalambo Falls (Zambia) the Late Acheulian level is dated 57300± 300 and 57600±750 (GRO–2644),[46] the Early Sangoan 43000±3300 (L–399 C).[47] I have shown above that Beach IV came to an end before but not long before the end of the Late Acheulian, and that it usually carries rolled tools, but at some places in Angola and the Cape unrolled of this stage. Beach V normally carries rolled and unrolled developed Sangoan. Thus the Sangoan culture arose between Beaches IV and V. If it is legitimate to extrapolate from the interior to the coast of southern Africa, as with some time-lag I consider it is, Beach IV would correlate with the Eem interglacial, which ended about 70000 B.P. (see table of isotopic dates below). Beach V cannot be Eem, but must belong to a Würm interstadial.[48]

The swampy, lagoon-fringed coasts of much of West Africa are unsuitable for the preservation of raised beaches; the soft sediments would easily be eroded, or diagnostic features like pebbles and beach sand would be buried and revealed only by extensive boring. Results of this sort have probably been obtained in exploring for oil in the Niger delta, but little has been published; and this region was sinking rapidly in the Late Pleistocene.[49]

I do not propose here to discuss in detail the Moroccan beaches, which lie outside West Africa. There is in that country a very fine series of marine and coastal deposits, but levels have been slightly distorted. At Casablanca Beaches III and IV (Sidi Abderrahman J-O and G) have telescoped and been stratigraphically reversed; the same seems to have happened at the Oued Lau south-east of Tetuan.[50] Otherwise the beaches are at fairly normal altitudes, VI about +2 m., V (Uljian) at +6–8 m., IV at +24 m., III at +18 m., II about +55 m., I about +100 m.[16] There is archaic Acheulian in Beach III, advanced Acheulian slightly rolled and unrolled Sangoan in IV, what looks like rolled Sangoan in V at Khemisset;[51] heavily rolled pebble-tools in Beach III may be derived from an older beach.[52] A similar series, with rolled pebble-tools in Beach I at Magoito, is described from Portugal.[53] In southern Morocco and Ifni, where the mountains run out into the Atlantic, there has been more intensive tectonic movement, and beaches are at very divergent altitudes;[54] only in the extreme south is it claimed that there has been no deformation; the same seems to be true in Rio de Oro.[55]

In Mauritania and at the mouth of the River Senegal only Beaches V and VI have been identified; as Beach V seems to rest on an ancient continental surface, the older pleistocene beaches have probably been downwarped and drowned.[56] Beach V at +4-5 m. overlies a lateritic crust and dunes; it was followed by a regression during a dry period, with redistribution of the dune sands, after which the sea rose to +1-1½ metres. During Beach V the Senegal had an estuary 60 m. deep; during VI the sea penetrated only a short way up the delta. Beach V transgressed as much as 90 kms. into Mauritania near Nouakchott, with an impoverished fauna.[57] Despite the volcanic nature of the archipelago, these two beaches are visible on Sal (Cape Verd Islands), and also the remains of one or more older beaches at varying heights.[58]

Around Dakar a beach is known at altitudes varying from +12 to +30 m.;[59] it is generally believed that only one beach is represented, and recent vulcanism has caused considerable warping. There is a little information about its fauna, but none on its archaeological content. So one can only guess that it is Beach V, and that all the older beaches are submerged. Beach VI is at fairly stable altitude, and at Pointe de Fann is associated with an Ultimate M.S.A. industry [fig. 36].[60] It immediately underlies the mesolithic at Tiemassas [fig. 48].

The drowned coast of south Senegal and Port. Guinea is unsuitable for the preservation of old beaches, and the whole area appears flooded by outward tilting in recent times. So no terraces occur in the very level valley of the lower Gambia.

In Sierra Leone marine levels at +100 +50 +23 and +10 m. have been claimed;[61] but beach deposits were found only on the highest, and the report lacks certainty. Recent work has established beaches at +55 +12 and perhaps +32 m. on the Freetown peninsula;[62] these altitudes correspond roughly with Dixey's three lower levels, and the two lowest may be III and IV or V.

Liberia is again swamp and totally unexplored; so is most of the Ivory Coast, where Beach VI is cut into a bar six metres high which may represent a degraded Beach V. The western Ivory Coast however faces slightly east, and like the coast of Ghana has been swept by currents which have prevented the deposition of pleistocene or earlier sediments. But its granite cliffs have no notches, and only an "Uljian" beach (probably V) survives in certain bays.[63] The top of the cliffs is at +50–60 m., and the rock often is covered by a lateritic crust. Tricart believes that most of the pleistocene beaches have been removed by faulting of the cliff margins, which has cut back to the pliocene peneplain. He dates the surface behind the quaternary, because its lateritization implies displuvial conditions, unlike the dense forest régime which this coast has today. A peneplain rising from a base-level about +50 m. would correlate well with the peneplain of Cape Three Points (Ghana), which rises from the remains of Beach I at about the same level.

West of the River Ankobra the coast of Ghana is a continuation of the strip-lagoons and tertiary sediments of the eastern Ivory Coast. In the western portion there are traces of marine levels at +1½ and +6 m., presumably the same as Beaches V and VI of farther west. At Bonyeri there is also a +13 m. level, and perhaps the remains of an early pleistocene peneplain about +45 m. No archaeological finds are associated with these terraces, and practically no remains are known anywhere in this region of extremely wet forest. Borings near Edu show that the coastal plain of the Tano consists of recent sediments which fill a pleistocene drowned valley.

The region just west of the River Ankobra is a large swampy lagoon, bounded by a low sand-bar. Rivers empty into the swamp, and have left old gravels devoid of artefacts. Until quite recently the Ankobra seems to have flowed into a lake with islands, which has been reclaimed by the formation of the bar. It was probably first drained by the cutting of the present channel during a eustatic low. Junner considered that the islands preserve remnants of ancient surfaces, probably of the plio-pleistocene peneplain. A few microliths have been found on them.

Between the River Ankobra and Takoradi is a rocky coast on which marine terraces are preserved. Near Takoradi the crystalline rocks are masked by carboniferous sands and gravels, in which it is more difficult to determine marine levels. There are traces of all the beaches on this stretch; but as man penetrated only recently into this forested area, they are not associated with artefacts, and other fossils have not been found. The pliopleistocene peneplain is in evidence, and at several places rolled pebbles at its outer edge or on the slope probably come from Beach I at about +55 m., though the beach has not been found *in situ*.

A hill at $+32$ m. overlooking the mouth of the Ankobra may be a fragment of the terrace of Beach II; but this has nowhere been certainly identified in Ghana. There are levels of Beach III with pebbles at about $+23$ m., and of Beach IV at $+12-15$ m., and a few notches at $+5$ m. near Axim which seem to represent Beach V. Storm-ridges and large pebbles of Beach VI are preserved in the exposed bays west of Cape Three Points, but there is little sign of this level on the more sheltered eastern side of the headland. Grinding-grooves on the rocks below H.W.M. at Mutrakni Point and inscriptions (perhaps of European sailors) below water at Nsama Cove may be evidence of a recent sea-level lower than the present; but neither gives cogent proof, as they lie above L.W.M. and the inscribed rocks may have fallen.

East of Takoradi raised beaches are preserved better than elsewhere in West Africa, and are frequently associated with artefacts of recognizable cultures. This coast consists mainly of pre-Cambrian rocks, masked by softer carboniferous sediments as far as Komenda and by Jurassic conglomerates for a short distance near Saltpond. It seems during the later Pleistocene to have been indented, and has been straightened recently by the formation of bars.

It is impossible to map in detail the form of the coast during the Early Pleistocene. It probably consisted of wide bays several miles deeper than the present ones, with ridges of harder rock forming long promontories. At the mouth of the Densu, Beach I is at the back of a deep bay, which has been filled partly by the capture of the River Densu through a gorge in the ridge; during eustatic lows of the Pleistocene it was incised by the river to -22 m. The Muni Lagoon near Winneba also was a wide bay; a concentration of pebbles five miles inland at $+42$ m. probably marks the neighbourhood of Beach I.

Other modern lagoons are drowned valleys, incised by streams during the Pleistocene. There is no evidence for bays before their incision. Sakumo Lagoon has two channels at -13 and -16 m. half a mile from the present mouth; and deep levels have been noticed in the small valleys west of Cape Coast. At Tefle near the mouth of the Volta there is a narrow meandering channel 30 m. deep, which must have been occupied by a small river, while the Volta probably flowed into the sea farther west.[64] Much of this incision seems to date from the last eustatic low. Many of the valleys must have been very steep, and there is no evidence for fossil dunes. The Amisa Lagoon, east of Saltpond, formed a ramifying estuary up to eight kilometres long, which has left pebbles up to $+22$ m., among which are unrolled Sangoan tools. When

E

the ocean rose, these valleys were filled with sediments, and the lagoons were closed by bars, most of which are recent. At Apam the bar was formed by Beach VI, on which two rough choppers were found. At Aboadi there is evidence for a bar belonging to Beach V, corresponding to that at Abidjan; there may have been others bars of this date, which were eroded during the subsequent eustatic low. The valley behind the Legislative Assembly Building at Accra must have been cut between Beaches III and IV.

The Geological Survey recorded beaches in Ghana at about $+55$ m., $+22-25$ m., $+9-13$ m., $+3-6$ m. and $+1-1\frac{1}{2}$ m.[65] These altitudes concord with my own observations;[66] the denial[67] of more than one pre-holocene beach, of varying altitude owing to warping, does not agree with the field evidence. All the Ghana beaches are lower than their estimated world-wide eustatic constants, progressively more so with age; this suggests that there has been very slight outward tilting on the continental margin, which will have reduced by a small amount the gradients of the larger rivers.

I have mentioned evidence for Beach I and its associated peneplain near Cape Three Points. The peneplain is probably preserved at $+60$ m. on the Amisian plateau at Saltpond, and to the west in degraded form. The platform behind Apam rest-house [pl. 8] seems to mark the level of the beach. A notch at about $+55$ m. near the mouth of the Densu seems to be the remains of its cliff cut in quartzite, and there are pebbles in this area coming down from about the same altitude. A few miles to the east Beach I has been found *in situ* and derived near Odorkor on the western outskirts of Accra. This beach nowhere carries artefacts.

A few flat-topped hills have been claimed as remains of Beach II at about $+38$ m.;[68] but the existence of this beach has nowhere been proved in Ghana or other parts of West Africa. See, however, plate 8 for a possible notch.

There are platforms and pebble-exposures of Beach III at $+22-25$ m. at several sites along the coast of Ghana. One of the most impressive used to be at Senya Beraku [pl. 16]. At Huni west of Cape Coast are large deposits of pebbles, mostly derived but extending up to an original level of $+23$ m. On many platforms are unrolled Sangoan artefacts, especially round the Amisa and Muni Lagoons. From Senya Beraku is a slightly rolled piece which may be Chellean, from Huni a typical rolled Chellean pick. Rolled flakes and pebble choppers have been found at the same level near Huni, Eja and probably at the mouth of the River Densu; these also could be Chellean, but are not diagnostic.

Included typical rolled artefacts are the most useful for dating a beach relative to the cultural sequence, because a stone tool will not tolerate wave-action for very long without losing its form. It is permissible to use also artefacts rolled in river gravels, which may with some certainty be referred to a particular eustatic stage. There is a Middle Terrace on the Pra at about 20 m. l.w., but nowhere has rolled material been found in the gravel, and it is doubtful if man penetrated so far west into the forest before Sangoan times. On the Volta, although no beach gravel has been identified nearer to its mouth than Tema (at about +25 m.), there is a clear terrace gravel at Toje and Sogakope about fifteen miles from the present coast, and gravel-spreads at the same level to the east suggest that the old mouth was near this point and that the whole of the modern lagoons and delta have been built out since the Middle Pleistocene. The associated river terrace has not been followed immediately above Sogakope, but can be picked up again at +29–30 m. S.L. and about 20 m. above the river near Kpong Agricultural Station, 91 kilometres upstream; and a little farther up, in what must have been a backwater at Poyonu, the gravel carries rolled Chellean tools. If one allows for outward tilting since Beach III, these gravels could have been at or just above the head of the estuary. The terrace is interrupted above this point by the Volta gorge.

Beach IV, usually at +12–14 m., is less apparent in Ghana than Beach III. Rolled artefacts have seldom been found in it, because it normally contains Late Acheulian material, and this culture only penetrated slightly into Ghana. In other parts of Africa as well as in West Africa it seems that the Sangoan developed in the pre-Gamblian interpluvial, and the Late Acheulian, with Beach IV corresponding to the Eem interglacial, belongs to the final stage of the Kamasian II pluvial, when forest blanketed the Guinea coastlands.

The best exposure of Beach IV is at Asokrochona railway-cutting between Accra and Tema, where it abutted on a low cliff on each side of a point at +14 m. (+43 ft.) [fig. 1]. It yielded rough rolled tools which seem to be small cleavers. Wave-cut benches, cliff-bases and remains of gravel occur at the same altitude elsewhere from Axim to Tema. Rolled pebble tools from Duakur near Cape Coast and hand-axes from Biriwa look more archaic than the Late Acheulian, so may be derived from Beach III.

Unrolled Sangoan picks have been found among the gravels of Beach IV. As elsewhere, the Sangoan people took advantage of large pebbles.

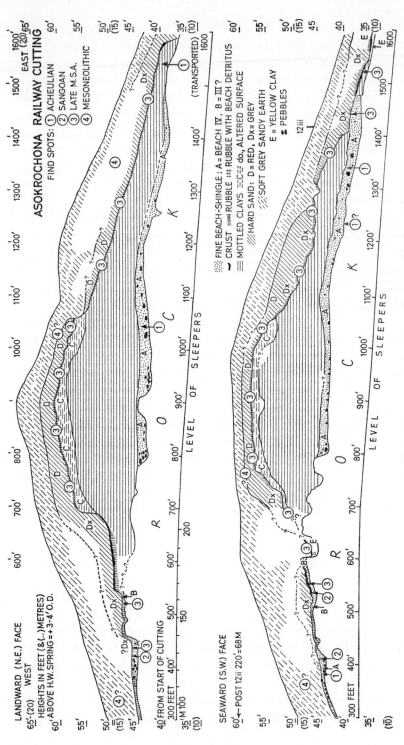

FIG. I   Sections of Beach IV and overlying deposits, Asokrochona, Ghana.

from Davies O., 1964 (2), fig. 64

At Asokrochona such tools lay *in situ* on the crust capping the beach [pl. 27]; and the same was probably true at Manprobi close to Accra, where many rolled Sangoan pieces, found in Beach VI, must be derived from a terrace of Beach IV, noticed a mile or two to the east, and demolished by erosion during the Flandrian transgression.

Beach V, at +6–8 m., is exposed at many places east of Takoradi. It appears to be separated from Beach IV by an interval much shorter than that between IV and III, and the Low Terrace of the rivers inland probably grades to both Beach IV and V. It sometimes carries unrolled Sangoan and M.S.A. pieces, e.g. a typical pick from Ankaful near Saltpond; some pieces are small and may be late in the Sangoan series. But no rolled material which is certainly Sangoan comes from Beach V *in situ* in Ghana.

Beach VI appears at a good many sites. At Manprobi it is overlain by clays containing Ultimate M.S.A. [fig. 32]. It alone yields molluscs, all of modern species. Mangrove-wood swamped by the rising ocean at Takoradi was dated 5570±70 B.P. (GRO 1194). In view of its importance in relation to soil-sections and the stratification of industries, it is better to postpone discussion to Chapter 3 (below pp. 136–9). There is evidence from Tema and Takoradi for a sea-level below present subsequent to Beach VI. It is known from many parts of the world that there have been minor fluctuations since the major post-glacial transgression.[17]

East of Ghana there is no reliable information about raised beaches until the mouth of the Congo, apart from a notice of a marine platform at +5 m. at Pointe Noire;[69] on it, at the base of red sands, were Lupemban picks. In eastern Ghana, Togo and Dahomey there are soft sediments known as Terres de barre, in which no marine terraces are preserved. Their date and nature is uncertain. They are probably largely illuvial, and are considered to be pliopleistocene; but in view of their great thickness they may well be in origin older. They have in places been redistributed as late as the Late Pleistocene, and cover the deposits of Beach IV at Asokrochona [fig. 1, pl. 27]. Similar sediments extend across Nigeria to the Cameroons fault, where recent vulcanism will have destroyed all beaches. On the coasts of the Cameroons and Gaboon there may be beaches, but no exploration has been attempted.

The Geological Sequence: River Terraces

River terraces are old valley bottoms which have been abandoned owing to incision and rejuvenation. The source of the river may be in mountains which themselves have not reached erosional maturity owing to recent uplift or exceptional hardness; therefore the longitudinal profile of a source-region is complex and often defies general principles. But from where the river emerges from the mountains, its mature profile is a slightly concave slope to the base-level.[70]

The ultimate base-level must be sea-level at the mouth. Sea-level relative to land may have varied locally owing to tectonic movements. These have been of importance on many African coasts. For instance, there seems to have been considerable submergence between the Congo (and perhaps the Cameroons fault) and the Cape between Beaches III and IV, and in Senegal and Mauritania between Beaches IV and V, if the raised beaches are rightly dated. Along the Guinea coast, excluding Nigeria, and in parts of Morocco tectonic movements have been minimal during the Pleistocene. Sea-level has varied also eustatically, and on stable coasts evidence has been given for a progressive drop of ocean-level, on which has been superposed a series of raised beaches corresponding to northern interglacials, and buried estuaries corresponding to glaciations.

Each lowering of sea-level must have caused rejuvenation of the estuary; but so far as we know from the smaller rivers of Ghana, there was not time for this to extend more than 30 kms. from the present coast. When longitudinal profiles of the lower Volta, the Comoe and some of the western rivers become available, we may find longer buried estuaries. Each rise of sea-level will have produced aggradation in the estuary, but probably not much farther inland. Consequently, near the stable Guinea coast river profiles have been determined not by the short-term eustatic variations but by the longer-term pleistocene drop of ocean-level; but for climatic reasons to be discussed below incision has not been continuous, and the terraces form a series of steps which can roughly be correlated with the stepped beaches.

A long river is almost certain to pass over rocks of unequal hardness, leaving bars which will break up the ideal longitudinal profile into a number of more or less independent reaches. Although each bar will slowly erode, only a maturity verging on senility could combine these reaches into a single profile. Such bars are well known at the cataracts of the Nile and on the Vaal-Orange.

Of the West African rivers which drain the interior of the continent, the middle and upper Niger flows over several bars, of which one, at Taoussa (Tosaye) is of extreme youth. But terraces at about 10 m. on the large tributaries in Nigeria, containing unrolled Sangoan and occasionally Acheulian pieces, so probably Low Terraces,[71] indicate an even profile during the later Pleistocene from at least Jebba and probably farther upstream to the head of the delta. On the River Senegal I have no information. There is at least one terrace gravel on the River Gambia near Kédougou, 600 kms. from the mouth, whence have been collected unrolled Sangoan pieces [fig. 14] and perhaps rolled pebble tools; but as no attempt was made to estimate its height, one cannot tell if it belongs to an even, unbroken profile.

The Volta, at the head of the Accra Plains, flows through a ridge of hard Togo-quartzite by the Akosombo gorge. Parts of this gorge have been deeply faulted during the Pleistocene, at Ajena and Senchi the river crosses very low rock-bars; comparison of terrace levels above and below the gorge indicates that earlier faulting had so disrupted the rock that its erosion has nearly been able to keep pace with that of the softer rocks upstream, so there is no true bar. Above Akosombo numerous very low rapids were swamped at flood-time and did not affect the profile of the river below the point where the Black Volta breaks through hard grits at Bui, 700 kms. from the mouth. There is here a bar 100 m. high, traversed by a series of rapids; above it terraces are telescoped like those of the northern Ivory Coast. There is a similar nickpoint on the River Oti below Yendi, 500 kms. from the Volta mouth; this seems to be a true nickpoint, marking what is probably the limit of headward pleistocene erosion but not determined by a bar of hard rock. Nickpoints of some of the smaller tributaries are not very far from their confluences, of the Daka at Wiae, of the Asukawkaw below Breniasi.

The short coastal rivers of Ghana have approximately even profiles to near their sources.[72] Though they traverse many types of rock, very deep weathering seems to have rotted resistant outcrops which could form bars. I have explained how in the Ivory Coast the watershed bends a long way to the north; but the coastal profiles of the rivers extend less than 250 kms. inland, where there must be either bars or nickpoints which have not been described. Above them terraces are telescoped as on the plateau. The coastal thalwegs of the Guinea forest must have been formed fairly rapidly; for artefacts of the same stage are found in the same terrace gravel at very different distances from the sea.[73]

River terraces are not easy to identify except by exposures of laid pebbles or river-sand on well-marked shelves [cf. pl. 19]. Shelves without pebbles may be structural. Except in regions with scanty vegetation, it is not reliable to trace scattered pebbles up to a maximum height, near which one postulates a former terrace gravel. A change of slope or rejuvenation point is a good indicator of the Low Terrace, which has been incised recently so that the latest valley has not had time to develop mature slopes [fig. 2; pl. 13].[74] The prehistorian is interested not so much in the terrace as in the gravel on it and in artefacts associated with this gravel.

A river terrace is an old valley floor, over which the former river probably pursued a changing course. Much of the old valley will have been removed by rejuvenation; but patches of gravel occur where the former course was markedly divergent from the present. In a valley several kilometres wide like the middle Volta, it is unlikely that any terrace gravel will have survived. But the present Oti meanders greatly in a very wide late-pleistocene valley, even incising its sides. Older thalwegs of the Oti were markedly divergent, and lines of terrace gravel cross the present course at sharp angles.

The sides of an old valley must have been eroded to some extent, and in arid regions the retreat of nearly vertical scarps has been rapid. In the humid climate of West Africa I have not seen evidence that the side of a valley is younger than the centre, so erosion probably broke down the talus and did not appreciably enlarge the true valley floor.

Near the Guinea coast rejuvenation, while dependent ultimately on the base-level of the sinking ocean, seems to have been controlled by climate and by the protection of vegetation. As far as it has been possible to correlate climatic and artefactual chronology, the cycle seems to have been as follows; I am taking as typical the southern orchard bush, where the climate is today mildly displuvial, but would become isopluvial without great increase of rainfall:

Onset of pluvial; displuvial conditions	Little vegetation cover or gallery forest owing to previous aridity. Increase of rainfall, especially stormy. Rejuvenation of unprotected valley floor in a fairly narrow channel.
Peak of pluvial; isopluvial conditions	Rock protected by heavy gallery forest. Pebbles in river-bed, accumulated from old valley floor and from incision of rock. Outside the river-bed only sand being moved.
Decline of pluvial; displuvial conditions	Slow deterioration of gallery forest, permitting some erosion of valley sides. As displuvial conditions intensified, exposure of much of the gravel in the river-bed and sometimes its lateritization. Valley sides tend to become protected by formation of lateritic crusts. The gravel may contain rolled artefacts of

	any period, including some derived from older terrace gravels; the latest will be contemporary, and unrolled artefacts must be later than the definitive abandonment of the gravel by the river.
Interpluvial; arid conditions	River running very low. Disappearance of gallery forest. This extreme is unlikely to have been reached in the present orchard bush.

In the coastal sector of Ghana, including the Volta Valley to a long distance inland, and to some extent in neighbouring countries where it has been possible to carry out detailed exploration, river terraces exhibit the following sequence, datable by a fair number of artefacts.

The High Terrace is usually at 30–35 m. l.w. [see fig. 2]. On the White Volta, which has no well-marked nickpoint, it tends to grade lower as one approaches the peneplain; at Yapei the High Terrace gravel, which has yielded many rolled pebble tools, is at 24 m. [pl. 18; fig. 4]. It grades towards the peneplain also near the sources of streams, for instance at Bawdua (22 m.) and Abuchen (10 m., perhaps the Middle Terrace); but its normal altitude is reported on the Tano, Ankobra, Pra and Ofin Rivers, perhaps also on the Comoe. The traverse illustrated from Todome on Dayi shows remains of a High Terrace, but the gravel does not seem to be *in situ*. There seem to be remains of the High Terrace gravel on the Volta near New Buipe at 28–32 m. and in the Kete Krachi and Yeji areas at 28–35 m. The only large collection of rolled pebble tools which it has yielded is from Yapei [fig. 4]; stray examples, less convincing because pre-Chellean material, not in itself very typical, relies largely on concentration for certain identification, have been found at Oda on Birim, Ofinso (perhaps with a Chellean pick), Otisu[75] and perhaps elsewhere on the lower Oti, and near Breniasi on the Asukawkaw.

It is unlikely that the High Terrace graded to Beach I, which is sterile of artefacts and is at + 50–60 m. along the coast of Ghana. At Accra and Cape Three Points this beach seems to be the termination of the plio-pleistocene peneplain, into which valleys have incised from early pleistocene times; and at Dumbai a higher gravel, without rolled arte-facts, has been identified at 50 m.; gravels of a similar height have been noticed elsewhere (Pasinkpe 40 m., on lower Ofin 50 m.). The High Terrace is more likely to grade to Beach II; for though this beach has not been identified in Ghana, there must have been a sea-level of the Cromer interglacial. By comparison with Natal, this beach should be contemporary with a well-developed pebble industry.[24] The High

Terrace gravels were probably abandoned by the rivers at the end of the first pluvial cycle (perhaps Kageran).

In the coastal sector of Ghana the Middle Terrace is normally at 18–25 m. above low water; especially in Togoland, where this industry is common, its gravels frequently contain rolled Late Chellean implements. The distribution of Chellean pieces is illustrated in the Todome traverse [fig. 2]; they occur rolled on the Middle Terrace, lightly abraded perhaps from slipping down hill rather than from river-action on the slope from the High Terrace, reused and so transported on the High Terrace. Chellean pieces, which were normally made of hard chert or quartzite, are naturally derived also on to the Low Terrace, perhaps at Todome, certainly higher up the River Dayi at Angeta and Hohoe. At the last the Middle Terrace is no longer extant; but its former existence higher than the top of the hill north of the town can be inferred from Chellean hand-axes in Low Terrace gravel at 13 m. on both slopes of this hill [pl. 14].

The Middle Terrace, often with its typical zone-fossil, the small rolled Chellean hand-axe, can be traced down the Oti from Atafie [fig. 7] and perhaps from Bladjai; rolled pieces in the gravel of the Low Terrace at Kitari may well be derived from the Middle Terrace, but are atypical. There are terrace gravels above the nickpoint at about 20 m. at Saboba, but nothing has been found to date them. Only at Pendjari gorge, close to the source, were two rolled cylinders flaked at one end on a terrace at 20 m.; this type, though not generally recognized, seems to be Chellean. What from altitude is likely to be the Middle Terrace has been observed at a few sites on all three branches of the Volta; a gravel at 19 m. at Yapei contains derived pebble tools from the High Terrace, and atypical rolled artefacts were found in the 20–25 metre gravel at Kandinga, which may be the Middle or the High Terrace, more probably the latter. But it is only near Kete Krachi and the Oti confluence that artefacts have been regularly found in what appears to be the Middle Terrace of the Volta, at Buafori Konkomba (from 20 m.), perhaps Mamata (from 22 m.); and these are not typical. There is rolled Chellean from the Middle Terrace opposite Akroso (22 m.) [fig. 7], and probably from Ntrubo, in a 20-metre gravel of a tributary far up the Asukawkaw River. Typical Chellean pieces have been found both in the Middle Terrace gravel *in situ* and derived at several sites along the River Dayi, at Hohoe and Wegbe (derived), Angeta (*in situ* and derived), Kpeve perhaps (*in situ*), Todome (*in situ*, fig. 2), and near the mouth (derived). This terrace gravel has been identified along the

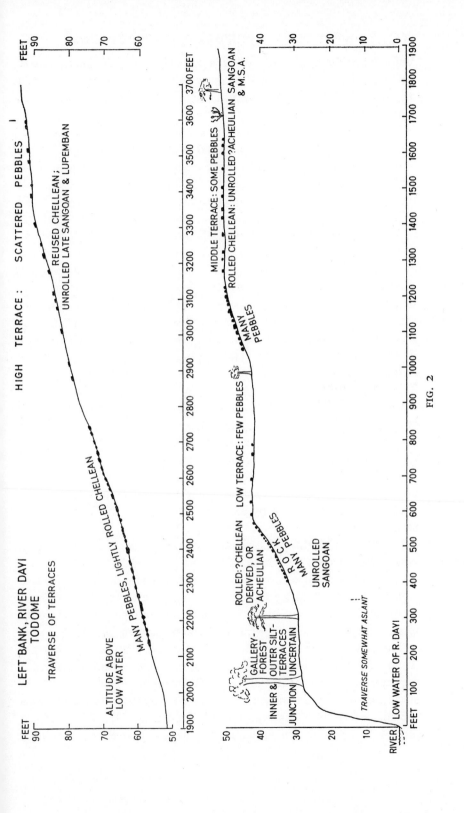

FIG. 2

Volta below the confluence. What is probably a broken Chellean hand-axe was found in it at Agoreke (about 25 m.), and the gravel at about 23 m. was identified at Mpeasem, close to the mouth of the Afram, but without rolled artefacts.

Below the Akosombo gorge, through which terraces have not been identified, the Middle Terrace gravel is well preserved near Kpong, and rolled Chellean implements have been found in it at Poyonu. This occurrence was nearly estuarine, and has been described in the section on raised beaches. The Middle Terrace undoubtedly graded to Beach III.

Along the rivers of Togo and Dahomey practically no occurrences of what could be the Middle Terrace are known. In the coastal sector of central and western Ghana the Middle Terrace is not uncommonly found, at heights comparable to the Volta Valley. But owing to the failure of the Chellean culture to spread west of the Pra River, associated artefacts are rare. Little is known of this terrace on the Densu and Ayensu; occasional rolled atypical artefacts derived on to the Low Terrace might be Chellean. Terrace gravels at about 20 m. are known all along the Pra, but have yielded only unrolled Sangoan material. There are good exposures along the Birim, owing to the activity of the diamond companies; and typical rolled Chellean pieces have been found at 18–20 m. at Edubia [pl. 17] and Ochereso. In the 18-metre gravels at Nsutam and Ekawso were probable rolled picks and other artefacts, though nothing has been found in the exposure a little farther upstream at Anyinam. This evidence, for what it is worth given the difficulties of exploration in the forest, suggests that the Chellean people may have reached the Birim Valley by an inland route from the Volta and not along the coast.

Gravels at a height which should indicate the Middle Terrace have been found on the Ofin, the Ankobra and perhaps the Tano; but there is no satisfactory means of dating them.[76] There are a few similar exposures with rolled atypical artefacts on the lower Nzi and perhaps on other rivers of the southern Ivory Coast, below the points where the terraces seem to be telescoped. No evidence is known from farther west.

The Low Terrace is normally at 8–12 m. l.w. On the Dayi River at Todome [fig. 2], where it is at nearly 13 m., there is a marked scarp to the Inner Silt-terrace; but at lower altitudes it often merges into the silt terrace or is distinguished only by a very slight step, and only where the silt terrace itself has been recently eroded does the Low Terrace, often with a gravelly scarp, stand out clearly, as near Kitari and Jimam on the Oti. The Low Terrace seems to grade primarily to Beach V; but it seems also to be associated with Beach IV. These two beaches were separated by a short interval, at most 30,000 years even if Beach V belongs to an interstadial of the Würm glaciation; so rejuvenation will have had little time to advance upstream, and the climatic stage which would encourage it in the interior probably fell between Beaches IV and V. It appears therefore that the same river terrace graded to both beaches except very near the estuaries.[77]

Being fairly recent, the Low Terrace can be identified at many places. Especially in narrow valleys it is often marked by a rejuvenation point or change of slope [pl. 13]. On the largest rivers, the Volta and Oti, the Gamblian Valley is so wide that the Low Terrace has sometimes been removed. Its existence is documented from the Ivory Coast to Nigeria. There is little doubt that when exploration is carried out in Liberia and farther west, it will be found there also.

In addition to rolled material derived from older terraces, the Low Terrace gravel occasionally contains rolled pieces which typologically look Late Acheulian; but in general it appears that the coastal region of Guinea was uninhabited between the Late Chellean and Sangoan invasions, so what should be the zone-fossil of this terrace is not found.[78]

Sangoan pieces, nearly all unrolled, are common on the Low Terrace gravel. The Sangoan culture must have reached the forest region during the pre-Gamblian interpluvial, but pebbles were easily available and had not yet been blanketed by soil and vegetation.[79] The 13-metre terrace gravel at Hohoe [pl. 14] is fairly well laid and appears to be *in situ*. Most of the rolled Chellean pieces lay on the gravel and at the base of the laterite sealing it; the erosion which destroyed the Middle Terrace and brought them on to the Low Terrace took place at the end of the pluvial cycle, when this gravel was reaching its final form. The unrolled Sangoan also lay on or above the gravel; a Late Sangoan core and miniature pick were high up in the laterite sealing it. At Angeta, on the other hand, none of the industries were clearly stratified above the Low Terrace gravel, which must have been still actively worked in Late Acheulian times. The occurrence of unrolled Sangoan pieces within the gravel would be due to digging for suitable pebbles after the gravel was left dry.

The Gamblian pluvial cycle marks the last stage of rejuvenation, which can be identified on practically every large stream in lower Ghana and neighbouring territories. Big rivers like the Volta and Oti cut valleys several kilometres wide, often not coincident with those of the previous cycle. These valleys may at times have been filled with water; for the buried basal gravels are rolled to a height of 10 m. above the rock floors.

The basal gravels are usually of fairly small size. They are composed of older terrace-gravels derived and of resistant materials eroded from the last rejuvenation. They rarely contain derived artefacts, perhaps because most of those incorporated in them were so much rolled that they are now unrecognizable.[80] They contain also rolled artefacts contemporary with a late phase of their formation, especially Guinea Aterian [fig. 29] throughout the area of its distribution in the savannah.[81] A rolled Lupemban pick, side-scrapers and one end-scraper were found in a thick deposit at Jimam on Oti. In the forest they have occasionally yielded indeterminate M.S.A.[82] They are normally 30–60 cms. thick and well laid. They seem to be the continuation of unrolled rubble on the valley sides, the rolling of the pebbles marking only the level which the river was able to reach when the rejuvenated valley was mature.

The gravels lie at the base of the valley-bottom sediments. Where good sections are preserved, they are usually overlain by 30–100 cms. of ferruginized grits. All these deposits seem to have been saturated with strong iron solutions, but only rarely did conditions allow the gravel and grits to become consolidated as block-laterite [pl. 21].[83] After the deposition of gravels and grits there was an unconformity, and frequently the grits were partly or wholly removed by erosion; for instance, at Jimam bands of consolidated sands and gravel are inter-calated, but the surface of the gravel is planed level.[84] The unconformity need not have lasted long. The gravels and grits are end-Gamblian passing into Post-pluvial I, and the inner silt terraces probably began to form at the beginning of Sub-pluvial II; so there was a gap of a few thousand years occupying the period of Sub-pluvial I and Post-pluvial II, which has been defined by Butzer in the Near East[85] but is not clearly identifiable within the tropics.

Most present-day rivers have incised to the base of the Gamblian valleys, though they are far less wide. They may therefore often be eroding and reworking the end-Gamblian basal gravels, especially the Oti. Smaller rivers have sometimes not reached the Gamblian rock floors. Where the modern river meanders, it may cut into the sides of the older valley, so that rock, sometimes capped by basal gravel, may be exposed up to 8 m. above modern low water. There are good examples of this on the Oti and Daka; and such places, being chosen for bridges because one abutment can be anchored on rock, may be well suited for examining basal gravels, as at Sabari on Oti. An unevenness in the thalweg, for instance former rapids in the river-bed through which the modern river has incised, may locally expose the Gamblian valley floor as a terrace above low water. At Jimam on Oti the old rapids have been completely levelled, at Ntrubo on Asukawkaw and Bui on Black Volta the gorge has been over-deepened and the rock terrace behind it incised about six metres.[86]

During the drier post-Gamblian period (Post-pluvial I–II), though the larger valleys were much wider than at present, rivers can have flowed only in the extreme bottoms, and because they were not confined by high banks, annual floods must have been lower. Recent incision into the inner silts has formed the modern high banks, but the inner silts are more recent than Post-pluvial I–II. However, post-Gamblian conditions of flow were not unlike the present day. The north abutment of Buipe bridge has sectioned an early holocene sand-bank, which rests on a thin basal gravel containing a rolled stone chopper. Its form resembles modern sand-banks. Its length cannot be estimated, its maximum height is 3 m. It was smothered by the inner silts.

At several sites in the savannah deposits of fossil strip-lagoons have been found, apparently resembling the lagoons now to be seen on top of the inner silts, and similarly acting as overflow channels during exceptional floods. These deposits consist of alternating bands of fine current-bedded sand and of bluish mud, in which are sometimes layers of leaves and other vegetable remains. At Jimam a small lagoon was incised into the basal gravel to a depth of 3 m. just above the end-Gamblian rapids. It may have been a backwater of a stream which already before the deposition of the inner silts was flowing into the Oti several hundred metres upstream, and it is sealed by the inner silts. Three layers of mud with decayed vegetable remains (either leaves or reeds) have been sampled. At Nalori or Limbisi[87] it was not possible to locate basal gravel or rock, and the lowest stratum was coarse sands. Lagoon-deposits occur to a height of 3·3 m. above low water, and consist of four thin layers of mud with leaves and twigs, intercalated with current-bedded sands [pl. 22–24]. The deposit is overlain with mottled inner silts. Scientific examination of the material has not been completed. The exposure is of considerable length, the mud layers coalesce downstream, and the macroscopic vegetable remains give out. At the rapids below Otisu there were layers and lenses of blue mud and sandy mud alternating with yellow and grey sands; twig fragments were found near the base. Just above Bator Gorge a section was recently dug in the deposits of an old backwater of the Black Volta. The height from water-level to the surface of the bank was 3·50 m., and the whole deposit consisted of muds, sands and peaty earths, apparently old soils. There were two main layers of leaves, one including kernels of Elaiis guineensis (oil-palm); and at several levels charcoal had drifted and sunk in the mud. Specimens have been taken for radiocarbon and palynological examination.

No cultural material has been found in these lagoon-deposits. As unrolled as well as rolled Guinea Aterian artefacts occur on the basal gravels, this culture must have continued during the unconformity.

Fossil fruits and twigs, apparently all of modern species, have been found at considerable depth in the gravels above Ankobra Junction,[88] near Takrowasi on Birim,[89] and on the gravels at Tapimarang on a tributary of the Birim.[90] There were pieces of wood in gravels at Asuboni.[91] Celts, beads, worked brass and other artefacts have been dredged from great depths in the gravels of both the Ankobra and Birim; so they cannot be regarded as basal gravels *in situ*, but clearly have been turned over not many centuries ago in search of gold.

It is not clear how dry Post-pluvial I–II was in West Africa, nor have isotopic dates been obtained. Both the evidence for lower rivers and the formation of the upper stone-line (below, p. 74) indicate conditions considerably drier than the Gamblian pluvial, and probably drier than today, when sheet-erosion does not seem to be prevalent except as a result of human interference.

South of the equator there seems to have been considerable aridity from about 12000 B.P., with blowing sands in the Zambezi Valley and an important stone-line at Kalambo Falls.[92] This is the 'Second Inter-mediate' period of workers in southern Africa, which is associated with the Lupembo–Tsitolian of the southern Congo and Angola (see table of dates, C–580–1, UCLA–172) and with the Magosian in Zambia (table of dates L–395D). The latter specimen need not mark the begin-ning of the dry period, as it was found in the stone-line. There seems at Kalambo Falls to be an unconformity at the base of the stone-line, as from very little below it comes the date L–399–I, 30500±2000. The Magosian need not have started exactly with the onset of drier con-ditions; a date for it from Pomongwe Cave, without climatic indication, is SR–11 15800±200. In Kenya there were cold, dry conditions, whether associated with the climatic change farther south or with the European Late Glacial (GRO–3048 12650±100, Cherangani, from near the end of this climatic period). Glaciers were retreating on Mt Ruwenzori about 14700±290 B.P. (I–556).

In the Nile valley, where the scheme of post-pluvial and sub-pluvial periods was devised by Butzer, Post-pluvial I started about 18000 B.P. with increasing desertification following displuvial conditions. This lasted until about 8000 B.P. (beginning of Sub-pluvial II), with a short wetter phase (Sub-pluvial I, about 11000 B.P., perhaps the equivalent of the European Younger Dryas).[93] The Nile near Wadi Halfa was depositing much silt in a period of low floods (Post-pluvial I), from well before 14950±300 (I–533) to 11200±285 (I–531–2);[94] conditions at its headwaters were therefore arid. Dates for erosion and probably high floods are 9325±250 (I–534), 8260±400 (M–804) and 7300±350 (I–530); the erosion was apparently interrupted, so these dates probably cover Sub-pluvial I, a weak Post-pluvial II and Sub-pluvial II. Fossil water from the Western Desert of Egypt has been dated before 19400± 1200 (the latest date, perhaps contaminated),[95] so the area apparently has enjoyed no excess of rainfall since 20000 B.P.

The Egyptian chronology ties in with Europe, where the change to warmth and aridity was marked not by the end of glaciation but by the first retreat from the Brandenburg maximum.[96] There were fluctuations, some of which like Alleröd may have been of a general nature, others were due to local circumstances caused by ice-melting in the Baltic and North Atlantic.[97] Aridity was not entirely the result of the cooling of the oceans by glacial melt-waters, as it was severe also in the northern Mediterranean region (Crete and Pyrenees),[98] which depends only moderately on river-water from glaciated regions, while incoming Atlantic water circulates anticlockwise so reaches the northern shores only after it has had time to become warmed.

The Maghreb and north Sahara also seem to follow roughly the European–Egyptian sequence. Post-pluvial I and Sub-pluvial I (not very closely dated) seem identifiable at Ain Metherchem, El Guettar and elsewhere,[99] Post-pluvial I perhaps at Haua Fteah[100] and not very commonly in Morocco (uppermost crust).[101] In the Saoura Valley a date from near the base of the Saouran deposits is 38000;[102] deposition was preceded by incision in the early part of the pluvial, with dry Mediterranean vegetation; the later Saouran sediments are sandy and arid, after which incision was renewed (interpluvial, followed by pluvial); there is another date for the second half of this pluvial of 6160±320.[103] There was a pluvial with Mediterranean vegetation near Touggourt, but no dates have been obtained.[104]

F

Older studies report a similar sequence on the southern edge of the Sahara. Tricart,[105] if one reinterprets his terminology, seems to describe a second period of dunes near Goundam between two periods when the Niger was able to spill over the bar of Taoussa (Tosaye); the second of these must be neolithic, the first is probably Gamblian. At the mouth of the Senegal the younger dunes date to some period between Beaches V and VI, i.e. between about 40000 and 6000 B.P. without precision.[56]

Recent work has, however, suggested that there was no marked aridification in the southern Sahara to correspond to Post-pluvial I–II in Guinea, the Nile Valley and the Maghreb. Quezel postulates a pluvial from about 25000 to 10000 B.P., the Saharan neolithic being contemporary with its last waning (ending about 4700). Indeed, the neolithic occupation was facilitated by partial desiccation which left dry land especially in the interdunes of southern Mauritania and Niger. The older pluvial with Mediterranean vegetation, previously thought to be Gamblian, must be pushed a long way farther back;[106] and the main period of dune-formation must be assigned no longer to the post-Gamblian but to a much extended interpluvial, whose dates neither correspond with any European interglacial nor with the Kamasian-Gamblian of the equatorial regions and the southern hemisphere.

These dunes are extremely difficult to date. In the coastal area they are older than Beach V (i.e. before 40000), but probably younger than Beach IV which has not been identified in Mauritania and Senegal. At Dakar they cannot be brought into relation with the Kalinian land-surface on Cap Manuel nor with the much distorted remains of Beach V. In Ténéré they are perhaps post-Acheulian and pre-Aterian.

For the central Sahara (Hoggar Ténéré, etc.) a good many neolithic radiocarbon dates have been obtained. The culture is thought to have flourished beside fairly numerous small lakes, among dry Mediterranean vegetation, and had been preceded before 8000 B.P. by a cool period with a damper arboreal flora.[107] The maximum of this pluvial was contemporary with the Aterian culture, for which early dates have been obtained from Morocco (27000–30000, UCLA 678 A–B) but none from the Sahara, where it was not replaced by blade-cultures and may have lingered late. The only radiocarbon date for what is believed to be the early part of the pluvial, which lasted without marked unconformity until the neolithic, is 21350 ± 350 (T–340–B) from Fachi (Niger). Perhaps more than a single date is needed to establish the length of the pluvial, especially as the sample may not come from the same lake as those of the neolithic series, and admittedly could not be associated with the main stratification of the basin.[108] The gap between this date and those of the neolithic (Fachi, GsY–285 8500 ± 350) is unsatisfactory.

At VII Inqua Faure pointed out that the evidence for pluvial conditions in the central Sahara from 20000 to 10000 B.P. consists of deep lakes, which could be maintained not by heavy direct rainfall but by abundant fossil water. Very large reserves must have accumulated during the Gamblian pluvial in parts of the Sahara.[95] If conditions in post-Gamblian times were dry and cool but not so severe as to mobilize active dunes, lakes could have maintained their levels for a long period.

At some period Mediterranean vegetation spread to Tibesti and Borkou, but no dates have been obtained.[109] Mediterranean pollen was not found in the neolithic shelter of Mossei (Tibesti); but this site may be later than those of the Hoggar and surrounding regions, and the pine and juniper charcoal may have been from dead wood.

The former history of Lake Chad has recently attracted attention; its level must have depended mainly on the climate of the wooded savannah to the south, whence today it derives the greater part of its water; but during pluvial periods local rain on the same latitude and in the present Sahara may have contributed.[110] It is not clear whether there has been epeirogenic distortion of the old strand-lines except in the Djourab, though the whole of the Chad basin is probably subsiding.

The present level of the lake is about 280 m. S.L. On the south and east are strand-lines at 285 m. (certainly Iron Age, Sub-pluvial III *ad fin.*) and 330 m. (Bama Ridge), a prominent feature which we might expect to be Sub-pluvial II. But if so it cannot be equated with Faure's dates from Niger, because the Ténéré sediments are at 350–400 m. In Nigeria no strand-line higher than 330 m. has been detected; and it may transpire that the Ténéré sediments belong to a number of small lakes. Faure assigns the sample from Fachi to the same lake as those from Ténéré; previous was the great formation of dunes, which he places in his great Saharan interpluvial (?–25000 B.P. or earlier; called by Tricart at the Niger bend Uljian). These may be the same dunes as those described by Grove east of Kano; he found no dunes which might date to Post-pluvial I–II, but a series which seems assignable to Post-pluvial III.

At the beginning of Sub-pluvial II, apparently about 7000 B.C., there was a marked change of climate in West Africa. The aridity of the previous stage, causing rivers to contract in their wide valleys and expose stretches of gravel, gave way to steady rainfall, probably not stormy, and perhaps without marked dry seasons. It has been suggested that there was a change from predominantly zonal to meridional circulation. Possibly the glaciers of Antarctica could become active only in a warmer period, when they would receive more snow; and their extension pushed northward the tropical rain-belt and caused meridional circulation in the northern hemisphere. There is, however, little evidence for the extension of inaccessible high forest far north of its present limits, so the total humidity of the wooded savannah cannot have been much greater than today.[111]

Sufficient exact dates are not yet available. It appears that this change of climate affected most of Africa and Europe. South of the equator there was the transition from the dry post-Gamblian to the sub-pluvial Makalian.[112] There was higher rainfall in the equatorial regions of the upper Nile and south of Lake Chad. It is not clear what happened in the Sahara. Recent French work, as has been described, maintains that the peak of the pluvial was earlier, and that it had spread from the north. We need a proper stratigraphy of the small Saharan lakes and evidence for the date and ecology of the Aterian culture. It is possible that pluvial conditions from the Mediterranean were overtaken by a spread of monsoon-rainfall from the south. At any rate, there were still many lakes in Sub-pluvial II,[113] and pasture for a fair number of large animals including oxen; winter-rain cereals were cultivated in the Hoggar.[114]

Butzer finds evidence in Egypt and the Near East for Sub-pluvial II, starting about 5500 B.C. and ending in a series of stages from the end of Naqada I (about 3600 B.C.) to the IV dynasty. The immigrant neolithic people of the northern Mediterranean almost certainly enjoyed conditions more genial than in Late Glacial times, but we do not know when these started. In Western Europe the Atlantic climatic optimum marks the peak of post-glacial warmth and rainfall.

It is possible therefore to summarize the climatic chronology of the Late Pleistocene, allowing for variations of perhaps 2,000 years at different latitudes:

40000–18000 B.P.   Wetter and cooler. Fluctuations in Europe. building up to the maximum of glaciation. Wetter in Maghreb, Aterian starts very soon after the regression from Beach V. Wet in Sahara, from a date which may not be before 30000, with probable survival of Acheulian culture. Wet in West Africa, Sangoan derivative cultures, Kalinian, etc. Cold on East African mountains and in Zambia.

| 18000–8000 B.P. | Dry. European Late Glacial with ice-retreat. Dry in Maghreb. Cool and perhaps still wet in Sahara. Dry in West Africa, basal gravels exposed, Guinea Aterian culture. |
| 8000–5000 B.P. or later | Wet. European Atlantic phase. Wet in Sahara, Aterian and neolithic. Wet in West Africa, inner silt terraces; Ultimate M.S.A. |

The climatic change in West Africa in Sub-pluvial II filled valleys, large and small, with marshes in which fine white silts were deposited to a height of up to 10 m. (8–10 m. above l.w., their thickness depended on the depth of the valleys). They blanket all previous formations, incised river-beds, basal gravels, older lagoon-deposits, and extend level to the sides of the old valleys. The meandering course of the Oti and other rivers indicates that they moved slowly among the marshes, with very little incision and probably a sharp decline in seasonal contrast. The white silts usually contain lateritic nodules, but seldom any larger material. Some nodules are rolled and seem derived; but there is a concentration near the surface where there has probably been incipient lateritization since the silts were deposited. At Otisu Rapids bands of ferruginization suggested that the silts had built up in stages. I have occasionally seen patches of ferruginous crust in the silts, probably due to local seepage of iron-charged water.

There is little evidence for artefacts occurring within the silts of the inner silt terraces; they would be either casual losses in the field or pieces washed in from elsewhere. On the silts in the savannah are frequently found microliths, but not usually in the forest of Ghana and the Ivory Coast, where the silt terraces remained too wet for occupation at the end of Sub-pluvial II. On many smaller streams, like the Tsawe at Chawenu, the silt was not high enough to avoid annual floods. On the Ofin near Dunkwa microliths occur at the back of the inner silt terrace 200 metres from the river, and on the slope behind it. Similarly, the Volta valley near Yeji remained too damp and liable to flood, except on a few elevations like Tunga, so microlithic sites lie on the rise from the silt-terrace to the Low Terrace, as at Kafaba and Kwayasi. At Kadelso there are microliths on the inner edge of the silt-terrace and on its central ridge. Rock islands among the silts were sometimes occupied, like the Kalowvi bridge (mesolithic) and Chukoto (Kintampo-neolithic). The formation of the inner silt terraces was contemporary not with the mesoneolithic but with the Ultimate Middle Stone Age. Important sites of this culture have occasionally been located on slopes overlooking the old marshes, such as Agoreke [fig. 34], Narago [fig. 35], and Kpafa. These pieces are usually slightly stained, because at the end of Sub-pluvial II there was a short displuvial period which permitted a certain amount of lateritization. Mesoneolithic microliths are hardly ever stained, being subsequent to this process.

The white silts had accumulated in wide marshes with little current. In Post-pluvial III the rivers began to incise deep and fairly narrow channels, perhaps owing to diminution of rainfall, certainly to a change in its incidence. I found evidence on both banks of the Volta near Usunfukrom for accumulation of sub-angular gravel within the inner silts, 30 cms. below their surface and the microlithic layer. In the gravel were rolled pieces which may be Ultimate M.S.A., but are not typically mesoneolithic. Thus late in Sub-pluvial II there were violent local flash-floods, in this case probably brought down by the Kalurakun River. The larger rivers began to form several channels, but after a while one predominated, leaving the others to carry small tributaries and as overflows during big floods, or as strip-lagoons. The main channels were 6–10 m. deep and up to twice as wide as present-day channels. Their steep fossil banks, the junction of the inner and outer silt terraces, have occasionally been noticed, at Bato on Oti, Dikpwie on Black Volta and Anincheche on Birim; but they are usually obscured by slip and by the gallery forest which covers the outer silt terraces. The rivers in these channels are today very low in the dry season, but fill them to overflowing during floods. The inner silts have therefore a low water-table in winter, and often support only acacias and other drought-resisting trees.

The microlithic layer on the surface of the inner silts is usually covered by up to one metre of soil, but in many places there has been wide, shallow erosion by local streams, which has exposed microliths and lateritic nodules. Such erosion may even have incised to the basal gravel, especially near the side of a Gamblian valley. At Dapola an eroded donga has been filled by the grits of the outer silt terrace.

At some date, probably fairly recently, the Sub-pluvial III channels contracted by the deposition along their sides of sandy silts of the outer silt terraces. These effectively mask the older banks except where rapids or sand-banks have forced the river out of its straight course; such places give also the best exposures of basal gravels and fossil pools. The lower part of the outer terraces often contains bluish sandy or clayey lenses; it looks as if accumulation has been round aquatic shrubs. The outer terrace is often embanked up to one metre above the inner, and sometimes spreads over it.[115]

At a few places in the savannah darker bands have been noticed near the top of the outer sand terrace, at Pwalagu at 120 and 250 cms. below surface, at Buipe Bridge at perhaps corresponding levels (the surface was here damaged), at Atunga near Yeji about 100 (thin layer), 130 and 150 cms. One grey band at 90 cms. depth on an incomplete section was noted farther downstream at Jifaji. They are interbedded with yellow sands. The dark bands are clayey and humic, and almost certainly indicate fairly prolonged periods of low floods, when thick vegetation could establish itself on the banks. At Pwalagu there were several thin varves above the highest band. At Atunga the section was capped by the midden of a village which is unlikely to have been established on the river-bank before the security of colonial occupation, and below it was sand indicating high floods. The two principal dark bands, noticed on both the Black, the White and the united Volta, probably correspond; the higher is unlikely to be younger than the second half of the nineteenth century, and may be older. The lower could be guessed to date 1800–50, perhaps 1750–1800. Both seem to indicate a change in incidence of rainfall, at a date which may significantly correspond to the northern Little Ice Age.

This account is of river terraces in the coastal areas, where rejuvenation has kept in step with falling sea-levels during the Pleistocene. Above the main nickpoints we find wide shallow valleys, which seem to have been incised not later than the Middle Pleistocene, often into a lateritized late tertiary surface or early pleistocene valley, for instance the middle valley of the Black Volta, the Comoe, and many in Upper Volta. At Nandom the bed of a wide tributary-valley is heavily lateritized; similar conditions have been seen elsewhere in northern Ghana and northern Dahomey. Industrial exploitation on the Jos Plateau (Nigeria) has revealed that such valleys were filled and incised three times, and in their basal gravels are found respectively Middle Acheulian, M.S.A. and early Iron Age material.[116] At this latitude incision and aggradation are likely to have taken place nearer the peak of a pluvial than on the coast, as rainfall would be low during interpluvials; so the periods when the basal gravels were exposed and worked will be Kamasian II (before the coastal Low Terrace), Gamblian (before the coastal basal gravels) and Sub-pluvial III. A Sub-pluvial II stage has not been identified. The lowest terrace is therefore the Middle Terrace, and a possible Chellean pick has been found near Nok in a gravel above the valley bottom. There is no Low Terrace, and the present basal gravels were first deposited in Kamasian II. Pre-Gamblian gravels occur in the valley bottoms in the dry upland valley of the Vaal. The burial of the gravels by aggraded silts has concealed all artefacts. This is why palaeoliths are hardly ever found in Upper Volta and other parts of the peneplain; they must be dug for in the bottoms of the valleys.

Urvoy,[117] near Niamey and Siguiri on the Niger, describes two phases only of erosion, and considers that the earlier is tertiary. There is a regular system of terraces at 40–50 m. below the plateau, undated but corresponding probably to the coastal High or Middle Terraces, incision to the valley bottoms (probably Kamasian II) and dune-formation in the valleys (in subsequent dry periods). He failed to find Fagg's complex picture of valley-filling because he had no complete cross-sections. On the Bagoe there are three terraces.[118]

As one approaches the peneplain, the terraces of the larger rivers are telescoped to form a sequence intermediate between the plateau and the staircase-formation of the coastal belt. At Alibori Bridge (Dahomey) what appears to be the Low Terrace is at 5 m. l.w., at Doufoumbara (Niger) perhaps at 6 m.[119] On the Black Volta above Wa rolled pebble tools occur in a gravel about 10 m. l.w. at Wizini Wessa and Poura, and on the Kamba, a small tributary, at 5 m. What may be the same gravel has been found at least as far downstream as Sara, probably as Chache; in other words, it may extend to the head of the Bui nickpoint. It is not certain that these pebble tools are *in situ* in this gravel; but the only higher gravel identified, at 30 m. or more, is sterile and seems to be a pre-quaternary peneplain-spread. So the 10-metre gravel of this part of the river is either the High or the Middle Terrace, and there was no Low Terrace stage. That it may be the latter is indicated by rolled pieces which could well be Chellean from a terrace at $2\frac{1}{2}$ m. above a tributary stream at Ypala, overlooking a wide, shallow valley in which alternate incision and aggradation of silts could have taken place since Acheulian times as on the Jos Plateau.

There are gravels containing rolled pebble tools also in the Ivory Coast, at Léraba Bridge at 12 m., at Tiendoukro on the White Bandama at 10 m. There seems to be a similar section at Aouen-Komoénou on the Comoe east of Ouellé.[120] Vogt, having worked above the Ivory Coast nickpoints, recognized only two terraces, the upper probably a plateau-gravel.[121] I have seen similar gravels at 10 m. on the Comoe east of Dabakala, and near the headwaters of the smaller rivers at even lower altitudes, at 5 m. at Gbadi Kaha on the White Bandama, at 6 m. at Fétékro on Nzi [pl. 25]. These gravels are sealed by massive block-laterite, which suggests that they are of early date (probably High

Terrace, as there seems to have been little lateritization at the end of Kamasian II, see below p. 73 and pl. 18); but no artefacts were found to identify them.

The Geological Sequence: Soil-sections

INTRODUCTORY NOTE. Geologists are attempting to abolish the term 'laterite' because it is irregularly formed and imprecise. The former objection is of little moment, considering the solecisms which they commit, e.g. the barbarous 'pisolite' as equivalent of 'pisolith'. The Gargantuan circumlocutions which they are trying to substitute for 'laterite' read so clumsily in a book which touches on the humanities that I have decided to retain this well-established term, but with precise significance. 'Laterite' here indicates superficial sediments which have been cemented by the deposition of insoluble iron salts. The cementation may be in the form of nodules (pisoliths) or of blocks (often nodules recemented). One finds also 'biscuity' or layered laterites, which seem to consist mainly of iron salts with little sediment occluded. Incipient lateritic nodules are the mottling of sediments, in which the iron salts have not yet hardened. 'Laterite' is here not used either for uncemented bright red tropical earths; or for weathered rock *in situ*, whence silica has been leached and only iron and aluminium salts remain; or for the hard ferruginized crust on top of such rock, but below the stone-line and the zone of recent sedimentation.

Every soil-cycle in sub-Saharan Africa was climatically controlled, and exhibits the effects of the pluvial-interpluvial rhythm. Each cycle normally started with a phase of erosion, which has left a stone-line; the lowest stone-line rests directly on weathered rock, and is the normal indicator of the beginning of recent sediments; for certain rocks in the forest are so rotted that they have lost all structure near the surface, so without the stone-line it would be difficult to discern where rock ends and soil begins.

A stone-line consists largely of fragments of quartz and other resistant rocks. It will be primarily a concentration of larger pieces in a period of erosion when finer particles are washed away. This process was sheet-erosion, and took place in a dry period when vegetation was spaced and could not afford complete protection to the soil; we do not often find fossil gulley-erosion on hillsides and plateaus, for gulleys have normally maintained and enlarged themselves. In the stone-line will be primarily pieces from quartz veins from the zone where rotten rock was humified and so liable to erosion; in the forest one often sees a vein rising regularly to the stone-line and spreading along it in a trail. A stone-line will contain also fragments of older stone-lines, usually much weathered, pieces of block-laterite, and material left on the surface, especially artefacts.

A true stone-line is a thin and sometimes discontinuous line of stones marking an old surface. In the forest are found beds of earthy rubble, little lateritized but containing fragments of old block-laterite [pl. 28]. There may at the base be no marked concentration of large material. These normally form on rocks containing much quartz, sometimes as talus at the foot of steep slopes, as below the Awudome Ridge (Transvolta); and in the forest there may never have been violent displuvial conditions to thin the vegetation and allow sheet-erosion to remove the finer soil and concentrate the stones. In addition, falling trees are liable to churn up the soil down to rock. The rubbles do, however, exhibit a similar stratification of artefacts as the soils and laterites of the orchard bush, with occasionally slight disruption.

Above a stone-line there was a build-up of soil when the climate became more humid and vegetation re-established itself. The soil is almost entirely fine particles, most of them probably from activity of termites, which seek their material not in the soil around them but from the top of the weathered rock. Fossil termite-nests have been found in block-laterite on Cap Manuel (Dakar).[122] Some soil must be aeolian, trapped by vegetation. With suitable topography, some will be illuvial. Stones are very rarely found in the soil; some may have been introduced by birds, others perhaps by man while hunting, but early man probably did not penetrate the forest under which soils would accumulate.

Under more displuvial conditions water-table would vary seasonally, and some of the soluble basic iron carbonate would be precipitated in the dry season and change to an insoluble hydroxide. Especially in clays this would result first in mottling, but the iron-concentrations would be little harder than the surrounding soil. As conditions became drier, or in better drained sandy soils, the concentration round a pebble or grain of sand would harden and become nodular.[123] Cementation of the nodules into block-laterite [see pl. 26] probably took place in the succeeding climatic cycle.[124]

Lateritization might interfere with tree roots, and with increasing aridity vegetation would become more spaced, so that sheet-erosion of unconsolidated top-soil could start, and larger pieces, especially artefacts, would be concentrated in a new stone-line on top of the nodular laterite. This is the beginning of a new cycle. It must be emphasized that lateritization takes place not on the surface but at some depth in the soil; therefore artefacts found in the stone-line do not belong to the level of build-up in which they occur but to an eroded level 20–30 cms. higher.

Laterite is practically insoluble chemically but easily breaks up mechanically, either by undermining of crusts or by abrasion in gravel (giving rolled nodules). Therefore a stone-line, and especially the basal stone-line, often contains fragments of block-laterite, which are proof of an earlier cycle of lateritization.

Where conditions have been unfavourable for lateritization, stone-lines may often coalesce, especially the pre-Gamblian and post-Gamblian. For instance, in many parts of the forest there is no trace of an independent pre-Gamblian stone-line and M.S.A. material occurs directly on rock, probably because there was insufficient hard rubble to form a thick but uncemented layer to separate the two stone-lines. Such profiles are seen especially in the coastal zone of Ghana, where quartzitic sandy soils are too well drained for iron salts to accumulate easily, and the rubble of the lower stone-line may largely have disintegrated (cp. fig. 3 and below, pp. 133–6). Under semi-desert conditions soils would have little termite-material and much blown sand, as apparently in Aïr;[125] there would be little lateritization, but also insufficient erosion to remove the dune-sand.

Nearly everywhere in West Africa the lowest stone-line belongs to the pre-Gamblian interpluvial and contains Sangoan tools [fig. 16]. The same seems to be true in other parts of sub-Saharan Africa, certainly in South Africa, where it is the equivalent of van Riet Lowe's 'youngest gravels' which yield Fauresmith material.[126] Hardly anywhere in Natal have I seen a soil older than this stone-line. In the Graben of East Africa there had been fairly continuous sedimentation through the Pleistocene; so apparently in the Maghreb, where French geomorphologists have mapped a series of pleistocene surfaces, each with its crust. Though West Africa is extremely stable, there must really be pleistocene basins with deep sediments. Almost certainly the old Niger delta and some of the former Saharan lakes are very old, but exploration has been confined to their margins. Hardly anything is known about the very deep sediments of Lake Chad. Lake Bosumtwi (Ashanti), probably formed in the pliopleistocene,[127] has deep sediments which have not been dated. Kumasi Hospital, on top of a hill, is built on pleistocene sediments in which the tusk of an elephant was found at a depth of $5\frac{1}{2}$ m.; these can have accumulated only under a topography very different from the present.

Rarely in West Africa does there appear to occur a soil-section which extends back to the Middle Pleistocene. At Edubia on the Birim [pl.17] there is a build-up on the gravel of the Middle Terrace:

	SUGGESTED STAGE
1 m. forest-soil	Holocene
Land-surface with a few microliths, probably mesolithic and M.S.A. mixed	Post-pluvial I, reexposed in Post-pluvial III
1–1½ m. clayey forest soil with lateritic mottling	Gamblian
Unconformity; erosion of clay; pockets of hillwash-gravel. Probably savannah	Kamasian II–Gamblian
A little clay, apparently much eroded. Probably forest soil	Kamasian II
Unconformity; truncation of lateritized gravel and presumably of capping sands	Kamasian I–II
50–100 cms. river gravel with rolled Chellean; gravel often heavily lateritized and truncated at surface	End Kamasian I
Middle Terrace at 20 m.	Middle Kamasian I

A clay deposit three metres thick overlies the Middle Terrace at Adiembra on Ankobra, on top of a hill; above it is a stone-line, and then another metre of clay to the surface.

On the High Terrace gravel at Yapei [pl. 18] there is a thick crust, but it cannot be dated. It may be partly pre-Gamblian, as the detrital gravel at the back of the hill, containing probably unrolled M.S.A., is sandwiched between two lateritic crusts, of which only the upper would be end-Gamblian. The section on the terrace is as follows:

	A little soil
0–135 cms.	Block-laterite, generally without pebbles
	? Unconformity
135–50 cms.	Small rubbly pebbles, probably a gravelly soil
150–330 cms.	Pebbles cemented by laterite; small pebbles water-laid near top, medium pebbles rather uneven lower down

Thick lateritic crusts are found in the drier savannah, often on surfaces which are believed to be pliopleistocene (in the Black Volta Valley) or even earlier (on remnants of an old surface in Upper Volta, and in Fouta Djalon).[128] There is no means of dating these crusts, and there has been a tendency to give rein to the imagination in guessing chronology.[129] There are very thick crusts on the basalts of Cap Manuel (Dakar).[122] The Kalinian [fig. 19] occurs about 30 cms. below the surface of the laterite, apparently before a renewed recent cycle of lateritization.

The weathered surface may have been exposed for a long period, as a much patinated pebble chopper was found at its base.[130] The date of the older laterites and basalts is unknown.

Near the coast of the Gulf of Guinea, however, a few artefacts found *in situ* provide some evidence. At Legon a fragment of an older pene-plain rises above the pliopleistocene surface. At its foot Sangoan picks were found in laterite at 90 cms. depth, above the stone-line. At Jigbe (Togoland) the stone-line with Sangoan overlies the base of a ferrugin-ized grit [pl. 32]. At Koloenu (Togoland) apparently a stream-gravel with unrolled Sangoan and perhaps Acheulian picks is embedded about half-way up a thick crust of laterite, so lateritization must have started in pre-Sangoan times, and one heavily rolled piece, not found *in situ*, looks Chellean. At Ataire (Togoland) the Sangoan stone-line (with a Hönderbeck core) is higher than the base of the laterite, which seems to fill hollows in the rock. Near Konakry Chételat describes[128] lateritic crusts which pass beneath the sea. This coast seems to have been sinking tectonically as well as to have been subject to eustatic fluctua-tions; yet it is likely that the oldest laterite is older than the Late Pleistocene.

From the regular occurrence of the stone-line with Sangoan material on rock one would conclude that West Africa was swept almost bare of soil in the pre-Gamblian dry phase; the same seems to have happened in South Africa and the Lower Congo. If the Kamasian II soils had been cemented, they should have resisted sheet-erosion and have survived. One is therefore led to conclude that at the end of Kamasian II con-ditions were unsuitable for lateritization, perhaps because the climate swung rapidly from isopluvial to arid; remains of pre-Sangoan crusts and pieces of laterite incorporated in the stone-line are in fact a survival from an older cycle; so also the massive crusts of the sub-Saharan savannah. The river gravels near the plateau which have been encrusted (e.g. Yapei pl. 18, Gbadi Kaha and Fétékro pl. 25) may well belong to the High Terrace. This conclusion is borne out by the sediments of Beach IV at Bishop's School, Accra. This beach should have been abandoned in Late Kamasian II; but as M.S.A. pieces were found embedded in it, it cannot have been lateritized before Late Gamblian times. At Asokrochona near Tema [pl. 27, fig. 1] the build-up starts from Beach IV, on which lay Sangoan picks embedded in a very thin siliceous crust not ferruginous.

The normal lower stone-line is composed of rock rubble, and is likely to yield Sangoan pieces [fig. 16], sometimes older material derived.

It may also be the gravel of the Low Terrace [pl. 14, 30]. In the savannah it is normally capped by about one metre of block-laterite, which is the Gamblian soil lateritized and partly eroded. In the forest there is usually uncemented rubble [pl. 29]. On this surface occurs the upper stone-line, with Guinea Aterian [pl. 26] or other M.S.A. [pl. 14, Late Sangoan; pl. 28, indeterminate], and above it again 10–20 cms. of laterite or rubble. This laterite may be nodular, or at least less well cemented than the lower; but if there are no indicator-stones or artefacts, it is very hard to distinguish the M.S.A. surface. The upper laterite seems to have accumulated during Sub-pluvial II.

There does not seem to be evidence in West Africa for an unconformity in the Gamblian laterite or other accumulation. South of the equator an intermediate stone-line was observed on the River Luki (Lower Congo),[131] though other Congo sections have only a single M.S.A. stone-line like those in West Africa. In some Natal dongas there are several lines of ferricrete and pebbles covering the M.S.A.[132] When it used to be held that the Gamblian pluvial corresponded to the Würm glaciation, these unconformities were thought to be the equivalent of Würm interstadials; but now that it appears that the Gamblian was shorter than Würm and covered at most Würm II–III (above pp. 41–2 and n. 48), the Gamblian ferricrete layers must be otherwise explained.

Local conditions may cause much greater depth of Gamblian accumulation. At Asokrochona [pl. 27; fig. 1] Beach IV is overlain by three or four metres of mottled clays, capped by a crust with rubble and M.S.A. flakes [fig. 31]. These clays seem to be slumped 'Terres de barre'. The original clays extend over a wide area in Lower Togo and the south-east corner of Ghana; they are probably illuvial and of uncertain date.

On the upper laterite or rubble are frequently found microliths [fig. 53, 1–23]; sometimes this zone, accumulated in Sub-pluvial II, consists of unlateritized sand [pl. 33], or at Tokuse of illuvial grits. In suitable places there has been a deep accumulation of Sub-pluvial II soil, in which the M.S.A. material is more finely stratified than usual; one of the deep sections excavated in Legon Botanic Gardens is detailed in fig. 3. At New Todzi about 150 cms. of red sandy earth with stratified neolithic and two zones of Late M.S.A. [fig. 30] overlay a line of lateritic nodules, below which were another 150 cms. of sterile red earth before reaching rock. Half-way up a gulley-filling at Little Legon was found a Levallois flake on a surface marked by a few stones [pl. 34]. There is a

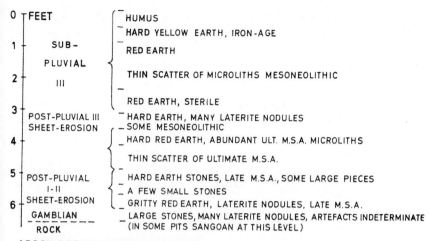

FIG. 3 Excavations by author in Legon, Botanic Gardens; soil-section of pit c29

similar deep accumulation, but not clearly marked by artefacts, in an old channel of the River Nzi at M'Bahiakro (Ivory Coast).

Above the mesolithic are one or two metres of modern soils. The neolithic surface often occurs 10–20 cms. above the base of these. At Legon Botanic Gardens [fig. 3] the stratified microliths were not sufficiently distinctive to draw a boundary between mesolithic and neolithic, and seem to belong to the earliest neolithic stage, with edge-ground celts but prior to pottery; pottery, either neolithic or slightly later, and small celts appear nearly at the top of the microlithic horizon. At New Todzi pottery and typically neolithic artefacts lay almost entirely above the microliths. At Somanya there was a good section with neolithic-B at 15 cms. depth and Late M.S.A. on an uneven surface of nodular laterite at 50–80 cms., but no mesolithic. At Little Legon [pl. 34] a surface is visible above the mesolithic, but it is Iron Age. On several road-cuttings at Akawle are levels of M.S.A. (on laterite), mesolithic (in one place 40 cms. higher) and early Iron Age pottery (apparently in shallow pits dug down to the mesolithic level); but the soil is not deep and there is no single section to show the three cultures in super-position.

If we may trust two radiocarbon dates just received from Ntereso (below p. 238). the last lateritization in northern Ghana must have been taking place not later than the middle of the second millennium B.C. The lowest level there is on laterite nodules or consists of pits dug into them; but on several sections this level was missing, and the second level was separated from the laterite by 15–20 cms. of sterile red sand.

Biological and Cultural Sequences

There is practically no pleistocene faunal evidence for West Africa. In the Chad basin has been found an early pleistocene fauna, including one hominid.[133] These have not yet been fully published. The next West African hominid is the skeleton from Asselar,[134] which is probably neolithic, though not directly associated with neolithic remains; neolithic fauna is common from the Sahara, but practically nothing even of this period has been identified farther south. Neolithic fauna is modern, and its only interest is evidence for the introduction of domestic animals. In any case, faunal evidence must be treated with caution in a continent which did not undergo spectacular changes of pleistocene climate; for relicts must have survived for a considerable time in remote regions. We would be most curious to know what type of man was responsible for the Aterian and other M.S.A. cultures; and one day we may find out, but West African soils are acid, and even recent bone is seldom well preserved.

The cultural sequence of the West African palaeolithic is described in detail in Chapter 3; but as African terms are unfamiliar in Europe, a table is here given for the ease of comprehending the chronological frame.

CULTURE	APPROXIMATE GEO-LOGICAL STAGE	EUROPEAN EQUIVALENT
Pre-Chellean pebble tools	Kageran pluvial and post-pluvial; Beaches I and II (in remoter areas)	Late Villafranchian, covering Donau and Günz
Chelles-Acheul	Kamasian I–II pluvials, Beaches III–IV	From near end of Günz to Eem or rather later
Sangoan	Pre-Gamblian interpluvial: Beach V	Würm I–II
Kalinio-Lupemban	Gamblian	Würm II
M.S.A.	Late Gamblian and early post-Gamblian, just until Beach VI when neolithic had already reached the Sahara	Late Glacial, up to Atlantic period

Table of Relevant Absolute Dates

NOTE. All dates are given B.P. unless otherwise stated. Laboratory numbers are quoted, where they are known, without other reference; in nearly all cases details can be found in *Radiocarbon*. Where a reference is given, the laboratory number has not yet been published.

EARLY-MIDDLE ACHEULIAN; KAMASIAN II

Y-142-8 >39000 Nok (Nigeria)

Evidence of deep-sea cores not satisfactory or abundant, and hardly any cores seem undisturbed so far back. The best are:

A-240, cold 100000–110000, warm 110000–150000, preceded by cold; perhaps covers the stages Warthe, Ohe and the end of Riss, Rosholt *et al.*, *Journal of Geology* lxix (1961), p. 162.

A-254-BR-C, very cold about 105000, preceded by cool to 140000, preceded by fairly warm; perhaps covers Warthe and Ohe, Rosholt *et al.*, *Journal of Geophysical Research* lxvii (1962), p. 2907.

LATE ACHEULIAN; BEACH IV

GRO-2644 57600 ± 750 Kalambo Falls (Zambia)
57300 ± 500 Kalambo Falls, second level from top; Clark and van Zinderen Bakker, *Nature* 201 (1964), p. 471

Deep-sea cores:

A-240, duration of Eem 93000–69000. Ref. above

A-179-4, maximum of Eem 97000. Ref. above, also Emiliani, *Bull. Geological Soc. America* 75 (1964), p. 129

A-254-BR-C maximum of Eem 98000 ± 8000, duration about 100000–70000, ref. above

Extrapolated date for end of Eem, 70000. Arrhenius, *Swedish Deep-sea Expedition 1947–8*, V 1

EARLY SANGOAN, BETWEEN BEACHES IV AND V; LOWER STONE-LINE

L-399C 43000 ± 3300 Kalambo Falls (Zambia)
40750 Kalambo Falls (Zambia) Clark and Bakker, *l.c.*
GRO-3211 >49000 Kalambo Falls (Zambia) Lowest Sangoan
GRO-3237 42000 ± 2000 Kalambo Falls (Zambia)
GRO-3196 40600 ± 1300 Kalambo Falls (Zambia) Late Sangoan
GRO-3228 37900 ± 1200 Kalambo Falls (Zambia) Above Sangoan
SR-8 42200 ± 2300 Pomongwe (Rhodesia)

G

BEACH V (DEVELOPED SANGOAN)

Africa:

W-246	>38000	Cape Flats. Emergent beach, stage uncertain
Y-468	37700 ± 2000	Sedgefield (Cape), +4 metre beach, ? tectonically disturbed, but there is a beach at the Wilderness at normal height of +7–8 m.

Outside Africa:

GRO-1473	47700 ± 1500	Gorham's Cave, Gibraltar; beach earlier than this date
W-185	>30000	West Australia, +3–4 metre terrace

Slight temperature-fluctuations are indicated in a few deep-sea cores, but dates are not consistent. The most important is about 50000 B.P. (Cores A-240, Alb. 13, P-126)

START OF GAMBLIAN PLUVIAL SOUTH OF EQUATOR; EARLY LUPEMBAN

UCLA-168	38000 ± 2500	Mufo (Angola); Lower Lupemban
UCLA-169	>34000	Mufo (Angola); Lower Lupemban
Lv-47	>30000	R. Basoko (Congo); Lupemban; said to be at start of an arid period
L-399A	>40000	Kalambo Falls (Zambia); relation to Sangoan-Lupemban transition not yet published

---

PLUVIAL CONDITIONS IN THE SAHARA

I-1787	>39900 ⎫	Bou Hadid, Saoura valley, from near base of
I-1761	38000 ⎭	sediments of second phase of pluvial; corrected dates. Alimen et al., *CRAS* 263D (1966), p.5.
T-340B	21350 ± 350	Fachi (Niger), well down in pluvial sediments

---

ATERIAN CULTURE

Algeria and Tunis:
Directly after Beach V

L-133A	7000 ± 200	Oued Djebbana, culture believed Aterian but doubtful; site not sealed

Morocco:

UCLA-678A	>30000	Lower Aterian ⎫ Dar-es-Soltan
UCLA-678B	27000-30000	Upper Aterian ⎭

Sahara:
Date for Bou Hadid (above) belongs to level of the latest Aterian in the Saoura Valley

W-85	34000 ± 2800	or probably older. Latest date for Mousterian from Haua Fteah (Cyrenaica); apparently no true Aterian

NPL-15B 6500 ± 108 Wadi Gan (Tripolitania); association with Aterian may be false

Guinea Aterian and upper stone-line:
I–2264 12400 ± 300 Jimam, peat above basal gravel

END OF GAMBLIAN PLUVIAL SOUTH OF EQUATOR: LATE LUPEMBAN OR TSITOLIAN

C-581 14503 ± 560 Mufo (Angola). Near end of pluvial; Late Upper Lupemban

C-580 11189 ± 490 Mufo (Angola). Just post-Gamblian. Lupembo-Tsitolian

UCLA-172 12970 ± 250 Calunda 3 (Angola). End-Gamblian. Lupembo-Tsitolian

GRO-3048 12650 ± 100 Cherangani (Kenya). Cold phase, ? Gamblian or under influence of European Late Glacial

NPL-38 31480 ± 1350 Kisese (Tanzania), claimed as Second Intermediate, but association may be wrong

L-395D 9550 ± 210 Kalambo Falls (Zambia). Magosian in stone-line

SR-11 15800 ± 200 Pomongwe (Rhodesia). Middle of Magosian level

POST-PLUVIAL I: SUB-PLUVIAL I

I-556 14700 ± 290 Mahoma Lake (Uganda). Retreat of Ruwenzori glaciers.

Correlation with European Late Glacial very uncertain; there was certainly a sharp rise in temperature before all the northern ice disappeared. There were at least two Late Glacial readvances of ice; one of these may be reflected in Sub-pluvial I, which is not proved in West Africa.

Rise in ocean-temperature:

Oldest reliable dates from deep-sea cores are

A 172-6 W-237 17500
Alb. 189 W-132 17200

In other cores the rise starts 15500-13000, and ends about 11000.

SUB-PLUVIAL II

EASTERN SAHARA
Deposits of Ténéré Lake:

T-338B	9240 ± 130	Agadem	
T-338A	8580 ± 110	Agadem, above last	Heights 350-400 m.; these
T-280	9150 ± 200	Bouloum Gana	samples may all be from the
T-279	6900 ± 150	Kandel Bouzou	same lake
T-341	7000 ± 100	Kafra	
T-361	7310 ± 120	Adrar Bous	From small separate lake
T-4013	5900 ± 140	Bougdouma	*Asequa* iii (1964), p. 11

Lacustrine neolithic:

Sa-100   5140 ±300   Adrar Bous, with fish-bones and Mediterranean vegetation

3350 ±200   Fachi, hippo bones. *Asequa* iii (1964), p. 10

CENTRAL SAHARA

Neolithic sites:

Sa-59   5410 ±300   Meniet, with fish-hooks and Med. flora
Sa-62   5030 ±300   Sefar, with Med. flora
Sa-65   4270 ±300   Jabbaren I
MC-14   5460 ±300   Jabbaren II, bovine
Sa-66   5470 ±300   Jabbaren II, bovine

NORTH SAHARA AND MAGHREB

L-134   8400 ±400   El Mekta, damp climate, Typical Capsian
L-133B   7000 ±200   Dra-Mta-el-Ma el Abiod, drier, Upper Capsian
Sa-217   6160 ±320   Beni Abbes. Conrad, *CRAS* 257 (1963), p. 2506

INTRODUCTION OF NEOLITHIC INTO NORTH-EASTERN AFRICA

W-98   6800 ±350   Haua Fteah. There are other similar dates for the transition to the neolithic

C-550-1   6391 ±180   Fayum
U-6   6130 ±110   Merimde, 180 cms. deep, the oldest date
M-803   5960 ±400   Abka, level 5, neolithic
C-753   5060 ±450   Shaheinab, the most reliable date
GRO-2805   5860 ±70   Dar-es-Soltan.

N.B. that dates from the Nile Valley are liable to be considerably too low.

GUINEA, ULTIMATE M.S.A.

Y-142-7   5440 ±110   Zenebi. Artefacts look old, may be derived into the deposit; above, p.67

SOUTH OF THE EQUATOR

UCLA-167   6830 ±120   Late Tsitolian, Mufo (Angola)
UCLA-171   4700 ±100   Late Tsitolian, Calunda 3 (Angola)
Lv-45   6030 ±190   Late Tsitolian, Mt. Gafula (Congo)
Lv-17   7840 ±190   Forest, no culture; Lemba (Congo)

BEACH VI

Y-466   6870 ±160   Groenvlei (Cape), just before transgression had reached −3 m.

GRO-1194   5570 ±70   Takoradi, when transgression reached modern S.L.

T–404   5570 ±120   Nouakchott, shells from +1-2 m. *Asequa* iii (1964)
L-398B   5970 ±130   Miramar, shells from +2 m.

6150 ±150   Miramar, shells from +2 m. Gigout, *SGFCR* (1961), p. 228

NOTE. The last three dates are likely to be too old, as shells often pick up dead carbon.

Dates of the Transgression and of subsequent fluctuations are a world-wide phenomenon, and are set out by Fairbridge, see note 17. The best absolute dates are:

First transgression about 6000–4600 B.P., with two slight regressions and maximum about 5120. Regression reached modern S.L. at latest about 4400. In West Africa there is evidence for only one regression, not associated with the cultural sequence. In other parts of the world there were at least two regressions, the later contemporary with the Roman Empire. The date in second millennium B.C. from Kouali Point (Algeria) W-658-9 may refer to the second transgression.

POST-PLUVIAL III

Sa-55   4680 ±300   Taessa, guano, indicating onset of drier conditions, but still with Med. vegetation.

Large fauna disappears from Egyptian rock-art after the neolithic, i.e. about 4900 B.P., see Butzer, K. W., 1958–9

Maximum in West Africa is after Beach VI.

European dates for dry maximum, about 1000 B.C.

South of the equator, probably neolithic:

Lv-46   3080 ±170   Mt Amba (Congo)

SUB-PLUVIAL III

Start of Iron Age,   Northern Nigeria:

Y-474   1750 ±50   Sample from clays overlying gravel which contained the Nok figurines, and probably not much later than the figurines, which must belong to the last phase of the gravel

Y-142-4   2875 ±70   Deposit below the figures

I-1458   2230 ±120   Nok-culture site, Taruga

I-1460   1975 ±120   Ropp, microlithic site near Nok.

For dates recently received from Ntereso see chapter 5, p. 238

Iron Age south of the equator:

Y-91   2920 ±80   Njoro (Kenya), stone-bowl culture

SR-24   1930 ±100   Situmpa Forest (Zambia), start of channelled ware

L-395C   1410 ±150   Kalambo Falls (Zambia), start of channelled ware

B-263   1240 ±120   Sanga (Congo), oldest date for Kisalian pottery

Y-587   1240 ±100   Feti la Choya (Angola), bottom layer

Ivory Coast:

U-266-4   990 ±70   Meaning of date uncertain until the site is published

NOTES

1. Cp. Blanchard, *L'Hypothèse du Déplacement des Poles*.
2. Aitken, *Physics and Archaeology*, ch. 7.
3. Over 1,000 years, *Radiocarbon* vi (1964), p. 32.
4. Ennouchi, *Anthropologie* lxvi (1962), p. 277; about 47000 B.P., GRN–2023, *Radiocarbon* v (1963), p. 171.
5. Monod T., 1964.
6. For discussion of the chronological consistency of deep-sea cores, see Davies, *GJS* iii (1963), p. 98.
7. Rosholt *et al.*, *Journal of Geology* lxix (1961), p. 167.
8. Evernden, Curtis and Kistler, *Quaternaria* iv (1957), p. 13.
9. See résumé in Howell, *Current Anthropology* (1962), p. 306. Dr Evernden announced at VII Inqua in 1965 that he has attained a much greater degree of accuracy, so that potassium-argon dating is now fairly reliable before less than 100,000 years.
10. This figure is probably too low, and a figure near 5730 is more probable, see *Radiocarbon* v (1963), pref.
11. Haring and de Vries, *Science* 128 (1958), p. 472.
12. Cp. *Radiocarbon* i (1959), p. 48, v (1963), pp. 287–9.
13. Witting, *Fennia* lxviii (1945), p. 1.
14. Cp. Blanc, *Soc. geográfica italiana Boll.* xcv (1958), p. 196; Castany and Ottmann, *RGPGD* i (1957), p. 46.
15. Bonifay and Maro, *SGFCR* (1959), p. 62; Arambourg, *ibid.*, p. 209.
16. Gigout, *CRAS* 247 (1958), p. 1363.
17. *Physics and Chemistry of the Earth*, vol. IV, pp. 160–73.
18. Tealham Moor (Somerset), 5412 ± 130, Q–120, Godwin, Suggate and Willis, *Nature* 181 (1958), p. 1518; Takoradi (Ghana), 5570 ± 70, GRO–1194, de Vries and Waterbolk, *Science* 128 (1958), p. 1552. These dates, like others in this book, were calculated on the old value of the half-life of radiocarbon, so may be slightly too low.
19. Zagwijn, *Geologie en Mijnbouw* xix (1957), p. 233; Blanc, *l. c.* (note 14).
20. Biberson P., 1961 (1).
21. Shukri, Philip and Said, *Institut d'Egypte Bulletin* XXXVII ii (1956), p. 395.
22. Davies and Walsh, *South African Journal of Science* li (1955), p. 277; Davies, *Inqua V Résumés*, p. 45.
23. Cp. Cahen, *Géologie du Congo belge*, p. 425.
24. Davies, *SAAB* vi (1951), p. 107; see Macfarlane, *SAAB* iv (1949), p. 95.
25. Breuil, *Anthropologie* xlix (1939–40), p. 13; Howell, *Current Anthropology* i (1960), p. 227, n. 5; Agache *et al.*, *SGFCR* (1963), p. 158.
26. Cp. those reproduced in Woldstedt, *Das Eiszeitalter* i, p. 229.
27. 'Examination of the Tertiary and Quaternary Changes of sea-level in South Africa' (*University of Stellenbosch Annals* (1927) V A 1).
28. Five stages at Durban above modern S. L., Davies, *SAAB* vi (1951), p. 107; probably four or five on Sundays River, Ruddock, *S. African J. Science* liii (1957), p. 373; perhaps three at Plettenberg Bay.

29. Martin, *Geological Society of South African Trans.* lxv (1962), p. 19.
30. Butzer and Cuerda, *Journal of Geology* lxx (1962), p. 398.
31. Occasionally unrolled, e.g. on the 16–metre beach at Cape Hangklip (Cape); also some at Punta de Giraul, Davies, *IV Panafrican Congress* i, p. 289.
32. There must have been warping here, as not only is Beach IV too high, but it overlies Beach III, contrary to the normal sequence.
33. Camps, *LAPE* iii (1956), p. 17.
34. Lorcin, *LAPE* ix–x (1961–2), p. 9; Roubet, *Bull. trim. Société de Géographie et d'Archéologie d'Oran* lxxvi (1953). p. 15.
35. Mabesoone, *Geologie en Mijnbouw* xlii (1963), p. 29.
36. Breuil and Zbyszewski, *Anais da Faculdade de Ciencias de Porto* xxvii (1942), p. 161; Zbyszewski and Teixeira, *Sociedade geologica de Portugal Boletim* viii (1949), p. 1.
37. For Lebanon see Garrod, R. *Anthropological Inst. Jour.* xcii (1962), p. 237.
38. *IV Inqua*, p. 547. For the Harbour Island bar at Alexandria, which seems to correspond to the 3–metre Nile terrace with Middle Mousterian and should be later than Eem, see also Shukri *et al.*, *l. c.* (note 21). For criticism of Zeuner and denial of the Epimonastirian see Butzer, *Journal of Geology* lxiii (1960), p. 626.
39. Gams, *Experientia* x (1954), p. 357.
40. Bonifay, *CRAS* 244 (1957), p. 3075.
41. Behm–Blanke, in *Hundert Jahre Neanderthaler*, p. 141; cp. Viete, *Geologie* vi (1957), p. 209.
42. Y-468; *Radiocarbon* v, p. 312.
43. Y-466; *Radiocarbon Supplement* i (1959), p. 159. This sample is slightly older than Beach VI, though there was no sign there of a positive sealevel of Beach VI. The absence of a positive Beach VI in certain parts of the world, especially in zones of subsidence with extremely flat shore profiles, is under examination.
44. Russell, *Science* 139 (1963), p. 9.
45. Curray, in Shepard, *Recent Sediments, Northwest Gulf of Mexico.*
46. Oakley, *Advancement of Science* xviii (1961), p. 425; Clark and van Zinderen Bakker, *Nature* 201 4923 (1964), p. 471.
47. Broecker Kulp and Tucek, *Science* 124 (1956), p. 164.
48. For further discussion see Davies, *VI Inqua* i, p. 279; Biberson, *SGFB* VII v (1963), p. 607. On the other side, Stearns and Thurber (*Quaternaria* vii, p. 29; *VII Inqua Abstracts*, p. 442) have been experimenting in the dating of molluscs by the ratio $Th_{230}:U_{234}$; it is too early to accord whole-hearted acceptance to this method. From molluscs from the western Mediterranean and Morocco they have obtained several dates for Beach V about 80,000 and for Beach IV about 125,000. If these dates are accepted, Beach V must be equated with Eem and IV with Ohe; the single finite radiocarbon date for the Acheulian at Kalambo Falls, which is very near the limit of radiocarbon possibility, must be rejected.

N.B. In the most recent literature (Kopp and Woldstedt, *Eiszeitalter und Gegenwart* xvi (1965), p. 37) it is indicated that Ohe is a misnomer for the interval between the Saale and Warthe glaciation, and Treene is suggested. This name has hardly become fixed.

49. Allen and Wells, *Journal of Geology* lxx (1962), p. 381.
50. Beaudet and Maurer, *Notes marocaines* xv (1961), p 13.
51. Biberson, *Société de Préhistoire du Maroc Bull.* N.S. 3–4 (1951), p. 9.
52. Biberson, *IV Inqua*, p. 705; id., *Quaternaria* ii (1955), p. 109; Biberson P., 1961 (1). He thinks that Beach III at Sidi Abderrahman is superposed on a regressive II, but continental deposits should separate the two beaches. That Beach III contains Beach II material reworked is more likely.
53. Breuil and Zbyszewski, *Serviços geologicos de Portugal Comun.* xxiii (1942) and xxvi (1945); Breuil, *Sociedade portuguesa de Antropologia Bol.* xvii (1959), p. 9.
54. Guilcher and Joly, *Recherches sur la Morphologie de la Côte atlantique du Maroc*; Hernandez–Pacheco, *CIAO* II i, p. 117.
55. Hernandez–Pacheco, *Instituto de Estudios africanos Arch.* XV lix (1961), p. 25.
56. Tricart, *Ass. des Géographes français Bull.* (1955), p. 109; Brigaud, *ESén* ix (1960), p. 53. There may be evidence for a much older beach in Mauritania, but it has been entirely reworked, see Tricart, *XVIII Cong. int. de Géographie* (1956), *I Rapport de la Commission des Niveaux d'Erosion* iii, p. 23.
57. Monod, *IRS Travaux* iii (1945), p. 33; Lecointre, *V Inqua Résumés* p. 104; id., *LAPE* v (1957), p. 261; id., *Quaternaria* vii (1965) p.16.
58. Tricart, *IFAN* 22A (1960), p. 1127; Lecointre, *SGFCR* (1961), p. 92; id., *Garcia da Orta* xi (1963), p. 275.
59. Hubert and Lenoble, *CEHSAOF* ix (1926), p. 185.
60. Corbeil R., Mauny R. and Charbonnier J., 1948; Corbeil R., 1951.
61. Dixey, *Geological Society of South Africa Trans.* xxii (1919), p. 112.
62. Gregory, quoted by Williams, *Asequa* 5–6 (1965).
63. Tricart J., 1957; id., *Recherches africaines* (1962), p. 31.
64. Hales, in a paper to Ghana Science Congress 1961, apparently not yet printed.
65. *ARGS* (1938–9), p. 22.
66. Davies, *II Panafrican Congress*, p. 259; Davies O., 1956.
67. Anderson and Brückner, *III Panafrican Congress*, p. 86. These authors have very recently admitted two pre-holocene beaches (*VI Inqua* i, p. 253); so when they examine the field evidence more carefully, they may yet come to admit Beaches I and IV.
68. Crowe, *Gold Coast Geological Survey Bulletin* 18, p. 30.
69. Lombard, *SAfr* i (1931), p. 57; Droux and Kelley, *SAfr* ix (1939), p. 80.
70. Such ideal curves are illustrated in Zeuner, *Dating the Past*, figs. 43–4.
71. Davies O., 1957.
72. Close to the sources nickpoints occur and terraces coalesce, cp. the study of the the upper Birim Valley by Hunter, *WASA* v (1959), p. 108.
73. E.g. rolled Chellean of similar type from the Middle Terrace of the

Volta and tributaries, from Poyonu Akroso Atafie and perhaps Dumbai, roughly 90, 230, 320 and 380 kms. from the Volta mouth; see fig. 7.

74. In fig. 2 the rejuvenation point of the Low Terrace of the River Dayi is clearly marked. In pl. 13 the rejuvenation point on the Ayensu is visible at the back. On the River Ofin at Ofinso the Low Terrace is cut by the road at 15 m.; on it was a rolled Sangoan pick.

75. The High Terrace is at over 40 m., but there was probably over-deepening of the bed because the Volta had in the present cycle incised below Oti at the confluence.

76. A rolled pick from Amanfinaso on the Ankobra (Davies O., 1964 (2), fig. 8 1) could be Chellean, but it was impossible to determine accurately the height of the gravel. There may also be one rolled Chellean pick from Ofinso.

77. E.g. at Kwanyaku 29 kms. from the mouth of the River Ayensu the Low Terrace is at 18 m., so would grade to Beach IV. As there was slightly rolled Sangoan material in the gravel, it would appear that the rejuvenation of Beach V had not spread thus far upstream before being overtaken by the much deeper rejuvenation of the Gamblian–Würm eustatic low, which formed the present valley floor.

78. Rolled Acheulian pieces: Nkunsia on Ankobra ?; Bawdua (find-site unknown, found in tailings of diamond-workings); Kwanyaku on Ayensu; Angeta on Dayi, very rolled pieces which appear to be Acheulian; perhaps Todome on Dayi; Bersingou and Wé-wé in upper Dahomey; slightly rolled in an old channel of the Mo River at Sabatei, unrolled on a small tributary close to Sokode (Davies O , 1957).

79. Sangoan pieces, rolled, Ofinso Kwanyaku: unrolled and perhaps slightly rolled, Jomuro on Tano; Kade on Birim: unrolled, confluence of River Ankobra and Mpintim; Twifu Praso on Pra, perhaps post-Sangoan; Dunkwa on Ofin, in the filling of a gulley in the gravel before soil accumulated on it (Davies O., 1964 (2), pl. II 4); Amoaku on Ofin; sites on the Birim, especially at Oda where the railway exposes the Low Terrace gravel in a series of cuttings for 2 kms. between the town and the bridge [pl. 19], Kade and Bunsu; many sites along the Ayensu; Apiakrom on lower Volta; but in general Sangoan pieces have not been found on the Low Terrace of the Volta save along its tributaries from the east, the Todzie (several sites), the Tsawe especially at Chawenu and Anum Jn., the Dayi (many sites), the Asukawkaw, and far upstream on the Mo and Kara, which are tributaries of the Oti; Anié and Amoutchou in the Mono basin; Bersingou and Kouniangou on small rivers in the Atacora Mts.; Alibori Bridge (upper Dahomey); and at several rejuvenation points on tributaries of the Niger.

80. Rolled Sangoan from basal gravels: Bremang on Ankobra, Nyinawonsu on Ofin, Bunsu and Wanchi on Birim, Diépouro in north Dahomey; rolled Chellean: Jani on Dayi.

81. Good sites close to the confluence of the Volta and the Daka; at Kukuo–Nawuni and Lungbunga on the White Volta; and at several sites near Wa on the Black Volta.

82. Bopa on Tano and several sites on the Birim, see Davies O., 1961 (1). A few pieces from the savannah are not obviously Guinea Aterian, but are difficult to identify.

83. The gravel at Lungbunga illustrated yielded Guinea Aterian artefacts (Davies O., 1964 (2), fig. 16 1–4); some of the pebbles are thought to be wind-eroded, probably during long dry seasons which would also provide the conditions for lateritization. Lateritization has been noticed at a few other sites, like Kukuo-Nawuni on White Volta and Lanto at the mouth of the Daka, also in northern Dahomey.

84. For ill-sorted basal gravel directly underlying the Inner Silt-terrace of the River Birim near Kibi, see pl. 20.

85. Butzer K. W., 1957.

86. A sketch of the bank of the Tano at Tanodumasi shows the river incising its granite bed, and leaving the basal gravels pendant and capped by sand and coarse grit, see Cooper, GSFNB 27/4/22.

87. Palynology in Africa viii, p. 65. Renewed investigation has revealed the outlines of a complex sequence, which must be tested by large-scale excavation. Radiocarbon dates will then be obtained. In the lowest level was a handled wooden instrument, perhaps a paddle; probably the remains of a dugout canoe; and other pieces of cut wood.

88. ARGS (1937–8), p. 8.

89. ARGS (1935–6), p. 10.

90. Junner, Geological Survey of Gold Coast Bulletin xii, p. 10.

91. Junner, GSFNB 14/3/31.

92. Clark and van Zinderen Bakker, Nature 201 4923 (1964), p. 471.

93. Butzer K. W., 1957; Butzer K. W., 1958–9.

94. Fairbridge, Kush xi (1963), p. 96

95 Münnich and Vogel, Geologischer Rundschau lii (1962), p. 611.

96. Cp. dates for rise of ocean temperature, W–237 W–132.

97. Cp. van der Hammen, Geologie en Mijnbouw xix (1957), p. 250; Jespersen, Neues Jahrbuch für Geologie und Paläontologie Monatshefte (1957), p. 541.

98. Guillian, Annales de Géographie 383 (71) (1962), p.1. Cp. pollen-diagram from Tenagi (S. Macedonia), van der Hammen et al., Geologie en Mijnbouw xliv (1965), p. 37, indicating sharp rise from steppe to oak-forest after about 13000 B.P. until 7900 B.P.

99. Leroi-Gourhan, SPF lv (1958), p. 546.

100. Higgs, Prehistoric Society Proc. xxvii (1961), p. 144; Hey, Eiszeitalter und Gegenwart xiv (1963), p. 77.

101. Choubert, Service géologique du Maroc, Notes et Mémoires 128 (1955), p. 9.

102. Beucher and Conrad, CRAS 256 (1963), p. 4465. Date later corrected, see above p. 78, Bou Hadid.

103. Conrad, CRAS 257 (1963), p. 2506.

104. Dutil Martinez and Quezel, SHNAN 50 (1959), p. 196.

105. Sols africains v (1960), p. 207.

106. Quezel and Martinez, in Hugot H. J. ed., 1962, p. 313; Rognon, IRS

Travaux xxi (1962), p. 57. This pluvial is possibly dated by the rolled Chellean found derived into the middle terrace in the Hoggar.

107. Quezel and Thébault, *Bull. scientifique et économique du Bureau de Recherches minières de l'Algérie* vi (1959), p. 59; Devillers, *SGFCR* (1948), p. 189; and reff. in note 106.

108. Faure Manguin and Nydal, *Bur. de Recherches géologiques et minières Bull.* iii (1963), p. 41.

109. Quezel and Martinez, in Hugot H. J. ed., 1962, p. 317; id., *SHNAN* xlix (1958), p. 230; Quezel, 'Mission botanique au Tibesti' (*IRS Mémoires* 4).

110. Grove and Pullan, in Howell and Bourlière, *African Ecology and Human Evolution*, p. 230 and bibliography; *Asequa* iv.

111. This conclusion is tentative, because it is not yet easy to distinguish Late M.S.A. from Ultimate M.S.A. save on geological evidence, so one cannot make a satisfactory distribution map of the latter.

112. Dates of well-defined Makalian phenomena are scanty: Lv–17 7840 ± 190, for forest growth at Lemba (Congo) in present grassland; Y–568 7530 ± 450 from Dura River (Uganda), in a phase of high lakes, may well be Makalian; UCLA–171 4700 ± 100 from Calunda 3 mine, Lunda, may be described as Makalian to fit the date. Concordant is L–395–D 9550 ± 210 for Magosian from Kalambo Falls, which is pre-Makalian.

113. Lhote, *SPF* xlvii (1950), p. 165; see Ch. 4 on harpoons from the Sahara. Some sites in the southern Sahara like Taferjit were flooded by rising lakes during the neolithic.

114. H. J. Hugot, personal communication. In his publication Hugot H. J., (1963) the cereals found at Meniet are not identified.

115. At Buipe Bridge, where the edge of the inner terrace may be eroded, the outer covers it to a thickness of as much as two metres.

116. For the general scheme see Fagg B., 1956. The reality was probably more complex than this scheme, which does not apply to sites like Zenebi, where the sediments are successively superposed outwash-fans.

117. Urvoy, 'Les Bassins du Niger' (*IFAN Mém.* iv), pp. 53–56; id., *Annales de Géographie* xliv (1935), p. 254.

118. *Asequa* iii (1964), p. 22.

119. Lambert, *SGFB* V vi (1936), p. 79.

120. Vogt, *Annales de Géographie* lxviii (1959), p. 193.

121. *Rapport provisoire de Mission en moyenne Côte d'Ivoire* (roneo), with review in *RGD* x (1959), p. 53.

122. Tessier, *Ann. Faculté des Sciences, Université de Dakar* iv (1959), p. 91.

123. Cp. Waagemans, *Bull. agricole du Congo belge* xlii (1951), p. 13.

124. Local conditions may cause immediate cementation; e.g. at Kuntunso (Ashanti) the latest nodules, immediately below the mesolithic, have formed a block-laterite.

125. Dresch, *Assoc. de Géographes français Bull.* (1959), p. 2.

126. Davies, *SAAB* iv (1949), p. 90; id., *Natal Regional Survey* I ch. I 5; van Riet Lowe, *SAAB* vii (1952), p. 143.

127. Smit, *GJS* ii (1962), p. 176. At the W.A. Science Ass. Congress in 1963 Gentner announced a date by potassium-argon of 1·3 million years, see *Zeitschrift für Naturforschung* 19a (1964), p. 150.

128. Cp. Chételat, *RGPGD* xi (1938), p. 5.

129. Maignien, 'Cuirassement des sols en Guinée' (*Mém*. *Service de la Carte géologique d'Alsace et de Lorraine* 16), tentatively suggests that lateritization started in the cretaceous, and dates the crust on each river terrace at Kankan by the terrace, whereas a crust may be much later than a surface. Similarly Brückner (*Eclogae geologicae Helvetiae* 50 (1957), p. 239; Brückner W., 1955) dates the laterites in Ghana far too early in the Pleistocene, because he did not know the artefacts associated with them; for correction of his scheme, see Davies O., 1961 (1). Brückner believes in an independent older cycle of lateritization, probably cretaceous, which produced the bauxites of Senegal and Ghana. He does not explain what was happening throughout the tertiary.

130. Hugot, *Asequa* 5–6 (1965), p. 26. At VII Inqua Hugot said that he had found several flaked pebbles, in a layer sharply separated from the weathered surface containing Kalinian.

131. Davies O., 1964 (2), p. 78.

132. Davies, in *Natal Regional Survey* I pt. 1, p. 24.

133. Coppens, *CRAS* 252 (1961), p. 3851; id., *SPF* lviii (1961), p. 756; id., *CRAS* 260 (1965), p. 2869; Monod T., 1964. Coppens (*VII Inqua Abstr.*, p. 75) says that the creature is of advanced type, intermediate between Australopithecus and Pithecanthropus.

134. Boule M. and Vallois H., 1932; Mauny R., 1961 (2).

SUPPLEMENT TO LIST OF DATES

Beach V or a later inter-Würm beach:

T–536	31100 ± 1200	North of Nouakchott, at 2·7 m. depth, perhaps end of beach
T–464	31400 ± 1700	Beach-rock, Bargny

Post-pluvial I:

I–1651	16300 ± 350	Top of Saouran sand
I–1991	14500 ± 190	Crust on Saouran terrace

Beach VI:

T–463	5470 ± 110	Beach-terrace at + ·4 m., Rao

Sub-pluvial III

I–2165	3160 ± 105	Diatomite, Koro Toro, indicating water 20 m. deep in Bahr-el-Ghazal

CHAPTER THREE

The Palaeolithic in West Africa

Pre-Chellean and Chellean Industries

Man is one of the weakest of the larger mammals. Even our earliest hominid ancestors probably had comparatively weak musculature, though it may have been more efficient in relation to weight than that of other animals. Above all, man was singularly unadapted to self-defence or to means of procuring food as soon as he turned from fruit-eating to predation and a taste for meat. He had no horns. His claws are not sharp. With the reduction of his canines his teeth have become useless for fighting.

His only chance of survival lay in the acquisition of tools, external objects which he could manipulate as substitutes for the natural organs which he lacked. Much has been written about the faculties which enabled him to make use of tools, and how adaptation of his faculties ran parallel with improvement of his techniques. To make and use tools he needed hands with muscles finely adapted for grasping, sharp and well co-ordinated near-vision, strong ankles which would give secure stance on two legs, a gracile and highly flexible body, herd-instinct and means of communication by which technical improvements could be transmitted. With these faculties man would find extraneous tools far more satisfactory than biological organs, because they could be adapted without delay to changing needs and environment. So the possession of tools enabled him to expand into ecological regions to which he had not been born, and to survive the violent climatic shifts of the pleistocene, during which other creatures had no alternative but to die out or to get out.

Many primates are capable of making use of an object to hand to satisfy an immediate need, even of adapting an object for their purpose. But while an ape will seize a stick to obtain food out of reach, he has not the foresight or imagination to carry a stick round, so that he may have it to hand in case he comes across food which he cannot reach. Certain highly domesticated animals have learnt, through their contact with human beings, to associate apparently irrelevant acts with desires which they wish to satisfy. But such forethought seems to be due entirely to domestication and has not been proved in the wild state.

Early man and his prehominid ancestors doubtless often used natural objects to hand. Even those species which were frugivorous and reasonably pacific would have to defend themselves against predators and probably to fight one another for mates, for which they would need at least clubs of wood or bone. The weakness of human claws and teeth would necessitate external means for perforating and cutting tough objects, and sharp points and blades could be provided in stone and bone. There would probably be need of stones for breaking hard fruits, perhaps also for pulping very tough food like tubers. Those species which took to meat-eating would be far more in need of tools, weapons to scare off fellow scavengers if they themselves scavenged the kills of carnivores, weapons to kill their own game, tools to cut skin which human teeth could not puncture.

Such objects were provided by nature, but their availability was very irregular, and they would almost always not be to hand at the critical moment. Here man's faculty of foresight stood him in good stead. He will have learnt to collect useful tools, and to carry them around in view of future foreseen needs. He will also have learnt to adapt the shapes of the pieces he had collected so that they would best serve his requirements. It is at this stage that we can begin to talk of man, the tool-maker.

Wood was in fact of little use to primitive man except for heavy clubs, until he possessed sharp tools or fire to shape it. Bones selected for particular purposes were of value, as has been demonstrated by Dart's studies on the osteodontokeratic culture of Australopithecus at Makapansgat. Such bones required a minimum of shaping, but they would exhibit signs of wear when used as clubs, rasps, points and so on. Critics of Professor Dart's theories were sceptical when confronted with an idea which ran against preconceived notions. They had been equally sceptical twenty years earlier of his Australopithecus from Taungs. Many are now becoming convinced when they see the material, look at the statistics of selected bones and of types of wear on them, and consider how such bones can have accumulated in or above the cave. It is to be hoped that other great collections of pleistocene bones will be critically examined to see whether they show purposeful selection or signs of use.

It is not by any means proved that Australopithecus of Makapansgat was an ancestor or even a close relative of man. He may well have developed his bone culture independently. But it is difficult to believe that man, once he had tumbled to the idea of using and shaping tools, did not take advantage of many of the specialized forms of bone which nature provided. He did so later; one need but mention the bone tools found in upper palaeolithic and neolithic contexts, antler-picks, scapula-shovels and so on. We have no critical appraisal of a large collection of bones from the earliest undoubtedly human sites, Chellean or Early Acheulian.

It was not at first easy to shape bone. Stone was less satisfactory than bone until the idea had arisen of artificially shaping it. Some pieces might have a crude sharp edge or point; but so often it was not of exactly the right shape. Moreover, sharp stones were not easy to come by except in arid regions where there was no soil, or among mountains subject to frost-weathering; neither region would in other ways be a particularly tempting habitat. In open country most stones would be buried beneath soil and vegetation. There would be available only the rounded pebbles in river-beds and on the sea-shore.

Therefore stone-users had from the start to shape their tools. This was not a difficult step to take. It would be easy to observe that pebbles, used for pounding or as missiles, would flake and provide a sharp edge. Stone pounders are not shaped tools. At Ain Hanech and Mansourah (Algeria),[1] with a Villafranchian fauna, there seem to have been only pounders. It is doubtful if the creature who used them can properly be described as a 'tool-maker'. The same seems to have been true at a much later date of the oldest level at Florisbad (Orange Free State).

Van Riet Lowe[2] set out an imaginative scheme of the development of the pebble tool. He probably regarded this as an exercise in theoretical typology, not to be treated too seriously. It certainly was not supported stratigraphically. Unfortunately French prehistorians, wedded to a rigid schematism in typology, have seized on van Riet Lowe's work and constructed on it theories which it will not bear.

Flaked pebbles by themselves prove nothing. This simplest form of artefact was commonly made at least until the Middle Stone Age. It provides a sharp edge; and conventionally, if shaped to a point, it is regarded as Chellean rather than pre-Chellean. Pre-Chellean pebble tools, to be acceptable, must occur in the proper geological horizon, and if possible with the proper fauna. If the horizon is a riverine or marine gravel, a large number of them must be rolled. It was easy for later men to mine a gravel and to leave in their pits their own artefacts; these pits would stratigraphically be indistinguishable, but the tools would be unrolled.

Strict criteria also must be applied to decide what is human workmanship. Selected pieces from the outwash of a tillite may be deceptive, though a large collection never looks convincing. Occasionally pebbles may undergo percussion-flaking at the base of a precipice or in cemented laterite. Pebbles nibbled round the edge in uncemented riverine or marine gravel are under suspicion. Nature can effect such flaking with violent water action, but very rarely can uncemented pebbles be split longitudinally, because there is a certain resilience in the gravel. The discovery of a good number of flaked pieces affords strong presumption of human activity; one or two flaked pebbles could more easily be of natural origin.

The old distinction of uniface and biface pebble tools, on which the theory of the Kafuan and Oldowan cultures was based, is not tenable. In East Asia these types are known as choppers and chopping tools, and occur together. In Africa also the distinction is technically meaningless. Once the idea of flaking a pebble tool had been grasped, its form would depend on the shape and thickness of the pebble, and to some extent on the purpose for which it was required. It must be admitted, however, that no satisfactory typology of pebble tools has been proposed, so they seem generally to have been multipurpose.

In East Africa pebble tools have been found stratified far back in the Villafranchian, especially at Olduvai Gorge. Even though there is no certainty about the date of Bed I,[3] there is agreement that it is over one million years old, consequently the pebble tools which it contains are far older than the oldest Chellean remains, which occur in some countries in Beach II (Cromer). Olduvai Beds I and II seem to be conformable,[4] but their very long duration has not been explained. The pebble tool therefore had a long independent history.

Pebble tools have been found rolled in the later stages of Beach I in South Africa[5] and Angola,[6] and at least in the Older Gravels of the Vaal.[7] Certain sites in the Congo do not seem to be geologically secure.

There is no proof of pebble tools north of the equator as old as those from East Africa. The exact date of Ain Hanech remains to be determined, and as I have explained, the stone balls thence are not true, shaped tools. Much of Biberson's material from Morocco[8] is open to challenge because of his preoccupation with typology, which is almost meaningless at this stage, and his failure to discuss his sites in geological detail and especially to demonstrate that the artefacts could not have been introduced by later men mining the gravel. However, acceptable artefacts were found in Middle Villafranchian deposits at Tardiguet-er-

Rahla, which belongs to the Moulouya stage regarded as the equivalent of the later Donau glaciations; and at least one or two rolled on a beach at Carrière Déprez (Casablanca) at +100 m., which must be a late stage of Beach I (Donau–Günz).

Rolled pebble tools were found in a gravel-terrace of the Tafassasset near In Afalaleh and at Kori Tizourigi east of Agades;[9] also on and above the highest terrace at Idjerane (possible Chellean).[10] The geology of the Saharan terraces needs careful study before these can be accepted as pre-Chellean. The same doubt exists regarding Aoulef[11] and the surface sites near Reggan,[12] where they are not stratified. From the Saoura Valley there is a good stratigraphy, and pebble tools have been claimed from the Villafranchian onwards.[13] The term 'Villafranchian' is often loosely used by French authors; here it seems to mean pre-Günz in the European sense, without reference to African pluvials. The pieces illustrated from Villafranchian deposits are unconvincing as artefacts. From the Mazzerian, which is equated with Günz, there seem to be one or two acceptable rolled artefacts, but the majority are unrolled and could be intrusive. From the arid post-Mazzerian phase, and even from the Late Mazzerian,[14] are already proto-Chellean picks, such as could occur in corresponding deposits in Europe.

In Ghana and neighbouring territories pebble tools occur rolled in the gravels of the High Terraces. They cannot be claimed as more than locally pre-Chellean, because this terrace probably graded to Beach II (above, p. 53), which overlapped the beginning of the Chellean. No typically Chellean pieces have been found in these gravels in Ghana, at Todome Chellean pieces from the High Terrace had been reused and so were not *in situ* [fig. 2]. West of the Ivory Coast the existence of pre-Chellean man is very dubious. The only likely site is at Laminia on the middle Gambia,[15] and there no geological study has been made of the terrace gravels, so the context of the rolled pebble tools is unknown.

There are few new sites to add to the distribution map which I made some years ago,[16] whence no clear pattern of distribution emerges. The High Terrace has seldom survived erosion, so there may originally have been more abundant material. The best site has been the 24-metre gravel at Yapei [pl. 18; fig. 4], whence ninety more or less certain artefacts have been collected, and doubtless many more have been lost, because it was impossible to watch the gravel-digging regularly. The gravel at Kandinga, a little farther up the White Volta, has yielded only one rolled pebble tool at present, but may be promising. There is probably a group of sites near the confluence of the Volta and the Oti;

H

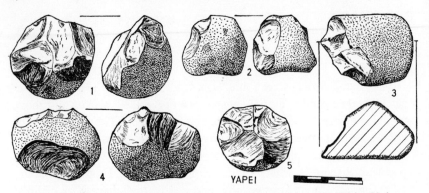

FIG. 4 Rolled pebble-tools from High Terrace, Yapei on R. White Volta

from Davies O., 1961 (3), p. 2

Otisu is the most promising. There is another group of probable sites in the Birim Valley, where now is forest. A terrace gravel of the Black Volta contains pebble tools in places; and there are other sites, very probable, on the Léraba and the White Bandama (Ivory Coast).

While the High Terraces in Ghana have been disappointing, the Middle Terraces, especially in Togoland, have yielded a rich harvest of Late Chellean tools. These terraces grade to Beach III, so belong to a different cycle from the High Terraces; there was a long interval between the very late pre-Chellean and the Late Chellean, during which we have no evidence and probably West Africa was uninhabited. This covered the Kamasian I pluvial, when forest may have extended far to the north. There does not, however, seem to be much sign of habitation in the northern savannah or southern Sahara. The Chellean pieces claimed from near Dakar[17] are probably Sangoan. I have mentioned a single piece from a higher terrace at Nok (Nigeria), which might be Chellean. The only site which typologically looks Chellean is the Mare de Toya near Yelimane (NW. Mali, fig. 5). There have been collected there without stratification five very crude pieces, which are rolled or heavily weathered. Several are made on large flakes. There are two hand-axes, a cleaver, and two large scrapers. Some other pieces, which are not artificial, were embedded in biscuity laterite; and there was from the same pan a little M.S.A. material, lightly patinated. The artefacts from Mare de Toya are reminiscent of some of the crude pieces published from Mauritania,[18] again unstratified. It would be reasonable to suggest that during the pluvial a Chellean province extended across the western Sahara from Morocco and the Saoura Valley to the River Senegal.

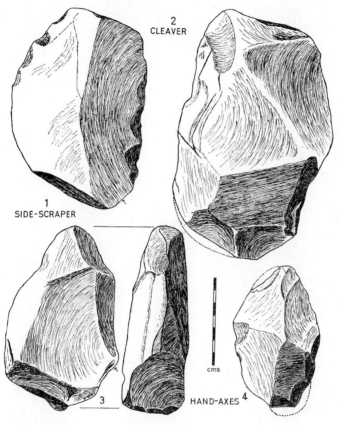

2
CLEAVER

1
SIDE-SCRAPER

3   HAND-AXES 4

cms

MARE DE TOYA   I.F.A.N. DAKAR So 48-37
FIG. 5

The Chellean in Ghana must belong to the end of the Kamasian I pluvial or the succeeding interpluvial. It is therefore stratigraphically late and typologically unlike the stray pieces from farther north. Most of it has been collected rolled in the gravels of the Middle Terraces and of Beach III, or else derived into lower gravels as at Hohoe and Angeta. A few pieces which may be Chellean were found on the slope above the Middle Terrace. They may have been transported thither at a later date [fig. 2]; and it is not unreasonable that Chellean people lived on sites overlooking the rivers as well as in their beds, as at Atafie Bato [fig. 7].

The distribution map [fig. 6] indicates occupation of the western flank of the Togoland mountains, along the Volta and Oti and on the lower course of their eastern tributaries. If these valleys had not been so inaccessible, more sites might have been found. The mountains were

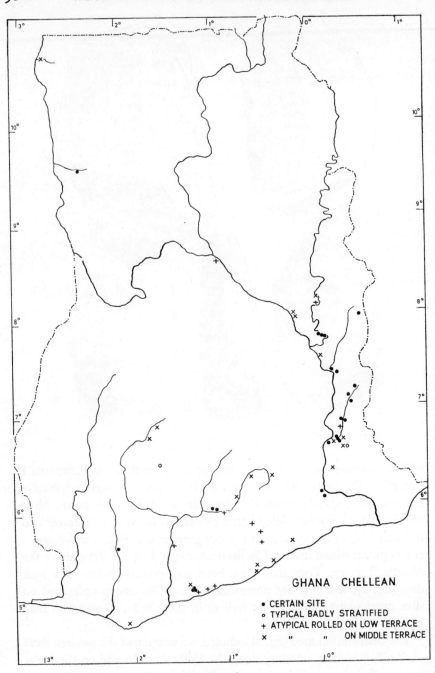

FIG. 6

probably forested; but as today, in an interpluvial the plains below them may have been open, with springs and streams. This must be the route by which the Chellean people reached Ghana, though the map shows a blank to the north, except for two probable Chellean pieces from the gorge of the Pendjari in northern Dahomey.[19] Thence one can reasonably reconstruct the route as far as the Niger gorge. But we are completely at a loss whence they had come, whether down the old

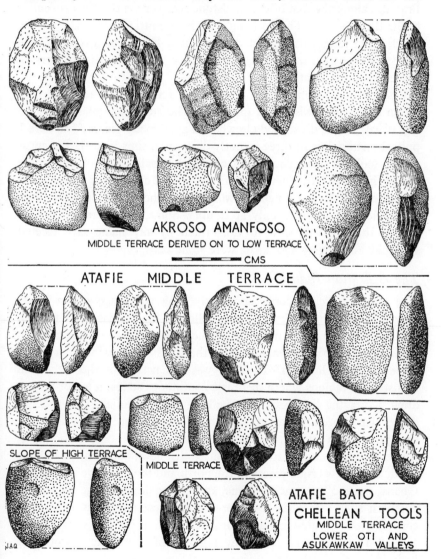

AKROSO AMANFOSO
MIDDLE TERRACE DERIVED ON TO LOW TERRACE
CMS

ATAFIE   MIDDLE   TERRACE

SLOPE OF HIGH TERRACE
MIDDLE TERRACE

ATAFIE BATO
CHELLEAN   TOOLS
MIDDLE TERRACE
LOWER OTI AND
ASUKAWKAW VALLEYS

FIG. 7

Niger–Tilemsi from the Hoggar, or down the Dallol Bosso from the Hoggar, or across northern Nigeria from central Africa; for none of these routes leads from a known centre of Chellean culture.

Not far below the Volta gorge the Chellean people will have reached the estuary, near which are the productive gravels of Poyonu and Kpong. Thence they spread along the coast, which may have been savannah as today, until they came up against forest near the River Pra; also along the foot of the sandstone scarp or via the Ayensu Valley to the Birim Valley. The outlying finds in Ashanti and the valley of the Black Volta cannot be explained. There may have been a route up the Black Volta, which we cannot trace because very little Middle Terrace gravel has been identified.

Chellean tools from Ghana are made of refractory stone, preferably Buem chert, otherwise hard quartzite. The stone-on-stone technique was usual. I have illustrated elsewhere a good many pieces;[20] so here I publish material from three recently discovered sites [fig. 7]. The most typical tool is a thick, short pick, on which usually some of the pebble surface has been left. There are various types of chopper or scraper, and in particular cylindrical pebbles worked to a chopper at one end. Very crude cleavers occurred only at Edubia. Some pieces are so roughly shaped that it is difficult to label them by any name save faceted spheroids; at Angeta and Ypala were stone balls.

The Acheulian Industry

The Late Chellean people apparently took advantage of an inter-pluvial to push into Ghana. There followed the Kamasian II pluvial, which seems to have been intense, to judge from the size of the Saharan lakes. Man probably cleared out of the forest zone, which may have extended to at least 11° N. This was the period of the Acheulian industry. In regions where there is a continuous series, it is not easy to draw a dividing-line between Chellean and Acheulian, and the two names have been combined in official Panafrican terminology; in Europe the term Chellean is almost abandoned. In West Africa, however, where it seems possible to make a sharp distiction between, on the one hand, a very few crude pieces in the north and the intensive industry of Ghana, worked by stone-on-stone, and on the other a large number of northern sites where the cylinder-hammer technique was used, it is convenient to divide Chellean from Acheulian at the end of the Kam-asian I–II interpluvial. In many regions this interpluvial would be included in the Early Acheulian.

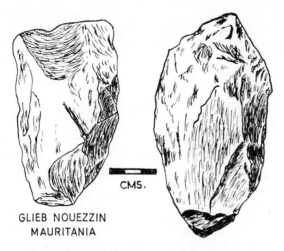

CMS.

GLIEB NOUEZZIN
MAURITANIA

FIG. 8 Acheulian pieces, Glieb Nouezzin,
Mauritania

by permission, from Mauny R., 1955, p. 467

It is impossible to subdivide the West African Acheulian on the basis of typological assemblages, because collection has been unmethodical and sealed living-sites have not been found. In a very few cases stratigraphical subdivision may be possible. Nor have any tools normally been found other than hand-axes and cleavers. Certain forms are believed by analogy with other regions to be Late Acheulian, such as small cordiforms and long lanceolate hand-axes.

Many rather massive Acheulian pieces are known from the southern Sahara [fig. 8].[21] Their rather patchy distribution probably depended on local geographical circumstances, such as availability of underground water, or on the hazards of modern exploration. Even during a pluvial the Sahara must have been dry, and not everywhere suited for habitation or for game.

Between 16° and 14° N and along the Niger a number of sites is recorded, especially in the Nioro region, as a result of careful researches by Fitte.[22] None of the material has been illustrated, and its geological horizon is not described. Some of it apparently occurred rolled in gravels, the chronology of which has not been worked out. These discoveries indicate how much could be found elsewhere in the northern savannah by detailed field-work. Stray pieces were collected much earlier in the same region, at Sarré (Senegal),[23] on the right bank of the River Senegal at Kayes,[24] and near the bend of the Niger at Goundam

LETJIEL, MALI, GUINEA

FIG. 9 Acheulian pieces, Letjiel (F. Guinea); no scale on original drawing

from Creac'h P., 1945, p. 419; by permission of I.F.A.N., Dakar

and Hombori.[25] An Acheulian site is recorded close to the Niger at Ansongo.[26] The territory of Niger has been less well explored. Comparatively few sites are known in the Sahara, though some of them, like Adrar Bous, are of great importance; and nothing Acheulian is recorded between 16° and 14° N.

This zone of the northern savannah includes the more favourable coastal region of Senegal. Although nearly all the material from around Dakar appears Sangoan or Kalinian, observations have revealed two Acheulian pieces from the University campus at Fann.

Between 14° and 12° N practically no Acheulian pieces are recorded. This zone may have been partly forested at the height of the pluvial, but I do not believe that it was permanently uninhabited throughout Acheulian times. Lack of finds must be due to lack of exploration and to the telescoping of river terraces on the plateau (above, pp. 67–8). This is my impression from the journeys I have made between Dédougou (3° W) and Maradi (7° E). A single typical Acheulian cleaver was found, along with much later material, in the Oueyanko Valley near Bamako.[27] I have classified as Acheuleo–Sangoan two or three sites on the right bank which have yielded cleavers, picks, hardly Acheulian in form, and large backed blades; but a better term which I now adopt is proto-Kalinian. Two large hand-axes, which may be Acheulian, were found at Keleyaga, one hundred kilometres to the east.[28] There is a hand-axe with other pieces unspecified from Letjiel near Mali [fig. 9];[29] from the illustration it could well be Acheulian.

I have mapped the distribution of Acheulian pieces in the middle and

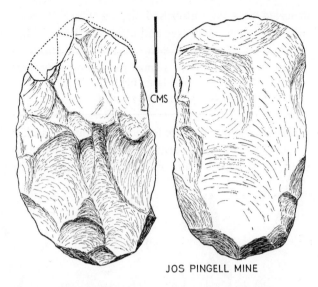

JOS PINGELL MINE

FIG. 10 Acheulian hand-axe and cleaver, Pingell mine,
Jos, Nigeria; both made on large side-struck flakes

southern savannah and forest;[30] some sites have been discovered
since, especially in northern Dahomey. The northern part of this area,
from 12° to 8° N, is today savannah. It includes the important Jos
Plateau, which perhaps would be better reckoned in the zone 14°–12° N,
because the isohyets bend southward towards the east. A rich collection of massive hand-axes and cleavers has been made from the
stanniferous gravels at several mines [fig. 10].[31] Methods of collection
have made it difficult to establish the total assemblage, though the
stratification is fairly clear (above, p. 67). Not very many have been
illustrated.

The sites on the Jos Plateau seem typologically Middle Acheulian,
and probably date from the Kamasian II pluvial. Six or seven sites of
a more developed Acheulian, characterized by long and rather narrow
hand-axes, have been located in the Atacora Mountains of northern
Dahomey [fig. 11].

Elsewhere in this zone there is a scatter of Acheulian pieces, most
perhaps not very early. I have found a few pieces in the valleys south
and west of the Jos Plateau,[32] and recent work, unpublished, may have
increased their number considerably. There are two important sites
near Sokodé (Togo). At one, Sabatei on Mo, the Acheulian was stratified beneath the Sangoan in the filling of a river channel. The other,

though unsealed, is a circumscribed site on which it was possible to collect tools other than hand-axes and cleavers; the inventory is[33]

hand-axes, 3 cordiform,	4 small piriform, 3 long ovate
cleaver, 1	large blades, 2
large side-scrapers, 2	quartz ball, 1.

Two fine piriform hand-axes were found at Legouansélandé a short way west of Sabatei. A single piriform hand-axe was picked up near the southern border of Upper Volta at Tiébélé, and there are pieces from

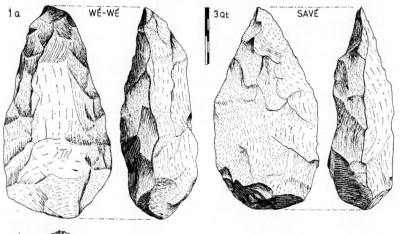

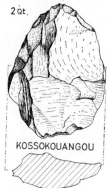

FIG. 11 Acheulian pieces, northern Dahomey

from Davies O., 1964 (2), fig. 31

Kongolo and Mamkuma in north-western Ghana [fig. 12]. None of the sites in the Ivory Coast can specifically be called Acheulian rather than Sangoan. The small group from Diarabakoko in south-western Upper Volta,[34] consisting of two hand-axes, a cleaver and two stone balls, would appear on typological grounds to be not very late in the Acheul-

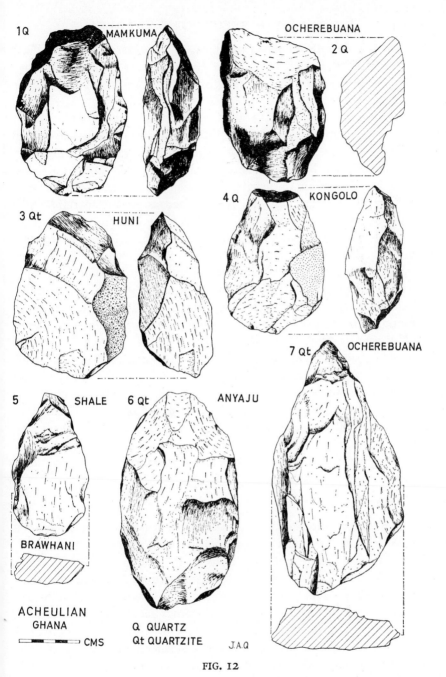

1Q MAMKUMA

OCHEREBUANA
2Q

3 Qt HUNI

4Q KONGOLO

7 Qt OCHEREBUANA

5 SHALE

6 Qt ANYAJU

BRAWHANI

ACHEULIAN
GHANA
CMS

Q QUARTZ
Qt QUARTZITE

J.A.Q

FIG. 12

from Davies O., 1964 (2), fig. 32

ian series. From F. Guinea three hand-axes are claimed as Acheulian: two from Pita,[35] found with a large side-scraper, are probably Sangoan or Lupemban; one from Fénaria[36] is hardly patinated and may well be post-Acheulian.

A good many small cleavers and finely worked hand-axes [fig. 12] have been picked up on scattered sites in south-eastern Ghana and central Togo, along the Togo–Akwapim range to the Accra Plains and thence westward along the coast. There are more sites than on the published map, but the pattern of distribution remains the same. It is difficult to be certain how far these can be classified as Acheulian rather than Sangoan; but one or two are stratified, and indicate a feeble Late Acheulian push towards the coast, soon to be followed by a more intensive Sangoan occupation. The two cultures seem to have arrived in the same climatic cycle and by the same route, along the Atacora Mts from the Niger. Mention has been made of the Acheulian stratified below the Sangoan at Sabatei (Togo). Small rolled hand-axes have been found in the Low Terrace gravel, along with unrolled Sangoan pieces, at Angeta on Dayi, Kpele-Beme (Togo) and Kwanyaku on Ayensu. At Asokrochona there were rolled Acheulian pieces on Beach IV, while the Sangoan lay unrolled just above the beach [fig. 1]. The hand-axes must therefore be older than the Sangoan, and can reasonably be described as belonging to an older industry. Rolled hand-axes from Bawdua on Birim and Sachiri on Nakwa, though not found along with unrolled Sangoan, are likely to be Acheulian. From this evidence at least a good many other hand-axes and cleavers, not rolled or stratified, may well be Late Acheulian.

The Sangoan Industry

The Sangoan culture belongs to sub-Saharan Africa only. Its relation with the Late Acheulian and the ecological conditions which caused its development are not fully understood. It made great use of a heavy pick, which seems to mark a degeneration from fine Acheulian technique, because it is clumsy, it has often been shaped by the outmoded method of stone-on-stone and it has neither the sureness of touch nor the aesthetic qualities of a fine Late Acheulian hand-axe. The cleaver seems to have been abandoned, but a smaller tool, the cleaver-flake, may have served the same purpose. At the same time, the Sangoans possessed a well developed Levallois technique, and were skilled at making smaller and finer tools from cores of Levallois type.

We can hardly suppose that man degenerated simultaneously over the greater part of Africa. So the apparent clumsiness of some Sangoan tools must have been dictated by their function. It seems that in all regions there was a stage when the heavy pick was predominant; but in some it probably gave way fairly soon before a lighter and better shaped tool, which characterizes the Early Lupemban. This change may have been associated with the development of the handle (below p. 118).

The Sangoan is found particularly in areas of higher rainfall, which in an interpluvial would be woodland. It is misleading to call it a forest-culture, as palaeolithic man would have difficulty in penetrating and supporting himself in true forest. It is common in the eastern Congo, East Africa, parts of Rhodesia and Natal. It probably originated some-where between Uganda and the Zambezi. It does not occur on the dry South African high-veldt, where the Fauresmith culture developed independently from the Acheulian and maintained its traditions much more closely. In western Rhodesia and South-west Africa, under conditions which are now semi-arid, there are Sangoan derivatives, which have usually lost much of their Sangoan character and especially the heavy pick, presumably become useless. In West Africa the Sangoan is common in wooded savannah, but thins out rapidly towards the Sahara. It did not penetrate down the Nile nor across the Sahara, save perhaps for some influences in Morocco.[37]

The Sangoan has been studied mainly in the interior of the continent; only in a few regions has it been possible to establish its chronological position by association with raised beaches. This is partly owing to the swampy and uninviting nature of much of the African coast, also to focusing of attention in central and southern Africa on the interior, where most Europeans have lived. There is, however, evidence for a few Sangoan pieces, rolled in Beach V or in estuarine deposits associated with it, in the Cape Province and in Angola. The Sangoan associated with Beach V gravels is, however, mostly unrolled, both in Angola and in West Africa. Unrolled picks, miniature picks and pebble choppers have been found with Beach V in Ghana; there was only one pebble chopper derived from a stream-gravel grading to Beach V close to the mouth of the River Densu, and such tools are not sufficiently typical to be called Sangoan. It thus seems that the Sangoan hardly reached the coast anywhere before the regression from Beach V.

The Sangoan usually occurs unrolled on the Low Terraces of West African rivers [see fig. 2; pls. 14, 30]. This terrace grades to Beach IV, and owing to the short interval between IV and V, thalwegs were adjusted to the lower beach only near the mouths. After Beach V it seems that rejuvenation proceeded upstream fairly rapidly; but one would expect a time-lag near the river sources, so Sangoan might appear rolled in the Low Terrace gravels of the more distant and smaller streams. In fact, slightly rolled Sangoan pieces have been found on the Low Terrace at Kwanyaku on Ayensu, not far from the sea; the river is small, and most of the Sangoan material on its Low Terrace is unrolled. In the Pra basin the Low Terrace carries only unrolled Sangoan; only high up the River Birim at Kade there was one slightly rolled pick in the gravel of the 8-metre terrace. In the Volta basin the Low Terrace consistently carries unrolled Sangoan, save perhaps for a point with faceted butt from Kpessidé (Togo) on a small tributary of the River Kara. Near the head of the Ouémé basin (Dahomey) there are perhaps rolled Sangoan pieces from Atchérigbé on the terrace of the River Zou, and probably rolled Sangoan as well as Acheulian at Wé-wé. There is a slightly rolled pick, probably derived from the Low Terrace of the River Kan at Dimbokro (I.C.). Only unrolled Sangoan pieces have been reported from the Low Terraces of tributaries of the lower Niger.

It is not possible to correlate exactly the West African Low Terraces with the river terraces of Central Africa, whence it is believed that the Sangoan originated; especially with rivers far in the interior. Rolled pieces which appear to be Sangoan have been found near the base of the gravel at M'Pila II–III and the Drain (Brazzaville);[38] but the rapids on the Congo make it impossible to connect the terraces of Stanley Pool with ocean-levels.[39]

The Sangoan appears regularly in West Africa on the lower stone-line, below the soils, now often lateritized, which accumulated during the Gamblian pluvial. It therefore flourished not later than the end of the pre-Gamblian interpluvial; pluvial conditions in due course favoured the forest and forced man to quit. Its chronological position is illustrated by the section at Asokrochona [fig. 1; pl. 27]; in Beach IV were pieces of rolled Acheulian, in the crust overlying Beach IV unrolled Sangoan picks, and the beach was covered by mottled clays, accumulated during the pluvial; on their surface was Late M.S.A. material [fig. 31].

Additions have been made to the Sangoan distribution map which I published in 1959. In particular, a few sites have been found in southern Senegal. I have therefore drawn a new map [fig. 13]. The picture presented is, however, very uneven; this I consider to be mainly due to the deplorable lack of exploration even in the Ivory Coast and especially in the territories to the west. I have omitted Nigeria because

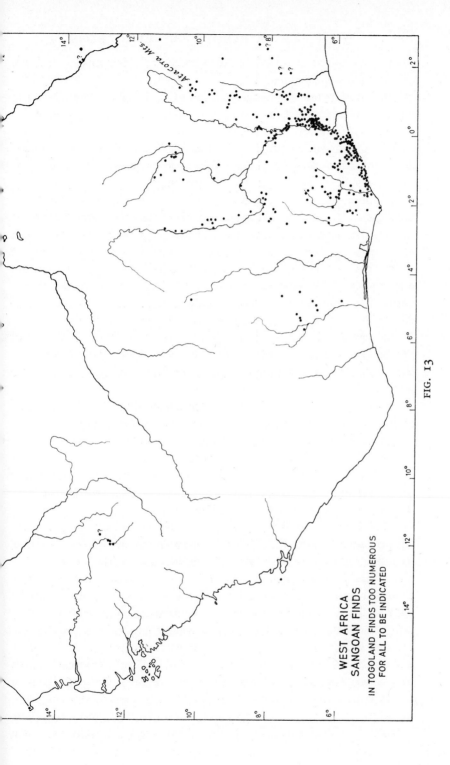

WEST AFRICA
SANGOAN FINDS

IN TOGOLAND FINDS TOO NUMEROUS
FOR ALL TO BE INDICATED

FIG. 13

I am sure that recent work has added much to the scatter of sites I was able to map some years ago.

The list of about 280 Sangoan sites in Ghana, 38 in Togo and 13 in Dahomey, contrasted with minimal numbers in the rest of West Africa may, however, reflect something more than intensity of exploration. The Sangoan people, like the Late Chellean, seem to have moved down the Atacora range, though they apparently preferred the intra-montane valleys rather than the western slopes. They had apparently come immediately from the Niger. There is some indication of them in Nigeria, but farther east there is a blank until Uganda.[40] Where it reaches the border of Ghana, the Atacora ceases to be a single massif and breaks up into several steep and narrow ridges, separated by wide valley floors on the surface of the older rocks, along all of which there are easy routes. The Sangoan developed during an interpluvial, whose aridity has been demonstrated by many types of evidence throughout Africa, most clearly in the western Cape (Sangoan on the dune at Koekenaap which overlies a gravel associated with Beach IV)[41] and in the Sahara (pre-Gamblian interpluvial believed to be responsible for the dunes of the south (above, p. 62) and for the great Ergs in the north).[42]

Groups stranded in a desiccating savannah about 12° N would be inclined to move southward into better watered lands along ranges which would attract rain and contain springs. The strike of the rocks in this part of West Africa is north-north-east; so storms from the Gulf of Guinea would move in this direction along mountains. The Akwapim–Togo–Atacora range is the most prominent of these storm-channels. Today a tongue of forest extends along it far into the latitude of the savannah, and anyone who has lived on the River Oti will have watched storms moving along the mountains even in the dry season. Another tempting route might be the northern ridges of the Tarkwa rocks, and in fact several Sangoan sites have been located on the Red Volta; but this route led southward to a dead end in the featureless plain of Tamale.

From the Atacora–Akwapim range the Sangoan people spread widely into Ghana, along the Volta and the Afram, along the coast and up the Pra and Ofin, and even along the western rivers in what is now very wet forest. I consider that in this interpluvial the forest contracted, making large areas accessible which would normally be closed. Even an annual reduction of 250 mms. of rain (20% at the present forest-margin) would turn large parts of the present forest into orchard bush, especially if more displuvial conditions prevailed. So I do not think that man would have great difficulty in reaching the western rivers of Ghana from the north; and if he already had some means of navigation, he could use rivers as lines of communication where the forest became too thick.

The scatter of known sites from the Ivory Coast, mostly along rivers, gives promise of a much denser concentration when proper exploration is carried out. The only piece which must be rejected is the 'hand-axe' from Bingerville,[43] first cited as Acheulian, then relegated to the Sangoan. It is a very crude pick of vein-quartz, little worked and hardly patinated; there is no compelling reason for classing it as older than the mesoneolithic.

North of 11° N three or four pieces have been found in the extreme south of Upper Volta. It would appear that 11° 30' N marks the limit of habitability in Sangoan times. The site at Carrière Tondubia near Niamey[44] I claimed as an adaptation of the Sangoan to dry surroundings; but just as the Bembesi variant in Rhodesia and South-west Africa is on the way to becoming proto-Stillbay, Carrière Tondubia may in fact carry a crude Lupemban, which had not been recognized in West Africa when the site was found. It lies on what even in an interpluvial must have been a seasonal river, though its sources in the Hoggar may have contributed little water. The repertory of picks (rare), miniature picks, cleaver-flakes, serrated blade-flakes, hollow scrapers, large tortoise-cores and 'Perdehof' cores seems more akin to the Sangoan than to the Kalinian of Bamako and Cap Manuel.

Mauny did something to fill the great gap to the west by the location, during a rapid reconnaissance, of five probable Sangoan sites in or near the upper Gambia near Kédougou (Senegal); these pieces are at Dakar, but have not been published [fig. 14]. Further exploration along the River Gambia would undoubtedly yield more.

Most of the old palaeolithic material from Dakar should be classed as Kalinian rather than Sangoan. At Pte. de Fann, in addition to some apparently Kalinian pieces,[45] two bifaces were found on the gravelly laterite, which look Sangoan.[46]

Several pieces at Dakar from Bakel (north-east Senegal)[47] might be Sangoan or Kalinian, but it is by no means certain that they are artificial.

The numerous and rich factory sites on the right bank near Bamako[27] seem to cover a long period, but have yielded nothing very typically Sangoan. Several of them are Kalinian or Lupemban. The most archaic have long narrow hand-axes, cleavers and blunt-backed blades. This material looks like the 'proto-Sangoan' from Luena (Katanga). It does not resemble the normal West African Sangoan, in which the cleaver is

I

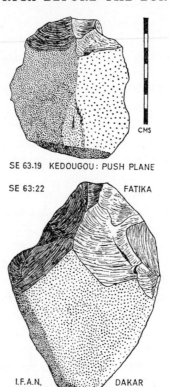

SE 63.19 KEDOUGOU: PUSH PLANE

SE 63:22   FATIKA

I.F.A.N.   DAKAR

SANGOAN, GAMBIA VALLEY

FIG. 14

rare if not absent and the pebble-butted pick common. It may be an independent local derivative from the Acheulian parallel to the Sangoan, or more probably a separate invasion from Central Africa, ancestral to the West African Kalinian. In the latter case, it is probably slightly later than the West African Sangoan, and followed a more northerly route at a time when the Gamblian pluvial was waxing and the northern savannah less uninviting than when the Sangoan people arrived.

There may be a little of this proto-Kalinian from farther north. At Kouga [fig. 15] two large picks were collected on the reg in addition to M.S.A. pieces; one is really a narrow cleaver. They could hardly be Acheulian, but could pass muster as Sangoan. There are two picks also from Boudou Kamara, one markedly Kalinian, the other more in the Sangoan tradition. Several sites also in Mauritania,[48] which yielded crude hand-axes made by stone-on-stone, are suggestive of the Sangoan. The material is unlikely to be Chellean, as formerly claimed, and is too crude to be classed with the Mauritanian Kalinian, to be discussed below.

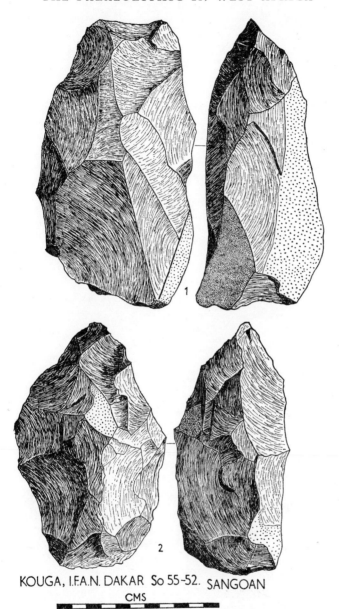

KOUGA, I.F.A.N. DAKAR So 55-52. SANGOAN
CMS

FIG. 15 Collection from Kouga, Mali; probably mixed, and
made on the regs around Kouga

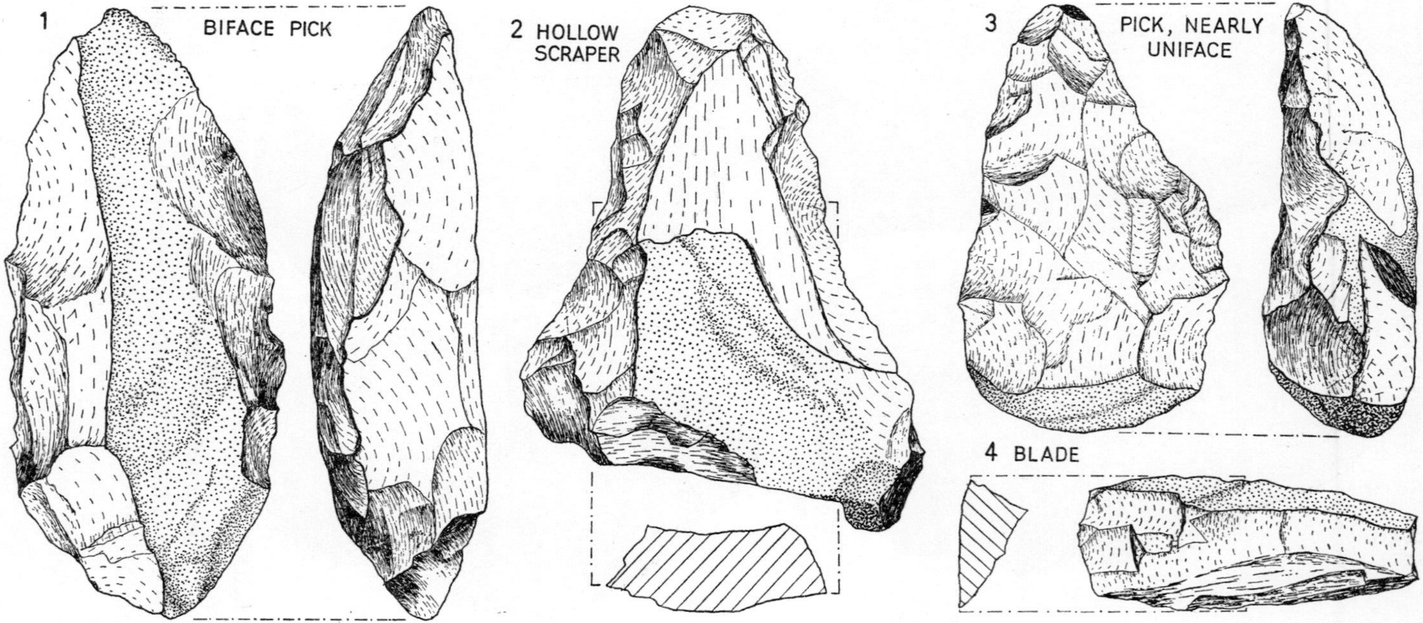

1 BIFACE PICK

2 HOLLOW SCRAPER

3 PICK, NEARLY UNIFACE

4 BLADE

FIG. 16a

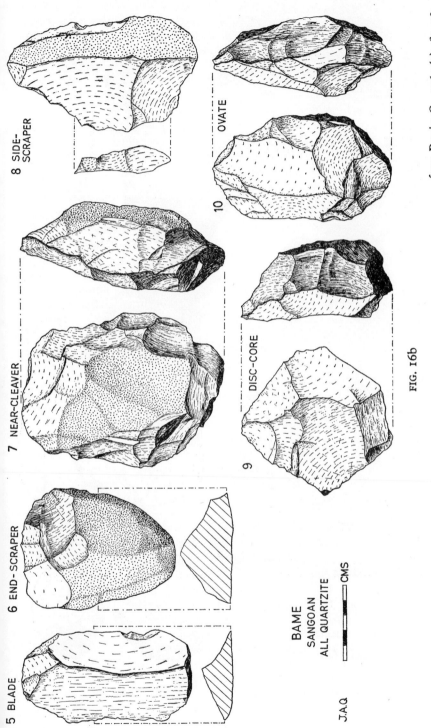

5 BLADE

6 END-SCRAPER

7 NEAR-CLEAVER

8 SIDE-SCRAPER

9

10

DISC-CORE

OVATE

BAME
SANGOAN
ALL QUARTZITE

J.A.Q

CMS

FIG. 16b

from Davies O., 1964 (2), fig. 18

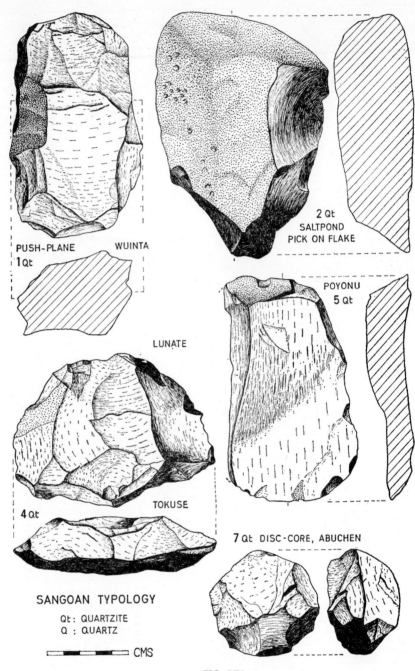

PUSH-PLANE WUINTA
1 Qt

2 Qt
SALTPOND
PICK ON FLAKE

POYONU
5 Qt

LUNATE

TOKUSE

4 Qt

7 Qt DISC-CORE, ABUCHEN

SANGOAN TYPOLOGY

Qt : QUARTZITE
Q : QUARTZ

CMS

FIG. 17a

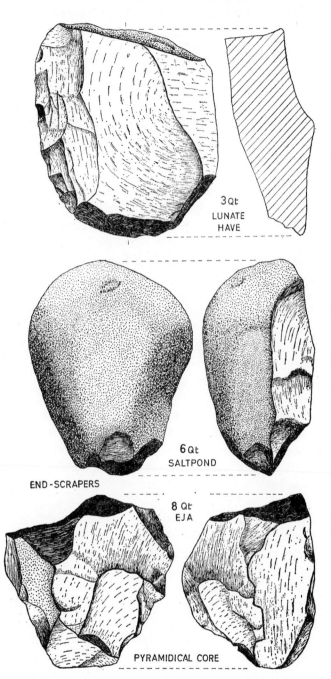

3 Qt
LUNATE
HAVE

6 Qt
SALTPOND

END-SCRAPERS

8 Qt
EJA

PYRAMIDICAL CORE

FIG. 17b

from Davies O., 1964 (2), fig. 37

The most characteristic tool of the Sangoan is the heavy uniface or biface pebble pick [fig. 14], made preferably of quartzite, quartz or other refractory stone, often by the archaic technique of stone-on-stone. Individual pieces, unstratified, may therefore be mistaken for Chellean. The most favoured material was large rolled pebbles, whence a few flakes were knocked off to shape the business-end, while the pebble surface was left on the butt and on one side, presumably to protect the user's hand. The pick seems to have been grasped in the palm and used downwards.

In what was probably the original Sangoan centre in Central Africa, the repertory of forms comprises picks, a few hand-axes, cleaver-flakes or Kombewa-flakes[49] replacing the Acheulian cleaver, rarely points and scrapers, and stone balls; also discoidal pyramidical and high-backed ovoid cores, whence must have been struck small flake tools which have not been identified.

In West Africa we find discoidal and pyramidical cores [fig. 17], also rarely Victoria West cores of Hoenderbek and Perdehof[50] types; where basalt or dolerite was used (especially in the Kalinian), Mfongosi-cores,[51] because two flakes naturally are detached simultaneously when a basalt block is bashed against a rock.

The commonest tool is the pick [figs. 14, 16, 17]. There are a few crude hand-axes and small ovates; perhaps no true cleavers but smaller sharp-edged cleaver-flakes [fig. 19] and near-cleavers [fig. 16]. There are probably a few large blades. A good many tools may be for wood-working [fig. 16], large end-scrapers, gouges (rarely), push-planes [fig. 14], side-scrapers, lunate scrapers [fig. 17], broad hollow scrapers, and rarely perhaps coarse awls. At Jani on Dayi, on the Low Terrace, was found an unrolled but heavily weathered trap-weight, a flat pebble with two nicks in the sides to hold a cord; it may be Sangoan, as may also the very large hand-axe from the Low Terrace at Hohoe, probably for a fall-trap, which I classed as Acheulian. Stone balls and pebble choppers are not uncommon in the Sangoan; they occur also both earlier and later. The Sangoan has often been found sealed in Ghana, but not in sufficient concentration to permit statistics; these could be obtained only by wide excavations of fossil land surfaces.

We have seen that the Sangoan reached southern Ghana just before the regression from Beach V and before the waxing of the Gamblian pluvial. With wetter conditions forest spread, and the Volta corridor was closed. The Sangoan was isolated near the coast, where for geographical reasons rainfall is low, and failed to participate in Kalinian-

Lupemban developments of the savannah, perhaps introduced by new immigrants. Thus a Late Sangoan appears to have lasted long in the Accra Plains. Ultimately it may have fused with the Lupemban when the forest opened, to form the Late M.S.A. of the Accra Plains (below, pp. 133–5).

It is difficult to distinguish stratigraphically the Late Sangoan. It has not been found in the soil or rubble accumulating above the Lower Stone-line. Many unrolled pieces on Beach V are probably late, and there is a site at Kpele-Beme (Togo) on the rejuvenation slope to the present valley, on a surface which must have been formed after incision had been well established at the beginning of the pluvial. The Late Sangoan apparently preserved the typology of the Early Sangoan, but many tools are small, miniature picks and hand-axes, small ovates, push-planes, stone balls; probably also small cores [fig. 17 7].

The Sangoan culture is the first in West Africa of which we can form a general picture; for though much Acheulian has been found on the Jos Plateau and the edge of the Sahara, no attempt has yet been made to collect in a systematic way.

The Sangoan was a woodland and waterside culture, which had been driven off the open grasslands by aridity. Presumably grassland animals had become scarce, and new sources of food had to be found. Its tool-kit does not suggest open hunting. We have to pass to the Kalinian lance-heads of the Gamblian pluvial to find hunting again. Traps were set, and one purpose of the Sangoan picks must have been digging; traps would catch woodland animals going to water, which do not live in large herds. Many tools indicate rough wood-working; and the distribution of the Sangoan suggests some form of river navigation, whether on bundles of reeds or in rudimentary canoes. Fish and molluscs may therefore have been available.

Sangoan man must have known fire. Traces of fire have been found at Choukoutien (perhaps Mindel), and from not much later (Riss or pre-Riss) in western and central Europe.[52] It is not proved to have been used in Africa before Late Acheulian times, i.e. hardly earlier than the Eem interglacial; the earliest site is Kalambo Falls.[53] By Sangoan times it must have been well established throughout the continent.

Fire in Africa would not have been of prime importance for warmth, though in deserts and mountains nights may be cold; nor would man often need to live in caves and require fire for protection. It would be of great use to him for making food digestible and for shaping wood.

I have mentioned the possibility that Sangoan man had some form of canoe. He would have had difficulty in felling a sound tree without burning, and it would have been very hard work hollowing it with crude stone tools. It is not certain if the Early Sangoan culture knew hafted tools; but a handle would be essential at least from Early Lupemban times for certain tools which have survived.[54] Shaping a handle of hard wood would be greatly facilitated by fire. A handle of bone may occasionally have been used earlier, but bone is not easily adaptable to the varied shapes of stone tools. Fire-hardened wood would be useful also for spears without a stone point.

The Sangoan pick was adapted for digging but not for many other uses; yet it is the commonest tool, often found stray. Sangoan man probably ate meat, and the pick may sometimes have been for game traps; but it is difficult to believe that tubers were not sought, especially the African yam, which must have been common in woodland. Meat might be rather indigestible without cooking, yams much more so; so knowledge of fire will have provided access to an important source of food.

Tubers, and especially yams, will easily sprout from the refuse thrown out round a camp. At first they would be wild; but Sangoan man may well have learnt to encourage them, and so practised what could be called a prelude to agriculture. Tuber-agriculture has been little studied. It is less specialized than cereal-agriculture, and may well go back very much farther. There is no real reason why the first attempts at planting may not date to Sangoan or Lupemban times. But apart from the shape and function of extant tools, evidence is almost unobtainable.

We have no evidence on the anthropological type of Sangoan man. His culture is in direct line of descent from the Acheulian; so he is likely to be a descendant of Atlanthropus and probably an ancestor of Rhodesiensis, whose date is not very much later.

The Kalinian and Lupemban Cultures

We have seen that Typical Sangoan does not occur north of 11° 30′ N in the central area of West Africa, though, with the northward drift of the isohyets and more genial conditions near the coast, sites have been found and probably more await exploration in the Gambia Valley and perhaps as far as Dakar [fig. 13]. But though its chronological position is uncertain, as it has not been found in geological stratification, there is reason to think that a parallel culture was developing on the middle Niger (above, pp. 109f). Its forms may have been determined by drier

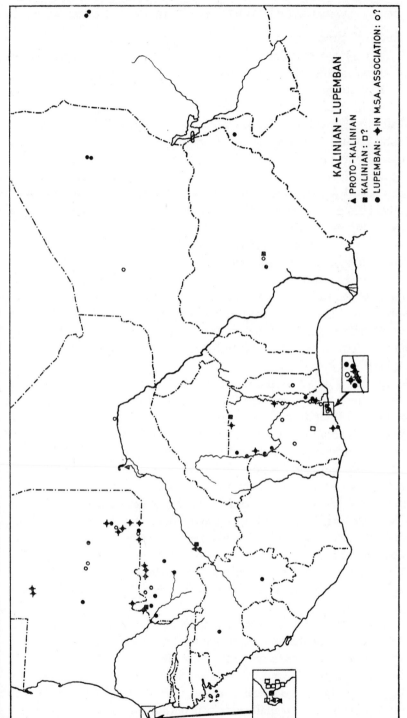

KALINIAN – LUPEMBAN

▲ PROTO-KALINIAN
■ KALINIAN: □?
● LUPEMBAN: ✦ IN M.S.A. ASSOCIATION: ○?

FIG. 18

ecological conditions in the northern savannah. It may have been derived by separate drift from Central Africa, and it seems to have remained in contact with Central African developments.

I have suggested that Kouga and the most primitive sites at Bamako should be classed as proto-Kalinian, and the more developed sites as Kalinian (Early Lupemban). Only one axe of Kalinian type has been found in Ghana, at Kunkoa in the extreme north. The Typical Sangoan took advantage of the pre-Gamblian interpluvial to occupy regions which are normally forest and orchard bush; at this time the northern savannah may have been sparsely inhabited. With the waxing of the Gamblian pluvial Sangoan people could no longer combat the extending forest; one group was isolated on the coast of Ghana; otherwise, Sangoan traditions were probably carried by two branches of the Kalinian in the northern savannah and the southern margins of the Sahara [fig. 18].[55]

I have described in detail the sites on the right bank of the Niger opposite Bamako. Careless collection by Waterlot and preconceived notions in Paris that the material is neolithic[56] have obscured its true nature until recently. Confusion was increased because neolithic settlers on the left bank had reused Kalinio–Lupemban pieces on their own sites, especially at Korofina.[57]

The material is a form of dolerite, which outcrops on the right bank. There are huge factory sites, where large flakes were detached from boulders. Mfongosi-cores are common. Levallois cores also were used. Most tools are more carefully flaked than in the true Sangoan industry, and the original surface was generally removed. The principal tool is a narrow axe with parallel sides, sometimes blade in the form of a gouge, and butt often square. There are a good many picks of similar form, and others flat on one face and domed on the other (tortoise-backed). There are large blades and side-scrapers, cleaver-flakes and stone balls, probably also large and thick biface spear-heads with pointed butts. The industry seems to have developed over a long period. I consider a site with smaller tools of similar types, including an awl, to be typologically later; it had also small uniface points, which may have been spear-heads.

Much similar material has been collected from Cap Manuel, Dakar; the typology resembles closely that of Bamako [fig. 19]. Here again, attention has been concentrated on the pieces derived on to the steep slope and Beach VI; so it was believed that the industry was neolithic, despite discordant technical features like Mfongosi-cores. The collections do in fact contain a few neolithic pieces, celts, some flint

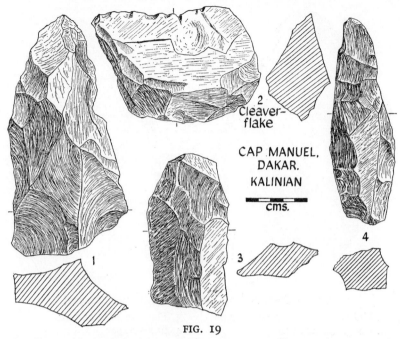

2
Cleaver-
flake

CAP MANUEL,
DAKAR.
KALINIAN

cms.

FIG. 19

microliths and a polished bracelet. It was not until 1960 that I was able
to demonstrate the antiquity of this culture by excavating a core and a
typical axe from a surface 30 cms. deep, at the base of the nodular
laterite, on the top of the Corniche; since then this surface has been
traced for some distance, and has yielded not only Kalinian but a
weathered pebble tool which may be older.[58]

Other sites near Dakar are probably Kalinian. Pieces illustrated from
Pte. de Fann and the University[45] seem typologically Kalinian. The
piece from laterite at Camp Gallieni, originally acclaimed as a hand-axe
and then denied,[59] is a broken tortoise-backed Kalinian pick. The site
at Almadies may be more recent. Several sites east of the city have
yielded material which is poorly illustrated, but could be Kalinio–
Lupemban. It is difficult, for instance, to place the collection from
Lguer [fig. 20], which is an atypical M.S.A., unlike the Ultimate
M.S.A. of Pte. de Fann [fig. 36].

At Dakar confusion between Kalinian and neolithic is less easy than
at Bamako. The neolithic people used only pebble choppers of basalt,
and did not collect palaeolithic pieces to be reshaped.

Numerous surface-collections from north-western Mali and Aouker-
Hodh (Mauritania) are described by the French as neolithic, but seem
typologically to be Kalinio–Lupemban. They occur especially along

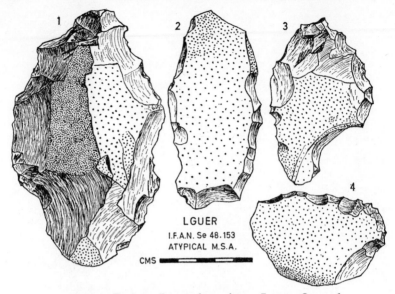

LGUER

I.F.A.N. Se 48.153

ATYPICAL M.S.A.

CMS

FIG. 20 Perhaps Lupemban pieces, Lguer, Senegal

1. Uniface of rostro-carinate type   3. Flat hand-axe or pick
2. Rough backed blade   4. End-scraper

the foot of the Aouker scarp, beside what was probably a lake, between Nara and Tidjikja. There is also neolithic here, but many of the sites lack characteristic neolithic forms. The most abundant collections were made on the right bank of the River Farah opposite la Bergerie, near Nioro; but the work was badly done by Waterlot and de Zeltner, several sites were mixed, and when Corbeil and Mauny went there in 1948 there was little left. The material is mostly shale; there are a few pieces of fine-grained granite, perhaps Sangoan or Acheulian. The main types [fig. 21][60] are small pyramidical and disc cores; biface points axes and picks; end-scrapers, some of spatula form; side and hollow scrapers; blades with signs of use but no trimming, some triangular; large discs; points from Levallois flakes; awls.

The collections from Boutounguissi in Paris[61] and Dakar appear to be mostly Lupemban. The tortoise-backed pick [fig. 22] and the long biface point [fig. 23] are paralleled at Bamako and Dakar. There is, however, no adequate description of the site, and there is a suggestion that material was picked up at random over a wide area. This might account for the inclusion of a few axes which look markedly neolithic [fig. 24], though none of them are polished; there is apparently one polished axe and one celt.

The Aouker sites have been described by the French as 'agricultural

NIORO, RIGHT BANK, R.FARAH: I.F.A.N. DAKAR So 45.36

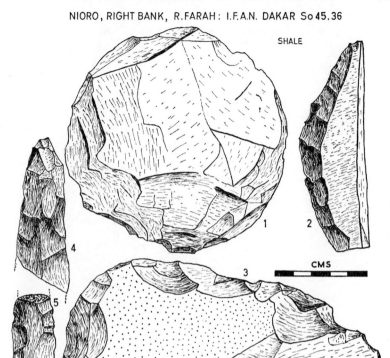

FIG. 21

neolithic'. Typologically they seem closer to Lupemban, and the material is quite unlike the normal Saharan neolithic of the region. One would have to assume a complete change of ecology and population within the few thousand years of the neolithic.

Stray pieces from far north in Mauritania and the Tilemsi Valley are suggestive of the Lupemban; but their distribution defies any coherent picture. We await particularly the publication of the great site of Richat (Mauritania), which typologically seems to yield a mixture of Acheulian, Lupemban and neolithic, without any stratigraphy or variation in patina.

All these sites in northern Mali and Mauritania are puzzling. Much of the material resembles Bamako and Cap Manuel. On many sites there is no good evidence for association with celts, hoes or microliths. But blades are abundant, and large discs are not found to the south, though common in the Nioro region; and few pieces are heavily patinated. Faceted butts and Levallois cores are uncommon, but the

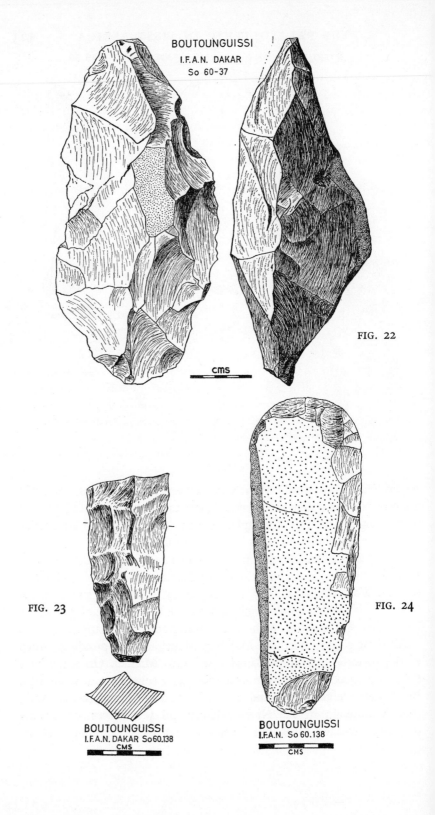

BOUTOUNGUISSI
I.F.A.N. DAKAR
So 60-37

FIG. 22

cms

FIG. 23

FIG. 24

BOUTOUNGUISSI
I.F.A.N. DAKAR So 60.138
CMS

BOUTOUNGUISSI
I.F.A.N. So 60.138
CMS

local shale splits naturally. The ecology suggests not hunting but scrounging for a good deal of vegetable food, probably in a pluvial, though the Aouker lake may have received much discharge from the upper Niger before Tosaye was breached. If the Sangoans and Lupembans had depended on tubers to an extent that they ultimately practised semi-cultivation, the Mauritanian industrial complex could be explained without describing it as 'agricultural neolithic', a phrase which has chronological overtones. Moreover, there is no other culture known in this area between the Acheulian and the neolithic, as the Aterian hardly spread so far south. A Kalinio–Lupemban offshoot could have become isolated and continued many millennia in the favourable environment of the Aouker lake, preserving most of its heritage and lasting even until the true neolithic replaced it.

There are scattered Lupemban picks and lance-heads from northern Nigeria and far out into the eastern Sahara, two picks from Kishuns (Cameroons), a pick and perhaps a spear-head from Nok,[62] crude blades from Izom (Nigeria), several lance-heads from Kawar[63] and from Ounianga Kebir (Tchad);[64] for Carrière Tondubia (Niger) see p. 109. A few obvious lance-heads are illustrated from the Sudan;[65] and it is possible that the origin which Huzayyin postulates for Egyptian neolithic bifaces[66] was an offshoot of the Lupemban coming down the Nile. These pieces seem independent of the Bamako–West Sahara industry, and may have been introduced separately from central Africa.

With the decline of the Gamblian pluvial, the forest will have receded and man was able to return to Ghana and other southern territories. A fair number of thin lance-heads and small slug-axes have been found in Ghana, nearly all without proved association [fig. 25]. I consider that these are advanced types, which should be classed as Late Lupemban. There is also much undifferentiated M.S.A. from Ghana and near by. Most of this may well be Lupemban, surface-collections having failed to provide typical pieces. The only well stratified piece is a rolled pick from the basal gravel at Jimam; in the same gravel were rolled fair-sized side- and end-scrapers, an unrolled uniface pick which also could be Lupemban, and several small rolled flakes which are more in the tradition of Guinea Aterian. An unrolled lance-head was found on the Low Terrace at Angeta. Sites with clear Lupemban association are disappointing. There was probably at least one on the River Pru between Prang and Yeji; but the records of the Geological Survey are confused. On the Low Terrace at Ypala there seems to be an association of an unrolled, short Lupemban axe and a broken piece which was either a

K

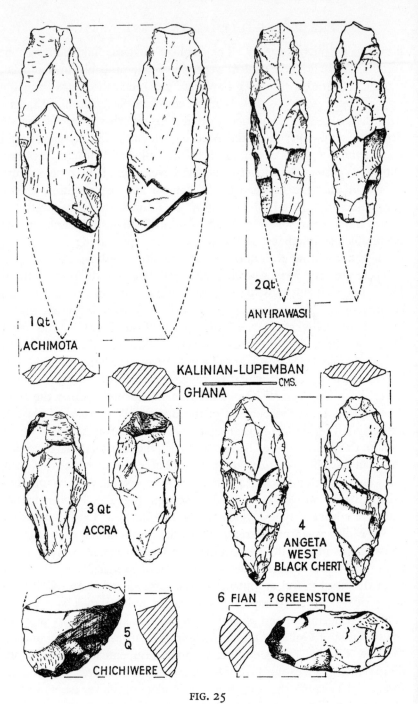

FIG. 25

from Davies O., 1964 (2), fig. 43 and Davies O., 1957

small ovate or the butt of a lance-head with stone balls. The material from Fian seems unified; but apart from a Lupemban slug all the pieces are atypical.

The Lupemban could have been introduced into Ghana from the northern savannah, perhaps from the Bamako area, though the lance-head is there rare. If we knew more about the industry in northern Nigeria and the eastern Sahara, we might find a closer link with this region. Independent immigration from Central Africa is unproved. The Lupemban probably spread widely in the orchard bush. A typical biface was found at Férédou (F. Guinea).[67]

Middle Stone Age Cultures

In Senegal and as far east as the middle Niger some sites have yielded an undifferentiated and atypical M.S.A. industry, often no more than a few flakes with faceted butts. Several of those reported round Dakar[45] fall into this category. Others have been listed by Mauny[68] without information on what was found, which probably amounted to no more than one or two formless pieces. The collection from Lguer [fig. 20] is reminiscent of Lupemban. At N'gor Hotel flaked basalt pebbles are being exposed below the turf (M.S.A. or neolithic?). It may well be that in addition to the well defined Kalinio–Lupemban sites which have been described, there is further material of this culture in northern Senegal, especially near the river, which has not been properly explored. The only stratified site in Senegal is Kidra (I.F.A.N. Dakar Se 48–38), where rolled flakes and blades and a chopper were found in the basal gravels of the River Falémé.

Some sites in north-western Mali are better defined. I have illustrated a small selection [fig. 26] of disc and pyramidical cores, Levallois flakes, blades and scrapers. These pieces are in quartzite, but otherwise would not be out of place in an assemblage from Bamako or Nioro. Most of the sites are in the northern savannah, a few in the Sahara. In only two cases is stratification recorded, and on neither site was there much typical material. In the upper valley of the River Baoulé a cordiform biface and blades with faceted butts were found in clay above the terrace gravel.[24] At Wassadan M.S.A. pieces were found in the topmost two metres of clay, overlying six metres of sands which rest on a terrace of the River Baoulé.[69]

From Ghana, Dahomey and the forest and bush-savannah to the south there is a good deal of undifferentiated M.S.A. It is not, however, worth discussion, because I am sure that it is either Lupemban or

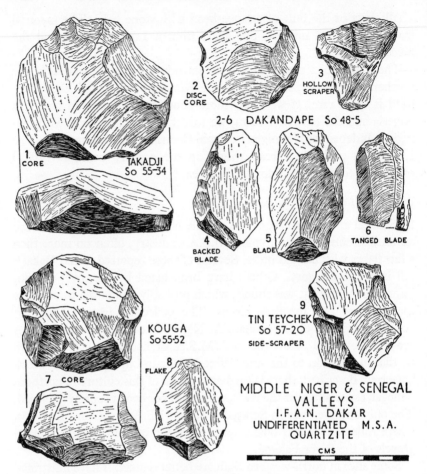

FIG. 26

Guinea Aterian, from sites which have yielded nothing recognizable. Some have been identified as M.S.A., principally from their position stratified on the upper stone-line or in basal gravels.

The Aterian culture is a specialized form of the Mousterian of Eurasia, using Levallois technique. It is characterized by well defined tangs, worked from both faces, both on points (probably spear-heads and perhaps arrow-heads) and scrapers. It is considered in North Africa that many sites which have been classified as Mousterian are really Aterian, but no pedunculate piece had been found.[70] In the Maghreb it appears immediately after Beach V,[71] and there are carbon dates before 30000 B.P. (see table above, p. 78). Much has been found in the Sahara, and it extends into the Saharan annexes of the West African

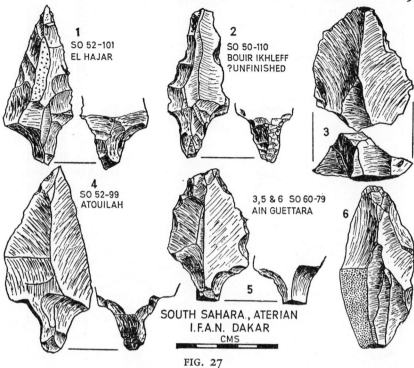

1 SO 52–101 EL HAJAR

2 SO 50–110 BOUIR IKHLEFF ?UNFINISHED

3

4 SO 52–99 ATOUILAH

3,5 & 6 SO 60-79 AIN GUETTARA

6

5

SOUTH SAHARA, ATERIAN
I.F.A.N. DAKAR
CMS

FIG. 27

territories, but not into the northern savannah. The most southerly piece claimed is a stray end-scraper from near Gao.[72] Other sites are known in the Tilemsi Valley,[73] and there is one piece from Hassi Badrina (Mauritania, about 18° N).[74] The Aterian is thought to start later in the Sahara than in North Africa,[75] and it probably lasted late, perhaps until the arrival of the neolithic, because no intermediate upper palaeolithic culture has been identified [fig. 27].

In the southern savannah a rather small industry of M.S.A. type has been widely identified [fig. 28], especially in Ghana where exploration has been most intensive.[76] There are also one certain and a few possible sites in Togo, several in northern Dahomey, and two in F. Guinea.[77] I have classed Dakandape (Mali) as undifferentiated M.S.A. [fig. 26]; the industry might be Lupemban, but the tanged blade suggests connection with that under discussion. To the same group may belong Yaoundé site I,[78] and probably many of the undifferentiated sites in the Ivory Coast and Upper Volta.

Most of the pieces are fairly small, often of fine-grained stone, a hard, brown, sandy shale that occurs in thin bands in the Silurian sandstones being popular. Pebbles were often used; there are some discoidal and

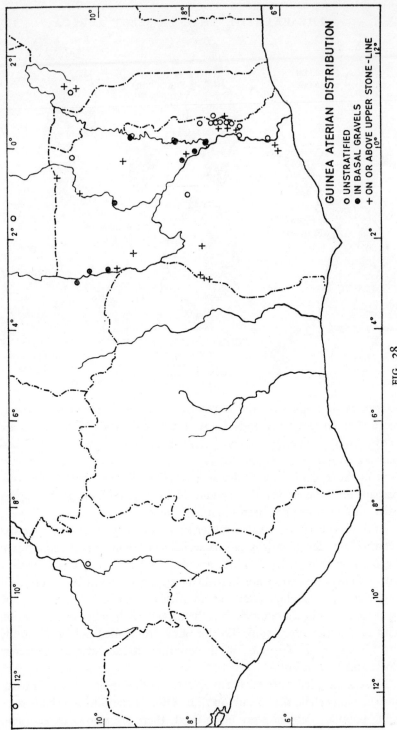

GUINEA ATERIAN DISTRIBUTION

○ UNSTRATIFIED
● IN BASAL GRAVELS
+ ON OR ABOVE UPPER STONE-LINE

FIG. 28

pyramidical cores. The main characteristic is a rudimentary tang, smaller than on Aterian points and often much less defined, nearly always uniface. Both tanged points and scrapers occur. Several are broken horizontally, which would not be expected if the points were used as weapons; they are blunted at the end and show wear along the edges; so I think that they were rudimentary drills. Other types are miniature picks, uniface or partly biface, sometimes the whole of one

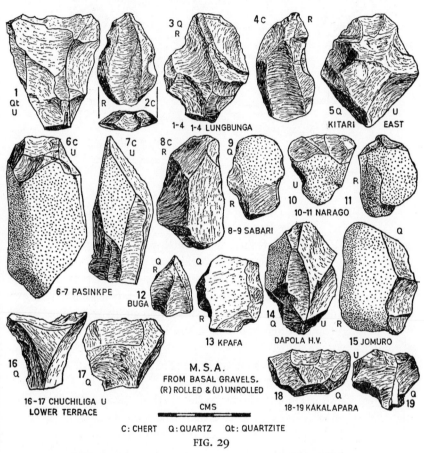

M.S.A.
FROM BASAL GRAVELS.
(R) ROLLED & (U) UNROLLED

C: CHERT   Q: QUARTZ   Qt: QUARTZITE

FIG. 29

1. Gouge
2, 4, 12. Points
3, 9, 13, 19. Tanged pieces
5, 14. Miniature picks
6. Push-plane
7. Blunt-backed blade

8. Side-scraper
10. End-scraper
11. Awl
15. Chopper
16. Hollow scraper
17. Chisel

18. Large Crescent

from Davies O., 1964 (2), fig. 16

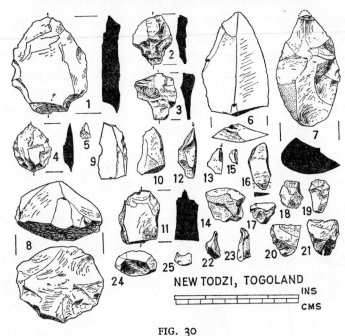

FIG. 30

from Davies, CISPP v (1958), p. 232, fig. 2; by permission
of the publishers, Verlag Gebrüder Mann, Berlin

face being left as pebble surface; small push-planes, gouges and others which seem to have been for wood-working; a good many points, some not tanged; many end-scrapers, but not many side-scrapers and very few pieces which could be described as hollow scrapers; a fair number of chisels, usually with wear on the blade, so unlikely to have been used as microtranchet arrow-heads; a few rather large crescents, some of which may be backed blades; backed and blunt-backed blades, occasionally notched and sometimes tanged; short awls; and a few pebble choppers [fig. 29 and 30].[79]

Known sites in Dahomey lie far to the north in the Atacora Mts. The material is perhaps more primitive than that from Ghana, if one may judge from the small amount which has been collected. At the same time, it does not resemble Lupemban. This would suggest that the origins of this industry are to be sought in the north.

I do not believe that it is an offshoot of the Lupemban, though a few pieces, like a tortoise-backed pick from New Todzi, are reminiscent of the Kalinio–Lupemban of the northern savannah. It does not contain the biface lance-heads and the slug-axes which are found on Lupemban sites in Ghana. Yet it must be approximately contemporary with the

Lupemban, as it occurs rolled in basal gravels, which at Jimam yielded a Lupemban axe. It is found rolled even at the sides of the valleys, which would be abandoned by rivers as the Gamblian pluvial waned. Moreover, it is not found in the forest and only just penetrates into the Accra Plains [fig. 28], the most southerly sites known being near Kpong, Somanya and Zaglekope; whereas in southern Ghana there are a good many sites of a distinct and more formless industry, which is more likely to be of Sangoan–Lupemban derivation. It is also unlike the probable Lupemban of the Jos Plateau. The rudimentary tang is hardly found in the Lupemban of Central Africa, but is known in the Tsitolian. However, the Tsitolian has many slugs and not many scrapers, and the tangs are usually chisel-shaped; and the industry from Ghana seems to have developed before the end of the Gamblian pluvial, before the rise of the Tsitolian in the Congo. So although an immigration of Tsitolian people, independent of the West African Lupemban, is possible, I prefer to look in another direction.

An entirely autochthonous development of this West African industry is also possible but unlikely, because with the spread of forest in the Gamblian pluvial most of Ghana seems for a time to have been uninhabited and must have been recolonized. I am inclined to look to the north. Perhaps as the Sahara grew drier, people of or influenced by Aterian culture pressed south. Thence came the idea of the tang, though technically the tang in Ghana is unlike that of the true Aterian. For want of a better name, I have called this industry of the southern savannah the Guinea Aterian; new names, unless proved to be unavoidable, are inconvenient and put a strain on the memory.

The geological horizon of the Guinea Aterian can be determined. It occurs rolled and unrolled in basal gravels, so was introduced before these were abandoned by shrinking rivers, but lasted for a considerable period, hardly, however, to the end of Post-pluvial I–II, as it has not been found in the overlying ferruginized grits which are capped by the inner silt-terraces. It occurs occasionally on the upper stone-line, so must overlap the end of the pluvial and the beginning of the post-pluvial phase. At New Todzi [fig. 30] it was stratified in deep soil immediately above a layer of nodular laterite which sealed sterile earth, perhaps of Gamblian date.

On the Accra Plains, south of the limits of the Guinea Aterian, is a non-descript culture which I believe to be a degenerate descendant of the Late Sangoan, probably refertilized by the Lupemban from farther north. There is little Guinea Aterian influence, though a few tanged pieces and certain tool-types could be paralleled there. I have explained how Sangoan

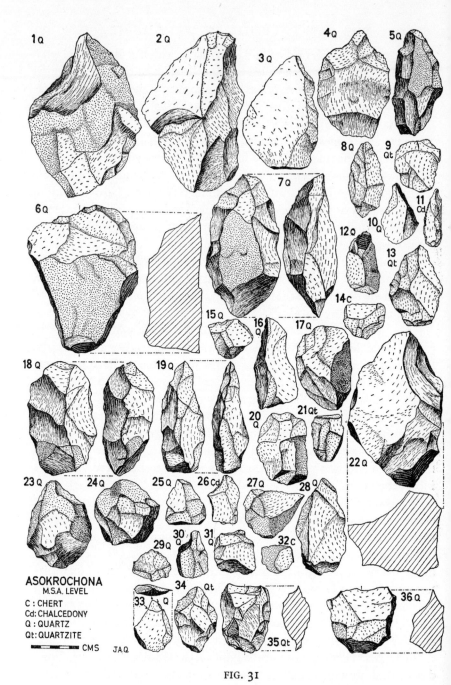

ASOKROCHONA
M.S.A. LEVEL
C : CHERT
Cd: CHALCEDONY
Q : QUARTZ
Qt: QUARTZITE
━━━━ CMS   JA.Q.

FIG. 31

from Davies O., 1964 (2), fig. 67

remnants may have survived in isolation during the Gamblian pluvial.

On the coastal sites, while there was knowledge of the Levallois technique, and pyramidical cores and flakes with faceted butts occur, preference was given to pebbles from former beaches, largely of quartzite. These were broken up into small picks and choppers, which it is difficult to classify culturally. There seem to be Sangoan reminiscences. From Accra Golf-course we have miniature picks and hand-axes, along with numerous pebble choppers and flakes. At Asokrochona [figs. 1, 31] Tema and probably Prampram there are sites on a lateritic crust overlying red sandy clays. The last are believed to be the Terres de Barre, which occur to considerable thickness east of the Volta and as far as Dahomey. Close to the coast they have slumped forward in Gamblian times, and overlie Beach IV. The lateritic crusts will have formed under displuvial conditions at the end of the Gamblian; so these sites are not older than Post-pluvial I. The marked difference from the material in and just above the Flandrian beach at Manprobi shows that they must be earlier than Sub-pluvial II, and cannot be classed as Ultimate M.S.A. Crude though the tools are, there is a much greater variety than at Accra Golf-course, where collections had to be made from derived material on a sloping surface, and smaller pieces may have been lost. The culture comprises [fig. 31] large picks and choppers, stone balls and push-planes or gouges; and of smaller tools crudely backed and blunt-backed blades, rough points unsuitable for weapons and perhaps used as scrapers or drills, a few scrapers, miniature picks, and a few chisels and awls. Occasional pieces seem to be intentionally tanged. The picks and wood-working tools are reminiscent of the Sangoan; Asokrochona, which yielded a larger collection and better stratified than the other sites, has several pieces like Lupemban axes.

Similar material of Sangoan tradition, with miniature picks, wood-working tools and stone balls, has been found scattered on the terraces at the mouth of the River Densu, west of Accra. There was no single site, and it was seldom possible to observe stratification; so probably most of the smaller pieces have been lost.

The Accra Plains are sharply defined by the Akwapim Ridge and the River Volta. They are open grassland, which even before human interference carried few forest trees. Immediately on the Akwapim Ridge forest started, and though there was a narrow strip of savannah along the coast as far as Sekondi, the relict Sangoan culture I have been discussing apparently does not occur west of the River Densu. The few small sites in forest and on the coast are, as I have said, probably

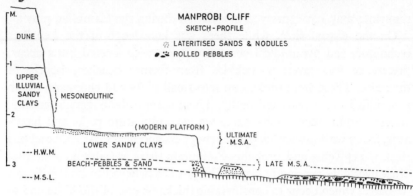

FIG. 32

from Davies O., 1964 (2), fig. 71

extrusions from either the Lupemban or the Guinea Aterian province, and form no unified or distinctive culture. The relict Sangoan did, however, flourish inland on the Accra Plains, especially on the west where detritus from the quartzite was more fertile than the gneiss elsewhere.

At Legon Botanic Gardens excavations were carried out in a deep soil which had been building up since Sangoan times [fig. 3]. Some pieces were collected in or just below the upper stone-line. A heavy pick and push-plane are paralleled on the coastal sites; so to some extent are chisels and blunt points. At Achimota cricket-pitch a scatter of objects was found at various levels in mottled clay.[80] There seems to have been no unified site, but objects were lost during the M.S.A. These include disc and pyramidical cores, flakes with faceted butts, a small pick, a pebble chopper and a slicer;[81] also microlithic scrapers, backed blades, and a chisel or microtranchet. At the base of the clay was a large gouge. Similar sites are known on the Accra Plains, but they have not yielded more than a few pieces.

The Ultimate M.S.A.

On the coast of Ghana, especially at Manprobi and Takoradi, it has been possible to associate the stratification of the M.S.A. with the well dated Beach VI [fig. 32]. On a few sites inland, like Legon Botanic Gardens and New Todzi, the depth of M.S.A. soil was considerable, and it was possible to define a slight hiatus by which an upper level could be separated from the principal M.S.A. horizon. In most soil-sections the M.S.A. horizon does not occupy more than a few inches, so no separation is feasible. Along rivers marshy conditions during Sub-pluvial II made life in the valleys impossible, so there is no industry of the inner silt terraces to be distinguished from that of the basal gravels; but sites

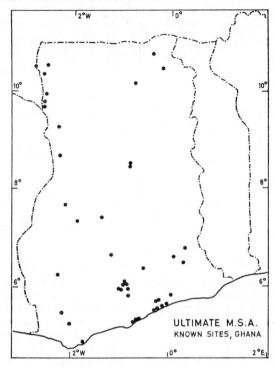

ULTIMATE M.S.A.
KNOWN SITES, GHANA

FIG. 33

have been found on slopes overlooking the marshes, which probably belong to this date.

In soil sections the true mesoneolithic, almost always unpatinated, occurs only on the laterite nodules or stone-line of Post-pluvial III. Pieces stratified just below this stone-line or showing initial patination are likely to be older. Patination is a fairly reliable indicator of date because it was induced only at a certain point in a climatic cycle, when displuvial conditions had set in and facilitated the chemical process. It is less reliable than geological stratification.

The sites which satisfy stratigraphical or other requirements to be classed as Ultimate M.S.A. have a culture of mainly M.S.A. affinities. There are, however, mesoneolithic influences, such as more numerous chisels and small burins and perhaps microtranchet arrow-heads. The relation of the Ultimate M.S.A. to the Flandrian Beach [see fig. 32] would make it roughly contemporary with Sub-pluvial II. This was a period when the neolithic was well established in north-eastern Africa and the southern Sahara, and all trace of the M.S.A. had disappeared. So it is not surprising that some mesoneolithic techniques filtered down

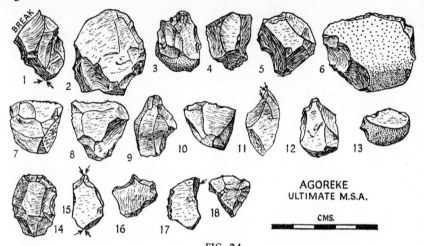

FIG. 34

Ultimate Middle Stone Age, Agoreke (Ghana)

1. Broken tanged blade probably used as burin, chert
2. Tanged end-scraper, quartzite
3. Awl, chert
4. Tanged blade, chert
5. End-scraper, chert
6. Core used as side-scraper or fabricator, chert
7. Chisel, yellow chalcedony
8. Chisel, chert
9. Hollow scraper and gouge, chert
10. Chisel, quartzite
11. Burin, ? dark quartz
12. Awl or burin, chert
13. Crescent-chisel, quartz
14. Tanged end-scraper, chert
15. Double-ended burin, chert
16. Awl, chert
17. Side-scraper and perhaps burin, chert
18. Chisel, chert

to the Guinea coast. Many M.S.A. sites may be of Sub-pluvial II; but I have accepted and mapped [fig. 33] only those which there is good reason to date to this stage.

The best stratified collection is from New Todzi.[82] The material is slightly patinated, and was fairly well separated from the Guinea Aterian below [fig. 30] and from the neolithic above. Most pieces are small, apart from a few Levallois flakes. A few rudimentary tangs may hark back to the Guinea Aterian. I illustrate here a collection from Agoreke, about fifty kilometres away [fig. 34]. It was made on the gravelly scarp from the Low Terrace to the inner silt terrace, with view over the wide marshes of the Volta. The typology is similar to New Todzi. There are crudely tanged pieces, end- and side-scrapers, chisels, blades, burins and awls. Pieces which at New Todzi could be described as points and crescents were not found at Agoreke, but there was not much time to search, and the site is now beneath the Volta Lake. The stratified collection from the Ultimate M.S.A. level at Legon Botanic Gardens has a similar assemblage, with the addition of a miniature pick and a push-plane, perhaps required for wood-working and derived from the relict Sangoan tradition of the Accra Plains. A small tanged biface point from Tema lay higher than the main M.S.A. level.

The pieces which were found in or just above the Flandrian beach at Manprobi and Takoradi are not numerous; but so far as they go, they concord with the assemblages I have discussed. A small group from Apam with tanged end-scraper, chisels and point seems to be slightly later than Beach VI. There is a rather better group with chisels, burin, point and flake with faceted butt from clays below Beach VI at Labadi. At Apam and Mankwadzi large choppers were found in Beach VI.

Two flakes from Pala, one slightly tanged and with faceted butt, had perhaps lain within the silts of the inner silt terrace. At Usunfukrom and the Sheribong mouth a violent flood, a little before the formation of the inner silt terrace, had brought down quantities of gravel which were overlain by white silts and then by the microlithic horizon, and capped 75 cms. of mottled blue clay resting on basal gravel and on rock. In the gravel were rolled artefacts, typologically not closely akin to the M.S.A., but from their stratigraphical position pre-mesoneolithic; there were small cores, blades and blunt-backed blades, one denticulated backed blade, one broken tanged blade, side-scrapers, chisels and an end-scraper. Up the Black Volta three sites have been found on slopes just above the inner silt terrace. Their position and the fact that the material does not look Guinea Aterian induces me to assign them to the Ultimate M.S.A. The most interesting is Narago at the mouth of the River Kule [fig. 35]; there are several large pieces as well as microliths. Another, at Dapola (Upper Volta), on the back of the inner silt terrace, has a mixture of Guinea Aterian technique and mesoneolithic tool-types. The third is at Kpafa.

At Chawenu an important site on a granite boss has yielded slightly patinated pieces of sugary quartz; this material was more favoured in the M.S.A. than the mesoneolithic, which preferred pebbles of crystal-quartz. Faceted butts are common, and there is a small pyramidical core. Tools include blades, burins, chisel and tanged end-scraper; also a short biface pick. From down the slope, probably derived from the same site, comes a well-made biface flaked axe, not polished and contracting slightly to the butt. There are others from Jani and Anum Jn. Such pieces are not otherwise known from Ghana, but are paralleled in the Late Lupemban at Boutounguissi [fig. 24; see fig. 54]. One or two rather cruder flaked axes have been found with M.S.A. slicers on Cape Three

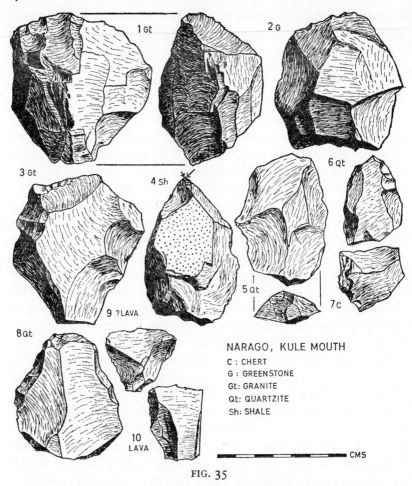

NARAGO, KULE MOUTH

C : CHERT
G : GREENSTONE
Gt: GRANITE
Qt: QUARTZITE
Sh: SHALE

CMS

FIG. 35

from Davies O., 1964 (2), fig. 62

Points. They might be precursors of the early neolithic edge-ground celt.

Ultimate M.S.A. sites are not limited to southern Ghana. There is a collection from the Nasuan bridge at Nakpanduri of disc-cores, pieces with faceted butts, side- and end-scrapers, awl, blades, point and chisel. Another with some faceted butts and a finely trimmed uniface point from Vako seems too well worked to be mesoneolithic and more advanced than most Guinea Aterian. At Maluwe an Ultimate M.S.A. level with disc-cores, faceted butts and a tanged chisel underlay the level of the mesoneolithic.

At several sites in the Birim basin, mostly on or just below the highest stone-line, small collections have been made. The pieces are unpatinated, but larger than most mesoneolithic material, and some of them have faceted butts and rudimentary tangs. The repertory is not particularly typical, chisels, awls, burins and blades, sometimes also rough scrapers; at Osenasi was also a disc-core. I consider on typological grounds that they are Ultimate M.S.A. or transitional. There are similar sites in the western forest at Awaso, and in Ashanti at Obenemasi. The displuvial at the end of Sub-pluvial II may have been so short that within the forest conditions did not favour patination.

In western Senegal there is another type of Ultimate M.S.A. The principal site is the Pte. de Fann, Dakar,[83] and there are others, without detailed stratification, around Dakar and Rufisque. At Fann the material occurs on the underlying laterite nodules and all through a bed up to 2 metres thick of sandy clay, on which is the Flandrian beach on the outer side of the promontory and on the inner a line of nodules, which probably marks the end of Sub-pluvial II and corresponds to the laterite on the Flandrian beach at Tiemassas (below, p. 177). Above the laterite are low dunes which carry neolithic. Rolled artefacts have not been found in the Flandrian beach. Though the industry lasted into Sub-pluvial II and may be termed Ultimate M.S.A., it may have started before this stage. The sandy clay contains a good many laterite nodules near the base, in the middle calcrete probably derived from shells at a higher level, and near the top little laterite. Its formation would therefore seem to have started in a dry period, which became wetter and less displuvial.

Stratification of the industry was not observed, as most pieces were picked up on the modern beach, whither they had been derived from the eroding cliff, and no excavation was made in the sandy clay. So the collection has to be taken as a unity, though there may have been development. The division by wear[45] cannot be accepted as significant unless it is supported by differences in level. As the published illustrations are not clear, I present a drawing of the main types [fig. 36]. These are small picks, backed blades, chisels, points, probably awls and various crude scrapers; burins, which have previously been listed, I did not notice. The retouch is often rather steep. Most pieces are uniface. Levallois cores were apparently not found, but a few flakes have faceted butts. I have illustrated one small blade-core. There was little attempt to provide tangs. The industry is certainly in M.S.A. tradition, and was dubbed 'Mousteroid' by its finders, without suggestion that it was contemporary with or closely akin to the Mousterian. It has no affinity with the Aterian or the Guinea Aterian, and it is difficult to

L

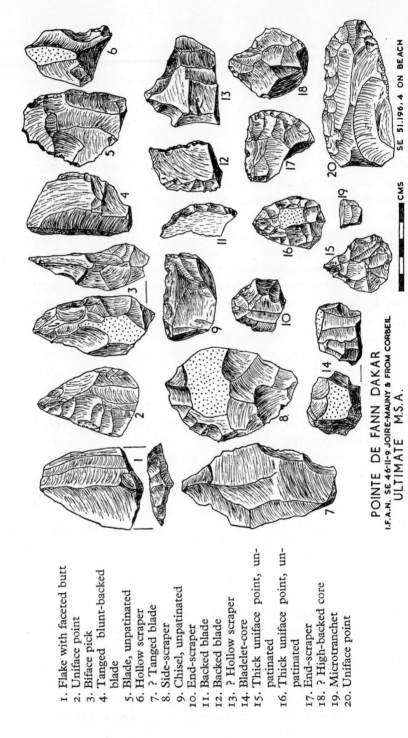

1. Flake with faceted butt
2. Uniface point
3. Biface pick
4. Tanged blunt-backed blade
5. Blade, unpatinated
6. Hollow scraper
7. ? Tanged blade
8. Side-scraper
9. Chisel, unpatinated
10. End-scraper
11. Backed blade
12. Backed blade
13. ? Hollow scraper
14. Bladelet-core
15. Thick uniface point, un-patinated
16. Thick uniface point, un-patinated
17. End-scraper
18. ? High-backed core
19. Microtranchet
20. Uniface point

POINTE DE FANN DAKAR
I.F.A.N. SE 46-II-9 JOIRE-MAUNY & FROM CORBEIL
ULTIMATE M.S.A.

CMS

SE 51.196.4 ON BEACH

FIG. 36 Ultimate Middle Stone Age, Pointe de Fann, Dakar: unpatinated pieces may be neolithic

trace any similarity to the western Lupemban. It was probably the work of a group which was early isolated from the North African Mousterian, and survived under Strandloper conditions until a date when the neolithic was already spreading in the Sahara. A similar culture is described in Rio de Oro.[84] There may be affinity with some Mousterian sites in Mauritania,[74] which are no more than unstratified surface-collections.

Just after Beach VI and before Post-pluvial III there was in Senegal a true mesolithic, apparently without pottery. The principal site is Tiemassas [fig. 48], and specimens have been found around Dakar. This culture is probably neanthropic and cannot be classed with the M.S.A., so I will discuss it in the next chapter. Near Bamako, the lower level at Kourounkorokale also seems to be a true mesolithic, if one can trust the report of the rather amateurish excavation.[85] It must be a fringe-culture of the neolithic of the southern Sahara. It also is most suitably discussed later.

NOTES

1. Arambourg, *SPF* xlvii (1950), p. 348; Laplace–Jauretche, *SPF* liii (1956), p. 215.
2. *Pleistocene Geology and Prehistory of Uganda* II.
3. Howell, *Current Anthropology* (1962), p. 306; Strauss and Hunt, *Science* 136 (1962), p. 293.
4. Hey, *Science* 139 (1963), p. 829.
5. Davies, *SAAB* ix (1954), p. 60; see also above, p. 39.
6. Clark, *V Panafrican Congress* i, p. 225.
7. Van Riet Lowe, *III Panafrican Congress*, p. 207. I feel little confidence in the specimens claimed from the Basal Older Gravels and from Makapansgat.
8. Biberson P., 1961 (2); Biberson *et al.*, *Bulletin d'Archéologie marocaine* iii (1958–9), p. 7.
9. Hugot, *LAPE* viii (1960), p. 325; Hugot H. J. ed., 1962, pp. 151, 166.
10. Bonnet, *SPF* lviii (1961), p. 51.
11. Hugot, *IRS Travaux* xiii (1955), p. 131.
12. Ramendo, *LAPE* xi (1963), p. 43.
13. Alimen and Chavaillon, *IV Panafrican Congress* ii, p. 3.
14. Chavaillon, *Les Formations quaternaires du Sahara nord-occidental*, pl. XXII.
15. I.F.A.N. Dakar Se 62.28.
16. Davies O., 1959 (1), fig. 1.
17. Corbeil R., 1951.
18. E.g. perhaps El Beyyed, Mauny R., 1955; cp. Biberson, *CRAS* 258 (1964), p. 3074.

19. Davies O., 1964 (2), fig. 31 5 and 8.
20. Davies O., 1964 (2), figs. 23–28, and see p. 143, nn. 25–29.
21. For Mauritania, see Mauny R., 1955. Generally Frobenius L. and Breuil H., 1930, which gives a fairly good summary of the collections at that time in Paris.
22. *SPF* lvi (1959), p. 453.
23. Laforgue, *Société de Géographie et d'Archéologie d'Oran Bull. trim.* xlvi (1926), p. 50.
24. Frobenius L. and Breuil H., 1930.
25. Armand, *SPF* xxxiv (1937), p. 506.
26. Lhote, *CPF* xiii (1950), p. 446.
27. Davies O., 1961 (2).
28. I.F.A.N. Dakar So 60–102.
29. Corbeil, *CIAO* I ii, p. 418.
30. Davies O., 1959 (1), fig. 2.
31. Braunholtz, *Geological Survey of Nigeria Occ. papers* IV; Balfour, *Man* xxxiv (1934), no. 25; Fagg, *CIAO* I ii, p. 435; Fagg B., 1956.
32. Davies O., 1957.
33. Davies O., 1957, p. 596.
34. Davies, *Archaeology* xii (1959), p. 172.
35. Corbeil R., 1951, p. 433.
36. *NA* 22 (1944), p. 7; Joire J., 1952.
37. Cp. the picks from Carrière Martin, Casablanca, and other sites, and the cleaver-flakes from Square de la Chaouia; Biberson, *Société de Préhistoire du Maroc Bull.* v–vi (1952), p. 3; Vaufrey, *Préhistoire de l'Afrique* I, pp. 38–40.
38. Droux and Bergeaud, *Revue congolaise* xxiv (1937), p. 211 and xxviii (1941), p. 137; Droux, in le Roy, *Encyclopédie maritime et coloniale A.E.F.*, s.v. Préhistoire, appendix.
39. Cp. Mortelmans and Monteyne, *IV Panafrican Congress* i, p. 97.
40. There are Kalinian and perhaps Sangoan pieces from southern Gaboon (de Beauchene, *Objets et Mondes* iii (1963), p. 3). One Acheulian hand-axe is published from Ubangui–Chari (Wulsin, *Harvard African Studies* x (1932), p. 79 and pl. XIII 704; Breuil, *SAfr* xxv (1955), p. 7); there are unpublished hand-axes, cleavers and Early Lupemban pieces from the same territory in the Musée de l'Homme.
41. Davies, *III Panafrican Congress*, p. 219.
42. The end of the Ougarta cycle in Kamasian II, Chavaillon, *Formations quaternaires du Sahara nord-occidental*, p. 320.
43. Creac'h P., 1945, p. 427; Alimen, *Préhistoire de l'Afrique*, p. 272; I.F.A.N. Dakar, CI 45–23.
44. Davies O., 1957, fig. 7.
45. Corbeil R., Mauny R. and Charbonnier J., 1948, p. 384.
46. Monod, *CEHSAOF* xxi (1938), p. 518; Corbeil, *NA* xvii (1943), p. 7; Corbeil R., 1951, fig. 8.
47. I.F.A.N. Se 48–40.
48. El Beyyed, 19° N, 9° W; Khat Takfoil, 19° 29′ N, 14° 45′ W; Oualata,

collection in Musée de l'Homme, 17° 15′ N, 6° 35′ W; Tarf Aguinjob, 20° 15′ N, 13° 10′ W.

49. Cp. van Riet Lowe, *Pleistocene Geology and Prehistory of Uganda* II, p. 55.

50. Cp. van Riet Lowe, *l. c.*, p. 54 and pl. XX i and XXIII.

51. Cp. Davies and Niddrie, *Natal Archaeological Studies*, paper 2.

52. Kukla Ložek and Barta, *Eiszeitalter und Gegenwart* xii (1962), p. 84.

53. Clark, *Current Anthropology* (1960), p. 318 n. 24; Oakley, in Washburn, *Social Life of Early Man*, p. 176.

54. Cp. Clark, *Soc. portuguesa de Antropologia Travalhos* xvii (1959), p. 257.

55. Davies O., 1965 (2).

56. *Anthropologie* xlv (1935), p. 247; Vaufrey R., 1947.

57. Cp. Szumowski, *NA* 72 (1956), p. 98, pl. I 2 6. Apparently Szumowski's 'shale-industry' (*SPF* liv (1957), p. 350) is a mixture of neolithic with a few older pieces, entirely from the left bank.

58. Hugot, *Asequa* 5–6 (1965), p. 26.

59. I.F.A.N. Se 47–62–1; Mauny, *II Panafrican Congress*, p. 473.

60. Vaufrey R., 1947, publishing Waterlot's collection; de Zeltner, *Anthropologie* xxiv (1913), p. 17; id., *SAP* VI vi (1915), p. 34 and VI vii (1916), p. 238.

61. Capitan, *Revue anthropologique* xxvii (1917), p. 283.

62. Perhaps much of the M.S.A. from Nok, stratified in the Gamblian basal gravels, is really Lupemban. But nearly all the pieces are atypical factory waste, mostly disc-cores and nondescript Levallois flakes. A few small and well worked bifaces might be Lupemban.

63. Noel, *Anthropologie* xxviii (1917), p. 353; Mauny, *SPF* lii (1955), p. 536, no. 6; Mascarelli and Mauny, *NA* 70 (1956), p. 38.

64. Arkell, *Kush* vii (1959), p. 15; id., *IV Panafrican Congress* ii, p. 353.

65. Arkell, *Old Stone Age in the Anglo–Egyptian Sudan* (Sudan Antiq. Serv., Occ. Papers 1); Clark, *Current Anthropology* (1965), p. 158.

66. *Soc. r. de Géographie d'Egypte Bull.* xxiii (1950), p. 175; *CISPP* iii (1950), p. 174; *Cong. int. des Sciences anthropologiques et ethnologiques C. R.* iii (1948), p. 112.

67. Joire J., 1952.

68. Mauny R., 1949; *SPF* xlv (1948), p. 68; *Encyclopédie maritime et coloniale A.O.F.*, s.v. Préhistoire. Cp. Bessac H., 1955.

69. Furon, *Anthropologie* xl (1930), p. 31.

70. Cadenat, *LAPE* 6–7 (1958–9), p. 13. For typology of the Aterian see fig. 27; and especially Balout, *Préhistoire de l'Afrique du Nord*, ch. VII; Tixier, *Bull. d'Archéologie marocaine* iii (1958–9), p. 107; id., *LAPE* 6–7 (1958–9), p. 127. For illustrations of some of the material from Ténéré, the only well published collection from the southern Sahara, see Hugot H. J. ed., 1962.

71. Camps, *LAPE* iii (1956), p. 17.

72. Lhote, *SPF* xli (1944), p. 103. This piece might have been transported more recently.

73. Amblard–Rambert and Gaussen, *SAfr* xxx (1960), p. 138.

74. Mauny R., 1955, p. 470 and ref.
75. Cp. Conrad, *CRAS* 257 (1963), p. 2506.
76. Davies O., 1958.
77. Creac'h P., 1945, pp. 418, 424.
78. Jauze, *Soc. d'Etudes camerounaises Bull.* viii (1944), p. 105.
79. For fuller analysis of the typology see Davies O., 1964 (2), pp. 116–21.
80. Davies O., 1961 (3), paper 2.
81. For discussion of M.S.A. slicers see Davies O., 1964 (2), p. 130. Some of the associated tools could be Lupemban or epi-Lupemban; but this particular form is not paralleled on other sites. It is to be distinguished from the small neolithic slicer of the northern savannah. There are similar tools associated with picks from Almadies near Dakar (I.F.A.N. SE–42–1–66 and 67).
82. See Davies O., 1964 (2), fig. 61.
83. Corbeil, *NA* 17 (1943), p. 7; Corbeil R., Mauny R. and Charbonnier J., 1948, p. 384; Richard 1955.
84. Cerda, *Inst. de Estudios africanos Arch.* 35, p. 81; Santa–Olalla, *El Sahara español anteislamico*, pl. xxx–xxxvii.
85. Szumowski G., 1956.

CHAPTER FOUR

The Neolithic in West Africa

Introductory

During the last forty years the neolithic stage in all parts of the world has come to be defined not by the diffusion of certain techniques of secondary importance but by man's mastery of his environment and food supply, which facilitated an explosion of population. During the palaeolithic man depended on hunting and gathering. Except at unusually favoured localities, where migration of big herds or fish-runs made food seasonally plentiful and easy to procure, a large area was required per head of population. For the food that was available man had to compete with animals stronger than himself, and his weapons were hardly adequate for self-defence. His existence was therefore precarious. He could make little provision against climatic irregularities, in Africa particularly drought; and even normal seasonal variations would render settled habitation in most regions very difficult. So to obtain enough food he had to wander, sometimes perhaps in a trans-humant cycle, in which he counted on annual seasonal return to particular settlements. But lack of permanent habitation made it impossible to accumulate more than a minimum of possessions, and the expenditure of labour in improving his environment was not worth while for the short time when he could enjoy it. So he lived from hand to mouth, and possessed no capital. At the same time, his existence did little to modify the natural order. He did not seriously change the landscape, and as a predator he took his toll of animal and vegetable life around him, but not sufficiently to alter the natural balance.

Control of food supply was exercised by the domestication of plants and animals. Agriculture involved settled habitation, at least for the growing season, in order to protect and harvest what had been planted; as there had usually been a considerable initial outlay of effort, men tended to remain for several seasons, until soil fertility was exhausted. Until in very recent times there has been some pressure of population on the land, the African peasant may often have practised a rotation of settlements, returning after some twenty years fallow to sites he had known previously. It is true that archaeology has not produced much evidence of cycles of reoccupation and abandonment; but a good many excavated sites have several levels, and it is usually impossible to estimate a short unconformity. Modern reoccupation of older sites not forgotten is common. In favoured areas intermittent occupation would be unnecessary, and high mounds would be formed. The Nile floods, for instance, refertilized the fields annually; the large sites in the Niger swamps were probably continuously occupied because of regular floods. The forest retains its fertility fairly well. But continuous dry farming cannot be practised in the savannah without scientific techniques which have been out of reach until very recently.

Many professional herdsmen are nomadic, especially in arid regions where they must range widely in search of fodder and water. Those who keep sheep or goats, whose requirements are less exacting than those of cattle, may often be based on a fixed settlement. Equally, small numbers of stock may be kept near a home as subsidiary to agriculture, as in southern Africa. It is probable that pastoral nomadism is not directly derived from food gathering, but is a reversion designed to fill an ecological niche in areas where agriculture would at best be chancy. Pastoralists need much more room per head of population than cultivators, but not normally as much as hunters. Yet on the grasslands of southern Africa and perhaps of West Africa enormous herds of game, still seen by European colonists, could permanently support a good many human predators, provided that other carnivores were chased away and there was no hindrance to movement of the animals. The farming of native African animals on large ranches in a semi-wild state for meat is seriously advocated today, because they are more fertile and less liable to disease than cattle, and they do less damage to the fragile African soils than agriculture.

West Africa today produces many food plants. It has profited by easy communications under European colonialism, which has transported and experimented with useful tropical products round the world. Some of the staple African crops, like maize and cassava, are of American origin, others, like plantain and coco-yam, from the Far East. Better species of yam and rice also have been introduced. A few of these may well have reached East Africa during the Middle Ages; but even when the Portuguese arrived, there was not a great deal available. There is practically no reliable evidence for interchange of plants between the Old and the New Worlds before Columbus, across either the Atlantic or the Pacific.[1]

The principal West African vegetable foods[2] were the African yam which is rather small, various forms of millet, and one species of rice (Oryza glaberrima). Other plants, now eaten as famine foods, may have been more widely used in antiquity. There is little evidence that the West African peasant did much to improve his plants. Scientific cultivation has been much practised in the Near East, including probably Egypt, India and China. The African peasant perhaps had less of the instincts of a devoted gardener, probably because he was not stimulated by pressure of population. Shifting agriculture, which is a form of predation, is unlikely to induce improvements.

The usual European cereals cannot be grown in tropical Africa, because they require winter rain and fairly long hours of daylight during the growing season. They have little resistance to fungus which is encouraged by summer rain. They grow well in a very dry climate with irrigation, as in Egypt, and wheat flourishes as far south as Ethiopia. It may have been grown in the Saharan neolithic, where Mediterranean vegetation indicates that there was mostly winter rain. Egypt and North Africa were the granaries of the Roman empire, practically the only regions which could produce cereals for export to feed large urban populations and the army. Some valuable types of wheat reached North Africa only in the Middle Ages.[3]

Several millets are native to Africa. They are summer-rain plants, which flourish in a fairly short but intense wet season, the land being left fallow for months during the winter. Above 10° N millet is a staple diet, to the south it has to compete with tubers and is used largely for brewing. In early days the seeds of many wild grasses may have been harvested and pounded for food. In the western part of the sub-continent rice replaces millet. It must have diffused especially from the swamps of the middle Niger and the Gambia Rivers; for it does not do well under dry farming even near the edge of the forest, except in swampy hollows.

Farther to the south yams will grow, but not generally west of the Ivory Coast. Even the small African yam produces a very large tonnage of food per acre in comparison with millet. It grows well in orchard bush up to 9° N and in favoured areas farther north.[4] Some form of proto-cultivation, originating in the discarding of the refuse of wild yams round a camp, is likely to extend far back into the palaeolithic (above, p. 118). This is a case where it is extremely difficult to draw the line between food gathering and deliberate cultivation.

There are valuable wild plants and trees. Many fruits are edible in their short seasons, some are available just before the rains, when stocks of cultivated crops are at their lowest. Some trees are planted for food, like baobab (in the orchard bush) and kola; many others grow wild but are protected and harvested. There is a good selection of oil plants. The oil-palm is of particular value in the forest, and in the savannah there is abundant shea-butter, farther east also sesame and castor oil.

There is a great variety of wild African animals, but little evidence that many of them have been domesticated. Domestication was apparently first practised in central Asia, and the techniques and probably the herdsmen were introduced into Africa at a time when their own ecology was thoroughly established, and there was little reason for beginning the process afresh with the species which they met. The Egyptians of the Old Kingdom herded gazelles into parks;[5] but this experiment of a wealthy aristocracy had no future. Huard claims rock pictures of domesticated antelopes at Gonoa (Tibesti).[6] Modern attempts show that eland and zebra can be partially domesticated. The donkey seems to be the only animal of African origin which has made an important contribution to human environment. The cat probably domesticated itself in Egypt. The Guinea-fowl is a West African bird; in Roman times it was known in North Africa and was called 'numidica', so it may have been domesticated in the neolithic Sahara.[7]

The dog attached itself to man in Asia before the neolithic. It is not proved to have reached Egypt and North Africa during the epipalaeolithic. Its talents as assistant of the hunter and herdsman have been little exploited by the African, it is sometimes used as a pet but seldom as a watchdog, and some tribes breed it for food, especially in the Sahara. It seldom appears on rock paintings.

Large numbers of cattle are shown in the rock art of the Saharan neolithic [fig. 46 7–8].[8] They must have been introduced from Asia or domesticated directly in the Nile Valley. In the Sahara we find paintings of long-horned *Bos Aegyptiacus* or related breeds. It is believed that in West Africa a short-horned breed, today kept by certain relict tribes, arrived earlier; but we have no evidence about its route. Cattle have certain requirements in fodder and water. With the desiccation of the Sahara at the end of Sub-pluvial II herds had to move south into the northern savannah. At the same time, they are liable to tsetse-borne diseases, and though they can be kept in wooded savannah with some gallery forest, they cannot survive long close to the forest, and their movement into southern Africa was conditioned by tsetse-free routes.

Sheep and goats are less exacting than cattle, but less mobile. They appear in predynastic Egypt. Droppings of sheep or goat were identified in the soil of a cave in the Monts Gautier (south-eastern Algeria, south of Djanet), in what is now absolute desert, along with traces of neolithic occupation and Mediterranean vegetation.[9] It is doubtful if the sheep is native to and was domesticated in Africa.[10] The African mouflon (Ammotragus) was native. It was a sacred animal, and appears frequently on rock drawings;[11] but it was probably not domesticated.

The domestic pig perhaps arrived in Africa by sea across the Indian Ocean, and may have interbred with African wild pigs. It is not clear whether the pigs now kept by some relict tribes in West Africa are of ancient strains. In much of West Africa pig-keeping was abandoned with conversion to Islam.

Horses and camels, though important in West Africa, do not belong to the neolithic economy, so will be discussed in the next chapter.

I have explained that the introduction of domestic plants and animals made for more permanent settlement. In fertile regions, where shifting cultivation was unnecessary, a surplus of food could easily be produced, so that villages became cities, cultural and political organization became complex, and part of the population could engage in specialized or non-productive work, government, war, metallurgy and other crafts. Without a regular food surplus, crafts could be no more than an amateur side-line, for which there was time in seasons when all hands were not needed in the fields. Urbanization in this sense, without the political overtones it has acquired from Greek history, developed early in Egypt, in the Maghreb probably not before Punic times, in the Niger Valley not before the Middle Ages, and southward towards the forest hesitantly and hardly before recent centuries.

The Saharan Neolithic

A proto-agriculture, based on tubers, may well have been practised far back in the palaeolithic. Archaeology cannot expect to detect its development. It is doubtful if it involved preparation of the ground. The heads would fall either into the holes where there had been digging for wild tubers, or on to the partly eroded ground round a camp, enriched by human rubbish; they would take root, and if men continued to occupy the same site, as concentration of implements suggests they did, they would have a crop ready to hand. Such proto-agriculture would not differ in conception from a proto-domestication of animals, either naturally in oases or in human-made enclosures. It is commonly supposed that the shy and savage animals which were selected for domestication must have become accustomed to contact with humanity under some such conditions in western Asia; it is difficult to believe that man was incapable of making rough enclosures to keep a herd within reach, if in the upper palaeolithic he was already capable of hunting by battue.

It is not, however, claimed that the proto-agriculture of the African equatorial region developed into true agriculture without being fertilized by the introduction of higher techniques from Asia. The predisposition was there. Negroid peoples spread into the Saharan oases. The Asselar skeleton, not closely dated but believed to be neolithic,[12] is of negroid type. Other neolithic bones from the Sahara[13] have been claimed as negroid, but have not been scientifically examined. The negro peoples had probably developed near the forest margin. Despite the technical difference between grooving and perforation of the butts of harpoons [figs. 42–43; below, pp. 163–5], it is difficult to believe that the idea of the harpoon was not carried by migration from Ishango, dated on geological grounds to not later than the seventh millennium B.C., via Early Khartum,[14] to the Saharan pans; and thus the negroes of the southern Sahara had come from regions where tubers were available and used. They may well have carried them with them. Wetter conditions at Khartum, and perhaps a longer flood-season, may have made yam-growing possible; and many tools from Shaheinab look like hoes, which seem to have developed in tuber-country. Indeed, a species of yam, which is poisonous unless carefully treated, grows today not far from Khartum, and is used as famine-food.

The knowledge of true agriculture and domestic animals must have reached Africa via Egypt. The suggestion of a route across the Straits of Bab-el-Mandeb has no archaeological support. The earliest dates from Egypt (Fayum, Merimde, Abka, see table p. 80) are not much earlier than 4000 B.C.; whereas there are dates from Haua Fteah (Cyrenaica) for the transition to the neolithic near the beginning of the fifth millennium. In the recent discussion on the predynastic development of the Nile Valley,[15] criticism was levelled at the accuracy of these radiocarbon dates, especially of that from Shaheinab. This must stand until it is proved that Shaheinab is not a fairly late representative of the culture in the Sudan or until an incompatible date is obtained from the preceding culture of Early Khartum. Historical Egyptian dates are, however, inclined to be too low,[16] so the neolithic dates may be too. But the other suggestion that the earliest Egyptian neolithic sites, before pressure of population increased the value of all irrigable land and

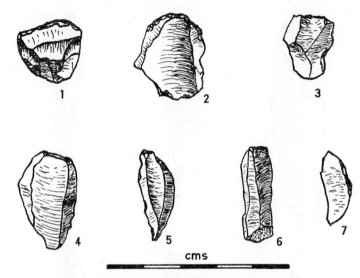

FIG. 37 Mesolithic pieces, Debeira West, Nubia

after Sandford and Arkell, Palaeolithic Man and the Nile Valley in Nubia and Upper Egypt, *pl. 42, by permission of the Oriental Institute of the University of Chicago*

forced settlement to the valley margins, were near the river, is more plausible, seeing that the Mediterranean would not have reached its present level until after 4000 B.C., so the valley would continue to be entrenched. This explanation would not apply to the Fayum, which is outside the main valley; except that the excavators believed[17] that the depression was partly or wholly desert until the Nile rose high enough to penetrate temporarily into it. No epipalaeolithic culture has been found in the Fayum area, and the neolithic occupation seems to be subsequent to the first flooding.

In view of the date from Haua Fteah, it is reasonable to suppose that agricultural techniques reached Egypt from Asia by 5000 B.C. Domestic animals must have arrived about the same time. They spread westward fairly quickly; for though proved neolithic dates from the central Sahara are not earlier than the fourth millennium B.C., there is a date from Dar-es-Soltan (Morocco) of 5860 ± 70.[18]

The sequence in Egypt from the epipalaeolithic [figs. 37–38][19] to the neolithic is interrupted. Certain forms may have reached Egypt from the south, perhaps the hoe, also the bone harpoon if it was not independently derived into northern Egypt from Eurasia. The site at Debeira West [fig. 37] appears to belong to the latest epipalaeolithic or

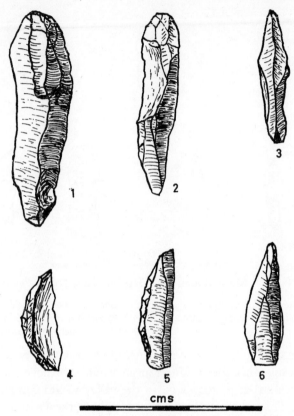

FIG. 38 Mesolithic pieces, Helouan, Egypt

after Sandford, Palaeolithic Man and the Nile Valley
in Upper and Middle Egypt, *pl. 39, by permission of the
Oriental Institute of the University of Chicago*

true mesolithic. It is clearly preneolithic. Geologically it dates to the
period when most of the Post-pluvial I silt had been removed. According to the radiocarbon dates recently obtained, this should be some
time after 9325 ± 250,[20] so at least 1,000 years before the arrival of the
neolithic. The industry with its blades, awls, end-scrapers and crescents
(rare) looks rather like the Guinea mesolithic, and may be an outlier of
an undifferentiated African mesolithic which did not reach the Sahara,
but gradually spread westward along the wooded savannah. The
Helouan material [fig. 38], not stratigraphically dated, is thought to be
just preneolithic. Capsian influence is unlikely, as there are no good
duckbills at Helouan. The industry is so much poorer than even the
Fayum B group, thought to be a reversion to a semi-nomadic culture

from the high level of the A group, that little connection can be traced. Other Egyptian neolithic sites are badly published, and there is now doubt whether the Tasian is an independent pre-Badari neolithic. The Beduin microlithic of Kharga[21] has a wider repertory than Helouan and Debeira West, and contains blade-scrapers, tanged microtranchets, awls, drills and various forms of arrow-head.

There appears to be a continuous sequence from the epipalaeolithic to the neolithic in Cyrenaica; but no detailed publication of Haua Fteah has yet appeared.

In the Maghreb there seems to be continuity to the neolithic especially from the Capsian, and it was the Mediterranean type of man who carried the Capsian and in due course imposed himself throughout the Maghreb in the neolithic. In the Oranian zone Capsian elements as well as specifically neolithic techniques like polished axes and pottery are added to the older culture, there was probably movement of population, and some of the older stock took refuge in the Canary Islands.[22] There is linguistic evidence for early cultivation of cereals in North Africa, though the archaeological evidence from the Maghreb neolithic is unsatisfactory.[23] On the western seaboard there seems to have been direct colonization of Oranian epipalaeolithic sites by Mediterranean and Iberian mariners.[24]

In the Sahara there is at present no evidence whether the mesoneolithic directly succeeded the Aterian, which almost certainly lingered late. In the Saoura Valley the intermediate Hémama industry has been identified,[25] presumably the counterpart of the Oranian. In the central Sahara continuity of human settlement would be expected if there was no catastrophic break in climate corresponding to Post-pluvial I, as French workers now maintain (above, pp. 62–3); and the earliest phase of rock art, depicting large wild fauna,[26] seems to be preneolithic [fig. 46]. But only on the southern margin, in the area of the epi-Lupemban (above, pp. 122–5), is there any suggestion of continuity from the palaeolithic to the neolithic.

It is not clear whence specifically neolithic arts reached West Africa, pottery and polished stone. The Fayum technique of leaving a ground edge and flaking the rest of a polished stone has been observed farther west in the Ténéré culture and at In Tecoufit [fig. 45 2]; normally the edge-ground celt seems to be a flaked axe superficially polished, so that only the most prominent parts of the flake scars would be removed. At Shaheinab flaking after polishing was practised only if the piece was to be reused.

Saharan and West African pottery does not resemble that from the

Fayum. There are from the Sahara wavy-line sherds, a technique derived from Early Khartum,[15] where the ornament was effected with the spine of a catfish. These sherds appear especially in the eastern Sahara,[27] most accessible from the middle Nile; but have been found as far west as Adrar Bous and Meniet.[28] The tool used in the Sahara is uncertain; some of the impressions from Meniet look like twisted cord.

At Meniet were zones of short walking grooves. They seem to have been made with a smooth tool, Hugot suggests the shell of Unio. Farther to the south walking comb is common. This decoration lasts in the southern savannah until after the sixteenth century. The comb impressions are sometimes straight [cp. fig. 44, Tin Ekiad], often curved especially on post-neolithic sites [figs. 81–82, 101: Reg de Zaki, Ait Nafane, Ntereso]. This feature suggests the use or at least the tradition of a denticulated shell. No West African freshwater mollusc is denticulated; but a degenerate Cardium edule is to be found in brackish sub-fossil deposits in the northern Sahara[29] and apparently near Bamako. Cardium impressions were much used in neolithic Spain and the western Mediterranean. There are a few pieces from western Algeria and in particular from Morocco,[30] probably introduced by colonists. Even if the sites in the southern Sahara be quite late in the neolithic, it is likely that the cardium pattern was carried south by pottery-makers, and so the western Mediterranean was a centre of diffusion of pottery into Africa. Where there were no cardium shells toothed stamps were made occasionally of bone or stone (a few are known from Mauritania),[31] more commonly of wood or reed; and the most southerly and latest sites where walking comb was used may well have established relations with the Guinea coast and imported thence other species of denticulated mollusc. Such shells certainly made their way up-country in Ghana during the last few centuries.

Information is scanty regarding neolithic sites in Tchad Territory, and many pieces are strays without association. There have been collected in the desert biface leaf-shaped points, points with rounded butt, occasionally blades and scrapers. A site at Niagri, 130 kms. east of Largeau, seems to belong to the Ténéré-culture. At Zouar (Tibesti) is a site of 'agricultural neolithic' with few microliths, waisted axes, celts, stone arm-rings and grindstones.[32]

Niger Territory has received more attention, because of the beautifully flaked Ténéré-neolithic which has frequently been found. The material usually is fine-grained green jasper, and admirable illustrations have been published, especially in the report on the Missions Berliet.[33]

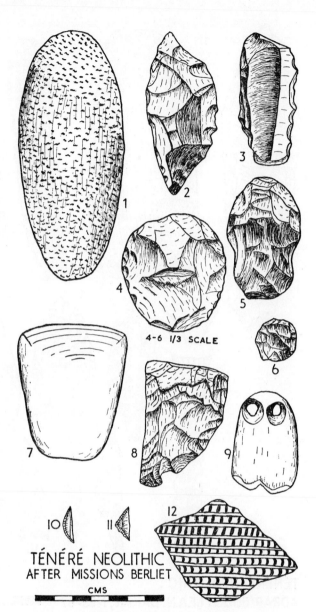

1. Pecked celt
2. Asymmetrical side-
   scraper
3. Denticulated blade
4. Flaked disc
5. Waisted axe
6. Thumbnail scraper
7. Celt of oval section
8. 'Egyptian' knife
9. Stone pendant
10. Crescent
11. Triangle
12. Sherd

4-6 1/3 SCALE

TÉNÉRÉ NEOLITHIC
AFTER MISSIONS BERLIET
CMS

FIG. 39 Selection of Ténéré neolithic, Niger

from Missions Berliet Ténéré-Tchad, *ed. H. J. Hugot, by
permission of Automobiles M. Berliet; 1–9 from article by
Hugot, pp. 149–78, pl. XI, XVII–XIX; 10–12 from article
by Tixier, pl. I and fig. 1, pp. 333–48*

M

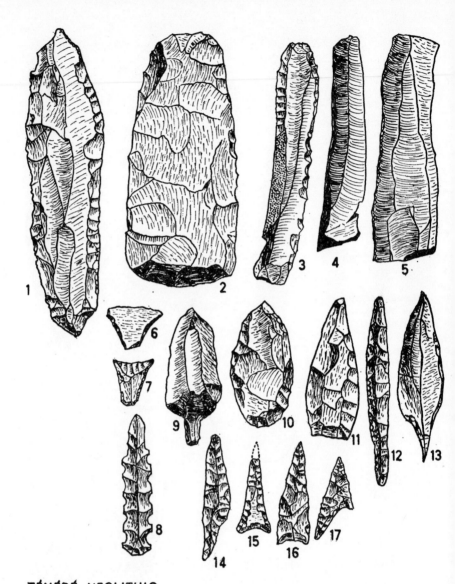

TÉNÉRÉ NEOLITHIC .
ADRAR BOUS: I.F.A.N. DAKAR, N53-87

CMS

FIG. 40

1. Double point
2. Axe or semi-gouge
3. Backed blade or side-scraper
4. Blunt-backed blade with traces of use
5. Backed blade with traces of use
6. Microtranchet
7. Microtranchet
8. Denticulated arrowhead

9. Tanged arrowhead
10. Leaf-shaped arrowhead
11. Square-based arrowhead
12. Double awl
13. Finely tanged Ounan point
14. Shouldered point
15. Eiffel-tower arrowhead
16. Hollow-based arrowhead
17. Shouldered arrowhead

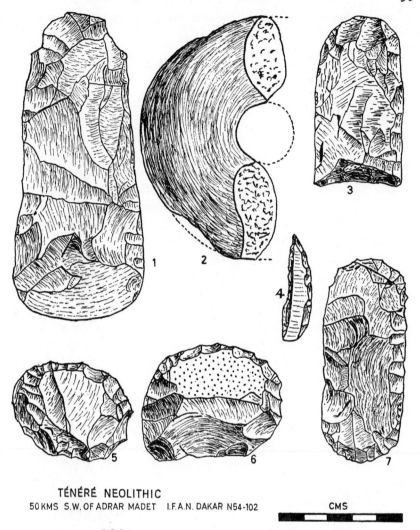

TÉNÉRÉ NEOLITHIC
50 KMS S.W. OF ADRAR MADET   I.F.A.N. DAKAR N54-102

CMS

FIG. 41 Of fine greenstone save no. 2, of coarse sandstone

1. Edge-ground celt
2. Perforated disc
3. Gouge
4. Awl, steeply backed
   on both edges

5. Disc-scraper
6. Disc-scraper
7. Double end-scraper

The first study of this culture was made by Joubert and Vaufrey.[34] As there is no comprehensive illustrated description, I have reproduced certain types from the publication of the Missions Berliet [fig. 39] and have added two unpublished collections in Dakar [figs. 40–41].

In addition to the Ténéré-neolithic, two neolithic cultures are distinguished in Niger, an 'agricultural neolithic' and a 'hunting and fishing neolithic'. Both of these extended a long way north-west of Agades, in a region of former lakes which today is less inhospitable than the Ténéré de Tafassasset. West of Aïr there were lakes near the heads of wadis which flowed into the depression between Aïr and Adrar des Iforas, drained by the Azaouak and Dallol Bosso. Before the breaching of Tosaye this was one of the main headwaters of the Lower Niger. East of Aïr a vast erg chokes the valley of the Tafassasset. Water is today very scarce, except beneath the cliffs on the east side of the valley. This valley drained ultimately into Lake Chad. There was probably little agriculture even in neolithic times, as most of the best settlements are on slopes above the erg, for instance on the north slopes of Aïr; so there may have already been much sand.

As far as is possible, I give a comparative table of the material of these three cultures. I have included references to the illustrations of the Ténéré-culture. This table must be regarded as of limited value, because all the collections are from surface, and some have not been carefully inventoried. There is no evidence whether the three cultures are contemporary; considering the duration of the Saharan neolithic, they may not be. The sole radiocarbon date is from a site of Ténéré-neolithic at Adrar Bous III, 5140 ± 300. [35]

The most northerly site of the Ténéré-culture reported by the Missions Berliet is at Guelb Berliet. [36] Ténéré-neolithic was found also at Er Roui on the Djado scarp. A kindred culture with fine flaking, flaked axes, awls, discs, drills and arrow-heads, but with a different form of matchet-knife and with jabbed pottery, was found at Fort Thiriet near Ghadames. [37]

Contacts of the Ténéré-culture with the Nile Valley have been claimed, partly because its beautiful flaking is suggestive of some of the best predynastic pieces, which are not very early. But the resemblance may be due to the fine grain of the material, and a coarser Ténéré-neolithic was made in quartzite (e.g. at Merguigara). There is only a generalized resemblance in forms; the specialized types of the Egyptian predynastic, the swallow-tail arrow-heads and fish-tail points, are not found in Ténéré. [38] The matchet-knife is an early Egyptian type. [39] The Ounan-point, of which most have come from near Taoudeni, is rarely found in a perhaps degenerate form in the Fayum and Kharga. A sub-spherical and a discoidal mace-head from Itchouma, [40] perhaps unassociated, are of Egyptian type, also one from Dourso cave, Tibesti. [41]

	TÉNÉRÉ	Fig.	AGRI-CULTURAL	HUNTING-FISHING
Arrow-heads: Tanged	rare	40 9	some	with wings
Leaf-shaped	rare	40 10	some	some
Shouldered	some	40 14, 17	some	—
Deep hollow-based	few		some	many
Shallow hollow-based	some	40 15–16	some	many
Denticulated	some	40 8	—	—
Triangular or square-based	some	40 11	—	some
Scrapers: Disc	some	41 5–6	—	—
Thumbnail	some	39 6	some	few
Asymmetrical side-	some	39 2	—	—
Double end-	some	41 7	—	—
Ounan-points	rare	40 13	—	—
Crescents and triangles	some	39 10–11	—	few
Microburins	many			
Microtranchets with concave sides	some	40 6–7	—	?
Drills and awls	some	40 12, 41 4	—	—
Blades: Ordinary	some	40 3, 5	—	—
Tanged-backed	some	39 3	—	a few
Blunt-backed	some	40 4	—	—
Denticulated	some		—	—
Burins	v. rare			
Flaked discs	some	39 4	—	—
Perforated discs	a few	41 2	—	—
Matchet-knives	rare	39 8	—	only Meniet
Axes: Flaked	some	40 2	—	—
Polished and flaked on blade	a few		—	—
Flaked and edge-ground	a few	41 1	—	—
Gouge-bladed	a few	41 3	—	—
Waisted	patchy	39 5	some	one hammer
Large pecked	many	39 1	many	?
Small polished	some	39 7	some	?
Hoes	a few		some	?
Stone pendants	rare	39 9	some	—
Bracelets	a few		many	—
Stone beads	rare		rare	—
Pottery	fine comb and wavy-line	39 12	comb and walking comb	some
Grinding material	one site		much	one site
Bone-work	?		much	much

The technique of flaking after polishing is claimed by Joubert and Vaufrey in Ténéré. Amazonite, found in the Fayum, is believed to have been brought from Eguei Zouma in north-eastern Tibesti,[42] far out in the direction of Ténéré. There are pieces also from the western Sahara.[43] The idea of mummification is perhaps common to Egypt and the Sahara; the mummy from Uan Muhaggiag (Fezzan) may be older than any neolithic in Africa, and belong to the earliest part of Sub-pluvial II.[44]

Other connections seems to be with the middle Nile near Khartum. If the radiocarbon dates are acceptable, they cannot be so early as those with the Fayum. The flaked axe, hoe and gouge are common at Shaheinab. There are not many gouges from the Sahara, several from Ténéré, and from Emi Zéridé near Itchouma.[45] Drill-points are found at Shaheinab. Wavy-line pottery indicates influence from the middle Nile valley as far west as Ténéré and sporadically farther. However, at Early Khartum most microliths are crescents, as contrasted with the variety from Ténéré.

These features seem to indicate fairly regular contact between Ténéré and the lower and middle Nile in the fourth millennium B.C. For the third millennium we have little evidence. From the second the stone lugged axes of Niger (below, p. 170) copy an Egyptian form. Strong influences from Middle and New Kingdom Egypt are claimed in the paintings of Tassili n'Ajjer;[46] but confirmation is required. The political and cultural development of Egypt may have temporarily severed contact with the desert barbarians.

It is uncertain how sharply we may distinguish the agricultural from the hunting-fishing neolithic of Niger; both these cultures extend far to the west of the present political frontier. Hugot claims some sites in Ténéré as agricultural neolithic. His criterion seems to be the presence of numerous querns,[47] pestles, grindstones (spherical and discoidal), large cylindrical pecked celts [fig. 61, below, pp. 195-7], and abundant pottery with comb impressions. There is a good deal of worked bone. Stone ornaments, bracelets and pendants, are more abundant. There are arrow-heads, but few other microlithic types. Sickles do not seem to have been found west of Kharga, the bone set with flint teeth from Columnata (Algeria) being unsuitable for cutting corn.[48] Tools which may be described as stone hoes must also have been for agriculture; they were found near Gossolorum (not in a unified collection), Tchigrine-Modjigo, and in Tchad Territory at Tohil.[49] From a long way to the south-west, in Cercle Tahoua, comes a miscellaneous collection which includes a good deal of agricultural neolithic, stone hoes, grindstones and querns, stone bracelets and pendants, celts mostly small, many types of arrow-head, thumbnail-scrapers, awls and blades.[50] The stone hoe seems to be represented, though unrecognized, among the 'axes' from Shaheinab; there are many examples from the Guinea savannah [figs. 69–70, below, p. 212].

If these sites east of Aïr were primarily agricultural, what was the economy of the Ténéré-culture? It contains arrow-heads, but apparently not more abundantly than the agricultural sites. Its main characteristic is a large selection of microliths, and many flaked axes and similar tools. The Ténéré-people do not seem to have been nomads; their tool-kit is too large and too numerous. They may have been herdsmen, though direct association with the rock paintings of cattle is unproved; they had subsidiary agriculture. But until a stratified site is found by which we can distinguish the chronological relations in Niger, it will be difficult to understand its neolithic cultures.

The hunting-fishing facies of the Saharan neolithic is noted especially for its fine bone-work. It is not probably radically distinct from the agricultural neolithic; perhaps at suitable sites, where were lakes with game and fish, more emphasis was laid on this aspect of the economy than on crops. Where there were lakes, a hunting-fishing economy was stressed also in the Ténéré-culture, for instance near the eastern headwaters of the Dallol Bosso basin at In Azaoua.[51]

The repertory of artefacts on hunting-fishing sites does not differ greatly from that of the agricultural neolithic, except for the highly developed bone industry. The material may indeed merely have survived better in swamps and pools which were rapidly desiccated than on agricultural sites with seasonal rainfall.

The most remarkable tool is the unilateral perforated harpoon [fig. 42],[52] which was almost certainly used for fishing. From nearly all the sites which have yielded harpoons, from Artiena and Goz-Kerki (Tchad) in the east to Meniet (Hoggar) in the north and Arawane (Mali) in the west, bones of fish and large aquatic animals are reported. From the most westerly site, Taokest (Mauritania), nothing except one harpoon seems to have been collected. The less satisfactory method of attachment by grooving the haft is found rarely and to the south, on sites of very divergent dates, Ishango (? seventh millennium), Early Khartum (? fifth millennium), Manga (Tchad, undated) and Ntereso [fig. 43] (Ghana, about 1200 B.C.); it will be discussed later. From a few sites like Meniet, Tamesna, Krimeng (Tchad) and Artiena[53] there are only fragments of harpoon, which do not indicate the method of

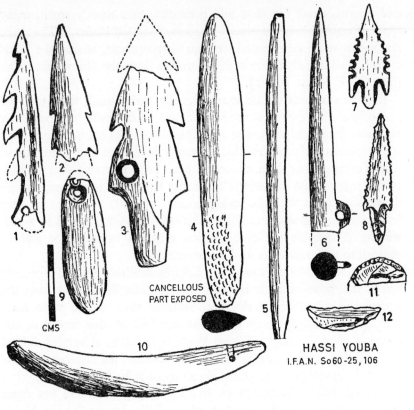

FIG. 42

1-3. Harpoons, bone   7-8. Arrowheads
4. Knife, bone   9. Pendant, ? shale
5. Blunt point, bone   11. Broken end-scraper
6. Perforated point, polished granite 12. Crescent
10. Anchor-shaped pendant, quartzite, perforated at end and
    without projection like several from Mauritania

hafting. Except for some Tchad sites, which are believed to be Iron Age,[54] all the perforated harpoons appear to belong to a single culture within a limited period. Of most the chronology is also climatically determined, because the Saharan lakes were drying up towards the end of Sub-pluvial II. Even so far south as Kourounkorokale,[55] where pottery and celts probably did not occur in the lower level with the harpoons and these belong to a pre-neolithic phase, they must be roughly contemporary with those of the southern Sahara.

The bilateral harpoon is rare, and most of those from Ishango are

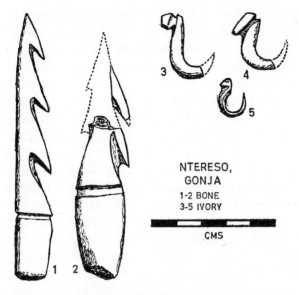

NTERESO,
GONJA
1-2 BONE
3-5 IVORY

CMS

FIG. 43

claimed to be barbed spears.[14] There is a single one from Shaheinab
and a very few from Early Khartum. There are two from Hassi Youba
[fig. 42], one at least perforated in a way which must imply use as a
harpoon. One and probably several from Tamaya Mellet are bilateral,[56]
so is one from Ntereso [fig. 43 2].

Hooks, probably for fishing, are rarely found both with and without
harpoons. The best collection is from the early Iron Age site of Ntereso
[fig. 43], where the only complete example had no barb at the point.
Plain hooks were found also at Meniet and Shaheinab (with harpoons),
and Teghaza (without harpoons). Other hooks are broken or are not
described. The only barbed hook is from Karkarichinkat-Sud,[57] a site
which yielded lacustrine fauna but no harpoons.

Apart from fishing equipment, the commonest bone object from sites
of the Saharan neolithic is a polished point [cp. fig. 42 6]. These have
been found on many sites, not only on those which have yielded fishing
tools. They are liable to turn up on any site in West Africa where bone
is well preserved. There is a number from Ntereso.

Other bone tools have rarely been found, daggers on a few sites, most
of which have yielded harpoons [fig. 42 4], blunt burnishers at Hassi
Youba [fig. 42 5] Karkarichinkat-Nord and sites on the upper Niger,
combs on several central Saharan sites but not farther south, polished
chisels at Gao and Ntereso. From Akreijit (Mauritania), along with a

rich neolithic inventory, is what is believed to be a gorge for fishing.[58] The curious piece from Hassi Youba [fig. 42 10] is too large to have served this purpose, and we do not know what it is.

Sites which have been carefully examined have yielded many artefacts in addition to bone fishing equipment. Pottery with varied types of decoration, some indicating connections with the Nile Valley, was found at Meniet,[28] on several sites in Niger and Tchad, and occasionally in the Tilemsi Valley. Walking-comb decoration, dominant at Ntereso [fig. 101], seems to have been found in small quantities at Kobadi only. There was probably no pottery from Kourounkorokale Lower, apparently also from Gao Dune Rosé and Gangaber. Statistics about pottery are, however, unsatisfactory, as it has often not been collected from surface sites and may have been destroyed by exposure.

Microliths again are subject to hazards of collection and of mention in reports. Arrow-heads, tanged and barbed, leaf-shaped, square-based and hollow-based are recorded fairly frequently from harpoon sites, the first type not from Meniet. Crescents and microtranchets also seem not uncommon. End-scrapers and awls have been collected and seem to be a regular item of the culture. Miniature celts are regular [fig. 60]. The larger edge-ground celt has been found occasionally, a pecked celt of cylindrical section only at In Guezzam [fig. 61; below, p. 197]. Small biface gouges and waisted or rilled hammers are sometimes mentioned. Stone beads are reported from Asselar Akreijit and Karkarichinkat-Sud only; but grooved stones indicate the use of beads of shell or bone, which have been rarely found as they seldom survive exposure. Stone bracelets and arm-rings [see figs. 45 1, 85 6] have been found here and there on sites both with and without harpoons. There are polished quartz lip-plugs from Gao-Hydrocarbures;[59] but the site seems to have yielded a mixture of neolithic and later material, so the association of these objects, which are otherwise believed to be fairly modern,[60] cannot be determined. Kobadi[61] and Hassi Youba seem to have been within the metal-age, unless there has been contamination; iron was certainly known in the latest level at Ntereso.

Many sites in the western Sahara had no access to open water, so their economy was geared rather to agriculture. This facies in eastern Niger has been discussed, the sites yield stone hoes and many grinding tools. Sites rather vaguely described as 'Toumbian', like Dounzou (western Niger),[62] probably also belong to the agricultural facies. There is perhaps a hoe from Karkarichinkat-Sud. This tool is of importance in the neolithic of the savannah and forest.

Pottery with walking-comb impressions is perhaps commoner on sites of agricultural facies than on those with harpoons. It has been found particularly in the Tilemsi Valley (Karkarichinkat-Nord and Sud, Tin Ekiad, fig. 44) and on the upper Niger (Kobadi, fig. 85, a site which yielded harpoons; Kourounkorokale Upper, whereas the harpoons apparently came from the lower, pre-pottery level). Pieces from Reg de Zaki and Ait Nafane [figs. 81–82], far out in the Sahara, may be of very late date. This decoration was perhaps a local development near the Niger bend owing to the presence of Cardium fossils in the old Niger delta (above, p. 156); or it may have become popular rather later than the climatic deterioration which caused the disappearance of the south Saharan lakes and the fishing communities which exploited them.

The Tilemsi Valley, a main route into the Sahara, has been more thoroughly explored than many other regions;[63] fairly large inventories have been made of surface collections from several sites.[64] Apart from one hook from Karkarichinkat-Sud, it has not yielded fishing equipment. The finds from the two sites at Karkarichinkat are listed [see fig. 60].[65] I am illustrating two unpublished collections. At Tin Ekiad (Tineganen), at Km. 98 from Gao to Tabankort, there is a rather scattered site. Apparently it has been visited several times. The collection at Dakar [fig. 44] contains:

Fairly thin bowls but no other form of pot; many are plain and some coarse; decoration consists of walking-comb impressions.
Lower and upper grindstones, no pounders.
Heavy stone bracelet of triangular section.
Small and miniature celts.
A few pyramidical and discoidal cores; many flakes, most are probably not utilized.
Scrapers, end-, disc- and side-.
Awls or drills, abruptly retouched on both sides.
Perhaps a slicer, of the type known from the neolithic near Bamako.
Arrow-heads, poorly made, tanged, leaf-shaped and denticulated.
Crescents.

From In Tecoufit [fig. 45], a site on the eastern margin of the Tilemsi Valley, come several types of arrow-head, miniature celts, a fairly large celt shaped by the curious technique of flaking after polishing, an unfinished sub-spherical quartz bead, several pieces of stone bracelet, and a few microliths.

With local modifications the South Saharan neolithic extends as far as the Hoggar. Meniet must be near its northern limit. For in Tidikelt

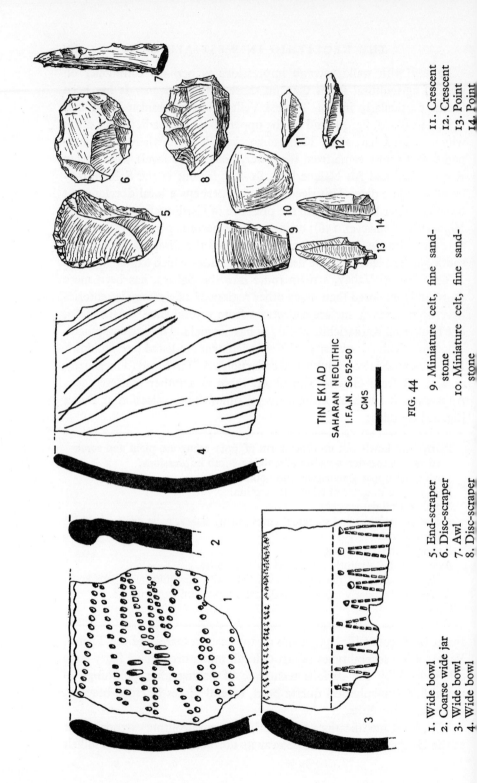

TIN EKIAD
SAHARAN NEOLITHIC
I.F.A.N. So 52-50

CMS

FIG. 44

1. Wide bowl
2. Coarse wide jar
3. Wide bowl
4. Wide bowl
5. End-scraper
6. Disc-scraper
7. Awl
8. Disc-scraper
9. Miniature celt, fine sandstone
10. Miniature celt, fine sand-
    stone
11. Crescent
12. Crescent
13. Point
14. Point

2-7 FLINT, 8 SANDSTONE

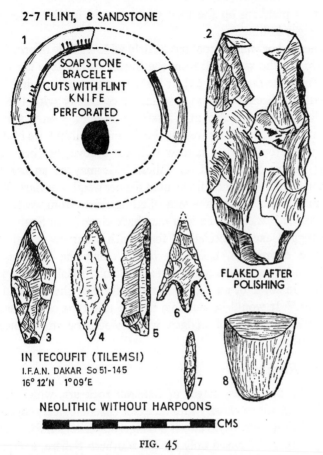

1

SOAPSTONE
BRACELET
CUTS WITH FLINT
KNIFE
PERFORATED

2

FLAKED AFTER
POLISHING

IN TECOUFIT (TILEMSI)

I.F.A.N. DAKAR So 51-145
16° 12'N   1° 09'E

3   4   5   6   7   8

NEOLITHIC WITHOUT HARPOONS

CMS

FIG. 45

there appears a different form of microlithic culture with geometric microliths and microburins, more closely akin to the Capsian.[66] There is a limited range of arrow-heads from the southern Sahara, without the fantastic variety described by Hugot.[67]

Tools which occur in the Saharan neolithic but are more important in the savannah and forest, like celts and hoes, will be discussed later. The rilled or waisted stone axe (hammer), which is comparatively uncommon in the south, is more suitably described at this point. They are fairly common in Niger and Tibesti.[68] There are at least three types, whose common feature is the use of a depression to hold the fastening of the handle. In fact, this is a wide-spread idea, wherever men were too ignorant or too poor to make a socket; and the handle could be of three forms: forked into which the stone tool rested, bent round the groove so that both ends were grasped,[69] or straight and fitting to a platform on the tool, which would involve more complex and stronger lashing.

The necked or waisted tool has a fairly wide shallow depression about two-thirds of the way back from the business-end. It is the only form known from the forest [fig. 65]. It is the commonest form in Niger, and has normally been found in association especially with the Ténéré-neolithic.[70] It occurs also in Tibesti, at Meniet,[71] on a few sites in northern Mali[72] and as far west as the fishing-neolithic site of Akreijit.[73]

The rilled tool, with a narrow well cut groove, has been found at Taferjit, Adrar Madet and on Tibesti.[74] It may be an early tool of Nilotic inspiration, as the rill was used for net weights at Early Khartum. There may be no connection with rilled hammers from western Algeria and Morocco,[75] whither the idea may have come from Spain.

The lugged axe, a specialized form with a narrow splaying border above the depression, has been found along the Tafassasset,[76] in Tibesti, and in a rudimentary form at Bamba (Mali).[77] It appears to be a copy in stone of an Egyptian metal form of the Old and Middle Kingdoms.[78] It would be possible to haft this type of axe into a perforated stick with use of wedges, which would be an advance on the lashed handle.

Saharan Rock Art

Mauny[79] proposed five stages of Saharan rock art, which he admits would be difficult to classify into an exact chronological scheme, owing to cultural time-lags. Style also is a dangerous criterion for chronology. His sequence was devised only for the southern Sahara, and cannot be applied to a site like Marhouma in the Saoura Valley,[80] where there is no tropical fauna and perhaps no domestic animals, so hunting will have remained important until a late date. I have added my suggestions as to the chronological stages:

1. Naturalist, with large tropical fauna	Early Sub-pluvial II
2. Bovidian, with little large tropical fauna; towards the end, sheep as well as oxen	Late Sub-pluvial II
3. Caballine	From about 1000 B.C.
4. Libyco-Berber, cavalry and beginning of camels	200 B.C.–A.D. 700
5. Arabo-Berber, camels, tifinagh inscriptions	A.D. 700 to present

Huard, with special reference to Tibesti, sets out a more complicated sequence[81] with transitional phases, especially between stages 1 and 2;

furthermore, in Tibesti stage 3 is rare, so 2 probably dragged on until the arrival of the camel.

The earliest stage appears to be preneolithic, without cattle, and can hardly start later than 6000 B.C. It should be possible to establish a geologico-climatic limit by means of patination, which requires displuvial conditions, and from formation of the shelters by disintegration of the rock under a humid climate, followed by deflation.[82] But these questions require further investigation.

It seems implied that rock art started rather suddenly. This should mean an invasion of artists, probably neanthropic, either into a Sahara which was recovering from aridity (e.g. Post-pluvial I–II), or to replace an earlier population of non-artists, who might be the last makers of the Saharan Aterian. That the invaders arrived before cattle is unimportant. The introduction of cattle would not necessitate an important new invasion, as hunting-people can readily adapt themselves to domestic animals.

Of the large tropical fauna, elephant and giraffe are common. Hippopotamus is portrayed rarely, though its bones occur in neolithic association, especially in the south Saharan lakes. Rhinoceros was retreating south-eastwards before the neolithic.[83] Bubalus antiquus appears in Algeria and the northern Sahara.[84] The elephant survived in North Africa and Tripolitania into Roman times;[85] the giraffe, by nature a steppe-animal, seems to have become extinct even later. The cattle paintings indicate large numbers of beasts. In a Sahara with such fauna there must have been not only open water but fairly lush vegetation, probably less so in Libya, and consequently a fairly high and reasonably dependable rainfall.

I do not propose to discuss Saharan art in detail, because it is a subject to itself, and topographically hardly falls within the limits of this book. I have included illustrations of a very few animals of different dates from the southern Sahara [fig. 46]. The important questions of horses, chariots and camels concern the Iron Age and will be postponed to chapter 5. I have already referred to Egyptian influences on Saharan art, the mouflon with solar disc, perhaps Egyptianizing figures from the Tassili. One other question is of archaeological interest: whether we can identify costume, tools and weapons on paintings of known stylistic phases.

The bow appears early in the bovidian period and perhaps occasionally earlier.[86] But the commonest early weapon is the throwing-stick, which is seldom assigned to Libyans on Egyptian monuments. On these the

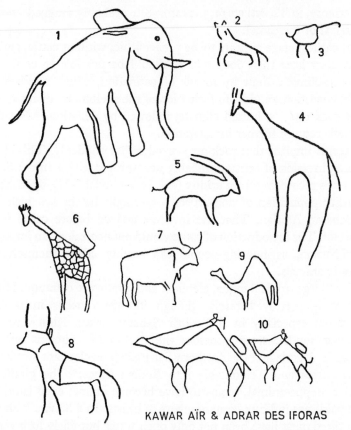

KAWAR AÏR & ADRAR DES IFORAS

FIG. 46 Selection of rock-engravings from southern fringe of the
Sahara

1. Djado	4. Agaouat	8. Anesok
2. Tadint	5. Adrar Zeline	9. Iférouane
3. Abezou	6. Arli well	10. Djado
	7. Orida	

*from Lhote, IFAN xiv (1952), p. 1268 ff., by permission of the author
and of I.F.A.N., Dakar*

bow is common, and Libyan archers with stone arrow-points are still
mentioned by Herodotus.[87] Bowmen are normally nude or clad in short
tunics or loincloths, without defensive armour or spear; they may carry
quivers on the back.[88] Their arrows are seldom shown in detail. There
is a suggestion in a reproduction from Enji (Aouker)[89] of barbed arrow-
heads stuck into a camel, so probably not of great antiquity.

There has been little attempt to associate the bovidian paintings with
archaeological deposits, and it is seldom certain that the paintings in

a shelter are contemporary with the remains in the floor. A typical neolithic assemblage with bones of oxen was found in the shelter of Aouanrhet (Tassili n'Ajjer).[90] There can be little doubt that most of the bovidian paintings are neolithic, though a few indicate men with iron weapons, so the keeping of cattle remained possible at least for a time during the Iron Age.

Horsemen may carry javelins, and contemporary with them are men on foot with large-bladed spears, almost certainly of metal. Spears without heads may be older and contemporary with the bowmen. Spearmen usually have small round shields, less commonly leather shields of figure-of-eight form.[91] They occasionally have swords, carried in scabbards at the waist.[92] The Saharan peoples may have had sufficient metallurgical knowledge to make an iron spear-head, which is little more than a plate. They are unlikely to have been able to forge swords, so unless these were smuggled or looted from the Roman empire, they are probably not earlier than the Arab invasions. Short metal daggers, large single-bladed knives, and what may be single picks or axes are represented. Basket-like saddles occur at Enneri Fofodé (Tibesti).[49] Spearmen commonly are shown with two or three horns on the head, which may be the ostrich feathers on Egyptian representations and were perhaps a mark of rank. They seem to have worn tunics, often rather longer than their predecessors. Robed figures may be contemporary.[93] Voluminous robes may have been worn by old men or priests at a time when the tunic was usual for warriors. Some robes are decorated with a panel in front or with chequer-pattern, especially in Aïr.[94] The long robe is worn by Libyans of rank on New Kingdom monuments, and was often richly ornamented.[95]

Extremely stylized engravings are fairly recent. They commonly show camels, and are often suggestive of woven material. Some on the walls of the Medracen (Algeria)[96] may have been added long after the construction. Camel-riders may carry small round or rectangular shields and spears or javelins.

The identification of weapons and tools on rock drawings does not give a satisfactory time-scale because little has been excavated in the Sahara, especially from the pre-Islamic Iron Age. Our most detailed and best dated representations are from Egypt; it is not certain that the same techniques and fashions were current at the same period in the central and western Sahara. However, when it is possible to carry out a large programme of detailed and careful archaeological investigation, and the activities of irresponsible collectors and local excavators

N

ministering to their demands are curbed, the Saharan paintings will provide an invaluable key to the material objects discovered.

The Copper Age in Morocco and Mauritania

Despite initial scepticism, evidence has accumulated that the chalcolithic Beaker-people established close relations with the Atlantic coast of North Africa. Beakers have been found at Dar-es-Soltan (with an archer's wrist-guard),[97] Rhar-oum-el-Fernan,[98] Gar Cahal level IIIa[99] and Achakar.[100] The contact must go back behind the Beaker-culture, if the making of cardial pottery came from Spain (above, p. 156); and beakers do not occur in the older neolithic levels in North Africa. There are other forms of pottery common to Spain and North Africa, such as the lemon-shaped vases from Volubilis and Achakar.[101] Whether there was colonization from Europe is less clear. Beakers have been found mainly in caves, which seem to have been regularly occupied by the local population. Important Beaker-settlements are not known, of a type which regular colonists would establish in a foreign country; but search may not have been in the right directions.

It is not surprising that the Beaker-people explored the African coast. Navigation had long been practised in the western Mediterranean, and Iberian ships had moved up the Atlantic coast of Europe, carrying the megalithic culture. The African coast may have been less inviting, with fewer natural resources and perhaps a less hospitable population. The prevailing northerly winds and currents, though not insuperable to navigators north of Cape Bojador, must have made the return voyage difficult.

There was probably fairly regular contact during the Iberian Late Neolithic and Chalcolithic.[102] There is little evidence during the later Bronze Age, and communication may have lapsed until the first Punic colonization of Morocco, perhaps as early as the seventh century B.C. (below, p. 254).[103]

The Mediterranean people introduced North Africa and especially Morocco to the use of metal. There was hardly more than a Copper Age, tin-bronze has very rarely been found, there is a tanged dagger of arsenical bronze of European chalcolithic type from Cap Chenoua near Tipasa.[104] But the rock engravings at Oukaimeden, presumably a sanctuary of the Iberian colonists, and elsewhere in the Atlas represent Iberian chalcolithic weapons such as riveted triangular daggers, halberds, leaf-shaped javelins and perhaps flat axes[105] along with human and animal figures of markedly African style.

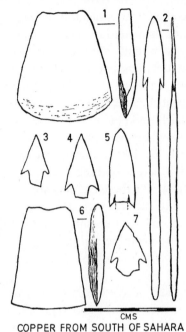

FIG. 47 Selection of copper objects
from Mauritania

1. Oued Initi,   6. Western
   west of Oualata   Mauritania
2. Marsa Djerida   7. 50 kms. NW.
3–5. Mts. Ibi, Adrar   Tichitt

by permission from Mauny R.,
1952 (1), p. 567

CMS

COPPER FROM SOUTH OF SAHARA

The knowledge of copper and apparently of its metallurgy reached
Mauritania at an uncertain date.[106] As the few pieces found [fig. 47]
are of archaic European types,[107] it probably was carried by chalcolithic settlers in Morocco. The centre of the industry must have been
the copper-mines of Akjoujt,[108] where vigorous late medieval exploitation has destroyed traces of older working. Whether the metallurgists
came by sea and were unable to return against wind and current, or by
the difficult overland route known in the Middle Ages and marked by
late chariot engravings[109] we do not know. But that contact from early
days was possible through the western Sahara is shown by stone
hoes of West African type from El Fahs near Tangier[110] and from
Cuatro Puertas in Grand Canary, presumably carried by immigrating
Guanches.

Other old copper-mines are known in West Africa, near Nioro,[111]
near Tessalit, and in Niger at Azelik and Marandet. But the only artefact of primitive type discovered outside Mauritania is one arrow-head
from Niger.[112]

The Preneolithic Fringe

It is beginning to transpire that around the neolithic focus in Africa there were cultures of neanthropic character and partly neolithic affinity, but without the principal characteristics of the neolithic. The evidence does not allow us to say whether they knew cultivation or domestic animals. They apparently did not know pottery and polished stone, and established habitation is doubtful. It is not suggested that these cultures were contemporary. Indeed, there are probably very large lacunae in our knowledge; for while we can form a fairly good picture of the whole Sahara, we know very little about what was going on round its margins except in a few discrete areas, Senegal, Bamako, Ghana, perhaps Nigeria, Niamey. From east of Lake Chad there is nothing.

The term mesolithic is unhappy in Africa. Yet these cultures are not epipalaeolithic, a word that can be applied to cultures with strong roots in the palaeolithic, like the upper Sebilian or Late Lupemban, but not to those which are feeling out towards the neolithic and seem to be intrusive and to displace the M.S.A. The term preneolithic is perhaps more exact.

A preneolithic phase may be characteristic of West Africa. It is to be located at all times beyond the area where climate and vegetation permitted the basic neolithic techniques. A few thousand years ago this was in the orchard bush and forest margins; today it is on the fringe of the desert. In the preneolithic zone, wherever it lies, cultivation is impossible or chancy. Population therefore cannot agglomerate. But scanty groups of men live on nomadic animals, whether wild or domestic; and the economy is hunting and herding, with a dash of brigandage against the cultivators.

The situation to the south and east of the Sahara cannot be disentangled, because exploration has been limited in the Sudan outside the Nile Valley and there is nothing from Equatorial Africa south of Lake Fittri. Mention has been made of a mesolithic collection from Debeira West (North Sudan) [fig. 37, above, pp. 153–4]; the absence of burins, microburins and backed blades rules out association with the epipalaeolithic of the Maghreb, and suggests an outlier of an undefined sub-Saharan mesolithic province. Some of the pieces recently published from Gaboon[113] suggest a preneolithic culture with Saharan influences, especially in the points, also resembling the preneolithic of Guinea, and with flaked axes, precursors of the edge-ground celt and similar to the epi-Lupemban flaked axe from Boutounguissi [fig. 24]. The Late Tsitolian of the Congo seems to be a complex culture which has not yet been sorted and properly arranged. In certain facies there is marked Saharan influence on types of arrow-head.[114] Though dates have been obtained for the Late Tsitolian (e.g. Mount Gafula, Lv-45, 6030 ± 190), it has not yet been possible to pinpoint the introduction of Saharan or neolithic forms.

TIEMASSAS. On the coast of Senegal a characteristic preneolithic industry has been identified. The type-site is Tiemassas, where pieces occur over a wide area beside the mouth of a lagoon, one of the few sources of drinkable water between Rufisque and Joal.[115] The only artefacts are finely worked stone tools, pottery celts and other remains have nowhere been found. The site is geologically dated. The artefacts occur on a thin crust of lateritic nodules, which in places overlie the fine gravel of the Flandrian beach, and underlie the low redistributed dunes which almost certainly belong to Post-pluvial III. On these dunes at Dakar occurs the Senegal neolithic. The lateritic nodules will belong to the displuvial phase of Sub-pluvial II, after the start of the regression from Beach VI. So the site may be dated to the second millennium B.C., probably to its second half.

The industry bears no resemblance to the Ultimate M.S.A. of Pte. de Fann, which lasted until the transgression of Beach VI and then apparently died out [fig. 36, above, p. 141]. The principal forms [fig. 48] are finely worked small bifaces, especially leaf-shaped points, in general larger and more clumsy than those of the Sahara and probably used for tipping spears rather than arrows. There are also chisels, disc-scrapers, end- and side-scrapers (rather crude), blunt triangular points probably used as scrapers, and awls. Harpoons, which one might expect on such a site, have not been found.

Hugot has suggested that the Tiemassas-industry is directly derived from a western offshoot of the south Saharan Aterian, found in the Adrar of Mauritania, which has very few pedunculate points. This is not unlikely as the tanged point occurs occasionally also at Tiemassas.

This culture has been identified three kilometres to the south at Pte. Sarène. There are almost certainly stray pieces of it, apparently unstratified, among the collections from the Dakar peninsula, for instance from Yof, Ouakam and N'gor.[116] It is noted there that biface lance-heads do not occur in association with the common neolithic biface arrow-heads. The unusual pedunculate point from N'gor Island,[117] which can hardly be Aterian but does not fit into the neolithic series, may well belong to the Tiemassas-culture.[118]

Tiemassas-points have occasionally been found with less typical microliths in the Bamako area, on a stratified level well below the

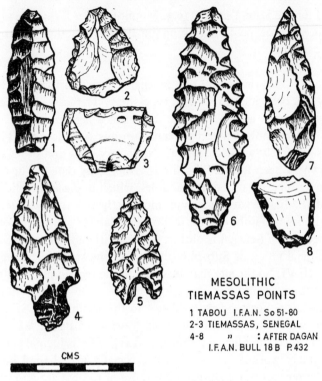

MESOLITHIC
TIEMASSAS POINTS

1 TABOU I.F.A.N. So 51-80
2-3 TIEMASSAS, SENEGAL
4-8   „   : AFTER DAGAN
I.F.A.N. BULL 18 B P. 432

CMS

FIG. 48

by permission of author

neolithic surface on the River Samanko, at Tabou shelter [fig. 48 1],[119] and as far east as Kakalapara on the lateritic nodules of the inner silt terrace of the Black Volta.[120]

THE MIDDLE NIGER. Sometimes associated with Tiemassas-points are blunt tanged points, uniface or biface, which I have called fish spears though their true purpose is unknown.[121] There is one from Tiemassas [fig. 48 4]. They have turned up on sites in the upper basin of the River Senegal, notably at Noumoubougou with an awl and side-scrapers. There are two crude ones, unstratified and unassociated, from Northern Ghana; and two tanged quartz bifaces, found in preneolithic context, from Ghana and Upper Volta[122] may belong to the same group.

Niamou [fig. 49], about 200 kms. north-north-east of Bamako, has none of the fine neolithic stone-work of the Senegal Valley and no pottery, only a very crude celt, two scrapers with a notch at the base, what may be a piece of a slicer, some small basalt flakes and several

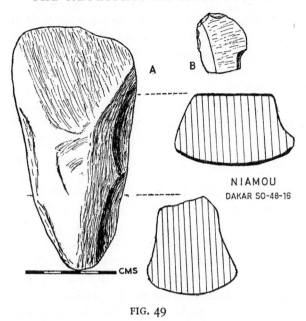

NIAMOU
DAKAR SO-48-16

CMS

FIG. 49

A. Sandstone axe, weath-
ered and with slight
lateritic crust

B. Basalt scraper, notched
at base.

pestles of rectangular section. Several pieces have a lateritic patination, so are probably older than the end of Sub-pluvial II. The collection may most suitably be classed with the preneolithic.

The most important site of this phase from the Niger–Senegal area is Kourounkorokale Lower. Although the report[55] is not everywhere clear and excavation techniques may not have attained modern standards, it seems probable that the burials were sunk into the lower deposit; so contamination with the neolithic of the upper level is likely. Many of the animal bones figured seem to be unworked fragments. The harpoons probably belong to the lower level, though they were found close to the burials and could be associated with them. Polished points and bone knives accompany harpoons fairly regularly in the southern Sahara. Some of the unpolished pointed chips may have been utilized; but without close examination it is easy to mistake natural for intentional fractures. One or two perforated bones and one piece clearly shaped at the end but to no obvious purpose [pl. VIII 28] must also be reckoned as artefacts. The shaped shells described can hardly be accepted without re-examination; there seem to have been no shell beads, such as were found at Ntereso.

Most of the stone industry claimed to come from the lower level probably did. As illustrated it is clearly much rougher and very different from the conventional neolithic of the upper level, with its points, blades, scrapers and crescents. If one may trust the illustrations, the lower level yielded blades and backed blades, chisels, awls, choppers and a variety of scrapers. There were a few pieces which could be described as flaked axes, smaller than those from Boutounguissi [fig. 24] and Chawenu (above, p. 139). There was no pottery and no celts. There does not seem to be anything which could be classed as Ultimate Middle Stone-Age.

There is no chronological evidence. The bone-work compares closely with the Saharan neolithic, and one stone piece [pl. IV I] seems comparable to the Saharan matchet-knives. But in general the resemblance is much closer to the pre-neolithic of the southern savannah, so the site must be included rather in the Guinea province. It is unfortunate that the material at Bamako has been badly stored and by 1960 most labels had disappeared; there is not much at Dakar. So it is impossible to re-examine it. The site looks unpromising and would hardly reward an attempt at re-excavation.

THE LOWER NIGER. A large and indiscriminate collection was made at Niamey–Est [fig. 50].[123] It cannot be guaranteed that a quartz lip-plug and several beads are not intruders, though bead-polishers could well belong to the site. There is probably one hoe, celts are doubtful, and there is an upper grindstone of shoe-last type which does not appear to be early. Most of the material is in quartz. There is one flattish pyramidical core and one bladelet-core. A few crudely tanged pieces may imitate Saharan arrow-heads. There are a few fine microliths, thin awls steeply trimmed on both edges, very small crescents, small gouges, a blunt-backed bladelet and end-scrapers. Two roughly flaked rods are reminiscent of the much smaller rods found in the Kintampo-neolithic of Ghana.

This site again seems to belong to the province of the southern savannah, with a few Saharan intrusions. Similar material has been found at Bac Niger, 80 kms up the Niger, with a winged point probably imitating a Saharan form.[124] Other sites around Niamey have yielded nothing typical.

THE SOUTHERN SAVANNAH AND FOREST. Large preneolithic or mesolithic collections have been made in Ghana, and the same culture

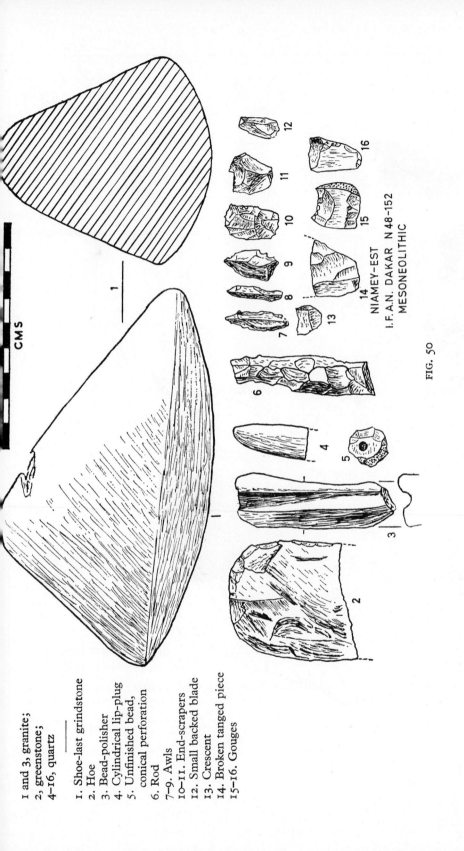

CMS

1. Shoe-last grindstone
2. Hoe
3. Bead-polisher
4. Cylindrical lip-plug
5. Unfinished bead, conical perforation
6. Rod
7–9. Awls
10–11. End-scrapers
12. Small backed blade
13. Crescent
14. Broken tanged piece
15–16. Gouges

1 and 3, granite;
2, greenstone;
4–16, quartz

NIAMEY-EST
I.F.A.N. DAKAR N 48-152
MESONEOLITHIC

FIG. 50

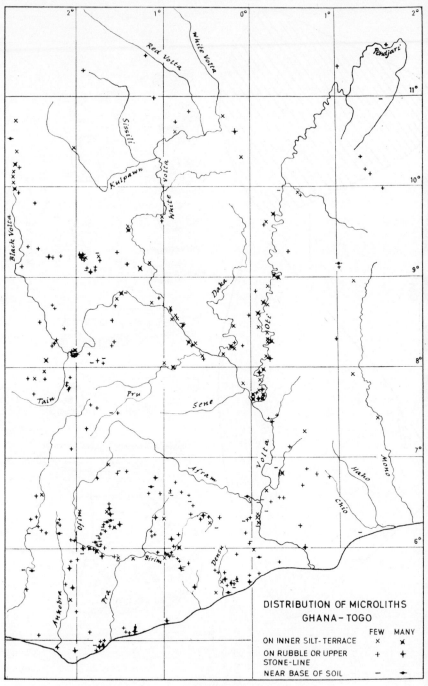

FIG. 51(a)

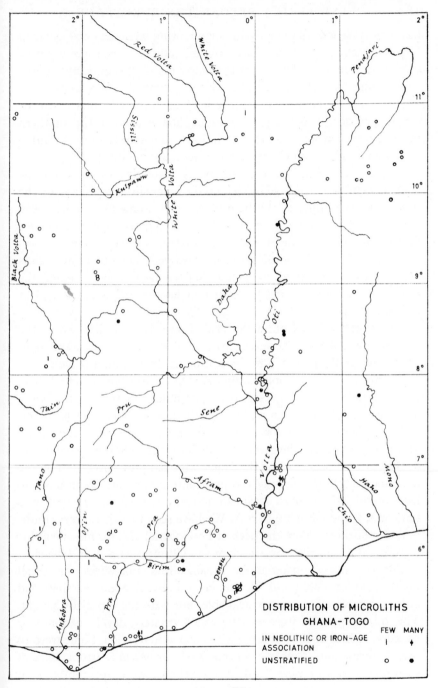

FIG. 51(b)

has turned up less abundantly in neighbouring territories and as far as Nigeria. Many sites have yielded only microliths, without pottery celts or hoes; where only a few pieces have been found, it is difficult to assert that the site is not in fact neolithic. But the number of sites known with a fairly uniform microlithic culture is so great [fig. 51] that it can be stated confidently that a pre-neolithic phase existed in the southern savannah, into which neolithic techniques and tool-types were introduced with only small changes in the microlithic industry.[125]

In southern lands the preneolithic is regularly stratified, on the laterite nodules which have formed on the inner silt terraces, and on the uppermost stone-line at the base of the soil. Sometimes it has been possible to identify the true neolithic at a slightly higher level [see fig. 3], but often owing to erosion or slow soil-formation the pre-neolithic and neolithic surfaces have telescoped. The quartz microliths are hardly ever patinated, indicating that they were deposited after the chemical processes leading to patination had ceased, near the end of Sub-pluvial II.

The stone-work of Kourounkorokale Lower is rather like that of the Guinea preneolithic. There are closer similarities to a site on the inner silt terrace at Bougouni. The desiccation of the southern Sahara must have driven neolithic people southward. One would expect to find them along the Niger. Desplagnes[126] describes numerous sites on the Niger up-stream from Labbezenga; but he left no exact record of localities, and the material was not kept separate. Either some neolithic people moved south towards the orchard bush, losing most of their techniques; or they ejected people along the Niger who had previously been on the neolithic fringe. In this way the preneolithic microlithic cultures will have reached the Guinea savannah and forest, where they fused with remnants of the Ultimate M.S.A. We have seen that there were south-bound influences before the peak of Post-pluvial III, for mesoneolithic features appear in the stone-work of the Ultimate M.S.A. of Ghana.

The commonest material for mesoneolithic microliths was small quartz pebbles. Pebbles of silcrete, chalcedony, fine-grained shale and other rocks were used where available, but were not especially sought. The quartz pebbles were usually rolled crystals, devoid of joints or fractures, which could not have withstood water-action. Some were of recent formation, pebbles concentrated in streams from ancient conglomerates also were used. Such pebbles were apparently often sought from considerable distances. They must have been difficult to flake, and for this reason probably had not been used by the M.S.A.

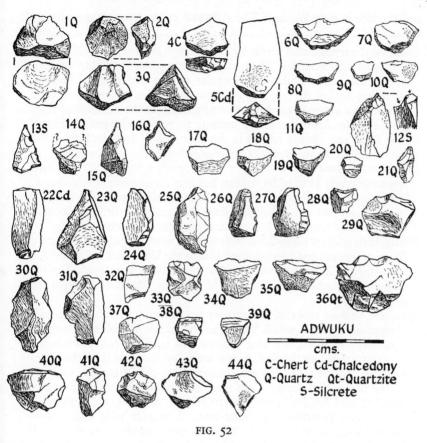

FIG. 52

from Davies O., 1964 (2), fig. 80

people. There is no evidence that they were broken on dimpled anvil-stones, which are not uncommon in Ghana but do not usually occur on mesoneolithic sites. They may have been broken by heating, which is apparently feasible.

From smaller pebbles there would be no cores. Larger pieces of quartz were sometimes fashioned into pyramidical or conical cores, which would give small flakes of Levallois type with faceted butt. More frequently flakes were detached from one side of a pebble, leaving chopper-like cores, while the flake would normally retain some pebble surface on the butt. Regular use of the microburin-technique is doubtful.

A fairly large and apparently early assemblage of microliths was found at Adwuku (Shai Hills). There seemed to be a similar collection from Babun on the River Afram; but this was lost in a boat accident, and the site is now flooded. The Adwuku collection contains [fig. 52]:

Chisels and microtranchet arrow-heads, common in all parts of Ghana and
neighbouring territories. They may be rectangular (probably chisels),
trapezoidal, semi-circular or triangular with a slight tang (probably
arrow-heads); but the tang is never so pronounced as in Egypt. I separate
chisels from arrow-heads somewhat arbitrarily on the evidence of wear
on the blade. Arrow-heads are unlikely to become chipped or dinted.
The chisel was already known in the Late M.S.A. It is doubtful if the
microtranchet arrow-head was introduced before the mesoneolithic.

Crescents, segments less than half a circle, nearly symmetrical. The back
is usually partly blunted by flaking, but may retain some pebble-cortex.
The edge may be formed by the intersection of two principal flakes or
of one main and one subsidiary flake. Crescents are believed to have
been used for arrows, perhaps mounted loosely as detachable barbs.

Blades, both primary blade-flakes with signs of wear, backed blades blunted
by steep retouch and blunt-backed blades, the blunt back being a single
flake-surface. Either this was struck after the blade was detached or the
blade was detached from a corner of the core. Blades of all types are
common.

Scrapers. Various types of end-scraper are common. Duckbills, an end-
scraper on a blade, which belong to the upper palaeolithic–Capsian–
Smithfield tradition, are rare because this tradition had not reached
West Africa, where the M.S.A. was immediately replaced by the mesoneolithic. I have separated end-scrapers from chisels by the convexity
of the blade. Side-scrapers are more amorphous, but fairly common.
Notched and hollow scrapers were rare at Adwuku, but have been
found fairly plentifully on other sites. A regular wide and shallow
hollow, such as occurs in the Capsian and Smithfield, is rare; so it
seems likely that the purpose which such scrapers served, whether for
shaving poles or fraying sinews, was not practised in West Africa.

Pieces with rudimentary tangs, usually blades or scrapers, appear in the
mesoneolithic in Ghana, and several are figured in the collection from
Koumi, near Bobo Diulasso.[127] Many are so crude that they can with
difficulty be described as tools. The rudimentary tang is found also
in the Guinea Aterian, and may be a survival. It seldom appears in
definitely neolithic association, except on long blades, which appear
to be a neolithic development.[128] At Adwuku were two finely worked
points with short tang, two also from the neolithic level at Legon
Botanic Gardens. Others from Babun were cursorily noticed before
the collection was lost. These may be unskilful adaptations of Saharan
tanged arrow-heads.

Short, blunt-nosed awls, usually made by trimming slight hollows behind
the intended point, are fairly common. They would be unsuitable for
perforating material like leather, but may have been used for smoothing
a perforation.

Two microlithic types which are moderately common are not represented at Adwuku. There were certainly in the preneolithic of Ghana a few simple burins [fig. 53 2, 30, 33, and 39]; apparently only the *bec-de-flûte* type, with the removal of one or more spalls, was used. Small untanged points are less certain. Most of those which Shaw illustrates from the neolithic site of Abetifi[129] may be discarded chips, or if held at another angle could be classed under a different heading. Pieces carefully trimmed at the point have been identified only in association with pottery. Drills have not been found in the mesoneolithic.

It would be difficult to recognize crudely worked macrolithic pieces except on sealed stratified sites. One or two have probably been found in preneolithic association, others will certainly turn up when large-scale excavation of old land surfaces can be carried out. Partially flaked small picks have been found in Togoland[130] and may be related to the two flaked axes thence (above, p. 139), which appear to have been in Ultimate M.S.A. association. They may also be related to the neolithic hoe and the edge-ground celt.

The vastly greater number of sites known in Ghana than in other territories makes it necessary to discuss preneolithic typology almost entirely with reference to Ghana. Small collections from neighbouring territories indicate, however, that essentially the same culture was widely distributed. A good assemblage from Koumi (Upper Volta) has been published.[127] A small group from Ropp (Jos Plateau)[131] seems comparable to the assemblages from Ghana. A collection recently published from Old Oyo (Nigeria)[132] exhibits certain differences. Crescents are dominant over trapezoidal microtranchets, and there are hardly any obvious chisels. Blades are rare, though pieces described as points may be blunt-backed blades. Scrapers are rare, the only clearly identifiable type being a thumbnail end-scraper. There are a few burins and awls, practically no pieces with rudimentary tang.

It is not easy to make comparisons farther afield, unless collections are published with full illustrations, because the terminology for African microliths is not well fixed. Microlithic industry similar to that from Ghana has been found in neolithic association in the caves near Kindia (F. Guinea), and will be discussed below. Kakimbon cave near Konakry is not well described.[133] The principal raw material is hematite, which would flake differently from quartz. There are said to have been celts, grindstones and grooved stones. Chisels, blades, microtranchet, endscrapers and apparently biface points suggest comparison with Tiemassas rather than with Ghana. One sherd is presumably neolithic.

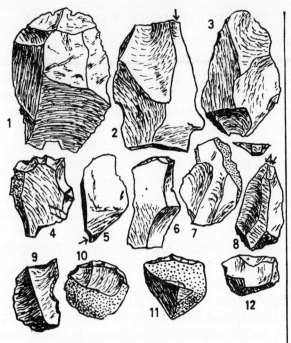

OKUMENI 4kms FROM F.R. BOUNDARY
ALL QUARTZ

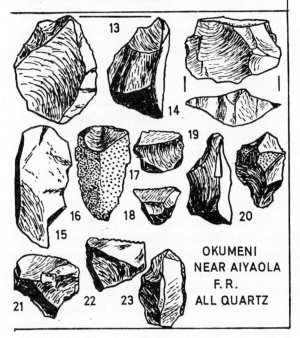

OKUMENI
NEAR AIYAOLA
F.R.
ALL QUARTZ

FIG. 53a

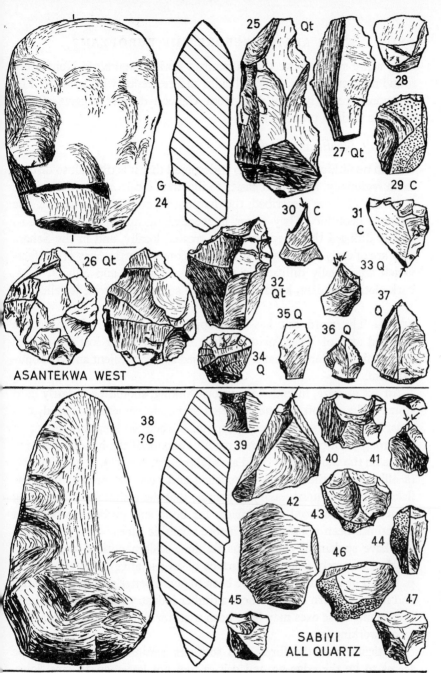

ASANTEKWA WEST

SABIYI
ALL QUARTZ

MESONEOLITHIC LARGER GROUPS: S.GHANA, ASHANTI

━━━━━━━━━━━ CMS

C: CHERT   G: GREENSTONE   Q: QUARTZ   Qt: QUARTZITE

FIG. 53b

from Davies O., 1964 (2), fig. 81

In white sands above the Lupemban horizon at Pointe Noire were found miniature cores, backed blades and crescents, with a hoe.[134] The collections recently published from Gaboon do not suggest affinity with the Guinea preneolithic.

Types of Neolithic Artefact

Certain neolithic artefacts are so widespread that it is difficult to discuss them regionally, and much easier to illustrate local varieties in a single synthesis. I have described the harpoons and waisted axes of the Saharan neolithic. They occur in wooded savannah, but are not so widely diffused that they cannot be treated locally, and in the Sahara they are of early date. I want here to speak more particularly of artefacts which are equally diffused in the forest savannah and Sahara, celts, bark-cloth pounders, kwes or perforated stones, and stone jewellery.

CELTS. The word celt has been applied, perhaps abusively, to the polished axes of West Africa. It has, however, so far lost its original connotation in Europe that it may be used as a convenient and economical term.

An axe or adze, intended for wood-working, should be of fairly hard stone. Celts of soft or uncompacted stone are sometimes found, and must have had some different purpose. A wood-working tool must also be strongly hafted. It could not readily function if the handle were tied on, as on the waisted and rilled axes (above, pp. 169–70). It gains greatly in efficiency if the surface is polished and does not present irregular flake-scars. It is unnecessary to assume that the technique of polishing stone was introduced into Africa, for bone and probably wood had sometimes been polished long before neolithic times.

I have spoken of the curious fashion, seldom noticed outside the Fayum, of partly flaking the surface of an axe after polishing (above, p. 155). The intention may have been to give a better grip to the handle; and in the western desert, where a timber industry can never have been important, these axes may have been used for some purpose other than wood-working.

Particularly in the forest and southern savannah the earliest type seems to be the edge-ground celt, a tool not less than 10 cms. long, shaped by flaking and then rubbed over, especially to give a keen blade which is usually convex, but also to remove irregularities on the faces. Thus traces of polishing may be seen on any part; but it was not deep enough to remove all flake-scars. An edge-ground celt is usually fairly

GALGROU
NEAR PONTYEBA H.V.

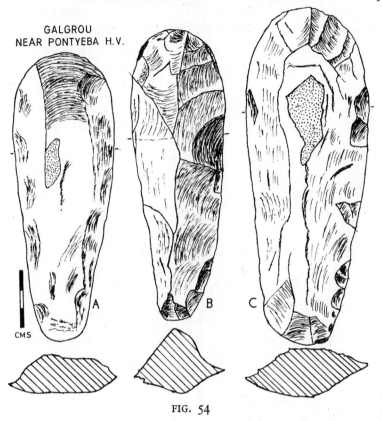

CMS

FIG. 54

thin, the surfaces are parallel, and the sides taper slightly to the butt, which is seldom, however, pointed.

This axe was perhaps at first flaked without polishing. From Galgrou (Upper Volta) come eight long axes, seven flaked and one edge-ground [fig. 54]; unfortunately there is no report either on the exact locality or on the association. Flaked axes are probably a development of the Lupemban culture [cf. fig. 24]. The Lupemban parallel-sided pick or gouge was made more serviceable for wood-working by being thinner, and the tapering of the blade gave a better hold when it was learnt how to fit it into a socketed handle.

Edge-ground celts are not uncommon in the southern Congo[135] and have been found in the ill-explored Equateur Province.[136] There is an interesting collection from the Mouka Plateau (Ubangui–Chari),[137] from sites on the concession of the Société Remina. One of two have been recently published from Gaboon,[113] and there are some from the Cameroons, but practically none are reported from Nigeria or Dahomey,

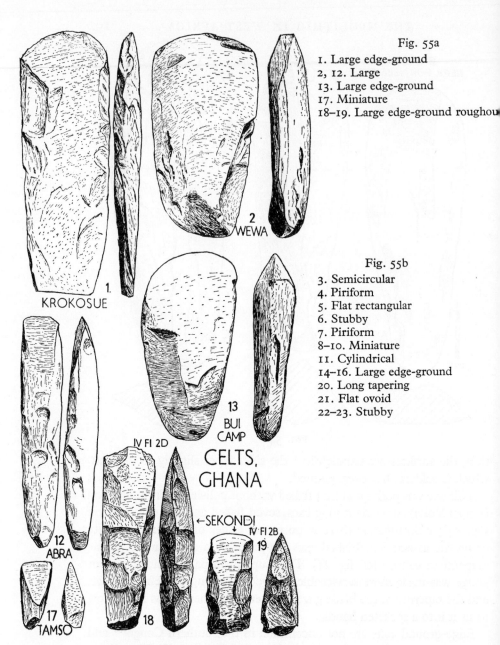

CELTS, GHANA

KROKOSUE

WEWA

BUI CAMP

ABRA

TAMSO

IV FI 2D

←SEKONDI

IV FI 2B

FIG. 55a Types of celt, Ghana

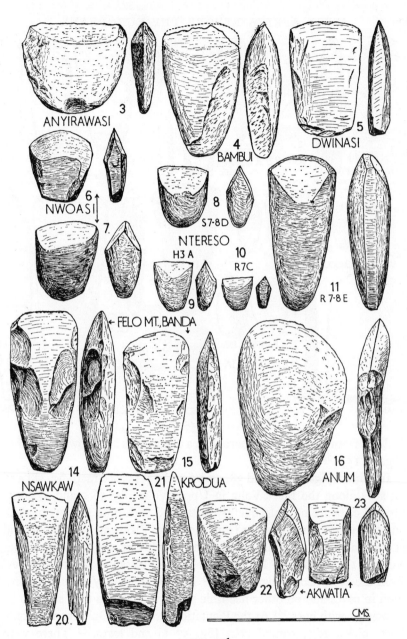

ANYIRAWASI
3

BAMBUI
4

DWINASI
5

NWOASI
6
7

8
S7-8D

NTERESO
H3A
9
10
R7C
11
R 7-8 E

← FELO MT., BANDA

14
NSAWKAW

15
KRODUA
21

16
ANUM

20.
22
AKWATIA
23

CMS.

FIG. 55b

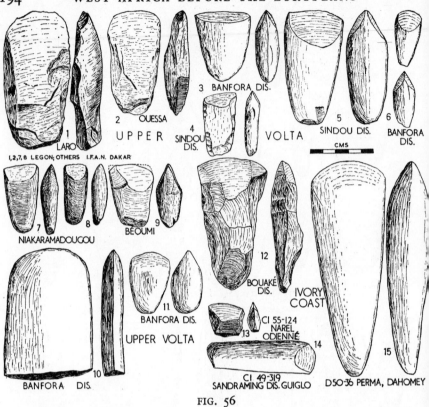

FIG. 56

Indeed, from the latter not more than a dozen celts are known altogether [fig. 56 15].[138]

In Ghana [figs. 53 24 and 38, 55 1 2 and 13–15; see map, fig. 58] and on sites along the Black Volta in Upper Volta [fig. 56 1 and 2] edge-ground celts are not infrequently associated with hoes (below, p. 214), and two of the limande-hoes from the Accra Plains are slightly ground at the blade. A good many were collected without association in Upper Volta in the districts of Banfora and Bobo Diulasso.[139] There are a few from the Ivory Coast [fig. 56 12].[140] In F. Guinea they are not uncommon in caves and on other neolithic sites, where again they seem to be associated with hoes.[141] At the Plantation Roullin at Dubréka were only hoes, picks, edge-ground celts [fig. 57 1] and kwes.[142] There were edge-ground celts also at Kakimbon cave.[133]

There are some edge-ground celts from Mali, especially from the upper Niger and upper Senegal valleys. At least one is illustrated from Kourounkorokale Upper.[143] There are perhaps some from Bamako, a rough one from Niamou [fig. 49 A], and one in a collection from near

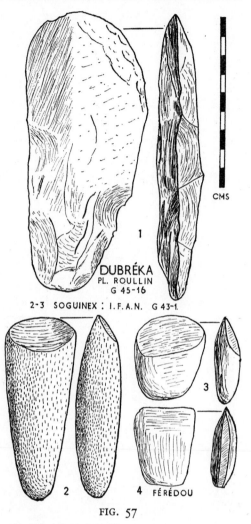

CMS

1

DUBRÉKA
PL. ROULLIN
G 45-16

2-3 SOGUINEX : I.F.A.N. G 43-1.

3

2   4 FÉRÉDOU

FIG. 57

Ségou [fig. 59 1]. Several have been found in the upper valley of the River Baoulé, west-north-west of Bamako, and one at Sénoudébou (Senegal).

The distribution of celts of form approaching cylindrical is in general more northerly than that of edge-ground celts, and complementary to it. Cylindrical celts are usually of hard eruptive stone, carefully shaped by fine pecking and ground only near the blade. The edge-ground celt is known in the Nile Valley and appears in the Ténéré-neolithic [fig. 41 1], but not otherwise in the Sahara and northern savannah.

Cylindrical celts are found in Niger in association with the

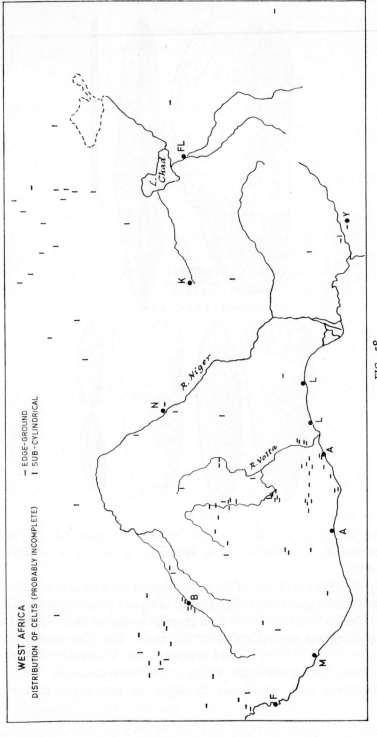

WEST AFRICA
DISTRIBUTION OF CELTS (PROBABLY INCOMPLETE)

— EDGE-GROUND
I SUB-CYLINDRICAL

FIG. 58

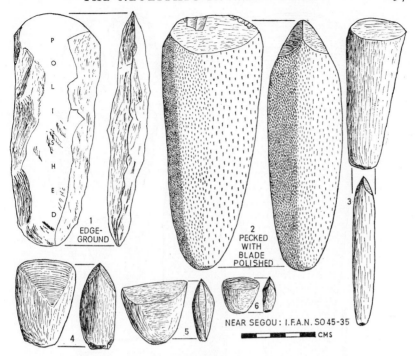

1
EDGE-
GROUND

2
PECKED
WITH
BLADE
POLISHED

3

6

NEAR SEGOU: I.F.A.N. SO 45-35

4

5

CMS

FIG. 59

Ténéré neolithic [fig. 61 2], at Ehi Mounto with a neolithic of more agricultural facies,[144] at In Guezzam which is a settlement of the hunting-fishing neolithic [fig. 61 1], and in some numbers in the southern part of the territory, in the zone of the Guinea mesoneolithic, where Labouret collected from Ct. Torodi near Say [fig. 61 8]. The piece from In Guezzam is unusual, in that it was pecked all over and the blade formed by flaking, not grinding. There are a very few from Tchad.[145] There are a good many from Nigeria, especially from the Jos Plateau.[146] They seem to drive a wedge between the Central and West African provinces of the edge-ground celt, and occur as far south as the districts of Bamenda and Bafia in the Cameroons[147] and perhaps also in northern Dahomey.[148] Very little information is, however, available about types of celt throughout this area.

In Upper Volta polished cylindrical celts have been collected in the districts of Ouahigouya and Sindou [fig. 56 5]. They are not known from the Ivory Coast, and only three examples have been found in Ghana, two of them on sites with markedly northern affinities and probably occupied by invaders, Ntereso and Bui; the third is a stray from Jirapa in the Geological Survey collection.

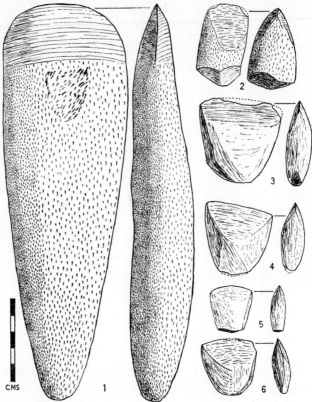

CMS 1

KARKARICHINKAT, TILEMSI VALLEY : 1-3 NORD 4-6 SUD

FIG. 60

None have been found in the Ivory Coast. There is a good number of pecked gouges from the Soguinex mines of F. Guinea [fig. 57 2]. They appear in northern Mali, near Ségou [fig. 59 2], in the Tilemsi Valley [fig. 60 1] and near Guir.[149] They have been rarely found in southern Mauritania.[150]

Most of those from Ghana and F. Guinea, which lie outside the normal area of distribution, are fashioned as gouges [figs. 55 11, 57 2]. Apparently the cylindrical blank was pecked all over and ground to a concave blade only on one face. One of the celts from Termitt–Sud also is ground to a gouge.

In fact, the cylindrical celt is not a very practical forester's tool. It is too thick to be an axe, and would be difficult to use as an adze. It could find specialized uses in the carpenter's shop; but most, from regions with hardly any trees, were probably not for wood-working. Some

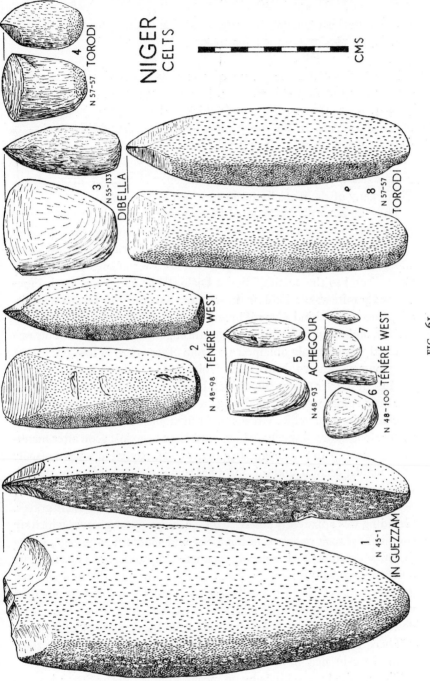

NIGER CELTS

CMS

4 TORODI
N 57-57

3 DIBELLA
N 55-133

8 TORODI
N 57-57

2 TÉNÉRÉ WEST
N 48-98

5 ACHEGOUR
N 48-93

7 TÉNÉRÉ WEST
6 TÉNÉRÉ WEST
N 48-100

1 IN GUEZZAM
N 45-1

FIG. 61

have not been sharpened. It is suggested that in the Sahara they are not unfinished axes but served for making the smooth, deep grooves of rock engravings.[151]

By far the commonest type of celt throughout West Africa is a stubby instrument 5–8 cms. long. In the northern zone [figs. 56 5–6, 59 3–4, 61 3–4] they are usually thick and sub-cylindrical, carefully polished all over. In the forest some are fairly thin with parallel faces [figs. 55 5 and 16, 56 4 7 8 and 14, 57 3–4, 60 3–4, 67 8]. Shaw[129] drew up an elaborate typology of those from Ghana, which at present seems meaningless, though local and chronological varieties may emerge when many of them are found in stratified association.

They are normally made of hard fine-grained stone which was ground to a sharp blade from both faces. Some of these stones patinate rapidly in the ground, so the serviceability of the original instrument is difficult to appreciate from modern finds. In the north-eastern Congo,[152] the Ivory Coast[153] and to the north of Fouta Djalon[154] hematite was used. Fine-grained granite was available in the southern Sahara.[155] In Ghana deposits of greenstone behind Cape Three Points and beach pebbles were exploited, and roughouts were exported throughout the forest.[156] This raw material was certainly obtained also from other areas. A few greenstone roughouts are known from Upper Volta and the northern Ivory Coast.

Most of the very short celts which have been found are rejects, which had been resharpened again and again until they could no longer be set efficiently in the handle. Greenstone roughouts are about fifteen centimetres long, and a few celts, which must have been lost soon after manufacture, are up to this length [e.g. fig. 55 12]. Roughouts were usually of triangular section, and this form has sometimes left traces on the finished celt [e.g. fig. 55 23]. This may be seen particularly on celts from Sekondi [fig. 55 18–19], which are mint-pieces made for deposit in graves. Grinding was apparently practised on the long narrow grooves which are common on rock outcrops in the forest and southern savannah. In the forest, where most rock is deeply weathered, advantage was taken of any outcrop, especially in recent valleys, or for instance the unweathered granite dome at Ntonsu, north-east of Kumasi. Portable grindstones were used. One was found with two celts, which had not been worn down to the stump, at Felo Mountain near Banda [fig. 55 14–15].

There is little information about roughouts in the northern zone. Hematite celts may have been made from river pebbles.

The polished stone axe is by no means confined to the Stone Age. As a cheap and serviceable tool it far outlasted the discovery of iron. The enormous numbers in southern Ghana could not all have been made by neolithic people, who were only beginning to penetrate the forest. At Sekondi celts were being used and made as late as A.D. 1500. Until modern times they have been collected for magical purposes, and can still be bought in the market at Kumasi. So the occurrence of one or two celts on a recent site without flakes or roughouts is no evidence of continuing utilization.

Occasional celts seem to copy metal forms, such as one of rectangular section from Bafoulabé.[157] From a diamond-working at Banankoro (F. Guinea) comes a long, narrow celt of dolerite with splaying blade, a form very unlikely to have been devised except in metal.[158]

In all areas are found miniature celts, in the Ténéré-culture [fig. 61 6–7], in other groups of the southern Sahara [fig. 60 5–6], on the upper Niger [fig. 59 6], near Dakar, in the Ivory Coast near Odienné [fig. 56 13], at Ntereso, probably a settlement in Ghana of invaders from the north [fig. 55 9–10], and in the Kintampo-culture, also probably of northern origin. They must have had a special purpose, presumably for some fine craft especially in the northern zone. Some of those found in hoards in Ghana may have been deposited ritually, so they do not essentially belong to the culture of the southern savannah and forest. At Ofuman one and probably several were found in a stream with some beads.[159]

Principally in the Ivory Coast [fig. 62][160] have been found unassociated a few celts up to sixty centimetres long, which would be too brittle for practical use and must have been ceremonial. One from Fama (Mali)[161] has painted bands. Their date is unknown. Several up to 35 cms. long, less exaggerated than those from the Ivory Coast, have been found in River Ofin, Tano and other rivers in Ghana, where they may have been offerings.[162]

BARK-CLOTH POUNDERS. In the Soguinex workings in F. Guinea, especially at Fénaria,[163] have been found stone pestles with crisscross scorings. There is one also from near Beyla.[164] They are believed to have been used for pounding bark cloth; their date is unknown. Similar beaters have been found north of Stanleyville.[165] Weaving in fact may have been introduced to the Niger Valley by the Arabs, who could have used either the hair of their animals or indigenous cotton. It was apparently uncommon in Roman times in the Maghreb, where leather was worn.[166] The horizontal loom, now usual in the savannah, would leave no archaeological trace like the weights of vertical looms common

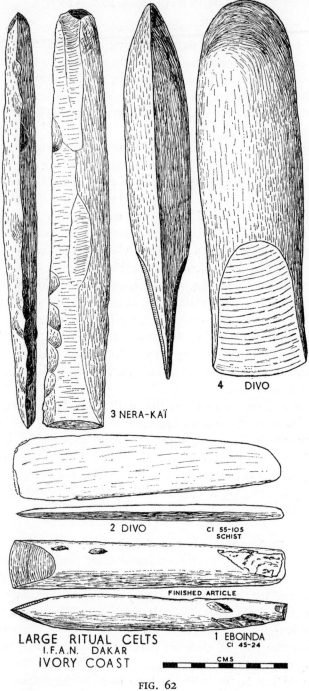

4   DIVO

3 NERA-KAÏ

2 DIVO   CI 55-105
                      SCHIST

FINISHED ARTICLE

LARGE RITUAL CELTS   1 EBOINDA
    I.F.A.N.   DAKAR   CI 45-24
IVORY COAST   CMS

FIG. 62

in Greece. Weaving probably was not introduced into the forest until late, because there would be nothing to weave. The little figures from Ahinsan in south Ashanti (seventeenth century) seem to be wearing something stiffer than textiles.

Pestles with a pecked surface have been found north-west of Bamako at Djiribougou, Bélé and Nioro.[167] In this region of dry savannah one would not expect bark cloth. There is a stone beater with marks of percussion, not on the end but on a convex face, from Kouga on the middle Niger.[168] Again its purpose cannot be determined.

KWES. The use of a heavy perforated stone for weighting a digging-stick was known in the Congo.[169] Their association is apparently pre-neolithic,[170] so they must have been unsuitable for the regular labour which agriculture demands.

Perforated stones may have been used also as trap-weights[171] or as club-heads, apparently depicted on South African rock paintings. They could have been anchors. It is unlikely that they were usually net-weights; in the neolithic of West Africa small pebbles, nicked to form a waist, probably served this purpose. These were particularly common at Ntereso, and would be much easier to make than kwes.

The finely shaped mace-head, a form probably derived from Egypt, has been mentioned in discussing the Ténéré-culture. A few shapely perforated stones from the southern savannah may also be mace-heads. If these had a ritual or ceremonial function, they could have been widely disseminated. A flattened sphere with biconical perforation, 15–16 cms. across and $6\frac{1}{2}$ cms. thick, was found with celts at Flampleu (Ivory Coast).[172] The broken oval kwe of sandstone from Tienfala, east of Bamako, does not look very practical and may have been ceremonial. Another well-worked disc-kwe was found at Yazore (Tong Hills, Northern Ghana).[186]

In West Africa there is no good evidence for weighted sticks for agriculture. A good many kwes have turned up in the Soguinex concessions and in deep-level auriferous river gravels in Ghana and other mining areas. They were probably used on digging-sticks for mining. A few have been found in gold-bearing sands also in the Congo; also on the upper River Falémé, the area which may have witnessed the first gold-mining in West Africa;[173] so such tools may have been diffused by miners in search of gold-bearing placers. There is no evidence whether the mining-kwe was derived, perhaps by a roundabout route, from the preneolithic digging-stick. It could have been an independent invention.

STONE JEWELLERY. The perforation of stone was developed at an early date for the manufacture of beads and bracelets. Often small, hard pebbles were worked under what must have been great difficulties. The commonness of biconical perforation suggests the use of a stick or reed with wet sand as an abrasive. Cylindrical perforations, which would be more difficult to make, are perhaps not older than the Iron Age.

The technique of perforating hard stone may well have been introduced into the southern Sahara from the Near East via Egypt. There seem to have been centres of production with a wide export trade. Quartz beads were made at Tarf Frékiké (Aouker).[174] Pink quartz was worked on the Gadaoui dunes near Gao[175], red flint near Arakat,[176] carnelian in the Tilemsi Valley,[177] amazonite at Eguei Zouma (southern Libya).[42] In western Ghana, near Wiawso and probably elsewhere, cylindrically perforated beads of black and pink hornblende-porphyry were made; there is reason to think that this industry goes back to neolithic times.

The dating of stone beads is extremely difficult, because they are dug up, put into circulation and reburied. They are not infrequently acquired on strings along with modern imported beads. Normally no great value is attached to them, unlike various types of glass, clay and paste bead, probably a few centuries old, which may command very high prices. One small quartz bead with biconical perforation I have found with microliths on the inner silt terrace at Bocanda (Ivory Coast) [fig. 63]. Consequently this type goes back to the mesoneolithic, but may have continued to be made for many centuries.[178] Most excavations yield a few beads; so a planned programme of investigation may give at least a series of *termini ante quos* for beads of different form and material.

Along with beads may be considered the irregular perforated pieces of quartz which are found abundantly in south-eastern Ghana and Togo and along the Mpraeso scarp into Ashanti [fig. 63].[179] They are irregularly smoothed on the outside; the very narrow biconical perforation is always carefully worked. They are too heavy to have been worn regularly as beads, as any cord thin enough to string them would rapidly chafe as the wearer moved. They may, however, have been worn on ceremonial occasions; and as they have been found in hoards and there is a strong tradition that they were money, they may have been mainly symbols of wealth. Two broken ones were found in the preneolithic level at Legon Botanic Gardens.

The manufacture of beads was a specialized activity. Bracelets, often

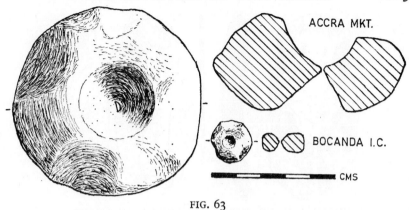

FIG. 63

from Davies O., 1964 (2), fig. 91

made of shale or sandstone, required less skill. The stone bracelets current today are of hard and attractive rock.[180] But this concentration of the industry may not be very old. Perhaps when glass bracelets began to be made at Bida, only the best stone could live up to the competition. Bracelets of shale are found in the Saharan neolithic at Meniet [cp. fig. 45], the Kintampo-culture of Ghana [fig. 74 20], and frequently in the neolithic caves of F. Guinea.[181] In the Oueyanko Valley near Bamako there was a factory for arm-rings of lateritized sandstone, which are found on neighbouring neolithic sites and may have been exported far afield. Stone bracelets were made from discs which seem to have been roughly perforated by pounding and then chipped to shape and polished. Wastage during manufacture was considerable.

The Neolithic Hoe-culture of the Forest

The stone hoe, presumably accompanying the regular culture of tubers, seems to have been superimposed in southern Ghana on the pre-neolithic. Regular culture implied clearings several miles across, in which rotational tillage could be practised. Two such clearings have been explored in Ghana, one at the foot of the Awudome range in Transvolta, the other around Aiyinabirim west of Wiawso [fig. 67]. Indications have been found of several others. They lie especially at the foot of ranges, where there was deep soil. Large numbers of hoes have been picked up wherever it was possible to examine below the surface; but settlements have not been identified except Krokosue, the centre of another clearing. Slight traces are known also of settlements in Kumasi.

P

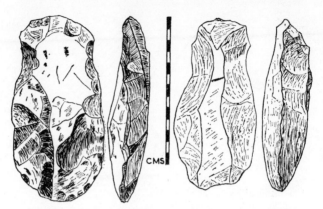

WAISTED AXES, BAMESSING near BAMENDA, CAMEROONS

FIG. 64

from Jeffreys, IFAN *xiii (1951), p. 1203,*
fig. 1 and 2, by permission

To deal with heavy vegetation it would be necessary to have picks, hoes and rough axes. These tools go back to a Lupemban ancestry. But the idea of systematic cropping as opposed to gathering and probably sporadic planting must have been inspired from the agriculturalists who were being parched out of the Sahara. The yam also may once have grown farther north; but its range was contracting with desiccation.

Tools which would more suitably have been used for working the soil than for wood have been found at Shaheinab and occasionally in the Ténéré-culture [figs. 39 5, 40 2; above, p. 162] and the agricultural culture of Niger. There is one in the collection from Niamey–Est [fig. 50 2].

With hoes there may have arrived very crude waisted axes. We have seen that this method of hafting was widely used in the southern Sahara, where various types of waist or rill are known. Many have been found near Bamenda,[182] some of which must be axes, others are probably hoes, for they seem to be field-waste and not to have been on settlements [fig. 64]. The axes may have been for cutting the sod, as there is little wood on the Cameroons grasslands. They occur farther east in the Cameroons, on the Cross River and elsewhere in eastern Nigeria; and they appear on the older sites on Fernando Po.[183] Round Bamenda there are also celts and picks, but nothing obviously pre-neolithic.

A very few tools with a slight waist have been found in Ghana [fig. 65]. Ntereso is a site probably of northern invaders. The piece from

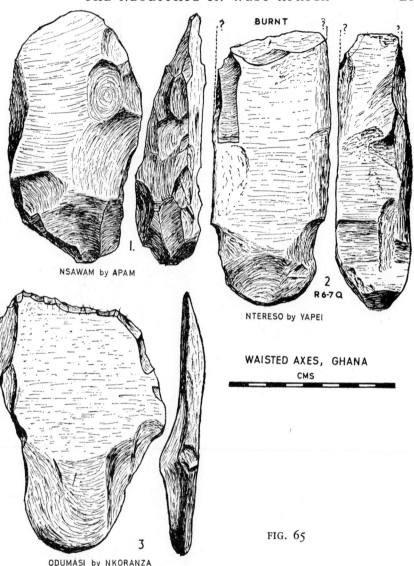

1. NSAWAM by APAM

BURNT

2
R 6-7 Q

NTERESO by YAPEI

WAISTED AXES, GHANA
CMS

3
ODUMASI by NKORANZA

FIG. 65

Nsawam was found with hoes and greenstone-flakes; and two from Mamomoho were in association with apparently early pottery.

I have mapped[184] the distribution of stone hoes, related agricultural tools and edge-ground celts in Ghana and territories to the west. There are practically no sites to add to this list. Though the edge-ground celt is more widely diffused than the hoe, it seems to belong to the same cultural complex. So probably do a few of the smaller celts, which have

been found among the prolific areas of hoes like Aiyinabirim [fig. 67 8].
A very short, broad celt [fig. 55 3] is rarely associated in Transvolta and
the Accra Plains. There is a similar celt in a collection from Divo
(southern Ivory Coast).[185]

Pottery does not seem to form part of the original hoe-culture, and
was not found at Legon Botanic Gardens or in Awudome. It was
probably introduced with the Kintampo-culture, and occurs on hoe-
sites in western Ghana (Kumasi, Aiyinabirim, Krokosue; fig. 67 12)
and F. Guinea, where the hoe-culture seems contaminated. Two hoes
from Ntirikurom bungalow [figs. 105 10, 107 10] may not be associated
with the medieval site.

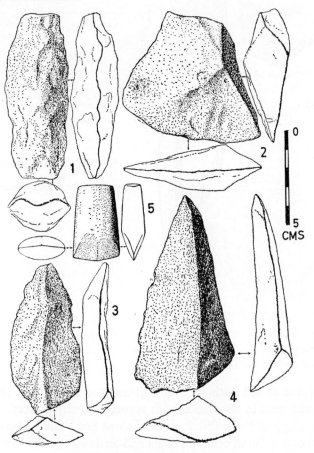

FIG. 66 Picks, Blandè, F. Guinea

by permission from Holas B. and Mauny R., 1953,
p. 1612

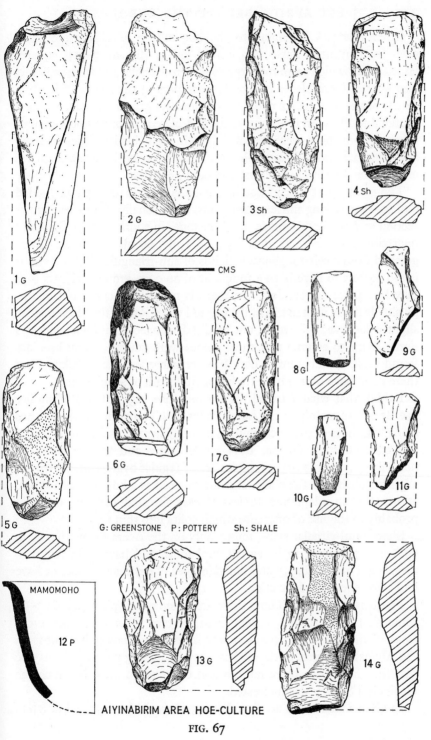

CMS

1 G
2 G
3 Sh
4 Sh
5 G
6 G
7 G
8 G
9 G
10 G
11 G

G: GREENSTONE   P: POTTERY   Sh: SHALE

MAMOMOHO

12 P

13 G
14 G

AIYINABIRIM AREA HOE-CULTURE

FIG. 67

from Davies O., 1964 (2), fig. 94

Other artefacts belonging to the hoe-culture of Ghana are small side-struck utilized flakes, apparently knives [fig. 67 9–11]; square-ended flakes which seem too large to be arrow-heads and were probably also knives; large blades and hollow scrapers in the Accra Plains [fig. 68 1]; perforated quartz pebbles occasionally; grooved bead-polishers; rounded mullers. In the Tong Hills, an isolated region in north-eastern Ghana, many hoes were associated with small blades, side-choppers and what are probably mace-heads;[186] there is much smashed quartz on the sites, but few microliths, no pottery or celts.

The commonest type of hoe in Ghana is a fairly thick parallel-sided tool 10–15 cms. long and less than 5 cms. wide, usually of sub-rectangular section and preferably made of greenstone, in south-eastern Ghana of quartzite or other tough rock [figs. 66 1, 67, 69 2]. It may be distinguished from a celt-roughout, which is of sub-triangular section; and it is too narrow to have been a roughout of an edge-ground celt. Its butt may be square or rounded, and there is normally a crude but distinguishable blade with marks of flaking and wear. Rarely the blade may be slightly concave; this would not be disadvantageous in a hoe, and it is unnecessary to assume that these pieces were gouges. Many hoes are found broken, and seem to have been resharpened after breaking; but there must have been a limit to the useful length of a hafted hoe.

I think that what I called the limande-hoe [fig. 68] was of similar use. It occurs mainly in the Accra Plains and Transvolta, on some sites along with hoes of sub-rectangular section. There are a few from central and north-western Ghana. It is rather larger and thinner than the normal hoe, and the best examples are of regular oval outline. Two are slightly polished at the blade. It could be used as a hoe, also as a spade. It may be an adaptation to less thickly forested country, or more probably to the use of quartzite which splits into thin slabs.

Short semi-circular slabs, found only on the Accra Plains [fig. 68 6, 69 1 and 7] appear to be agricultural tools, and have been found in association with ordinary and limande-hoes. They may be hoes or have had some specialized function.

Frequently along with hoes there are found rough picks [fig. 69 3–5], some short and stubby, others from western Ghana and the Ivory Coast[187] rather thin. There are many from near Wiawso, but not from the Aiyinabirim area. Some of these may be mining picks; or it may be that they have been more noticed and collected in areas in which the Geological Survey was interested.

In Ghana stone hoes are found stray, as would be expected of a tool

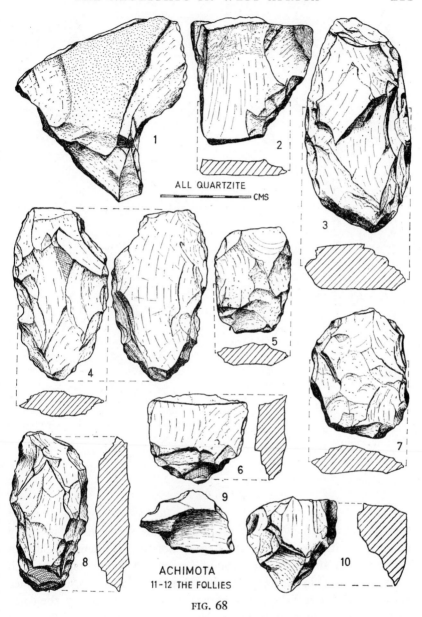

ALL QUARTZITE
CMS

ACHIMOTA
11-12 THE FOLLIES

FIG. 68

from Davies O., 1964 (2), fig. 107

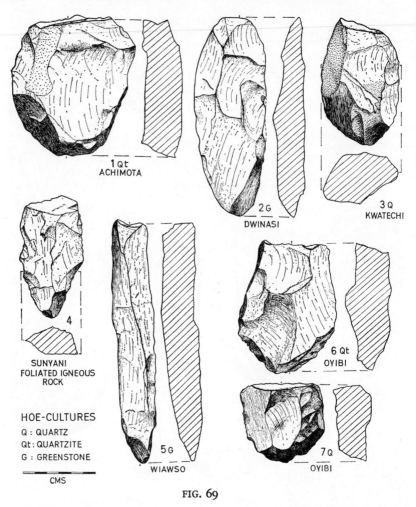

FIG. 69

from Davies O., 1964 (2), fig. 98

used in the fields. Where in association, this seems to be normally neolithic, without pottery at Legon Botanic Gardens, Achimota Cricket-pitch and other sites round Legon and Achimota, only with microliths at Ofin Bridge opposite Dunkwa, on an erosion-surface above Beach VI at Takoradi. Where they occur with pottery, the complex seems still to be neolithic, at New Todzi, Christian's Village and Krokosue. Unlike celts, there is no good evidence for stone hoes having continued to be used until late in the Iron Age, except on one or two remote sites like the mouth of the River Sheribong above Yeji. It is for this reason probably that they have not been recognized by ethnographers.

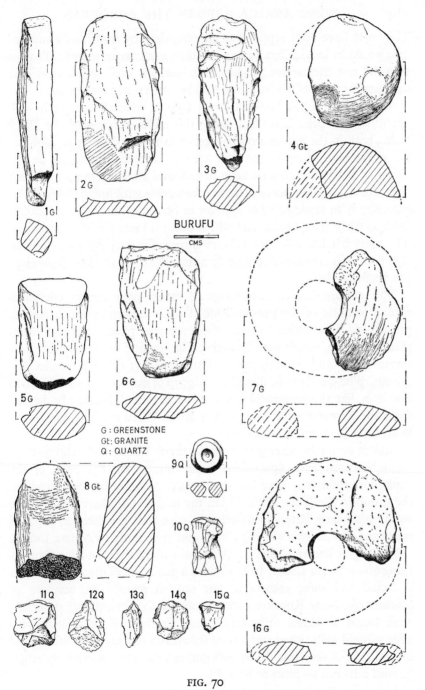

BURUFU

CMS

G : GREENSTONE
Gt: GRANITE
Q : QUARTZ

FIG. 70

from Davies O., 1964 (2), fig. III

They may have been replaced at an early date by iron; badly smelted iron would be less ineffective as a hoe than as an axe or weapon. Peoples who did not themselves produce iron perhaps used wood, as still in the remoter parts of Ghana, for a tool between a hoe and a rake.

An offshoot of the hoe-culture of Ghana, which seems to be still neolithic, has been identified along the middle course of the Black Volta, both in the extreme north-west of Ghana and in Upper Volta as far as Boromo. Many of the sites are on the inner silt terrace or just above it. Unassociated hoes have been found all the way up the Black Volta from near Bui, many of them comparable with limande-hoes. The difficulty is to separate what appears to be a neolithic without pottery from an early Iron Age culture which occupied many of the same sites. The most reliable collection is from Burufu [fig. 70], because the Iron Age pottery is concentrated slightly nearer the river and hardly overlaps the neolithic site.

This culture has an assemblage of rather poor quartz microliths similar to those of the pre-neolithic of the southern savannah (above, pp. 185–7). In addition to hoes, there are amorphous rods and sharp pieces of stone, which may be picks; edge-ground celts; probably perforated discs and perhaps polished mace-heads; rubbers, pestles and querns. The quartz bead illustrated [fig. 70 9] may be intrusive. Certain elements, like the perforated discs and some microliths, may be derived from the Kintampo-culture; but the Black Volta neolithic has in the main little in common with this.

Almost certainly other groups in northern Ghana and neighbouring territories developed specialized local cultures on the basis of the stone hoe; some may have lasted very late. Mention has been made of the group in the Tong Hills.[186] On the middle Oti short uniface hoes were found near Kitari in association with oval grindstones, a pitted stone and sherds with walking comb; and apparently stray near Jimam.

Nothing is known about the prehistory of Liberia, and hardly anything about Sierra Leone. In F. Guinea a good deal of material has been collected and some excavated, but not all reports are accurate or informative. Near Konakry picks, probably for agricultural purposes, were found at Massa M'bombo[188] and Koutaya,[189] hoes along with edge-ground celts, kwes and a long flaked rod but no microliths at the foot of Mt. Kakoulima.[190] At Kakimbon cave were apparently edge-ground celts but no picks or hoes.[191]

About eighty kilometres inland, caves and open sites near Kindia[192] have yielded remains apparently of more than one culture; but much of the material has been mixed. On some sites there were certainly hoes, picks, celts, discs, kwes and large knives; others seem to have yielded little but microliths. In at least the agricultural caves there was pottery, at Grotte de Ségéa [fig. 71] heavily ornamented sherds with sharp impressions suggestive of chip-carving (perhaps post-neolithic, but reminiscent of Blandè). At Bandé Bokhon cave, with hoes and celts, were small blades, hollow scrapers and microtranchets. A wider range of microliths, including awls and backed blades, must have been found in some of the caves. This microlithic culture seems akin to that of the wooded savannah of Ghana, and northern intrusions are not recognizable.

Agricultural tools in essentially similar association are reported from caves and open sites farther north in F. Guinea. The collection from Oualia near Télimélé[193] has picks, edge-ground celts, awls, few scrapers, concave blades, with such northern elements as leaf-shaped and lozenge-shaped arrow-heads and a perforated mace-head. About 65 kms. farther east caves round Pita have been examined.[194] The inventory contains, along with hoes, pottery, celts (some edge-ground) and a gouge, a number of elements which seem derived from the middle Niger:

Almond- and lozenge-shaped arrow-heads; a few microtranchets.
Points and scrapers; awls and hollow scrapers rare.
Sickle-shaped blades and discs; most blades are backed and trimmed, a few denticulated.
Polished rods of red schist, perforated at one end.
Perforated stones rare; a few thin polished bracelets.
Grooved stones for polishing beads and bone needles.
Three engraved stones with network pattern, reminiscent of the terra-cotta 'cigars' of the Kintampo-culture.
Perforated mace-head.
Waisted hammer.

There is apparently similar material from caves on the northern side of Fouta Djalon near Kinséa;[195] also in P. Guinea at Nhampasseré.[196] Hoes were found on an open site at Du'bere on the River Boe. At Nhampasseré there were sherds with square-toothed comb impressions.

Stone hoes have been rarely found near Bamako, but apparently in contexts which differ markedly from the southern savannah; so they seem to be an intrusive element into a northern neolithic culture, which will be described below. There is one from Kourounkorokale Upper, one from Bamako Grottes, one from Bamako–Bankoni, one from Mori-babougou.

A few of the sites reported in the Nioro shale area seem to be genuine neolithic, though the majority are Lupemban. I have suggested that some of the Lupemban material may have been used for proto-agriculture (above, p. 125). The illustrations of the pieces from Fangala[197] seem to show a neolithic industry, hoes, edge-ground and small celts, large blades, hammer-stones, discs, microtranchet. In caves near Zig (Aouker) hoes and edge-ground celts are said to occur without pottery or microliths, these being found on dune-sites.[198] A few stone hoes are reported from surface collections in north-western Mauritania and Rio de Oro. One was picked up on the slope beneath the cave of Cuatro Puertas (Gran Canaria); it need not be associated with the late red-polished pottery from the cave.

The stone hoe is probably descended from the Lupemban pick and axe; not in Ghana, where there is little evidence of continuity from the Lupemban to the neolithic. It does not occur south of the River Congo, though there has been much exploration along the southern fringe of the Congo basin. There are, however, a good many hoes from Dolisie[199] and other sites between Brazzaville and Pte. Noire.[200] There may be some from Gaboon. They have been found in the Uélé Valley, and pieces from the Mouka Plateau[137] are very lightly polished and not far removed from hoes.

It is from Equatorial Africa that I am inclined to bring the hoe to Ghana. It could also have been developed in the epi-Lupemban shale industry of northern Mali and eastern Mauritania (above, p. 122), and have been brought south by refugees from climatic deterioration. A source in this direction would account for the stray hoes from the neolithic of the upper Niger, where they are obviously out of place in a microlithic industry of different character.

The Kintampo Neolithic

In the lower basin of the Black Volta, as far west as the Ivory Coast border, have been found many sites of a neolithic culture which was generally not associated with hoes.[201] The map which has been published[202] presents a picture of its known distribution, though half a dozen new sites have been discovered since it was compiled. Though the curious terracotta 'cigars' have been known since the earliest days of field-work in Ghana,[203] proper collection to give a general conspectus of the culture was not started before 1952, in the neighbourhood of Kintampo. This town does in fact seem to be fairly central to its distribution; so the name Kintampo-neolithic is not inappropriate.

There are outlying sites as far south as Kumasi, which must be a very early clearing in the forest, and as the Accra Plains. 'Cigars' themselves, however, were transported in later times, apparently as magical objects, and have been found on sites as late as the eighteenth century. The Kintampo-neolithic was fused with an invading northern culture, which adopted many of its characteristic artefacts, including 'cigars'. The best-known site of this mixed culture (below, pp. 277–83) is Ntereso [figs. 43, 98–103] on the White Volta, not far from the home-land of the neolithic; another site has recently been located far to the east, at Nandikrom between the River Daka and Oti.

Most neolithic sites are in concealed positions, beside streams (Tolundipe), among rocks (Kintampo, Pumpuanu), on prominent hills (Wenchi, Jema) and on islands (Lake Kpiri, Chukoto). At Lake Kpiri a circle of pieces of burnt daub about two metres across had probably been the remains of a round hut, and there are at least six other daub-concentrations. Fragments of baked-clay cylinders found at Christian's Village near Achimota must be the remains of clay houses built on very light frames of wattle or sticks.

The pottery which has been found on these sites is fragmentary and weathered. Jars and wide bowls can be recognized with commonly heavy rolled rims. Decoration was usually by comb impression on the body and occasionally on a cordon. Few sherds are sufficiently well preserved to identify walking comb, which characterizes the culture of Ntereso [fig. 101].

It is likely that the Kintampo-neolithic, which seems to be intrusive, introduced pottery-making into Ghana. Sherds have been found on neolithic sites in Northern Ghana, which do not yield characteristic artefacts of the Kintampo-culture; but so far as can be judged, the pottery is similar. The sherds from the lower level at Bosumpra cave look genuine neolithic.[204] Pottery has been found also on hoe-sites in the south-west. The open cup [fig. 67 12] and decoration in narrow zones at Mamomoho and the heavy overhanging rims from Krokosue[205] are unlike the Kintampo-neolithic and are more closely paralleled at Ntereso.

The same appears to be true of the closely decorated sherds from Blandè shelter,[187] but few profiles are published. The pottery from Grotte de Ségéa [fig. 71] looks more advanced than the neolithic, but is not very far from Blandè.

The 'cigars' [fig. 72, 102] are of hard-baked terracotta. They are of flat oval section, carefully scored on both faces, usually horizontally and

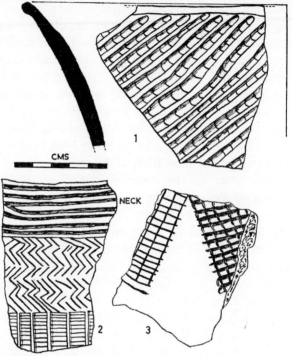

GROTTE DE SÉGÉA, KINDIA : I.F.A.N. G54-41

FIG. 71

vertically. A few have diagonal scoring, on some it is irregular. The surface is often rubbed, and nearly all are broken. The most complete are rounded at one or both ends, on many the butt is squared. Only of very few can the length be measured. The longest is about 22 cms. [fig. 102 6]; it was found on the base of one of the pits of the first period at Ntereso. Kitson mentions one of the same length from Tolundipe.[206] A very few are made of fine sandstone,[207] lightly scored with patterns similar to those of terracotta. Many have been perforated near the butt by pecking after baking, especially from Ntereso. They usually broke under this treatment.

No satisfactory explanation has been given of their use. Any suggestion must take account of their abundance, their material which would not stand up to severe abrasion, and their usual present broken condition. They would be particularly unserviceable for pounding bark cloth (above, pp. 201–3). They might have been used in pottery-manufacture, but why so many and so broken?

There are no exact parallels to 'cigars' from outside Ghana. Stones

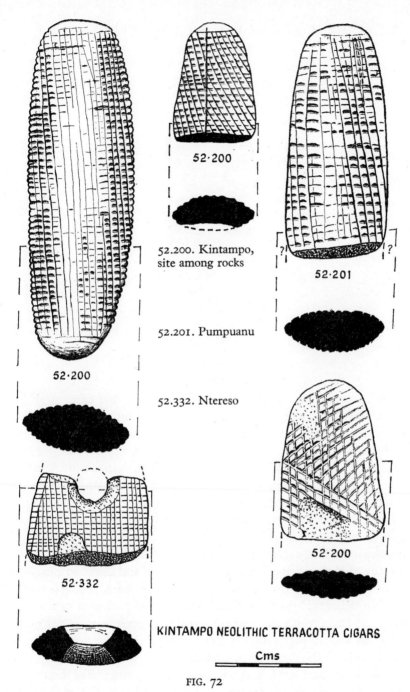

52·200

52.200. Kintampo,
site among rocks

52·201

52.201. Pumpuanu

52.332. Ntereso

52·200

52·201

52·332

52·200

KINTAMPO NEOLITHIC TERRACOTTA CIGARS

Cms

FIG. 72

*from Davies O., 1959 (2), p. 296; by permission of the Musée royal de
l'Afrique centrale, Tervuren*

60km S.W. ARAWANE
I.F.A.N. DAKAR So 60-48

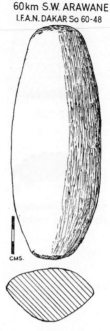

CMS.

FIG. 73

scored with similar designs were found in neolithic caves near Pita (F. Guinea).[208] They are of rectangular section and not identical. From the northern savannah and the Sahara come several long stones, in shape resembling the 'cigars' of Ghana, but not scored. The one from near Arawane [fig. 73] has marks of pounding on the end. A broken cylinder from Dinguira-Sud [fig. 76 2] may well belong to the same group; it is of sandstone, so too soft to be part of a pecked celt. A cylinder of smoothed granite from Karkarichinkat–Sud, of oval section 49 × 20 mms., is quite like the 'cigars'; but both ends are broken. It appears to be finely scored on the surface, probably by a polishing tool. A stone, slightly more pointed than the 'cigars' and about 20 cms. long, with small pits on the surface, is illustrated from Port Etienne.[209] At Ti-n-deher (Hoggar) was found unassociated a stone of oval section 8 × 3 × 1½ cms., with sharp vertical and almost-horizontal scoring on the faces and a small perforation at one end.[210] This is the nearest parallel in the north to the pieces from Ghana.

If we look southward, long smoothed stones, rather like 'cigars' but unscored, are known from neolithic sites in the Lower Congo. They are usually slightly curved lengthways, with the tip turned up. A stone piece from Ntereso is likewise curved. The similarity may, however,

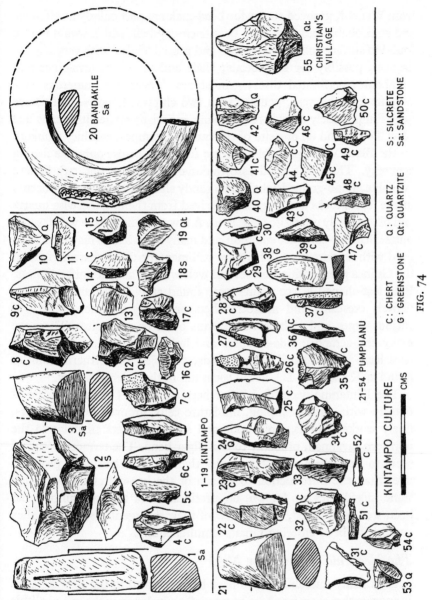

from Davies O., 1964 (2), fig. 116

FIG. 74

1–19 KINTAMPO

21–54 PUMPUANU

55 CHRISTIAN'S VILLAGE

20 BANDAKILE
Sa

KINTAMPO CULTURE

CMS

C : CHERT   Q : QUARTZ   S : SILCRETE
G : GREENSTONE   Qt : QUARTZITE   Sa : SANDSTONE

be due to Saharan influences on the neolithic of the Congo (above, p. 176), traceable also in microliths and other artefacts.

The Kintampo-culture, apart from pottery and 'cigars', comprises small and miniature celts (above, p. 201), apparently no edge-ground celts; hoes probably only on mixed sites like Christian's Village, probably one

Q

from Wenchi; grooved stones for bead-making, particularly at Ntereso, and so probably beads of shell or ostrich-eggshell, which would not be found in surface collections; stones and reused 'cigars' with very narrow grooves, possibly for seed-beads; shale and sandstone arm-rings and roughouts; perforated discs; grindstones. There are numerous net-weights from Ntereso, pebbles with two chipped hollows. They have been found widely elsewhere in Ghana, especially on neolithic sites like New Todzi; and on one site of the pure Kintampo-neolithic, Chukoto on the Black Volta, probably because they were of use only to a fishing economy. There is a good assortment of microliths [fig. 74]. Where available, a fine-grained light brown sandy shale was preferred; it occurs in the Volta rocks and in gravels derived from them. Otherwise quartz and occasionally quartzite were used. A few microliths have well faceted butts. Bladelet-cores are common, and many small blades may have been used without trimming. There are rudimentary tangs characteristic of the Guinea preneolithic, and several well-worked tanged uniface points. Fine leaf-shaped biface points were found at Fiakwasa and Chukoto. Chisels crescents and microtranchets are fairly common, blades of various types and awls less so. Burins occur on some sites. There are many end-scrapers; side-scrapers and hollow scrapers are rare. Some sites have yielded small chipped rods, an object of northern affinities found at Kaballa (S. L.), near Dakar and in the Tilemsi Valley.

The Kintampo-neolithic has northern affinities. The introduction of pottery with comb-stamping, miniature celts, grooved bead-polishers, finely worked points, stone rods and stone bracelets all point to the northern savannah, probably to the Niger bend. The terracotta 'cigars' seem to have their nearest analogies there. This intrusion is probably later than the introduction to Ghana of the hoe-culture. But though some mixed sites are known, no stratification of the two cultures has been well established, and in view of their divergent distribution they could have been entering Ghana simultaneously.

The Neolithic of the upper Niger

A good many microlithic sites have been revealed in the Bamako area. It appears that there was here an unconformity between the pre-neolithic and the neolithic. At this latitude the aridity of Post-pluvial III may have led to blowing sand, though there is no evidence for dunes. At least one metre of sterile sandy soil seems to have accumulated. In the Samanko Valley, though there is no single section, it is clear that the preneolithic with a Tiemassas-point and fish-spears lies at the top of laterite nodules, far below the neolithic, which is a few centimetres from the surface. Neolithic people may therefore have occupied the area rather late, at least later than the beginning of Sub-pluvial III. It is not implied that they necessarily had vacated the whole area; they had certainly vacated exposed places on the left bank and in tributary valleys, while perhaps continuing to reside where there was more shelter and less dust. Only a long stratification either of a soil or of an occupation-site would provide an answer to this possibility.

The most productive site has been the upper level at Kourounkoro-kale cave, where the artefacts seem homogeneous and not exposed to the disturbances which the lower level has suffered.[55] Szumowski excavated a second cave at Ntekedo, but very little of the material has been identified. There are from Kourounkorokale fairly small celts, a few kwes and one hoe; a good many microliths of quartz and dolerite, crescents, microtranchets, chisels, end-scrapers and thumb-nails, blades and probably blunt-backed blades, awls, and rather rough points. Some microliths have rudimentary tangs. Typical of this region are slicers, thin sandstone slabs ground usually to a wide convex blade but otherwise quite unshaped, unlike a celt. Slicers were found at Ntereso, being part of the Sudanic equipment brought by invaders to this site. Much pottery came from the upper level, whereas the lower probably had none (above, p. 166). Most sherds are decorated with comb impressions, and there is some walking comb, a few pieces curved in cardial style. One or two pieces seem to recall the wavy-line pottery of Early Khartum, though they must be very much later. There are also jabs and maggots. There are similarities with Ntereso but not identity. There seems to be a wider range of decoration than any site yields in Ghana. The range is certainly much richer than that of the Kintampo-neolithic, but for climatic reasons sites round Bamako may be later than the neolithic of the southern savannah. There are some resemblances also to the pottery from Blandè, again not extending to identity.

Surface sites in the Oueyanko and Samanko Valleys and the environs of Bamako as far as the River Baoulé, 83 kms. west-north-west of the city, have yielded much neolithic material [fig. 75]. But it is difficult to classify because of the state of the collections in the Bamako museum, and Szumowski in his publications[211] did not describe the assemblages clearly and separately. They had apparently been unscientifically collected even before Szumowski's time. There are pieces and flakes of dolerite, including Lupemban artefacts probably brought from across the river to manufacture into edge-ground and fully polished celts and

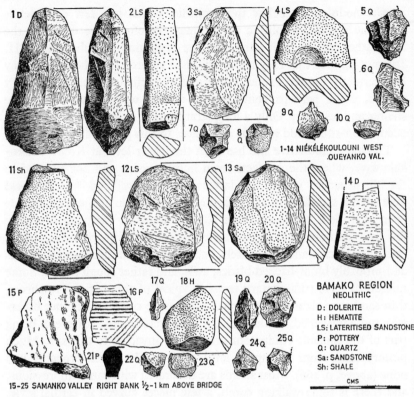

FIG. 75

from Davies O., 1964 (2), fig. 97

perhaps occasionally into gouges, hoes and picks; slicers; discs of shale perforated and unperforated; grindstones; bracelets; large sandstone kwes; little pottery, perhaps because the sites have been long exposed; in sugary quartz microtranchets, chisels, crescents, awls, end-scrapers, side-scrapers, hollow scrapers, burins, a few microburins, backed and blunt-backed blades, a few points. A few pieces have rudimentary tangs.

The site at Kobadi, north of Ségou, may be intermediate between the Sub-pluvial II neolithic of the Saharan fringe and the very late neolithic around Bamako. It has been badly collected, and in general not published. The harpoons point northwards; they were found in Kourounkorokale Lower. But the pottery and the massive arm-ring [fig. 85 6] look late, even Iron Age.

Otherwise practically nothing neolithic has been reported east of the neighbourhood of Kayes. Dinguira-Sud[212] yielded, along with one or two hoes and a rather banal microlithic assemblage, two probable

DINGUIRA-SUD : I.F.A.N. DAKAR SO 48-7

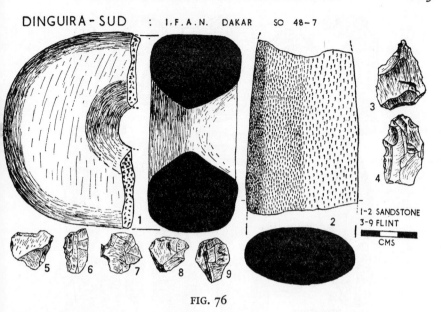

I-2 SANDSTONE
3-9 FLINT

CMS

FIG. 76

1. Broken perforated stone
2. Flattened cylinder, ? broken pecked celt
3. Awl
4. Backed blade
5. Chisel
6. Backed blade
7. Tanged piece
8. Thumbnail-scraper
9. Steep end-scraper

slicers [fig. 76]. The tanged point looks like a poor imitation of a Saharan piece. De Zeltner records[213] many sites along the river above Kayes; but few of them have yielded anything interesting or typical.

The Neolithic of Dakar

West of the River Falémé there has been hardly any exploration until the Dakar peninsula. There probably are sites along the River Senegal; the only one reported is at Dendoudi, yielding flakes and cores, a few crescents and backed blades. Unlike the prevailing blank, the Dakar peninsula is covered with sites. Intelligent observers and the facilities round a city for examining the subsoil have put at our disposal a great number of collections.[214]

The term Neocapsian, which has been applied to the Dakar neolithic, is unsatisfactory and should be abandoned. The culture, though of Saharan affinity, is not closely connected with the Capsian of the Maghreb. Its date seems to be as late as the neolithic of Bamako. It normally occurs on the low dunes which mark the final stage of Post-pluvial III,[215] exposed on shallow erosion-patches.

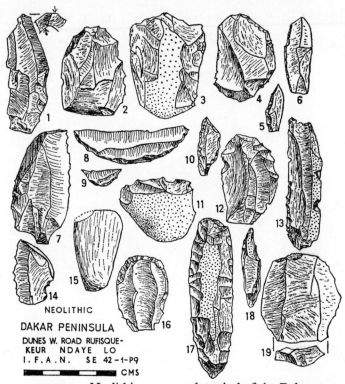

NEOLITHIC

DAKAR PENINSULA
DUNES W. ROAD RUFISQUE-
KEUR   NDAYE   LO
I . F . A . N .   SE 42 – 1 – P9
CMS

FIG. 77 Neolithic stone-work typical of the Dakar area

1. Burin	11. Biface pebble-chopper
2. Rough biface	12. End-scraper
3. Rough axe	13–14. Blunt-backed blades
4. End-scraper	15. Celt, sandstone
5–6. Backed blades	16. End-scraper
7. Tanged blunt-backed blade	17. Biface end-scraper
8–9. Crescents	18. Steep-backed drill
10. Trimmed point	19. Flake with faceted butt

The material is usually flint. Basalt occurs on a few neolithic sites, perhaps not of the younger group. I have illustrated [fig. 77] a fairly representative series from one of the sites near Rufisque.[216] In addition to these types, microburins, flaked rods and pieces in Y (a Saharan group) occur rarely. There are a few biface arrow-heads; the fine work of the preneolithic of Tiemassas seems to have disappeared. Grindstones, grooved stones for bead-making, small and miniature celts and stone bracelets occur. On most sites there are small sherds of tightly orna-mented comb-impressed pottery.[217] This is not easy to illustrate; but the Iron Age continued neolithic traditions, so the pots from Bel-Air [fig. 94] give a good idea also of the neolithic wares.

The absence of markedly Iron-Age material from Dakar suggests that in this eccentric area a sub-neolithic culture survived very late. We do not know what the Portuguese found here. There is little information until we reach the seventeenth-century settlement on Gorée Island.[218] But the great shell-mounds along the coast of Casamance (below, p. 273) indicate the primitive Strandloper-culture of the coastal dwellers of West Africa so long as every outlook was oriented inland and before the ocean ceased to be an impenetrable barrier and became a highway of communication.

NOTES

1. Merrill, *Chronica Botanica* xiv (1954), p. 161.
2. Cp. Portères R. *et al.*, 1962; Okiy G. E. O., 1962; Portères, *Société de Biogéographie C. R.* xxviii (1951), p. 16.
3. Erroux, *SHNAN* li (1960), p. 143.
4. Chevalier, *Revue de Botanique appliquée* xxix (1949), p. 609.
5. Dechambre, *Société de Biogéographie C. R.* xxvii (1950), p. 147.
6. *Notre Sahara* xii (1959), p. 17.
7. Werth, *Grabstock Hacke und Pflug*.
8. See Espérandieu, *II Panafrican Congress* p. 551. Most publications of Saharan painted sites show some cattle. For bibliography to 1954, see Mauny R., 1954 (2). There have since been a good many large publications, especially by Lhote (west Sahara) and Huard (Tibesti, etc.).
9. Quezel and Martinez, in Hugot H. J. ed., 1962, p. 326.
10. Espérandieu, *I Congreso arqueologico del Marruecos español* (1953), p. 121.
11. The best known are in North Africa, cp. Vaufrey, *Archives de l'Institut de Paléontologie humaine Mém.* 20, pl. XXXVIII and XXXIX. Some of the more sketchy drawings of ovines with a disc on the horns are almost certainly mouflons, see Huard, *IFAN* 23B (1961), p. 499.
12. Boule and Vallois, *Archives de l'Institut de Paléontologie humaine Mém.* 9; Monod, *Historia naturalis* i (1946), p. 81.
13. Mauny R., 1961 (2).
14. From both sites both types of harpoon, see de Heinzelin, *Scientific American* 206 (June 1962), p. 105; Arkell, *Early Khartoum*, pl. 46–48.
15. Arkell and Ucko, *Current Anthropology* (1965), p. 145.
16. The reason has not been determined. In the discussion cited much was made of specimens being taken from European museums where they had been contaminated by soot. This explanation would be more convincing if the soot of modern cities were not largely derived from coal-burning, so the carbon is dead. Damon *et al.*, in a paper at the Int. C_{14} Dating Conf. (Pullman, U.S.A., 1964), suggest that the atmospheric flux varied with climate and was high at the Altithermal, thus giving dates which historically can be proved too low.

17. Caton–Thompson and Gardner, *The Desert Fayum* i, p. 14; id., *Geographical Journal* lxxiii (1929), p. 20.
18. GRO–2805, *Radiocarbon* vi (1964), p. 355; almost certainly from the neolithic deposit, though this is not clearly stated in the text.
19. Sandford and Arkell, *Palaeolithic Man in the Nile valley in Nubia and Upper Egypt*, pp. 79–80; id., *Palaeolithic Man in the Nile valley in Upper and Middle Egypt*, pp. 119–20 (University of Chicago Oriental Inst. Publications).
20. I–534; Fairbridge, *Nature* 4850 (13/10/62), p. 108.
21. Caton–Thompson, *Kharga Oasis in Prehistory*, pl. 94–99.
22. See the admirable summary of the situation by Balout, *Préhistoire de l'Afrique du Nord*, p. 453; also Maître, *LAPE* xi (1963), p. 132.
23. Camps, *Massinissa* I, ch. B (*Libyca Archéologie–Epigraphie* viii).
24. For instance, Gar Cahal (Tarradell, *Tamuda* ii (1954), p. 344; see above, p. 174). It is not clear whether there was an interval between levels IIIb and IV.
25. Chavaillon, *SPF* C.R. (1964), p. lxxxviii; id., *SPF* lxi (1964), p. 84. The industry, still little known, may be transitional between the Aterian and the Oranian.
26. Mauny R., 1956; Huard, *Encyclopédie mens. d.Outremer* v (1955), p. 366.
27. Arkell, *IV Panafrican Congress* ii, p. 283; Huard and Massip, *SPF* lxi (1964), p. 105.
28. Hugot H. J., 1963, especially pl. XVIII–XIX. Huard and Massip identified one from Kobadi and a few near Dakar; but they need re-examination to determine if they really belong to the Khartum group. They also illustrate sherds with walking grooves from Toboï (NW Tibesti). Degenerate wavy-line ornament occurs rarely at Ntereso (Ghana), and survived in the Volta valley until, or was reinvented in, recent centuries.
29. Monod, *Société de Biogéographie Mémoires* vi (1938), p. 145.
30. El Khril; Jodin, *Bull. d'Archéologie marocaine* iii (1958–9), p. 249: Gar Cahal level IIIb, above, n. 24.
31. Laforgue and Saucin, *CEHSAOF* (1925), p. 145; I.F.A.N. Dakar M 47–45.
32. Huard, *IEC* 17–8 (1959), p. 12. Cp. recent mentions of neolithic sites with pottery with comb impressions in zones and patterns near Largeau; Courtin, *SPF* C.R. (1965), p. cxxxv; Huard and Massip, *SPF* lxi (1964), p. 105.
33. Hugot H. J. ed., 1962, especially the analysis by Tixier, p. 333; also Hugot, *LAPE* viii (1960), p. 328.
34. Joubert G. and Vaufrey R., 1946; also Mauny, *IFAN* xi (1949), p. 144.
35. Hugot H. J. ed., 1962, p. 71.
36. There is little there indicative of extensive agriculture as Hugot suggests; a few grindstones could have been for seeds of wild grasses. The economy seems to have been hunting with perhaps some fishing.
37. Savary, *SPF* lviii (1961), p. 605.

38. The last occur occasionally in the Congo Tsitolian, but may have been derived up the Nile and not via West Africa.
39. Caton–Thompson and Gardner, *The Desert Fayum* II, pl. XLIV 10.
40. I.F.A.N. Dakar N 49–285.
41. I.F.A.N. Dakar AF EQ–41–8.
42. Dalloni and Monod, *Mission au Fezzan* VI.
43. E.g. one piece from Kobadi, I.F.A.N. Dakar So 55–29; from near Tombouctou, Gaubert, *Soc. française de Minéralogie Bull.* xli (1918), p. 38.
44. Mori and Ascenzi, *Rivista di Antropologia* xlvi (1959), p. 126.
45. Noel, *Anthropologie* xxviii (1917), p. 351.
46. Lhote, *A la Recherche des Fresques du Tassili*; Lhote, *Die Felsbilder der Sahara*; Lhote and Breuil, *II Panafrican Congress* p. 67.
47. Cp. the factory site for querns at Grein, Hugot H. J. ed., 1962, p. 176.
48. Cadenat, *LAPE* viii (1960), p. 239.
49. Dalloni, 'Mission au Tibesti' (*Académie des Sciences Mémoires* 62 (1935)).
50. *CEHSAOF* (1933), p. 299.
51. Lhote, *CPF* xiii (1950), p. 426.
52. Mauny, *SPF* xlix (1952), p. 469; Monod T. and Mauny R., 1955.
53. Courtin, *SPF* C.R. (1964), p. cxxix.
54. Coppens, *SPF* lix (1962), p. 265; Courtin, *SPF* CR (1965), p. lxx.
55. Szumowski G., 1956.
56. Kelley, *SAfr* iv (1934), p. 137, pl. IX.
57. I.F.A.N. Dakar So 53–1. Balout, *Algérie préhistorique*, p. 165.
58. Monod T. and Mauny R., 1955, fig. 4.
59. I.F.A.N. Dakar So 52–44.
60. Davies O., 1964 (2), p. 246.
61. The absence of microliths from Kobadi must be due to incompetent collection.
62. Lhote, *CPF* xiii (1950), p. 446. The term was misapplied widely in West Africa until it was abolished at the First Panafrican Congress.
63. Mauny R., 1952 (2); Monod, in *Mission Augiéras–Draper*; Amblard–Rambert and Gaussen, *SAfr* xxx (1960), p. 123; id., *NA* 84 (1959), p. 97; Gaussen, *SPF* lix (1962), pp. 100 and 175.
64. It must be admitted that large collections seem to have been recently made in the Tilemsi Valley, but only a few pieces from them have been published, without any inventory. One cannot but deplore the continued activities of archaeological jackdaws.
65. Mauny R., 1952 (2); Hugot, *LAPE* v (1957), p. 225; Gaussen, *NA* 105 (1965), p. 19.
66. Hugot, *LAPE* iii (1955), p. 291.
67. Hugot, *LAPE* v (1957), p. 89.
68. Kelley, *SAfr* xxi (1951) p. 197; Kennedy, *Antiquity* xxxiv (1960), p. 354.
69. Schnell, *SAfr* xviii (1948), p. 127.

70. E.g. In Azaoua, Lhote, *CPF* xiii (1950), p. 436; probably area of Gossolorum, Hugot, *LAPE* viii (1960), p. 328; Areschima, Hugot H. J. ed., 1962, p. 166.
71. Hugot H. J., 1963, pl. XIII.
72. Tabankort, transported in modern times; *Mission Cortier 1908–10*, *Notice de Préhistoire saharienne*.
73. Musée de l'Homme 35·128.
74. Schneider, *Recherches congolaises* xxvii (1939), p. 41.
75. Ruhlmann, *Soc. de Préhistoire du Maroc, Bull.* x (1936), p. 1.
76. Reygasse, *CPF* xi (1934), p. 577.
77. Kelley, *SAfr* v (1935), p. 154, pl. XXIII.
78. Cp. Petrie, *Tools and Weapons*, pl. II–VII.
79. Mauny R., 1954 (2).
80. Alimen, 'La Station rupestre de Marhouma' (*IRS Mémoires* I).
81. *Encyclopédie mensuelle d'Outremer* v (1955), p. 366 and vi (1956), p. 317; *Notre Sahara* xii (1959), p. 17.
82. Perret, *Cahiers Charles de Foucauld* x (1948), p. 81.
83. Mauny R., 1956.
84. Fuchs, *Archiv für Völkerkunde* xii (1957), p. 128.
85. Aurigemma, *Africa italiana* vii (1940), p. 67.
86. Cp. Huard, *Notre Sahara* vii (1959), p. 33.
87. VII, ch. 69.
88. E.g. Aozou (Tibesti) (Monod, *Rivista di Scienze preistoriche* i (1947), p. 30); Oued Djorat (Tassili n'Ajjer) (Lhote, *Cuadernos de Historia primitiva* iv (1949), p. 27, no. 627).
89. Hubert Laforgue and Vanelsche, *CEHSAOF* (1921), p. 388.
90. Lhote, *Acad. des Sciences d'Outremer C.R.* xvii (1957), p. 345.
91. Monod, *l. c.* (note 88); Frobenius, *Hadschra Maktuba*, pl. 79.
92. Jacques–Meunié, *SAfr* xxix (1959), p. 23; Fuchs, *l. c.* (note 84); Huard, *IEC* vi (1953), p. 149, pl. IX; Huard, *IFAN* 22B (1960), p. 134.
93. E.g. El Gleitat (Monod, 'Contributions à l'étude du Sahara occidental', *CEHSAOF Publ.* A7); Oued Sedaden (Lhote, *IFAN* 14 (1952), p. 1292, no. 276), figure with two spears and knee-length robe; similar from Tagant (Senones and Puigaudeau, *SAfr* ix, p. 43).
94. Rodd, *Royal Anthropological Inst. Jour.* (1938), p. 99.
95. Bates, *The Eastern Libyans*.
96. Flamand, *Les Pierres écrites*, p. 180.
97. Ruhlmann, *La grotte préhistorique de Dar-es-Soltan* (Coll. Hespéris 11); *Germania* xxxiii (1955), p. 22; del Castillo, *Congreso arqueologico del Marruecos español* (1953), p. 163.
98. Balout, *Préhistoire de l'Afrique du Nord*, p. 470.
99. Tarradell, *Tamuda* ii (1954), p. 344.
100. Jodin, *CPF* xv (1956), p. 564.
101. Ruhlmann, *Soc. de Préhistoire du Maroc Bull.* vii (1933), p. 3.
102. Camps, *Revue africaine* 104 (1960), p. 31: Jodin, *Bull. d'Archéologie marocaine* v (1964), p. 11.
103. Jodin, *Bull. d'Archéologie marocaine* ii (1957), p. 9.

104. Camps, *LAPE* viii (1960), p. 263.
105. Malhomme, 'Corpus des gravures rupestres du Grand Atlas' (*Publ. Service des Antiquités du Maroc* 13 and 14).
106. Mauny R., 1952 (1); Mauny, *IFAN* xiii (1951), p. 168; Crova, *CPF* viii (1912), p. 702.
107. Martin, *Cuadernos de Historia primitiva* iv (1949), p. 111.
108. Mauny, *III Panafrican Congress* p. 249; Bessac, *IFAN* 20B (1958), p. 352.
109. Mauny R., 1947 (1); Mauny, *Bull. de Correspondance saharienne* ii (1948), p. 9.
110. Santa–Olalla, *Cuadernos de Historia primitiva* II i, p. 47.
111. Mauny R., 1961 (1), pp. 306–8.
112. Mauny, *SPF* lix (1962), p. 332.
113. Farine, *Sites préhistoriques gabonais*; de Beauchene, *Objets et Mondes* iii (1963), p. 1.
114. E.g. near Kikwit, Bequaert, *CISPP* iv (1954), p. 29; probably also near Lac Léopold, van Moorsel, *Folia scientifica Africae centralis* iii (1957), p. 70.
115. Dagan T., 1956.
116. Corbeil R., Mauny R. and Charbonnier J., 1948, fig. XII 1 3 6 and 13.
117. Mauny, *NA* 57 (1953), p. 7.
118. For attempt to link Tiemassas with a culture parallel to the Aterian, see Hugot, *CRAS* 260 (1965), p. 2861.
119. I.F.A.N. Dakar So 51–80.
120. Davies O., 1964 (2), fig. 74.
121. Szumowski, *SPF* liv (1957), p. 350, pl. III 13–14.
122. Davies O., 1964 (2), fig. 78.
123. Mauny, *IFAN* xi (1949), p. 151. It is not clear how the collection was made. It is suspected that a body of soldiers was lined up on the parade-ground and told to move across, picking up every stone seen.
124. Davies O., 1964 (2), fig. 83.
125. The number of microlithic sites recorded is: Ghana 489, Togo 25, Dahomey 20, Nigeria 7, Upper Volta about 35, Ivory Coast about 25. These numbers mean little, because outside Ghana and Togo no great effort has been made to collect or to publish this unattractive industry.
126. *Plateau central nigérien*, pp. 22ff.
127. Creac'h P., 1945, p. 425.
128. Davies O., 1964 (2), pp. 179–80.
129. Shaw C. T., 1944.
130. Davies O., 1964 (2), p. 171, fig. 79.
131. Fagg, *Proc. Prehistoric Society* (1944), p. 68. The date of 1975 ± 120 (I–1460; Fagg, *Man* lxv (1965), no. 8) recently released for Ropp probably indicates that it was a relict-culture. This date could just be fitted into the short chronology for Nok, but is far later than the first level at Ntereso, which yielded a developed neolithic.
132. Willett, *IV Panafrican Congress* ii, p. 261.
133. Hamy, *Muséum d'Histoire naturelle de Paris Bull.* v (1899), p. 336 and

vi (1900), p. 337; Hamy, *Cong. int. d'Anthropologie et d'Archéologie préhistoriques* xii (1900), p. 232; Hamy, *Anthropologie* xii (1901), p. 380; Jelinek et al., *SPF* lxi (1964), p. 492.

134. Droux and Kelley, *SAfr* ix (1939), p. 80.

135. Bequaert, *Soc. belge d'Anthropologie et de Préhistoire Bull.* lviii (1947), p. 315.

136. Bequaert, *ibid.*, liii (1938), p. 32 and lvii (1946), p. 182.

137. Breuil, *Anthropologie* xliii (1933), p. 222.

138. Cp. *NA* 79 (1958), p. 70.

139. Mauny, *NA* 73 (1957), p. 18.

140. Imbert, *SPF* vi (1909), p. 442; Combes, *Ass. française pour l'Avancement des Sciences C.R.* xxxviii (1909), p. 830; Laforgue, *CEHSAOF* viii (1925), p. 130.

141. Hue E., 1912; Guébhard, *Bull. de Géographie historique et descriptive* xxii (1907), p. 408.

142. Joire J., 1952, pl. III.

143. Szumowski G., 1956, pl. XII 3.

144. Hugot H. J. ed., 1962, pl. XII.

145. Gaden, *Anthropologie* xxx (1920), p. 513.

146. Fagg B., 1956, fig. 15.

147. Fourneau, *SAfr* v (1935), p. 67, pl. V 4; many in the Jeffreys collection in the Pitt–Rivers Museum, Oxford.

148. Cp. Maurice, *NA* 79 (1958), p. 68.

149. Roman, *Ass. rég. de Paléontologie et de Préhistoire de Lyon Bull.*, v (1935).

150. At Adafer: Laforgue, *Soc. de Géographie et d'Archéologie d'Oran Bull. trim.* liii (1932), p. 120.

151. Lefebvre, *LAPE* xi (1963), p. 137. Cp. also the blunt hematite celts from the Uélé basin (van Noten, *Man* lxiii (1963), no. 24).

152. Schouteden, *Revue zoologique africaine, Bull. Cercle zoologique congolais* iv (1927-8), p. (14).

153. de Zeltner, *CPF* ix (1913), p. 264.

154. Houdaba (*NA* 13 (1942), p. 22); Sénoudébou (Guébhard, *SPF* ix (1912), p. 428.

155. Elb Techerit (Szumowski, *NA* 72 (1956), p. 98, pl. 2 3 2-8 and pl. 2 4-5).

156. See map, Davies O., 1964 (2), fig. 89.

157. I.F.A.N. Dakar So 41-6.

158. Joire J., 1952, pl. IV 20.

159. *ARGS* (1923-4), p. 10; Kitson, *GSFNB* (25-26/11/23).

160. Holas, *IFAN* xiii (1951), p. 1174.

161. Mauny, *NA* 86 (1960), p. 40.

162. See Balfour, *Royal African Soc. Jour.* xii (1912-13), p. 1.

163. Mauny, *NA* 61 (1954), p. 1.

164. Hubert, *CEHSAOF* viii (1925), p. 287.

165. Bequaert, *Soc. belge d'Anthropologie et de Préhistoire Bull.* lviii (1947), p. 244.

166. Camps, *LAPE* xi (1963), p. 169.
167. I.F.A.N. Dakar So 47–41, 55–144, 45–36.
168. I.F.A.N. Dakar So 55–56.
169. Bequaert, *Soc. belge d'Anthropologie et de Préhistoire Bull.* lix (1948), pp. 20 and 81; Doize, *Musée du Congo belge Ann.* D I 1 iii; Schnell, *Plantes alimentaires et vie agricole de l'Afrique noire*, p. 45.
170. Mortelmans, *Soc. belge d'Anthropologie et de Préhistoire Bull.* lviii (1947), p. 151; Lenk–Chevitch, *ibid.*, lx (1949–50), p. 12.
171. Cabu, *Musée du Congo belge Ann.* D I 1 iv.
172. Bequaert, *Soc. belge d'Anthropologie et de Préhistoire Bull.* lix (1948), p. 118.
173. Mathelin de Papigny, *Con. int. d'Anthropologie et d'Archéologie préhistoriques C.R.* xv (1931), p. 320; below, p. 248.
174. Mauny, *Revue coloniale belge* (1/8/1949), p. 492; I.F.A.N. Dakar M 49–169.
175. Lhote, *SPF* xxxix (1942), p. 277.
176. Furon and Pérébaskine, *CEHSAOF* xii (1929), p. 88.
177. Gaussen, *SPF* lix (1962), p. 100.
178. The bead from Niamey–Est (fig. 50 5) may be intrusive.
179. Davies O., 1960.
180. Lhote, *IFAN* xii (1950), p. 456.
181. Delcroix R. and Vaufrey R., 1939–40; Hue E., 1912.
182. Jeffreys, *IFAN* xiii (1951), p. 1203; id., *III Panafrican Congress* p. 268.
183. Panyella, *Inst. de Estudios africanos Arch.* xiii (1959), p. 23.
184. Davies O., 1964 (2), fig. 88.
185. Mauny, *NA* 86 (1960), p. 40; I.F.A.N. Dakar CI 55–105.
186. Davies O., 1964 (2), fig. 99.
187. Hoes and pick from Tubalo; hoes from Assakra and probably from near Bouaflé; picks and hoes from the rock-shelter of Blandè, just in F. Guinea (fig. 66) (Holas, *IFAN* xii (1950), p. 999 and xiv (1952), p. 1431; Holas B. and Mauny R., 1953).
188. Hamy, *Muséum d'Histoire naturelle de Paris Bull.* iii (1897), p. 282.
189. Schnell, *SPF* xlvi (1949), p. 442.
190. Schnell, *NA* 27 (1945), p. 4.
191. Hamy, *Anthropologie* xii (1901), p. 380.
192. Delcroix R. and Vaufrey R., 1939–40; Joire J., 1952.
193. Desplagnes, *SAP* lviii (1907), p. 59; id., *Journal officiel de l'A.O.F.* (2/2/1907).
194. Hue E., 1912; Guébhard, *Bull. de Géographie historique et descriptive* xxii (1907), p. 408; id., *CPF* v (1909), p. 281.
195. Creac'h P., 1945, p. 423.
196. Mateus, *CIAO* II iv. p. 377; id., *Bol. cultural da Guiné portuguesa* ix (1954), p. 457 and figs. 8–14.
197. Vaufrey R., 1947, figs. 10–11.
198. Laforgue, *Soc. de Géographie et d'Archéologie d'Oran Bull.* xliv (1924), p. 267.
199. Sadoul, *CIAO* I ii, p. 459.

200. Droux and Kelley, *SAfr* ix (1939), p. 71; Bergeaud, *Recherches congo-laises* xxiii (1937), p. 163.
201. Davies O., 1959 (2).
202. Davies O., 1964 (2), fig. 113.
203. Kitson, *Geographical Journal* xlviii (1916), p. 380; Balfour, see n. 162.
204. Shaw C. T., 1944, fig. 7.
205. Davies O., 1964 (2), fig. 95 5–6.
206. *GSFNB* (15/2/26).
207. Davies O., 1959 (2), fig. 6 19.
208. Hue E., 1912.
209. *NA* 10 (1941), p. 27.
210. Maître, *LAPE* ix–x (1961–2), p. 125.
211. *II Panafrican Congress* p. 664; *NA* 72 (1956), p. 98. Cp. Creac'h P., 1945.
212. Mauny, *SPF* xlv (1948), p. 68.
213. *SAP* VI vii (1916), p. 238.
214. See Corbeil R., Mauny R. and Charbonnier J., 1948; Richard, *IFAN* xiii (1951), p. 1181; Laforgue and Mauny, *CEHSAOF* xxi (1938), p. 533.
215. Joire, *NA* 31 (1946), p. 4.
216. Cp. the description of Waterlot's collection in Vaufrey, *Rivista di Scienze preistoriche* i (1946), p. 19.
217. Mauny R., 1951.
218. See Mauny, *NA* 96 (1962), p. 127.

CHAPTER FIVE

The Early Iron Age

The Introduction of Iron to West Africa

West Africa had no Bronze Age and practically no Copper Age. Gold, easy to recover native from placers, was probably known in pre-Roman times. Tin, also easy to recover from placers and easy to reduce to metal, had been smelted on the Jos Plateau at least as early as the first century A.D.

The working of iron is a more complicated process. Native iron occurs nowhere in the earth's crust except in Greenland. Iron-ore is seldom found in placers, except the magnetite-sands known in some countries, which yield a high-grade ore concentrated usually from weathered granite.[1] Elsewhere ore must be mined. As its value is usually patchy and low-grade ore cannot normally be smelted, it must be carefully hand-sorted after extraction.

The richest ore mined consists of hard concentrated deposits in old rocks. Such ore-bodies were attacked in several places round the Mediterranean in pre-Roman times. They often occur opencast, which would avoid the problems of underground mining; not that in many parts of Europe and probably of Asia underground mining had not been practised with some engineering skill in the Bronze Age. Deposits in rock have been mined in various parts of West Africa, perhaps not very anciently, especially from the quartzites of Togo. But they would be unattractive to people with primitive techniques and tools. The ore is hard to break and often difficult to smelt in primitive furnaces.

Soft ores of recent formation would therefore appeal to men without experience in iron-working. In northern Europe precipitates of iron salts in bogs were popular; some contain harmful impurities like phosphorus. The beds are too thin to appeal to an industrialist, but could easily be dug by peasants. In Africa also there are recent superficial deposits, the lateritic crusts. An ancient crust is hard, but usually brittle; recent laterites are often nodular. The difficulty is that most laterite is poor in iron; very careful comminution and hand-sorting is needed to give a usable furnace charge. Below the crust also there are zones of concentration, especially in the forest where the rock has completely rotted and most of the silica has gone into solution. Stringers of high-grade hematite are described in rotten rock just below the stone-line; at Kumasi there is evidence for these having been mined, whether as ore or pigment.

The smelting of iron-ore does not require a very high temperature (800–900° C), but could not be carried out except in some form of constructed furnace, be it no more than a hole in the ground, or without bellows except under favourable conditions of natural draught (strong regular winds). Iron was discovered only after many centuries of the use of copper and bronze. Earlier pieces which have been recorded seem to be native meteoric iron or occasionally pieces reduced by chance. They had no economic significance, and often served as jewellery. It is true that iron unskilfully smelted would be of less use for many purposes than bronze. But if it had been known as a metal, it would certainly have been produced now and then. The difficulty for the bronze-smith was that iron-smelting requires a radically different technique. One heats copper-ore until the copper melts, as one does with more easily fusible metals. The melting of iron requires a temperature higher than was attainable throughout antiquity; and the addition of carbon, which reduces the melting-point, needs special skills. But iron-ore reduces long before it melts; only one must know how to stop the smelting without trying for impossible temperatures. Furthermore, the iron-bloom which comes out of the furnace looks unpromising. It needs frequent heating and hammering to express the slag and yield a piece of metal, which even then is likely to be too soft to be serviceable.

The very complicated techniques of iron-smelting were at least partly worked out in eastern Anatolia about 1500 B.C. Some attempt was made to keep them secret; but with the weakening of the Hittite state they were rapidly diffused through the Near East and into Europe. Iron, however, did not at once supersede bronze, except where bronze was difficult to procure; for though iron-ore is common, the unsteeled metal is of little use for tools and especially weapons, which must be hard, sharp and rigid.

Iron was occasionally imported to Egypt in the nineteenth dynasty; but local ores do not seem to have been found or local fuel was not available to smelt them, so Egypt practically remained in the Bronze Age until the Assyrian conquest in the seventh century. The Punic settlers in the Maghreb and the Greeks in Cyrenaica had access to overseas supplies of iron. It is unlikely that the natives whom they found possessed any, though it does not follow that they were totally ignorant of it.

An important industry of iron-smelting was established at Meroe and other sites in the Sudan[2] after 400 B.C. but before the first century B.C., and continued until about A.D. 330. Previous to the fourth century B.C. little iron has been found in graves in the Sudan, and it must have been imported from Egypt and probably from overseas. Very large slag-heaps have been found round Meroe.

One would expect Meroe to have been the centre of diffusion of iron-working in Africa. There were apparently regular routes from the middle Nile Valley to Lake Chad, though they may not have been continuously used. Many features of West African culture, especially in the royal ritual,[3] appear to be pharaonic, and are most likely to have reached West Africa after it had become sufficiently civilized to adopt them (i.e. after the mesoneolithic), and through the pharaonic successor-state of Meroe. Unfortunately, though Sayce speaks of furnace remains at Meroe, no description of them has been published. While West Africa has in recent times used high furnaces, the most primitive type of bowl-furnace, with pot-bellows, is described by Russegger in Kordofan in 1844.[4] The bowl-furnace appears very early on Egyptian monuments, and one would expect continuity through the centuries in Kordofan. If Meroe used the shaft-furnace, it would be surprising that a more archaic type survived in the region nearest the Nile Valley. We cannot assume that the shaft furnace was introduced to West Africa by Europeans from the coast. It is more likely to have formed part of the original industry.

It is further argued that the modern tribes eastward from Lake Chad are primitive, so it is unlikely that any important cultural practice came from this direction. Consequently, it is suggested that the knowledge of iron-smelting was brought to West Africa across the Sahara from the Maghreb.[5] There is, however, almost no evidence for iron-smelting in the Sahara,[6] where lack of fuel would be an insuperable obstacle. Saharan peoples later obtained their iron ready fashioned from their neighbours in the savannah. It is true that while the bowmen on Saharan rock paintings probably used stone arrow-heads, as Herodotus describes,[7] in the caballine period large-bladed spears, almost certainly of iron, were common (above, p. 173). But the date of these paintings is uncertain, and the swords which these people sometimes wear are unlikely to be earlier than the Roman empire and may be Arab. The

R

chariots depicted on Saharan paintings can hardly have been constructed without metal; but it is now thought that the style of flying gallop may be inspired by Roman rather than by Mycenean art,[8] and the carts which the Garamantes used[9] may have been of simpler construction and not exposed to such strains that metal bolts and pins would be necessary.

Pot-bellows are known from Egypt, and are described as common in the Cameroons[10] and Equatorial Africa. The essential principle is a pair of vessels, which may be of pottery or of wood; these are inflated and deflated by moving a leather cap up and down. In Africa this was done with the hands, in Egypt with the feet. Pot-bellows occur in north-western Ghana and among the Bassari (Togo), where the pump-bellows are a specialized and more efficient form.

Bag-bellows on the other hand are found in North Africa and the Sahara. They are more easily portable by nomads.[11] They overlap occasionally with pot-bellows, for instance at Atakpame (Togo) and in the Cameroons.

Nearly all our evidence about West African iron-working is in fact ethnological, and we know practically nothing about practices in the first millennium A.D. It seems on the whole probable that iron-smelting was diffused on an industrial scale from the middle Nile Valley. This would suit the large slag-heaps at Bochianga near Koro Toro on the Bahr-el-Ghazal, associated with painted pottery of Nubian type, though it cannot be of very early date.[12] A limited knowledge of iron may, however, have reached parts of West Africa from the Sahara, for instance at Ntereso by invaders from the Niger bend.

NOTE. This account of the diffusion of iron-working to West Africa is complicated by two radiocarbon dates just received from Ntereso. This site (pp. 277–82), near the White Volta in northern Ghana, contained three cultural levels, which seem to have succeeded each other with practically no interval and probably did not last very long; a duration of not more than one century for the whole occupation would not be unreasonable. No iron was found in level I, or perhaps in II; but several pieces from III indicate that by that time iron was known, though there is no evidence for its being smelted on the spot. A date of 3190 ± 120 has been received for the final phase of level I (SR-61), 3580 ± 130 for level III (SR-52). Both samples were satisfactorily stratified and from fairly large pieces of charred wood. The second date must be rejected, in view of the known history of iron-working; either the sample has been contaminated by earlier material, which with charcoal is difficult to explain though it can easily happen with calcareous matter, or the charred wood came from the centre of a long-lived tree and its growth was several centuries older than its deposition. The first date, for level I, is not in contradiction to present archaeological knowledge. It implies, however, that iron-working reached West Africa before the eleventh century B.C.; how and whence we cannot tell.

The knowledge of iron may have reached the west coast by cultural diffusion, not across the Sahara but from sub-Roman Morocco (below, p. 255), and not from the Punic but from the Roman world. The first evidence for iron weapons in Toucouleur country (Senegal) is El Bekri (A.D. 1067); by the fifteenth century iron was well known along the coast and was probably brought from the interior (not necessarily from farther east than the upper Niger, and very probably from inland Senegal).

About the form of the furnaces we can only guess until evidence is forthcoming regarding those at Meroe. If iron-working was in fact diffused from Roman North Africa, high furnaces would have come with it. They are unlikely to be a recent importation, as each furnace had to be broken down and patched before reuse; the continuous process which was developed in medieval Europe was unknown in Africa.[13] High furnaces were seen in operation about 1900 in Bassari [fig. 78] and Akpafu (Togo).[14] While presumably more sophisticated than the original types, they must closely preserve the tradition and are worth study by archaeologists. The industry at Akpafu is certainly not old; it was started within living memory. These iron-working areas (Akpafu and the western edge of Bassari around the ore deposit of Shieni) come out clearly on the map of Ghana [fig. 80].[15] Iron slag occurs sometimes in dated horizons, but the dating of furnaces is much more difficult. The high furnaces at Kouga and Tindirma (Mali) probably belong to the medieval mounds with painted pottery [fig. 84].[16]

On the other hand, very primitive modern furnaces of the bonfire type are described near Jebba (Nigeria);[17] and the furnaces at Ola–Igbi, though more advanced,[18] do not belong to the true shaft type. So it is possible that in parts of West Africa the high furnace was not original but has been introduced in the Middle Ages, and has overlain an older iron industry which would be directly associated with Egypt and Kordofan. This problem can be solved only if early iron-smelting sites are found and properly excavated.

I have included distribution maps of known iron-working sites in West Africa and in Ghana [figs. 79–80].[19] The former does not mean a great deal, as some of the industrial areas are small, it is difficult to obtain chronological data, with the result that sites may be distributed over ten centuries or more, and exploration and recording have been so patchy that important centres are almost certainly omitted. It is

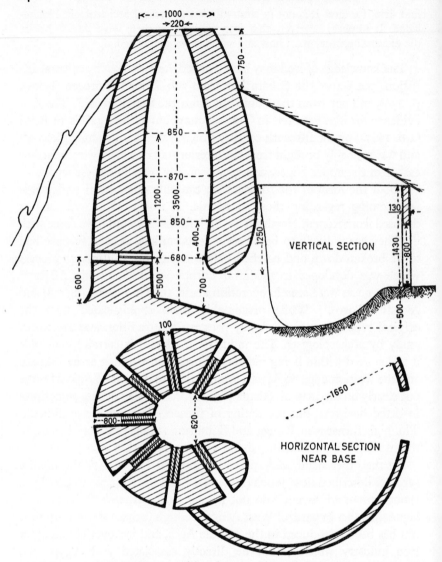

FIG. 78 Iron-smelting furnace, Bassari, Togo

from Hupfeld, Mitteilungen aus den deutschen Schutzgebieten
xii (*1899*), *p. 180*

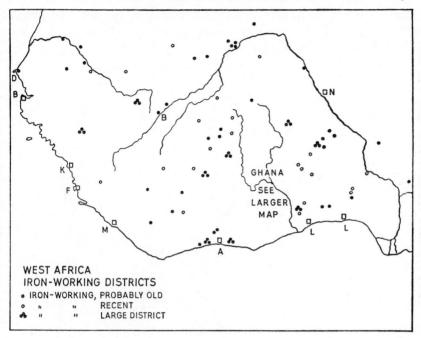

WEST AFRICA
IRON-WORKING DISTRICTS
• IRON-WORKING, PROBABLY OLD
○ „   „   RECENT
♣ „   „   LARGE DISTRICT

FIG. 79

clear that in the past some tribes have worked iron much more intensively than others, and have probably traded it to their neighbours and
far afield. Many iron-workers seem to be relict tribes; it is natural that
conquerors exploited their subjects for the hard work of metallurgy.
In some regions iron-working was witnessed by travellers a century or
less ago; in others it seems to be much older.

The map of Ghana [fig. 80] is inserted to illustrate the large number
of small sites. This is probably true of the whole of West Africa. Each
slag-heap contains the slag from a few furnace charges. Smelters moved
on probably when their furnace could no longer be repaired or fuel in
the immediate vicinity had been exhausted. The map shows concen-
trations of iron-working. Of these, north-western Ghana (Lawra and
Tumu districts) was still smelting iron during this century, Akpafu
is no older. The concentration around Yeji and Salaga is much older
and clearly of former importance; fair-sized trees are growing on some
of the very numerous slag-heaps; pieces of slag have been found on
early modern and late medieval sites in the district. There was a good
deal of smelting on a small scale on the edge of the savannah in north-
western Ashanti. The absence of sites in the northern part of the forest
is notable, and there is evidence that this belt was until recently largely

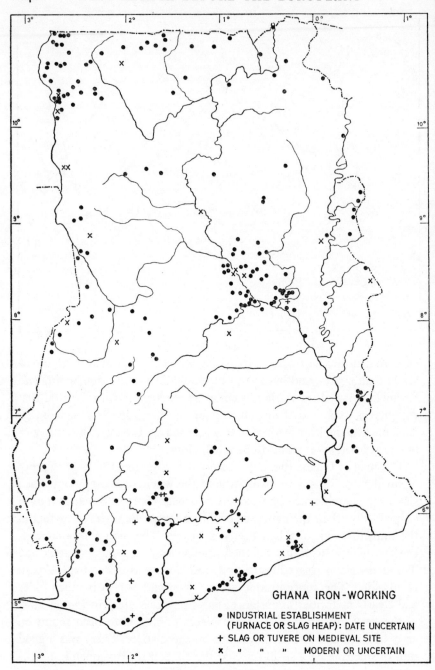

GHANA IRON-WORKING

● INDUSTRIAL ESTABLISHMENT
(FURNACE OR SLAG HEAP): DATE UNCERTAIN
+ SLAG OR TUYERE ON MEDIEVAL SITE
✗ " " " MODERN OR UNCERTAIN

FIG. 80

uninhabited. In the forest there was clearly an active local industry, undeterred by the difficulty of obtaining dry fuel. Most of the slag-heaps are fairly large, and may have served local needs for a long period. Near the coast in Gomoa and near Achimota there are small slag-heaps, probably of a more industrialized economy, stratigraphically recent.[20]

Hardly ever is there indication of exact date. Pieces of slag or tuyere are, however, found in habitation sites which can be dated approximately. Some smelting sites, especially in southern Ghana, seem to go back to the later Middle Ages, a good many probably belong to the last four centuries. when the country was progressing culturally and economically on Atlantic trade and was no longer a backwater on the fringe of the great empires of the Niger Valley.

Roman and Post-Roman Penetration along the Nile

During the first millennium B.C. the lands of the Mediterranean and the Near East, where civilization above subsistence-level was rapidly developing and was being spread by commerce, imperialism and scientific curiosity, were bounded on the south by an almost insuperable barrier of desert. The routes through this zone were difficult, to be attempted only by local experts. The little trade and information which came from beyond the desert did not seem to justify the hardships and dangers of attempting to cross it.

At the eastern side of Africa two channels seemed more inviting, though they were not free of danger, the Red Sea and the Nile. It had been known for a long time that there was a way into the Indian Ocean, and both the Ptolemies and the Romans greatly developed this route for commercial purposes. The Ptolemies were able to obtain easily the products of tropical Africa, to the Romans there were the even more inviting riches of India and the East. Along the African coast, however, there was no attempt to penetrate the interior, though ships rounded the Horn and sailed at least as far south as the modern Tanzania. No Mediterranean influence has been observed in Ethiopia before the founding of Axum in the first century A.D.[21] By the third century Axum was becoming a civilized state, and in the fourth or fifth century[22] it was converted to Christianity under Ezana and established contact with the Nile Valley with the overthrow of Meroe.

The Red Sea is barren and dangerous to navigation. It was a highway for ships which wanted to go farther. The Nile Valley was a goal in itself. In the Middle and New Kingdoms Egyptian armies had penetrated south of the border of Egypt, often in search of gold; explorers had gone much farther.[23] With the break-up of the New Kingdom there had grown up at Napata a state which seems to have been completely African in its social organization,[24] but was strongly influenced by pharaonic civilization and ritual. Relations with Egypt were uneasy, as Egypt broke up and fell under the domination of Asiatic empires. Napata did not repeat her seventh-century attempt to reconquer Egypt for a pharaonic successor-state. Under Persian rule there was probably little contact between Egypt and Nubia, and Herodotus knew practically nothing about the lands beyond Syene. The Nubians, after the threat by Cambyses, withdrew their capital from Napata to the more remote Meroe.

The Ptolemies, who were enterprising business-men, were anxious to open up the Nile Valley, and obtained the co-operation of the able Nubian king, Ergamenes. But with the weakening of the Ptolemaic kingdom communications again lapsed. When Augustus annexed Egypt he wanted a secure southern frontier, and was interested in the people beyond it. After a raid on Napata[25] and an attempt to annex as far as the Second Cataract, the frontier was established at Hiera Sycaminos,[26] where there is said to have been an important market.[27] Romano-Egyptian pottery, glass and bronzes were imported to Nubia, which was developing into one of the semi-civilized states within the orbit of the Mediterranean world. The chain-pump for irrigation and the wine-press furthered its development. Nero was able to send two centurions to explore the Nubian kingdom.[28] They apparently reached the Sudd, beyond which navigation was impossible.[29]

The collapse of the Meroitic kingdom in the fourth or fifth century A.D. probably led to anarchy in the middle Nile Valley. There had been disorder even earlier on the southern border of Egypt, so that Diocletian withdrew his troops from Hiera Sycaminos to Syene. Nubia again came within the orbit of the Mediterranean world with the arrival of Christian missionaries, dependent on Alexandria, in the sixth century A.D.

But although there is evidence in classical authors for penetration up the Nile Valley, there is nothing about contacts with the west, along the route which must already have been in existence through Kordofan and Darfur to Lake Chad. In neolithic times there must have been desert tracks much farther north, certainly from the Nile Valley to Tibesti; we do not know if they were still in use. The route through Darfur would, it is true, leave the Nile south of Meroe, which was very nearly the limit of ancient geographical knowledge. Nevertheless, it would seem that the radiation of culture from the Nile Valley into West

Africa[3] may not have taken place within the Roman period. The art of iron-smelting should have been carried across then, if the knowledge of iron in West Africa was derived from Meroe. Yet the only clear archaeological evidence for contact from east to west is the painted pottery from Bochianga on the Bahr-el-Ghazal,[12] associated with an important iron industry. It may have been refugees from the wreck of the Nubian state and the Arab conquest who brought the arts of civilization to the west. About the eighth century A.D. communications may have been easier, as there is evidence for some northward extension of the summer rainbelt.[30]

The Pre-Islamic Sahara

The Sahara was by no means uninhabited in the Iron Age. Conditions may have been slightly more hospitable than today, as desertification is progressive with exhaustion of fossil water and increase of blown sand. There were already large ergs, which were practically uninhabitable; but considerable areas must have had moderate water supplies, some pasture, and to judge from the number of tombs, a fairly high human population.

Nor were communications impossible. Herodotus[31] describes an expedition of some Nasamones from eastern Tripolitania to a land with marshes and a large river, in which was a big settlement of negroes. This tale may be satisfactorily combined with a plausible reconstruction of the route which Herodotus describes[32] from Augila to the Straits of Gibraltar.[33] It is unlikely that there was a route across Africa behind the Maghreb, straight across the Grand Erg Occidental; but there is an ancient route southward from Tripolitania through the eastern Fezzan to the oasis of Kawar and now to Lake Chad. It is reasonable to suppose that in Greek times it diverged to the east and reached water farther north in Djourab; for so long as the Bahr-el-Ghazal was flowing,[34] Lake Chad was not the terminus of the equatorial rivers.

Attention has been paid to paintings and engravings of horse-drawn chariots.[35] They are more or less strung out on two routes, from the Fezzan (whence there were tracks to the coastal cities of Tripolitania and Cyrenaica) south-west to the Hoggar and thence south to the Tilemsi Valley and Gao, and from the southern side of the Atlas roughly parallel to the coast through Mauritania and thence turning sharply east to Lac Faguibine near the Niger bend. Both these routes avoid the main ergs; the western has to cut across dunes to reach the Niger, but all the sites are near water-points on the reg.

Most of the chariots are very light vehicles with two four-spoked wheels. They often have only a driver and no accompanying warrior. They are unsuitable for transport. Attention has particularly been drawn to the flying gallop of the horses.[36] Certain stylistic details have been claimed as typically Aegean, and it has been suggested that the drivers were Bronze Age sea-raiders, who reached Libya at the end of the thirteenth century B.C. and in due course settled inland. The chariots have been brought into connection with Herodotus' story[9] of the Garamantes, who chased the Troglodytes (cave-dwellers, perhaps in Tibesti or in Tassili n'Ajjer) in four-horse cars.

The chariots of the eastern route may perhaps belong to the first millennium B.C., though a charioteer from Tassili n'Ajjer has a broad-bladed iron spear.[37] I am doubtful about direct derivation from the Mycenean world, in view of the centuries involved. Those of the western route are mostly more stylized,[38] and some of them are four-wheeled carts. This route is first mentioned in literature about A.D. 750,[39] but is likely to have been in use much earlier. It has, however, been pointed out that the flying gallop is common for circus chariots on Roman mosaics.[8] It is not unlikely that, especially on the west coast in Morocco and Mauritania, it is really derived from the Roman world and is unconnected with the Aegean Bronze Age. Among a large group of engravings at Oued Lar'ar (Sud–Oranais) are perhaps two scythed chariots.[40] These were used by the Pharusii in this region in Roman times.

The horse, which appears to be the animal harnessed to Saharan chariots and carts, had been a more recent domesticate than the ox and sheep, and reached Africa with the Hyksos invasion of Egypt in the seventeenth century B.C.[41] Cavalry instead of war-chariots came into use gradually in different parts of the Mediterranean world. Homer hardly knows riding in Greece. In Libya it is suggested that chariots went out of use in the early third century B.C., as they are still recorded in the campaigns of Agathocles;[42] they lasted much later in the Sahara.[43] Charioteers occasionally carry spears with broad metal blades and small round shields.[37] These are commonly carried by riders, and some spears have two long perforations.[44] They had largely gone out of use by the cameline period.

The horse is not sufficiently hardy to be used satisfactorily in most of the Sahara. There had been wild camels in Africa during the pleistocene; possibly a few are represented on the earliest Saharan rock drawings, but it is difficult to date them on stylistic evidence.[45] There are a few remains and representations of camels from predynastic and early dynastic Egypt.[46] They then apparently became extinct, and do not reappear until the first millennium B.C., when they were reintroduced to Egypt perhaps by the Assyrians. It is probable that the camel was nowhere domesticated before the second millennium, so there is no proof of a continued tradition of breeding them in Africa from neolithic times.[47]

The Ptolemies probably possessed a few camels. By the first century B.C. small numbers had reached the Maghreb. The earliest literary record of them is Caesar's capture of twenty-two from King Juba.[48] An inscription of Massinissa speaks of a leader of 'gyml', a word which in later Berber came to mean camels;[49] but its connotation in the second century B.C. is doubtful. The camel appears on coins of L. Lollius of 39 B.C. as a symbol of Cyrenaica. It is, however, seldom mentioned in Africa in Latin literature, even by North African authors, because it is of minor importance in the coastal regions and Tell, where writers lived.[50]

From at least A.D. 200 a camel-corps formed part of the Roman garrison, especially of those provinces which bordered on the desert, like Tripolitania. Of about A.D. 100 is an inscription of Ti. Flavius Stephanus, 'praepositus camellorum', who seems to have been in charge either of the ivory trade or of catching elephants for the Roman circus. In A.D. 370 Romanus demanded 4,000 camels from Leptis Magna.[51] If by that time the Roman army made considerable use of them, it is almost certain that the nomads behind Tripolitania and probably farther west possessed them, and they could already have begun to use them for trans-Saharan traffic.

The use of camels apparently overlaps that of horses in Saharan rock art [see fig. 46 9–10]. They perhaps reached Tibesti and Ennedi fairly early, where there is no true caballine stage.[52] It is, however, dangerous to date rock pictures on stylistic criteria. The Arab conquests were effected with cavalry. There is no good evidence when the camel became common in the central Sahara or when the horse disappeared. Lhote[36] has tried to work out the indications from rock engravings; but they lead to few positive conclusions and no positive dates. Undoubtedly the camel greatly assisted trans-Saharan trade and traffic. It was really the Arabs who opened up West Africa to the Mediterranean world, and it may not have been until quite late in the first millennium A.D. that camel-convoys became regular on trans-Saharan routes.

There is in fact extremely little material evidence for pre-Arabic contact between the Mediterranean and West Africa. Before the Roman empire there were current a few travellers' tales, based on actual voyages by Africans (above, p. 245). The geographer, Ptolemy, whose sources are partly Hellenistic, knows nothing about tropical Africa.[53] He has filled up the empty space between the Roman *limes* and the equator with muddled duplications of North African names and a few names of tribes and mountains which may be inventions or derived from some unknown and inaccurate source. Herodotus[54] speaks of gold from the island of Kyrauis, which could well be near the upper Niger; and the gold in the tale of silent barter on the Atlantic coast also could indicate that the famous medieval goldfields were already in production. But this evidence is vague, it could refer to goldfields much nearer the Mediterranean, and there is no sign that in ancient times gold was being regularly brought across the Sahara.

There are accounts of three Roman expeditions into the Sahara. Cornelius Balbus in 19 B.C. apparently reached or received envoys from the Fezzan.[55] Roman objects become common at Garama, and merchants were probably installed there under a client-kingdom. The Mount Giri, 'where the gems come from', could perhaps be Eguei Zouma, between the Fezzan and Tibesti, with its amazonite quarries (above, p. 162). But identifications in Tassili n'Ajjer and the Hoggar are no better than guesswork, aimed at proving that Balbus followed the chariot-route perhaps almost to the Niger.[56] Even if some names are genuine Saharan, a Roman general would include in his triumph-list any place or people he had ever heard of. The best interpretation suggests that Balbus was operating around and north of the Algerian shotts.

Towards the end of the first century A.D. Septimius Flaccus and Julius Maternus, perhaps members of the same expedition, penetrated a long way south from the Fezzan to Ethiopia and the fabulous land of Agisymba. They must have reached the savannah where there was plenty of big game; the mention of rhinoceros shows that they did not follow the chariot-route south-west towards the Niger. Like the Nasamones many centuries earlier, they could have reached the Eguei and Djourab depression, which would then have been a huge oasis at a latitude which was climatically Saharan.

In the late second century A.D. Roman armies were pushing southward from Tripolitania, in order to protect the civilian province along the coast.[57] The first inscriptional evidence is from Commodus. Septimius Severus, a native of Leptis Magna, was interested in the hinterland and perhaps in trans-Saharan trade,[58] and occupied posts on the road to Cydamus (Ghadames) and perhaps as far as Garama (Djerma).[59] Thus for a time much of the Fezzan came under Roman control. There may have been more rain then than today, as the cemeteries of Garama and Ghat lie on the slopes and not in the now desert valley-bottoms.

South of the Fezzan there is no evidence for Roman penetration. Very few coins have been found south of the *limes*, and many of them do not resist criticism.[60] There are several from the line of the eastern chariots, which is a natural route avoiding the ergs and may have been used in Roman times, even if it was not the route taken by Roman expeditions. The most interesting find was at the fortress of Tin Hinan, near Abalessa (Hoggar).[61] What appears to have been a walled settlement, probably the capital of a Saharan kingdom, was later used as tomb of a chief; unfortunately, the excavation was hardly up to modern standards. In the tomb was jewellery of African origin, bracelets of gold, silver and iron, beads of gold, silver and coloured stone, and a steatopygous amulet of plaster. The gold may have come from the Niger Valley (above, p. 248); silver was probably not produced in West Africa, so Roman coins may have been melted up. There were also Roman lamps and pottery, engraved glass and three glass beads, and a wooden bowl impressed with a coin of Constantine I. It is clear that a few Roman objects found their way south, and that at least one route across the Sahara was occasionally used. Roman pieces may turn up on important sites in West Africa, for they found their way into chiefs' treasures. But they were probably often hoarded, and they can with difficulty be used for dating local material. Abalessa, for instance, must be later than A.D. 320; there is no reason why it should not be as late as the sixth or seventh century. Drawings of camels and early tifinagh inscriptions, apparently contemporary with the building, do not suggest a very early date.

Gold-production on the upper Niger and perhaps in other areas had probably started in pre-Islamic times. The earliest Arabic mention of gold from the kingdom of Ghana in southern Mauritania is by El Fazari about A.D. 800.[62] The method of medieval working deep-level gravels implies a long apprenticeship in surveying and mining. We do not hear of Arab prospectors penetrating barbarian lands to the south; so it is likely that the techniques were developed locally by Africans, and the gold trade became important when there were outlets for it.

The Saharan peoples of this period were nomadic and probably of Berber stock and partly Berber culture, as shown by the tifinagh alphabet derived from Neopunic. The acquisition of the camel, partly perhaps by theft from Roman troops, greatly increased their numbers and wealth. In the second and third centuries A.D. the Roman frontier had been pushed out to the edge of the desert. Diocletian withdrew outlying garrisons, leaving a fringe, especially in Algeria, of more or less responsible tribal states ruled by kings and aristocracies, as a buffer against the less controllable nomads of the true desert.[50] Towns gradually decayed in these native kingdoms, the episcopal organization was weakened, and there was a reversion to tribal life. States were less stable, and texts from the fifth and sixth centuries A.D. suggest the rise here and there of strong rulers who were able temporarily to combine many tribes, just as had happened in pre-Roman times in Numidia and on the European fringes of the civilized Mediterranean world. In the sixth century there seems to have been pressure on these Berber states by the more dangerous camel-nomads from the south, owing to increasing population or perhaps desiccation, and probably to a drift of people westward in the Sahara.[63] They were reinforced in the seventh century by Arab immigrants, also refugees from desiccation. The Berber peasants took refuge especially in the mountains, where they were able to resist Arabization and may have remained for a period Christian and perhaps Donatist.

Many funerary monuments in the central Sahara are believed to be of the pre-Islamic Iron Age, bazinas or tumuli and chouchets or small towers. Both types occur in Roman Algeria and spread southward with the expansion of the Berber nomads.[64] A group of cairns with rough peristaliths and central megalithic chambers, undated, is described at Guelta de Zli in the Mauritanian Adrar.[65] Complex and V-shaped forms may be later developments. Around Tin Hinan are many chouchets and horizontal slabs marking tombs. This was probably the capital of an important kingdom. Another centre was Tefedost, where tumuli contained tightly flexed bodies with baskets, one iron spear, one bronze bracelet, two metal leg-rings, one faience bead and some beads of limestone and quartz.[66] There are similarities to material from Gao and Killi. But in general very little is known of political centres, and few tombs have been opened. The site of Ghana, the first of the medieval Sudanic empires, has not been identified.

Dates have been obtained from pre-Islamic tombs in the Fezzan, but not from the Hoggar. They indicate that the pre-Islamic culture survived into the later centuries of the first millennium A.D. From Tajerhi we have 1190 ± 120 (Sa–78), from El Barkat farther west 1330 ± 120 and 1680 ± 150 B.P. (Sa–92 and 93).[67]

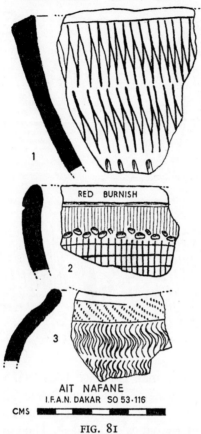

RED BURNISH

1

2

3

AIT NAFANE
I.F.A.N. DAKAR SO 53·116
CMS

FIG. 81

Similar tombs have been found in Tibesti and Ennedi, along with villages of tower-huts and stone circles which yielded nothing on excavation and may have been sheep-shelters.[68] The tombs contained practically no grave-goods; there was evidence that the bodies were buried in leather sacks. Huts at Fada in western Ennedi yielded celts, stone bracelets and sandstone tools;[69] iron does not appear before a late stage, perhaps fifteenth-century. Some tumulus-tombs seem associated with painted caves containing traces of habitation.

There are in the central Sahara a few monoliths, especially several sculptured ones round a tomb at Tabelbalet.[70] Portable sculptured stones with crude human or animal representations, doubtless of religious significance, have been found especially in Tuareg country.[71] There is no clear evidence that Saharan sculpture is ancestral to the monuments of the Niger Valley and farther south [fig. 83, below, pp. 260f, 274f, 293].

Little has been recorded about early Iron Age pottery in the Sahara,

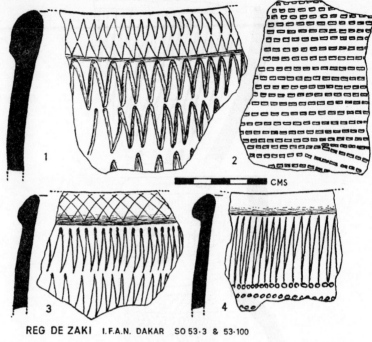

REG DE ZAKI   I.F.A.N. DAKAR   SO 53-3 & 53-100

FIG. 82

and among nomads it may not have been much used. The finely decorated heavy overhanging rims from Adrar Madet (Niger)[72] and Reg de Zaki north of Tessalit [fig. 82] suggest skeuomorphs of basketry which was found in the tombs of Tefedost. The taste for tight decoration at Ait Nafane [fig. 81] and the reticulate patterns [cp. figs. 81 2, 82 3] are also suggestive of basket-work, though I have shown that walking grooves and comb probably go back technically to Mediterranean cardial pottery (above, p. 156). It looks as if pottery from a settlement at Ghezendi (N.E. Tibesti) was moulded on to baskets to receive its decoration.[73]

These sites which have yielded early post-neolithic pottery must have been more or less permanent habitations. The shell-breccia found at Ait Nafane indicates a former pool. The Saharan peoples may not have made great use of pottery, but they cannot have lost the art, as they brought their styles to their settlements in the savannah, like Ntereso, where pottery was abundant [figs. 99–101]. They may also have brought the first knowledge of iron, though its industrial production probably came later from the east. The savannah in fact remained in the neolithic stage until the northerners began to push southward.

Phoenicians and Romans on the Atlantic Coast

There is scattered literary evidence for navigation in the Atlantic outside the Straits of Gibraltar in pre-Roman times. But geographical information was vague, none of our accounts are at first hand, and mariners' tales have certainly been mixed with genuine reports.

As we have nothing in the fragments of Hecataeus (sixth century B.C.), our earliest source is Herodotus. He tells of the Phoenician circumnavigation of Africa from east to west under Necho in the seventh century B.C.[74] Opinions are divided on whether this tale is true. The navigators would have encountered very great difficulties from adverse currents off West Africa. Mauny has frequently maintained that no one before the Portuguese, with their advanced practice in navigation, was able to round Cap Bojador in a northward direction. At any rate the attempt, if it was successful, was not repeated, and these Phoenicians are not known to have made any impact on African cultures.

Herodotus tells also[75] of an attempt by Sataspes in the sixth century to circumnavigate from west to east. He passed Soloeis, which was probably Cap Spartel;[76] no one knew how much farther he went. Herodotus[54] had also heard from a Carthaginian source of the silent barter of goods for gold on the west coast of Africa. This tale was still current about this coast in the thirteenth century A.D. Mauny[39] considers that the gold came from southern Morocco behind Agadir; but even if it came from the Sudanese goldfields much farther south, it may have been transported overland to a market not beyond the reach of ancient Mediterranean ships.

The Periplus of Hanno purports to be a translation of a Punic inscription of the sixth century B.C., commemorating a voyage of colonization and exploration down the Atlantic coast of Morocco. Much ink has been spilled in trying to resolve the difficulties and contradictions of its geography. It has recently been shown[77] that it is a forgery of about 300 B.C., based on Herodotus and perhaps on one or two details picked up at Carthage, but of no independent or documentary value.

There are two other texts of perhaps the late fourth century of rather more importance. Euthymenes of Massilia, not extant, spoke of crocodiles in a river which may have been the Draa. Pseudo-Scylax, a periplus written about 330 B.C. and fraudulently attributed to the explorer of nearly two centuries before, repeats travellers' tales about the African coast, but mentions two place-names, Lixus which is well known, and Cerne, perhaps a legendary name but not improbably

s

equated by the author or by a reliable source (? Hecataeus) with the settlement on Mogador Island.

Polybius sailed outside the Straits in 147 B.C., probably not very far. The next important account was that of Juba II, whose fleet in the first century B.C. reached the Canary Islands and supplied valuable detail to Roman geographers.[78] So far as we can gather from Pliny and Ptolemy, Juba's data were not always accurate as to distances and directions, and he probably attached to places he had discovered mythical names derived from Hanno or from Egypt, such as Theon Ochema (probably Cape Ghir), Hesperiou Keras (near Cape Juby) and the Fortunatae Insulae (in Juba certainly referring to the Canary Islands, in older literature wholly mythical or possibly sometimes referring to Madeira).[79]

There is probably no independent literary source later than Juba, though there was certainly navigation during the Roman empire as far as Mogador. Excavations carried out on the island[80] have proved the reality of the settlement. Above a scattered neolithic site were found three periods of Mediterranean occupation, in the seventh to sixth centuries B.C., late first century B.C. to about A.D. 50, and early fourth to sixth centuries A.D. In intervening periods there were occasional visits by Mediterranean ships. The second period of occupation was that of Juba, who established a factory for purple dye; heaps of *Purpura haemostoma* have been found along the coast. The earliest expansion may not have extended far beyond Mogador. Herodotus' story of silent barter for gold must go back to this phase. Theories to bring Punic or Roman explorers to Mauritania or even the River Senegal are unacceptable.[81]

Lixus and Banasa, not far south of the Straits, were continuously occupied from before 500 B.C., the date when the first settlement at Mogador was abandoned.[82] As might be expected, stray Punic finds have been made along the Moroccan coast, most of them probably carried to the natives by trade; but there may also have been Punic settlements, especially at Sala which was important in Roman times.

In the interior of Morocco Volubilis had grown up round a Berber shrine from perhaps the third or second century B.C.[83] It was developed by both Juba II and the Romans.

The Roman province of Tingitana extended as far south as Sala and Volubilis, and there was doubtless political control beyond the official frontier. Diocletian abandoned most of the province about A.D. 285.[84]

The last inscription from Volubilis is dated 283, but the town was soon reoccupied, the new houses being poorly built. It appears that the excavators paid little attention to this level; but the town continued to exist, and was besieged by the Muslims in 684. It probably became the capital of a Berber kingdom, perhaps of the Baquates,[85] a semi-client tribe. They, however, disappear not much later, and it would appear that Romanism underwent an eclipse in interior Morocco in the fourth and fifth centuries, there is hardly a trace of ecclesiastical organization, and perhaps the whole country reverted to barbarism. It is therefore surprising to find a vigorous revival in the sixth century. Evidence starts for an organized church and probably more settled conditions in Orania about A.D. 450. There were Catholic bishops there is 484, and a good many Latin inscriptions are known west of the Oued Chelif in western Algeria. The evidence for Morocco is later. Christian inscriptions between A.D. 599 and 655 have been found at Volubilis. There was a civilized state and apparently a Catholic ecclesiastical organization, based on Roman traditions.

Morocco lies at the northern end of the western trans-Saharan route, which despite its difficulties was much used in the Middle Ages. At first it ran fairly far to the west, just east of the border of the present Spanish Sahara, to Awdaghost.[86] It had been in use in pre-Islamic times, for it follows the western line of chariot engravings.[35] These are probably of late date. At the southern end of the route was the kingdom of Ghana, the first of the organized states of the Niger Valley, already directing the traffic in gold by A.D. 800, according to Al Fazari. I would suggest that the political organization and civilization of Ghana was directly derived from the sub-Roman states of Morocco, which seem after an eclipse with the withdrawal of Roman garrisons to have pulled themselves together in the seventh century; especially from Volubilis, where government literacy and ecclesiastical organization was established in the capital of what at that date is a nameless kingdom, for the Baquates had disappeared from view for several centuries.

Thus it was that West Africa came into the orbit of the Mediterranean world, at first fitfully via the eastern chariot-route and the perhaps ephemeral state of Abalessa, then more firmly via the western route and the well-established kingdom of Ghana. In the seventh century came the Arabs, who though fanatical and destructive, soon absorbed and spread the civilization of the Near East; and being desert-dwellers were better equipped than the Romans and their peasant successor-states to tackle the formidable problem of contact across the Sahara.

The Nok-Culture

A remarkable series of terracottas and pottery has been found in stream-gravels near Nok, on the edge of the Jos Plateau. The gravels belong to the last stage of aggradation of the valleys,[87] and appear to have been rolled during Sub-pluvial III. They may have been deposited at an earlier date, for instance in Late Gamblian times. All the finds have been made in course of mining, and there has been no large-scale controlled excavation, which might throw light on details of the stratification.

Deposits near the sides of the valleys seem to have contained only Acheulian implements, so presumably are Late Kamasian. The overlying silts were twice eroded to bedrock. The latest erosion was by narrow channels, into which it appears that artefacts of the Nok-culture were thrown. These include[88] terracottas and pottery, tuyeres and iron-slag, iron axes, tin beads, querns, celts, hoes, bracelets, quartz lip-plugs, quartz cylindrical and disc-beads; perhaps also kwes.[89]

Sherds and terracottas are fragile and could not have survived rolling in the gravel; they must therefore have been dumped at the very end of the minor pluvial, when the gravel was ceasing to be rolled and was about to be sealed by silts. This feature enables us to date the culture by the radiocarbon tests which have been made (see table above, p. 81). The date of 2875 ± 70 (Y 142–4)[90] probably indicates the incision. The artefacts in the streams cannot be much earlier than 1750 ± 50 (Y 474), a date obtained from peaty clay sealing the gravel. This was not the earliest stage of the culture, as a date has been obtained from Taruga of 2230 ± 120 (I–1458).[91] The culture may thus reasonably be placed in the last centuries B.C. and the first century A.D. Dates about 500 B.C. which have been claimed are unacceptably early.

The gravels were not sealed, so objects could have got into them during the whole of the thousand or more years when they were exposed. But most of the other objects found, especially the evidences of metallurgy, should a priori be late. Some of the stone tools could be older, but should exhibit more signs of rolling.

The evidence for the Nok-culture is unsatisfactory, because true habitation sites have not been found. It has been suggested that objects were thrown into streams for ritual purposes, in which case they were probably selected and do not give a full picture of the culture. Moreover, in publications attention has been concentrated on the remarkable terracottas [pl. 36]. These appear to be of African style; the sharp-cut lines they often exhibit in details of feature suggest the influence of wood-carving. There does not seem to be direct inspiration from the Mediterranean or the Nile Valley, though the knowledge of metallurgy presumably came thence. So far as anything has been published on the pottery, it does not seem to belong to the general Saharan and West African tradition, and may also be derived from the Nile Valley, as may the technique of making terracotta statues, however Africanized their style. Whether the contact was due to immigration, perhaps of prospectors, we do not know.

Stray terracottas of the Nok-culture have been found over a large area of Northern Nigeria, apparently from the Niger–Benue Valleys over the whole of the Jos Plateau. They have not been found as far north as Kano. As further sites are frequently being discovered, it would be premature to venture a distribution map. It is not clear whether there was a continuity of technical tradition from Nok to the much later terracottas of Ife, or if the Ife art was independently introduced into Nigeria.[92] The Nok-culture is likely to have played some part in the formation of the Sao-culture around Lake Chad (below, p. 318), for the style of some Sao statuettes can be paralleled at Nok.

Undatable, but perhaps contemporary with the Nok-culture, are a few rather poor paintings of cattle, the best known being at Birnin Kudu, east of Kano.[93] The contents of the Birnin Kudu shelter were sherds, amorphous stone flakes, a stone bracelet, a quartz lip-plug and fragments of iron; this assemblage could be roughly contemporary with Nok. Paintings have been found round the northern and eastern sides of the Jos Plateau. They are far more naturalistic than the stylized figures of Hombori and Bamako and the linear engravings of Ghana, which may be associated with fairly recent initiation-cults (below, pp. 296–7, pls. 44–5). They could be the work of neolithic Saharans who had moved southward. Saharan types of painting were found by Mr. P. Carter at Nabruk in the extreme north-east of Ghana, and have just been published (see bibliography).

Fagg associates the Nigerian paintings with rock-gongs and rock-slides. The latter had ritual significance elsewhere, for instance in Portugal.[94] The gongs are slabs of rock which emit a booming sound when struck; some of them seem to have been intentionally propped so that they would resound.[95] They are found in many parts of the world, often show marks of striking, and frequently are associated with super-stition and sometimes ritual. Their uncanny character could have attracted attention independently in many places, and there is no evidence that the idea of the rock-gong has been diffused from a single centre. They have been found in Ghana and elsewhere in West Africa, unassociated with cattle paintings; so it is doubtful if the Birnin Kudu remains form part of a single cultural complex, or how widely[96].

The Great Iron Age Cultures of the Middle Niger

NOTE. This section is fairly concise, owing to the very full treatment of this area by Mauny in his recent book, *Tableau géographique de l'Ouest africain au moyen age (IFAN Mémoires* 61).

The Middle Ages was a period of great prosperity and civilization in the middle Niger Valley. There is a fair number of historical notices; but it is not the purpose of this book to discuss the history, but the material culture. One empire rose after another. The reasons may have been largely political. At the same time, political organization may have outrun means of communication. Powerful monarchs would require concentration of population round their capitals, and the fragile African soils are likely in a region of low rainfall to have been over-exploited. Irrigation, so far as it was practised, could also be dangerous, as it is liable to make the land saline if unskilfully applied. It is thought that the caliphate ruined parts of lower Mesopotamia in this way.

So far as we know, the old Niger delta in the Middle Ages was not more extensive than today, and there was no scope for irrigating to the north. The channel from near Tombouctou to Arawane was blocked by a terrace (now 5 metres high) since the Niger overflowed the bar at Tosaye.[97] It would require deepening for about 30 kms. northwards to enable water to flow from the Niger along it. The outlet to the north-west, into the Oualata–Tichitt basin, may be less blocked, as Sonni Ali about 1480 planned to dig a canal from Ras el Ma to Oualata.[98] So the channel was probably still traceable and the idea did not seem visionary at that date.

The basis of West African prosperity was its gold, which was welcome in the Middle East and in great demand in medieval Europe, where short supply of precious metals greatly hindered economic development. The most important goldfield was Wangara, a large area on the upper Niger, upstream from just north of Siguiri,[99] where there were rich placers in deep-level tertiary gravels.[100] It has been suggested that the gold had been discovered in pre-Roman times; but the difficulty of communications across the Sahara restricted its output; it was unimportant until it could be profitably sold. It was known to the Arab world by A.D. 800, and was of great importance by the time of El Bekri (eleventh century).[101] There were numerous caravans on the Saharan routes, which came to the markets for gold at the principal towns on and north of the Niger. But merchants were never allowed to penetrate to the real mining areas farther south. They sold for gold wares from the Sahara and the Mediterranean, largely luxury goods, seeing that the trade was controlled by the chiefs, weapons, the all-important commodity, salt, which has always been in demand among the partly vegetarian peoples of the Niger Valley, but not food or bulky goods which could not stand high costs of transport.

The goldfields of the Falémé Valley were probably discovered at an early date. The more remote goldfields to the south-east were hardly developed before the later Middle Ages, perhaps by prospectors from Wangara or the Niger cities. There was a good deal of gold-working in Lobi territory and along the Black Volta, also farther south in Ashanti and the Ivory Coast. Most of the placer-gold here is fairly accessible and seems to have been dug largely for local use; the reef-gold in Ghana was probably not worked before Portuguese times. Gold was not reaching the coastal peoples of the Ivory Coast or farther west from the interior. The first gold that the Portuguese noticed was at the mouth of the River Pra. It was the reorientation of trade to the ocean which encouraged the exploitation of the southern goldfields.

The numerous habitation mounds, especially in the swamps of the old Niger delta between Ségou and Tombouctou,[102] where rice would grow well and it was not difficult to have a surplus of food, suggest that a prosperous population occupied the countryside and was less concentrated in a few urban centres than today. There is evidence for millet as well as rice, and some sites seem geared to an agricultural economy with many grindstones, like Macina–Nord.[103] Others were inhabited largely by fishermen. The bone harpoon was no longer in use, and evidence for fishing is provided by numerous terracotta net-weights from Douna Fatoma Ke–Bozo and Ségoubougou.[104] These have been found also on the River Senegal at Gaoudal and Tiaski.[105]

The earliest Sudanic empire was that of Ghana, which was consolidated before A.D. 800 and probably brought to an end in 1077. Its centre was not far from Koumbi–Saleh, north-west of Nara,[106] where there has been found the merchants' city described by El Bekri, which was destroyed in the middle of the thirteenth century [pl. 38].[107] This city was mainly Muslim. The royal city was pagan with possibly Christian influence; but until its site is discovered and excavated, we cannot understand its culture.

Although small excavations have been carried out, there is inadequate

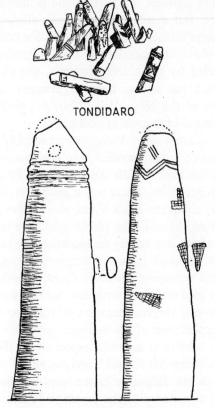

FIG. 83 Monument of standing stones,
Tondidaro, Mali

*by permission from Mauny R., 1961 (1),
p. 131, from Desplagnes, La Géographie
xiii (1906), p. 84*

evidence for detailed chronology of the sites in the middle Niger
Valley. There were a few impressive and undoubtedly pre-Islamic
monuments. The most important was the two groups of megaliths at
Tondidaro,[108] which were barbarously looted and destroyed by French
officials in the early part of this century. No discernible plan has been
recorded. Individual stones were carved in the shape of phalli and
apparently of human heads and with geometric designs [fig. 83].

There were other groups of standing stones near the Niger lakes,
especially at Kouga, where there are also important tumuli. At Sandiki
Vadiobé near Lake Débo was a grave with one pointed and three squat
flat-topped menhirs; the tradition was recorded that the first was male

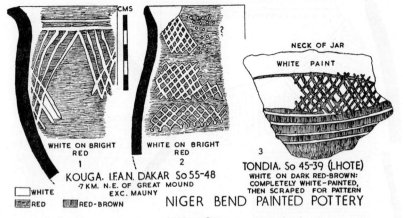

KOUGA. I.F.A.N. DAKAR So 55-48
·7 KM. N.E. OF GREAT MOUND
EXC. MAUNY

WHITE ON BRIGHT RED 1

WHITE ON BRIGHT RED 2

3 TONDIA. So 45-39 (LHOTE)
WHITE ON DARK RED-BROWN:
COMPLETELY WHITE–PAINTED,
THEN SCRAPED FOR PATTERN

WHITE   RED   RED-BROWN

NIGER BEND PAINTED POTTERY

FIG. 84

and the others female.[109] Farther upstream, not far from Bamako, are the standing stones of Moribabougou which project out of a cairn; originally there were apparently two.[110] Szumowski excavated and found no burial, but a few sherds, an iron blade and arrow-heads, one celt and remains of iron-smelting. In the relict area of Hombori, where pagan construction may have lasted late, are monuments of standing stones containing iron and copper objects, stone beads, ivory plaques and small animal figurines.[111]

There is no satisfactory information when painted pottery was introduced to the Niger Valley. There are bright red sherds and a few painted white on red from the old cities of Awdaghost,[112] destroyed perhaps in 1055, and Koumbi Saleh of later date. The latter are nearly all from small bowls with cordons which may have supported lids. The designs are bichrome and fairly simple, with a particular taste for dots. Red-polished and painted sherds were collected near the megaliths at Tondidaro.[113] There was much white-on-red ware from the excavated tumulus at Kouga [fig. 84], associated with iron-smelting, stone buildings and standing stones.[114] A date of 950 ± 120 B.P. (Sa–76) was obtained from this tumulus. Kouga seems to be so important and extensive a site that test excavations do not help to understand it. There are sherds all over the reg not far from the tumuli, many of them with impressions of millet, wheat and perhaps maize.

We do not know the origin of this painted pottery; nor can we be certain that in the Niger Valley there was an earlier Iron Age phase with only impressed sherds. At Kobadi, which appears to be sub-neo-lithic with harpoons, stone bracelets and other early material (above,

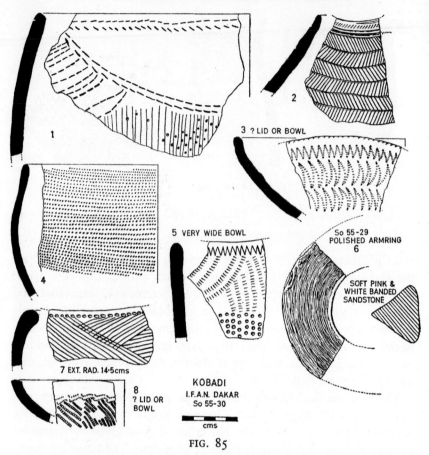

FIG. 85

p. 224), were many sherds with tight impressions, coarse comb and millet-cob [fig. 85]; a probable crucible indicates that the site is just into the metal age, unless it was reoccupied and the collector did not notice two periods of habitation. In village mounds at Kélébéré, south of Djenné [fig. 86],[115] and at Fatoma, north of Mopti [fig. 87],[116] was found elaborately impressed pottery believed to be pre-Islamic; at the latter also a little metal, barrel-shaped beads of polished granite, a quartz bead with biconical perforation, and a bracelet of black glass with irregular white streaks.[117] In a tumulus at Killi, south of Goundam, was undecorated pottery and pieces of copper and bronze [figs. 88–89].[118] Two mounds at Djindjin yielded mostly painted pottery, the others impressed. There was certainly much overlap between impressed and painted wares, and in the southern Sahara paint seems to have been much less used. The advanced and almost rusticated impressions from

FIG. 86 Impressed sherds, Kélébéré, Mali

by permission from Szumowski,
NA 70 (1956), p. 37, pl. V

Tin Eguelay not far north of Tombouctou [fig. 90], found with a few painted sherds, can hardly be older than the very late Middle Ages. At Ait Nafane [fig. 81], much farther north, were the more archaic walking grooves not unlike the material from Ntereso; but there was also a little paint.

Bamako was in the earlier Middle Ages on the fringe of civilization. It lay too near the goldfields for it to be wise to permit scholars, travellers, merchants and technicians to reach it. Szumowski excavated several

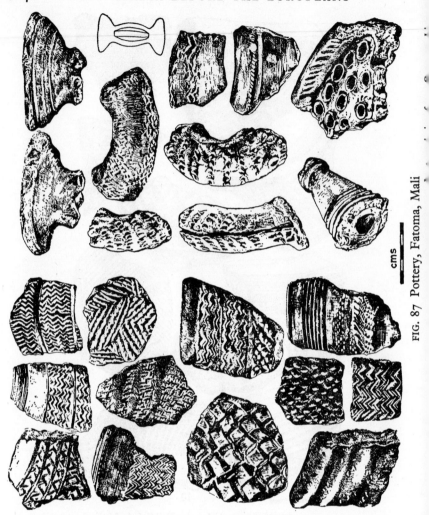

FIG. 87 Pottery, Fatoma, Mali

funerary mounds in the region. They yielded iron bracelets and beads, also pottery heavily ornamented in sharp relief from Diguidiguiba. on the north-west side of Koulouba Hill,[119] apparently sophisticated and of quite late date as it probably bears mealie-cob impressions. Paint was rare; a little was used on pots with roulette-ornament from a tomb at Bamako, T.S.F.[120] Graves in the Oueyanko Valley yielded hardly anything except sherds (undescribed) and a few celts. There was only comb-impressed pottery in the cave-burials farther south at Kanguikourou.[121] This material seems to be more archaic than the approximately contemporary painted pottery from Gonja (below, pp. 314–15, figs. 114–5).

FIG. 88 Pottery from tumulus, Killi, Mali

from Desplagnes, L'Anthropologie *xiv (1903), p. 162*

In the thirteenth and fourteenth centuries possession of the goldfields permitted the rapid rise of the empire of Mali, whose wealthy sultan, Mansa Moussa, became a by-word in the Muslim world. His capital was upstream from Bamako, probably between the Niger and the San-karani. It may have been at Nieni, where there are mounds. Very little exploration has been carried out in this remote area on the borders of

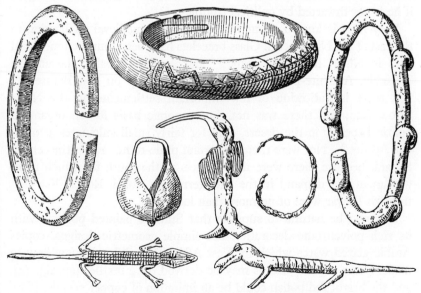

FIG. 89 Metal-work from tumulus, Killi, Mali

from Desplagnes, L'Anthropologie *xiv (1903), p. 165*

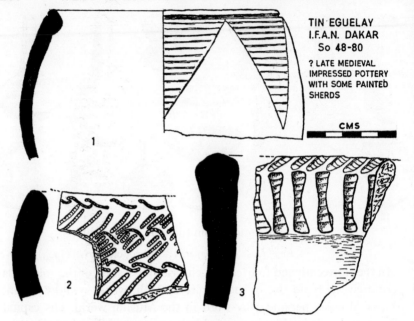

TIN EGUELAY
I.F.A.N. DAKAR
So 48-80

? LATE MEDIEVAL
IMPRESSED POTTERY
WITH SOME PAINTED
SHERDS

CMS

FIG. 90

the modern Mali and F. Guinea, and no important remains are recorded. It would seem that a rich harvest awaits some future archaeologist, if he is not thwarted by political troubles.

Very little is known about the extension of medieval civilization to the east of the Niger bend. Glass bracelets have been found on medieval sites in Niger, like Anissamane[122] and Azelik, probably the ancient Takedda. A white-painted sherd was picked up on Erg Brusset.[123] But there is indication of few important settlements on the Niger below Gao, and there was not the economic basis for an organized political society in the desert, only for fairly small sultanates at oases like Agades.[124] Nor were there important trade-routes across the central Sahara, because there were no products to the south for which there was an urgent demand in the Mediterranean world. Routes like that through Kawar were of no more than local use.

It would be natural to suppose that Sudanic painted pottery, with its rich polychrome decoration but simple geometric designs, copies Arabic glazed wares which in West Africa they did not know how to make. Some of the patterns may be derived from textiles [cp. fig. 84], and the bright red polish could be an imitation of copper vessels. If so, the painted pottery would be entirely post-Islamic, though the techniques could have been acquired by pagan peoples. On the other hand, simple painted designs appear on pottery from North African dolmens, and become richer but still extremely formalized about the first century B.C.[125] Such pottery must have survived as an undercurrent beneath Roman civilization, for it is clearly ancestral to modern Kabyle ware. So it is not impossible that knowledge of the painting technique spread thence to West Africa, in which case the painted pottery there could even be pre-Islamic. The use of red paint to emphasize impressed designs was common as early as Ntereso, so must have arisen in some phase of the Saharan neolithic.

The pottery of the Niger Valley is usually painted on a bright red or dark red base, which is a slip on yellow clay [see fig. 84].[126] From Kouga there is also red or black on yellow, one trichrome sherd with both red and black on yellow. Tricolour ware (white on dark red on yellow, dark red on white on yellow, black on white on red, etc.) is not very common, quadricolour rare. From Koï Goureye there are a few sherds painted white, on black and red, on grey with comb-impressions. Sometimes the whole surface was painted white, and either scraped to enable the reddish base to show through and form a pattern, as at Tondya [fig. 84 3], or with patterns over-painted in red or red-brown, as at Koï Goureye [fig. 91] (with socketed iron spear-head, terracotta stoppers and perhaps lip-plugs and grindstones). Tondya yielded a few sherds with millet-cob impressions. Comb-impressions and fine

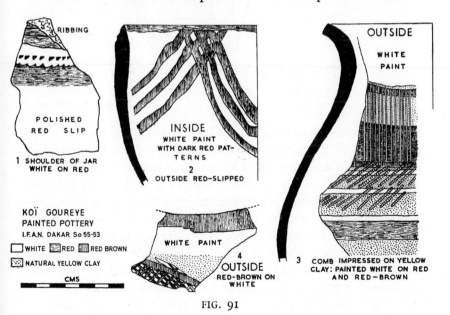

RIBBING

POLISHED
RED SLIP

1 SHOULDER OF JAR
WHITE ON RED

KOÏ GOUREYE
PAINTED POTTERY
I.F.A.N. DAKAR So 55-53

☐ WHITE ▨ RED ▥ RED BROWN
▨ NATURAL YELLOW CLAY

CMS

INSIDE
WHITE PAINT
WITH DARK RED PAT-
TERNS
2
OUTSIDE RED-SLIPPED

WHITE PAINT

4
OUTSIDE
RED-BROWN ON
WHITE

OUTSIDE

WHITE
PAINT

3 COMB IMPRESSED ON YELLOW
CLAY: PAINTED WHITE ON RED
AND RED-BROWN

FIG. 91

FIG. 92 Statuette, Djenné-Kaniana, Mali

by permission from Vieillard, IFAN *ii* (*1940*),
p. *349*, pl. XI

incisions subsidiary to paint are occasionally found [fig. 91 3]. Ribbing emphasized by paint occurs at Toggal Danewal near Sorguéré and at Ténouma; it may be a late or a local development.

Reports are frequently not clear whether a mound was for habitation or funerary. The former were presumably built up over a considerable period. The latter contain single burials, sometimes in jar-coffins as at Kaniana near Djenné.[127] There were there several human representations in terracotta, one small seated figure being well known;[128] I have reproduced another [fig. 92].[129] There are statuettes also from Nantaka,[130] Kami[131] and Koubaye.[132] Statuettes and pottery were found by Szumowski in much poorer mound-graves at Bamako–Bankoni and

N'koumi, and there are terracottas of a man struggling with snakes from near Mopti.[133]

One of the largest funerary mounds is El Oualadji, which was twelve metres high.[134] It was excavated long ago by Desplagnes, before the development of modern techniques. In the centre was a wooden funerary chamber with a shaft to the surface. With the bodies were many ornaments and arms of metal and sherds similar to Koï Goureye [fig. 91]. Other great funerary mounds near the swamps of the Niger were worse treated than El Oualadji. In many cases no report was published and the material has disappeared.

A good many mounds have yielded copper jewellery, especially arm-rings, and a few iron objects. Some of the copper may have been imported; but in the Middle Ages local sources, in Mauritania and around Nioro (above, p. 175), were worked and copper was probably fairly abundant. It has not been determined whether some of the material is of bronze or of brass. Both of these alloys must have been imported if they were used. But objects of gold are rarely mentioned, which is curious seeing that West Africa was the gold-land *par excellence* in the Middle Ages. Gold jewellery is reported from a grave-mound in Aklé, north of Lake Faguibine.[135] As I have said, the gold was not produced locally but came from farther south. Its traffic may have been strictly controlled, so that it became a royal monopoly; and while the great sultans possessed plenty, they did not distribute it to their people, but used it entirely for export.

There is reason to think that at its zenith this Sudanic culture was largely pagan, even if it owed lip-service to Islam. True Muslim sites like Gao may have been as prosperous, but seem less luxurious and probably more puritanical. There was little stratification in the test-pits sunk in the old city.[136] The pottery is bright red and ribbed, with a few comb and cob impressions, but few painted patterns in white on red. One sherd resembles pieces from Koumbi Saleh. There was also painted plaster and marble slabs and gravestones. There is similar material from In Begaouen up the Tilemsi Valley.[137] Inscribed gravestones have been found at Tombeau des Dia near Gao.[138] It appears that the Niger Valley was losing its sensuous African outlook and was being drawn more closely into the Muslim world.

Muslim Sudanic architecture remained African. The very thick clay walls built on wooden frames, still to be seen at mosques and important houses, the pillared clay portals, the simple patterns of unbaked bricks and the curious mosque-towers, short and squat with the ends of the

T

wooden frame projecting in all directions (what I have called porcupine-mosques), have no counterpart in the Near East and were an African development in a region which had little good stone or long timber [pl. 49]. This style was carried south by the Muslims into the Ivory Coast and north-western Ghana. In areas of higher rainfall flat-roofed clay buildings need constant repair, so what is seen today is modern construction in traditional style.

The use of earth for building necessitated large clay-pits. These may be seen round any African village today; they are usually rubbish-pits, and when flooded in the wet season become foul and breed mosquitoes. In Northern Nigeria clay was dug for the huge city walls from great pits in the soft mesozoic clays, and these pits stored water in the dry season. At the same time, the use of earth provides one special difficulty to the archaeologist in Africa. Buildings collapse, and their mud walls are naturally dug for new constructions. Their earth is mixed with the scatter of artefacts on the ground, so that sherds and sometimes other things become incorporated in later buildings. This may happen again and again, so it is extremely difficult to find a true stratification, and any level identified will certainly contain older material. Nor are levels easy to determine. There are sometimes paved floors; but levelled earth walls containing sherds look very like ordinary habitation-deposit. Only if a building is burnt, may there be a thick layer of burnt daub, preserving prints of the timber framework, to serve as a marker between one level and another.

The Iron Age in the West

Wealthy burial tumuli have been excavated near Rao, at the mouth of the River Senegal.[139] The burials, which were much disturbed by earth movement, had been made within wooden chambers covered by mounds at least four metres high; as the mounds seem to have settled considerably, an original height of 8–10 metres is not un-reasonable. They contained a good many pots of simple shape, bowls, beakers and jars, unpainted but closely decorated with elaborate designs, largely scorings and jabs, apparently without comb-impressions. More important is a massive iron sword, almost certainly not of local manufacture, and other fragments of iron, copper arm-rings and other objects, beads and jewellery of gold [fig. 93] and somewhat de-based silver, including a magnificent gold pectoral [pl. 50], two lidded copper pots almost certainly of North African origin, beads of carnelian and glass and a few of quartz which may be derived from a neolithic

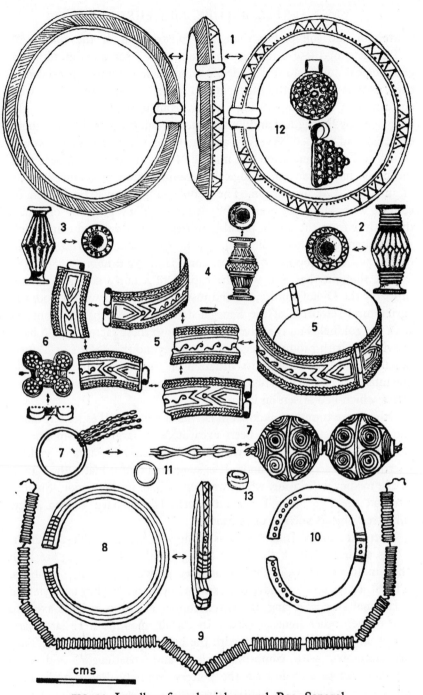

FIG. 93 Jewellery from burial-mound, Rao, Senegal

by permission from Joire J., 1955, p. 288, fig. 1

scatter in the soil earlier than the construction of the tumuli.[140]

The date of these tombs is uncertain. The excavator, arguing on genealogical and historical evidence from their obviously pre-Islamic rites, assigns them to the thirteenth to fourteenth centuries. The well cut carnelian beads suggest importation from India, which was greatly developed by Portuguese and Dutch traders; but it is possible that some carnelian had reached West Africa through the Arabs, though one would expect to have found it on the middle Niger. It does not appear that the beads have been mineralogically examined and pronounced to be of undoubted Indian origin. The people of Rao must have been in contact with Morocco, presumably overland. They probably obtained their silver from the north, possibly in the form of debased coin which was melted up. Their gold is likely to have been of West African origin, and their copper could have come from Mauritania.

It is thought that Rao was the capital of a fairly important state, probably the Djolof empire, which must have drawn its wealth from the agricultural resources of the Senegal delta, and perhaps had contacts with the goldfields on the River Falémé. Both these factors would have provided it with products needed in and beyond the deserts of Mauritania. In the Middle Ages its situation on the coast would give it no advantage. When the Portuguese reached Senegal, they found six small states which had arisen on its ruins.

Other large tumuli are known in northern Senegal,[141] especially along the river. Most have not been excavated. A large grave-mound at Soubalou–Boumba,[142] more than 240 kilometres upstream, yielded sherds but no sensational finds. It is suggested that it marks the capital of the medieval Tekrour, which was somewhere in this region. Smaller sites on the river, like Tiélao on Morfil Island, have yielded a few imported objects such as glass beads.

There are many Iron Age coastal sites in Senegal. Those near St. Louis at the mouth of the River Senegal and in Casamance are high shell-middens, on which are sometimes growing very large baobabs. The St. Louis middens have been studied by Joire.[143] They have yielded occasional sherds, a ring of twisted copper and iron, a bone axe and one or two other bone artefacts. In certain mounds were large jars, which must be contemporary with the build-up of the middens. They are decorated with comb-impressions and striations,[144] and seem distinctly more archaic than the pottery from the Rao tumuli. Joire cites historical evidence that the harvesting of oysters was still practised in the early eighteenth century. But almost certainly the climax of the industry was pre-European, and probably goes back to the earliest Iron Age, perhaps to the neolithic.

In the lagoons and estuaries of Casamance, southward from Joal and across the River Gambia, are the remains of a much larger industry of molluscs. There are very many large middens, in some of them burials.[145] The industry was flourishing about A.D. 1500, when dried oysters were widely traded inland. Stone beads, copper bracelets, comb-impressed sherds and iron have been found in the mounds; but the evidence does not extend back to the neolithic. A few stone chips do not belong to any well defined industry. There are some European imports.[146] About the time of our era the ocean was slightly lower than today, and the creeks may not have become suitable for oysters until the Rottnest or Dunkirk transgression about the fourth century A.D.[147] The middens stand on estuarine clay which has not been exactly dated; it may belong to the Flandrian transgression. Their bases have not been carefully examined to determine their relation to the clay.

The area between St Louis and Joal has no breeding-grounds for oysters; but the coastal dunes and rocks, especially on the Dakar peninsula, were thickly inhabited in the Iron Age as in the neolithic. It appears that on a few sites at Dakar, such as Bel Air–Hersent, the Iron Age material is stratified above the neolithic;[148] and stratified pottery can be definitely identified as Iron Age [fig. 94]. Pottery shapes and ornamentation seem to have varied little over many centuries; so sites, where no stratification was apparent, cannot be satisfactorily classified. Mauny's account of neolithic pottery[149] applies as well to the early Iron

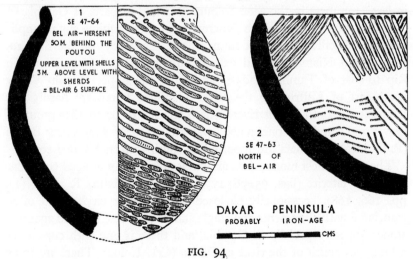

1
SE 47-64
BEL AIR–HERSENT
50 M. BEHIND THE
POUTOU
UPPER LEVEL WITH SHELLS
3 M. ABOVE LEVEL WITH
SHERDS
= BEL-AIR 6 SURFACE

2
SE 47-63
NORTH OF
BEL–AIR

DAKAR PENINSULA
PROBABLY IRON-AGE
CMS

FIG. 94

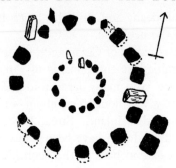

TOMBE DU ROI, SINÉ

FIG. 95 Plan of megalith, southern
Senegal

*based on Jouenne P., 1930, p. 323, fig. 2
by permission from I.F.A.N., Dakar*

Age, and some of the pieces he discusses are likely to be of this date. Bead-rimmed jars seem to be Iron Age rather than neolithic. Some sherds at I.F.A.N. (Dakar) with heavy grooves and no fine ornament may be very late, perhaps post-medieval or at least comparable with the Rao tumuli.

The most impressive sites in Senegal are the megaliths, which occur in large numbers in the Siné Saloum area and in parts of Gambia.[150] The distribution map which Jouenne publishes requires slight amplification. Megaliths are most numerous in the valleys of the Saloum, Bolong and Niammaro, and extend rather scattered from Nioro du Rip to east of Tambacounda[151] and from the upper Saloum Valley north-east of Kaffrine to the River Gambia. There are hardly any monuments south of this river. There appears to be another group of graves and standing stones a good way farther to the south, near Bafata (P. Guinea).[152] Others are reported in south-eastern Sierra Leone.

The commonest monuments are circles of roughly dressed columnar blocks of laterite (figs. 95–96; typical plans in Mauny R., 1961 (1), pp. 166, 168), occasionally enclosed within larger circles, and often associated with alignments and single standing stones. Isolated standing stones appear especially in Gambia, and there is one with cup-marks a long way south of the river at Dibito (Cer. Kolda). There are some

FIG. 96 Shaped stones from megaliths, southern Senega

1. Lyre-shaped stone,
   Maïssaring-Bero
2. Lyre-shaped stone,
   Diam Diam

3. Stone with disc, Siné
4. Stone with ball,
   Paya ma

after Jouenne P., 1930, p. 329, by permission from
I.F.A.N., Dakar

tumuli. Stones may be carved to a ball or boss on top, and not uncommonly are doubled, in what Jouenne calls the form of a lyre. Jouenne associates with the megaliths various cup-marks, ring-engravings and long oval grooves. They may have had a practical significance, for grinding celts and food, as in the forest and southern savannah; but their occurrence in some numbers just in this area suggests that they were of ritual importance.

Burials and pottery have been found in a good many megaliths, cremations in a few. Iron spear-heads, copper bracelets and quartz beads are occasionally reported. The grave-goods seem on the whole disappointing, perhaps because of careless excavation. Some circles contain more than one body. Bowls of rather angular profile are illustrated by Jouenne. They are in general undecorated and unpainted, but some of them red-polished, which suggests influence from Muslim copper-ware.

Jouenne's illustrations are not easy to reproduce, and his material is not at Dakar. So I have illustrated pottery from several tumuli on the River Bandiala [fig. 97], excavated by Monod in 1939. The site

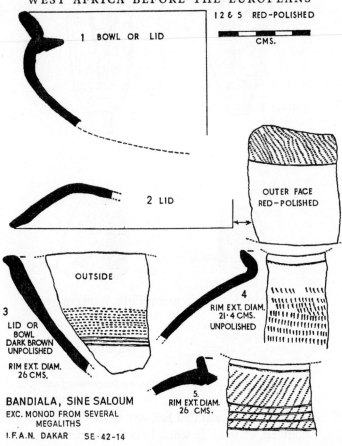

FIG. 97

seems to be roughly contemporary with the megaliths, though farther to the west and very close to the coast. Though there are shell-middens close by, the tumuli do not appear to belong to their inhabitants. This material has not been published, save for an illustration of one pot by Joire and a note by Mauny.[153] Some of the pottery is bright red and polished, a good many pieces have fine comb-impressions. The lidded bowls are not very closely paralleled in Senegal, though a few pieces from Rao and from the megaliths appear, from the internal flange on the rim, to have been made to carry a lid. The tumuli contained also iron spears and rings, copper bracelets made from rods 8–9 mms. in diameter, an open oval ring and some beads of bone.

Mauny, arguing from the absence of modern traditions, regards the Senegal megaliths as pre-Mandingo, i.e. earlier than the fourteenth century. There is no direct evidence for their date.

Practically nothing is known about the Iron Age between Senegal and
the Ivory Coast, not much until one reaches Ghana. The few scraps of
information, set out mostly by Mauny, make no coherent picture, and
need not be repeated. The whole of this area must have been within the
barbarian fringe, beyond the ken of the civilization of the middle
Niger and beyond the goldfields. Groups of people lost in the Guinea
forest must have made pottery, of which we have a few collections [cp.
fig. 71, probably Iron Age], probably smelted a little iron, and indulged
in pagan rites of which occasional stone circles and monoliths preserve
the memory. Most of the region is badly explored, large parts not at all.

The Iron Age in the South

At Ntereso, situated on a scarp above the White Volta, has been excavated
part of a village with an original culture which seems to belong to the
earliest Iron Age. Although a preliminary report is in press,[154] it will be
some time before the final report can be prepared. So it is worth while
giving here a provisional account of the site and finds, which may be
modified in detail when all the material is worked over.

There were three periods of occupation, apparently not separated by
long intervals, so the culture is essentially homogeneous. A scatter of
Gonja material lay in cultivation-soil above. The three periods were
marked by considerable accumulations of burnt daub, indicating that
each was brought to an end by fire, but not necessarily by hostile attack.
The first period is represented by little more than large and deep
irregular water-holes, which after the fire were filled with practically

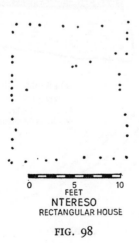

0   5   10
FEET
NTERESO
RECTANGULAR HOUSE

FIG. 98

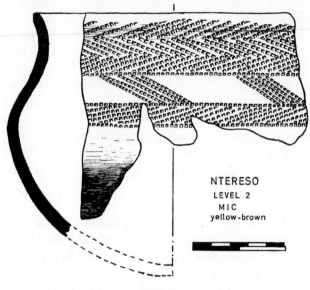

NTERESO
LEVEL 2
MIC
yellow-brown

FIG. 99

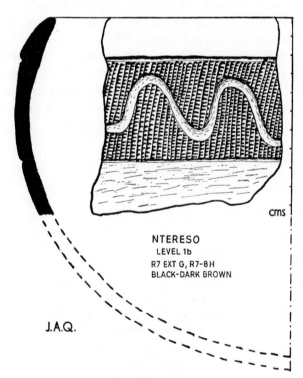

cms

NTERESO
LEVEL 1b
R7 EXT G, R7-8H
BLACK-DARK BROWN

J.A.Q.

FIG. 100

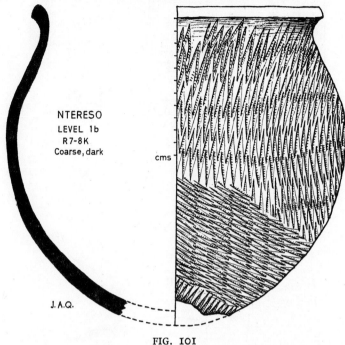

NTERESO
LEVEL 1b
R 7-8 K
Coarse, dark

cms

J. A.Q.

FIG. 101

all the habitation-earth on the site, and sealed with masses of burnt daub. The second period yielded the plans of two more or less rectangular houses [fig. 98] and a few narrow cylindrical wells. The third was less well defined, but there was little development in the artefacts.

The houses of the second period were roofed with poles and thick clay, laid horizontally. The walls were of poles, and probably grass matting, as there is no trace of clay structure. One house appeared to have a small porch and a screen inside the door. The remains of burnt daub indicate that the houses of the first period were similar, and not only poles but carved wood, presumably discarded, was used for the roofs.

Both coarser and finer pottery were heavily ornamented, almost entirely with comb-impressions, often with walking comb or grooves [figs. 99–101]. Some of the finer pieces are thin and polished with bands of paint. Shapes are simple, there is practically nothing except wide-mouthed jars and bowls. The rims are often partly rolled over, but seldom as much as in neolithic wares. Occasionally they overhang, a form probably derived from basketry. Overhanging rims which look like copies of basket-work were found at Adrar Madet (Niger) (above, p. 252) and Nieni (F. Guinea), and such profiles were much developed in the later medieval Akan pottery of the forest (below, p. 284).

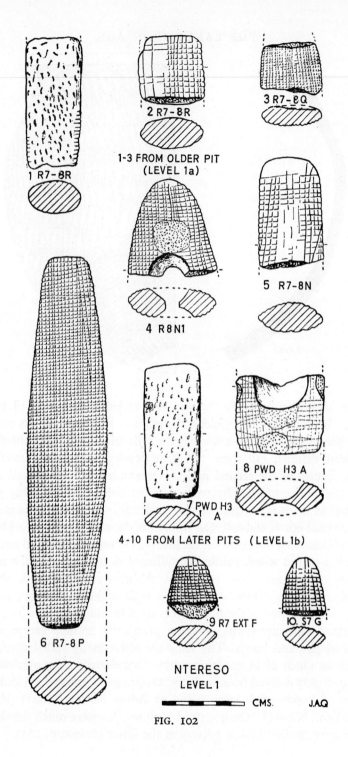

1 R7-8R

2 R7-8R

3 R7-8Q

1-3 FROM OLDER PIT
(LEVEL 1a)

4 R8N1

5 R7-8N

7 PWD H3
A

8 PWD H3 A

4-10 FROM LATER PITS (LEVEL 1b)

6 R7-8 P

9 R7 EXT F

10. S7 G

NTERESO
LEVEL 1

CMS.   J.A.Q

FIG. 102

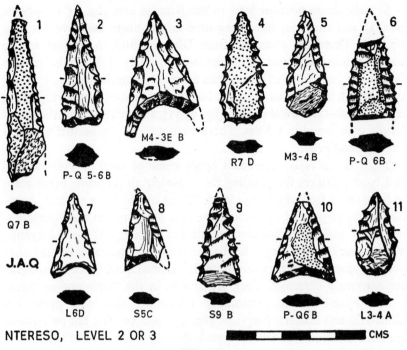

M4-3E B

P-Q 5-6B

R7 D

M3-4 B

P-Q 6B

Q7 B

J.A.Q

L6D   S5C   S9 B   P-Q6B   L3-4 A

NTERESO, LEVEL 2 OR 3   CMS

FIG. 103

A very little iron was found in the third level. There was no evidence for smelting below the Gonja level.

There is a large number of terracotta 'cigars' [fig. 102] from all levels. They are identical with those of the Kintampo-neolithic [fig. 72], except that many seem to have been perforated after baking, and usually broke in the process.

Fragments of terracotta spoons look forward to modern Akan culture, where they are used ritually. They were found at the seventeenth-century site of Ahinsan (south Ashanti). There were two stylized animal figures in terracotta, one probably the handle of a spoon, the other a small lizard, apparently stuck on to a vase.

While most of the microliths are of poor quality, there was a fine series of stone arrow-heads, which persisted through all levels [fig. 103]. There are leaf-shaped, hollow-based and square-based, but no tanged and barbed examples. These and no other types were found at Asselar,[155] not very far from Arawane, whence for other reasons it appears most likely that the intrusive Ntereso-culture had come. It seems to be derived not from the well-watered Tilemsi Valley but from the uplands north of the Niger bend.

Several slicers point at least to the Bamako area [fig. 75 11; above, p. 223], and they may have been used farther north but have not been noticed. There are examples from Dinguira-Sud. A waisted axe or hammer, much burnt at the business-end [fig. 65 2], is a Saharan type (above, pp. 206–7). Most of the celts are small or miniature [fig. 55 8–10] types which are common near the Niger bend (above, p. 201), and there is one of sub-cylindrical section [fig. 55 11], also markedly northern and hardly ever found in Ghana. There were none of the normal southern edge-ground celts.

There are several very small beads made of shell of Volta oyster, and bead-polishers for grinding them. Nearly all the stone beads seem to have come from the Gonja level. There are bracelets of shale, horn-blende-porphyry and sandstone; the first are found in the Kintampo-neolithic; sandstone bracelets recall the industry of the Oueyanko Valley, near Bamako. Reference has been made to the use of hornblende-porphyry for beads in the neolithic of the Ghana forest. Stone net-weights are extremely common. They are known in the Kintampo-neolithic.

The bone-work is particularly interesting and well preserved. Unilateral and bilateral harpoons [fig. 43], grooved but not perforated, are not a Saharan type and are paralleled only from some of the earliest sites like Ishango and at Manga (Tchad) (above, pp. 164–5). The fish-hooks have parallels in the Sahara (above, p. 165). There is a good series of bone points and other pieces with slight traces of polishing.

The Ntereso-culture is a rather unassimilated mixture of Kintampo-neolithic with an invading group from near Arawane. There is nothing to prove that the two invasions, from the same general region, were not nearly contemporary and that the two cultures did not survive side by side; so the very early date for Ntereso (SR–61, 3190±120, above, p. 238) does not imply that the Kintampo-neolithic was earlier still. The rich ornamentation of walking comb on the pottery is paralleled in the southern Sahara [figs. 81–82], but apparently not in the Kintampo-neolithic. The flat-roofed rectangular house is almost certainly northern; so are the arrow-heads, the fish-hooks and other minor finds. The 'cigars', the net-weights and a few other features are typical of the Kintampo-neolithic and cannot be derived from elsewhere. It is strongly to be suspected that the northerners were conquerors who took over the women of their victims.

Three other sites apparently of the Ntereso-culture are known in Ghana. One has yielded little evidence, the second only a scatter of apparently northern flints and celts without location of the actual habitation. The third, at Nandikrom between the River Daka and Oti, has recently been discovered. There seems to have been little depth of earth, which was largely overturned in bulldozing for road-works. On the site was found a good deal of comb-impressed pottery, burnt daub with pole-impressions, 'cigars', small celts and bead-polishers. The pottery seems on the whole to correlate with the third level at Ntereso; but without excavation of the remaining undisturbed area, it is difficult to form a decision. Ntereso itself, before excavation, had furnished no Saharan arrow-heads and no beads; it seemed to be a variety of the Kintampo-neolithic.[156]

Though other elements of this culture disappear, during the centuries which make up the Middle Ages walking-comb decoration on pottery survived. Deep deposits of such archaic pottery have been excavated by Mr. R. N. York at Banka Road and at Kadengben; another site remains to be tested at Tomaklaw, where heaps of burnt daub, fallen into an erosion-gulley, seem to mark sites of individual huts.

Especially the form of the overhanging rim inclines me to think that the Ntereso-people were proto-Akans, and that their descendants are to be found in the late medieval hilltop-sites and entrenched fortresses of the forest zone. Unfortunately, practically nothing is known from Kumasi, a neolithic clearing which one would expect the migrants to have visited or occupied on their way south.

In the extreme south of Ashanti, in Fanti country and in Akim medieval sites are known, either on steep hilltops or within fortified enclosures. The pottery is heavily decorated, often with overhanging rims suggestive of basketry. It has been mooted that the abandonment of such pottery for a more architectural style, with complicated profiles and less emphasis on surface-decoration, was due to large-scale introduction of metal vessels by the Portuguese, who bought brass at Aachen for export to their colonies.[157] There is at present no direct evidence for this suggestion; but details such as oral tradition regarding individual sites, the appearance of maize and of tobacco-pipes suggest that the striking change in pottery-style took place in the sixteenth century.

In the western forest of Ghana are many steep isolated hills, favoured as sites of modern bungalows, and so the vegetation and humus is cleared often to reveal a medieval habitation (cp. the site on the top of the hill at Kwapong; see map, fig. 104). These sites are not apparently fortified; but they were protected by their position, and may have relied on palisades. The hilltop was perhaps levelled. In addition to pottery, they usually yield a few celts and grindstones, sometimes celt-roughouts, poor quartz microliths which may be strike-a-lights, grooved stones for

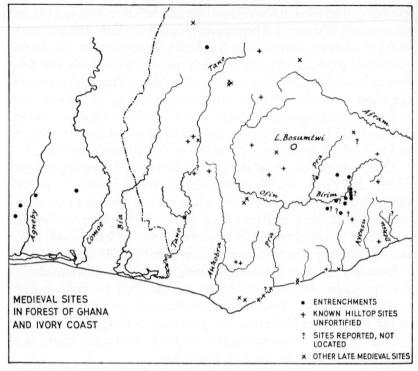

MEDIEVAL SITES
IN FOREST OF GHANA
AND IVORY COAST

• ENTRENCHMENTS
+ KNOWN HILLTOP SITES
  UNFORTIFIED
? SITES REPORTED, NOT
  LOCATED
× OTHER LATE MEDIEVAL SITES

FIG. 104

grinding. Iron has not been found except at Tarkwa, but would probably be revealed in a corroded state by excavation.

The only site of this type which has been published is Nsuta, not
far from Takoradi, where the whole hilltop was removed in mining
manganese.[158] In addition to pottery and celts, there were cylindrical
quartz beads and traces of iron-smelting, which have been found elsewhere on medieval sites in south-western Ghana (above, pp. 241–3). The
site was apparently still occupied about A.D. 1700, as a piece of a square-
faced Dutch gin bottle and one or two pipes were found on it.[159] Several
bobbin-shaped quartz beads are unusual; broken examples reused were
found on the fifteenth-century site of Sekondi.

All the pottery from these sites is fairly heavily ornamented, and
overhanging and ledge-rims are common. I have therefore thought fit
not to reproduce groups already published, but to illustrate a fairly large
and varied collection from cuttings on a site not previously known,
Ntirikurom in south-western Ashanti on the border of Sefwi [figs.
105–7]. There was from a few centimetres to one metre of habitation-
earth, but no evidence for more than one period of occupation. As could

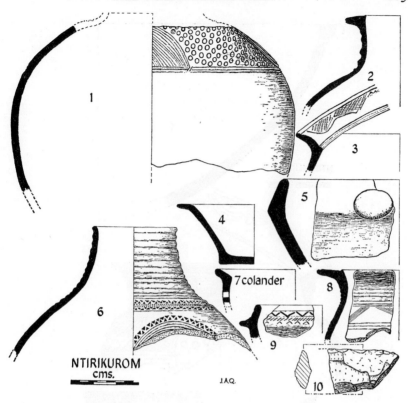

NTIRIKUROM
cms.

J.A.Q.

FIG. 105

be expected, the deposit is deepest on the sides of the hill, where it had accumulated by natural erosion.

Other hilltop sites with similar material are the residential area at Tarkwa, which yielded celts and a little pottery and microliths, but seems not to have been intensively occupied;[160] and Monkey Hill (or Government Hill), Obuasi,[161] with pottery with overhanging rims, celts, iron slag, grindstones, and a 'cigar', probably transported in medieval times; this was the principal area of habitation, though finds have been made all round Obuasi. Both of these sites were cleared for occupation in areas where there were miners trained to observe the ground. This is an indication of what many other places may yield when they become accessible and are properly examined. A single jar with overhanging rim and a plain bowl were found on top of the hill at Saltpond; one of them contained many rough stone beads. So Saltpond also may have been a medieval hilltop site, destroyed by modern levelling. The site at Odumparara Bepo, recently and perhaps anciently exploited to

U

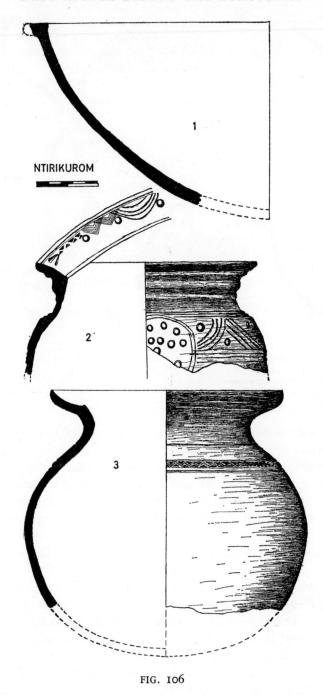

NTIRIKUROM

FIG. 106

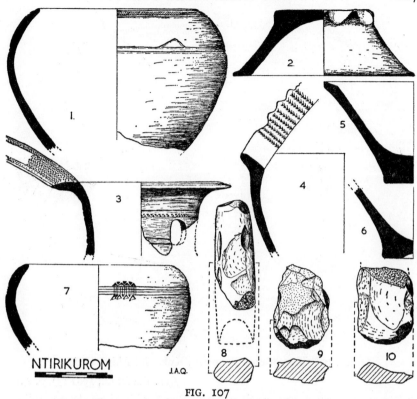

NTIRIKUROM

J.A.Q.

FIG. 107

make bauxite beads,[162] may also be one of the hilltop medieval sites;[163] it yielded pottery, celts, grindstones and perforated stones, also perhaps a bobbin-pendant of mottled polished granite. But the whole assemblage cannot with certainty be identified in the British Museum, and some of it was seized by the then governor of the Gold Coast.

Archaic pottery, usually with celts, is found on sites which are not prominent. While the main centres were presumably fortified, there must have been peasant villages in the forest, which had to be sited for convenience rather than security. Bekwai is on a low hill above a swamp. Some remains appear medieval, there are also European imports. There was evidence of iron-smelting and a perforated quartz pebble. Two small sites with pottery like that from Nsuta have been revealed on road-cuttings at Agona. The main occupation at Bosumpra cave, Abetifi, is late medieval.[164] Here again a remote and concealed site was selected, presumably for security.

East of the River Pra, and especially near the Birim Valley in Akim, people using similar pottery and a few celts occupied entrenched forts [map, fig. 104], which are not concentrated on hilltops but spread over

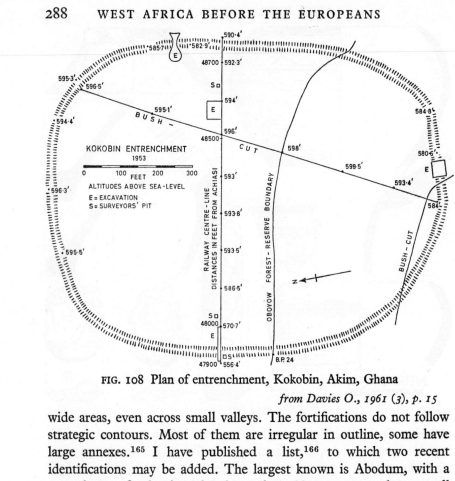

FIG. 108 Plan of entrenchment, Kokobin, Akim, Ghana

from Davies O., 1961 (3), p. 15

wide areas, even across small valleys. The fortifications do not follow strategic contours. Most of them are irregular in outline, some have large annexes.[165] I have published a list,[166] to which two recent identifications may be added. The largest known is Abodum, with a central area of sub-triangular shape about 880 × 500 m. and two small annexes. Akwatia, conveniently situated at the mines residential area, is roughly rectangular with several gates, about 850 × 550 m.;[167] Kokobin [fig. 108] is unusually regular and fairly small; it may be late, and had a very thin occupation-layer.

These entrenchments can be identified by one or two banks, usually fairly low, and a shallow fosse. It appeared at Kokobin that the bank is no more than upcast from the fosse, which was the principal feature of the fortification. When it was sectioned by a railway-cutting, it was a surprise to see that it is five metres deep [pl. 39]. At no other entrenchment has so deep a section been taken, and it is extremely difficult in a small pit to determine whether one is digging rotted rock or fill. It is likely that all have very deep ditches. At Akwatia a pit was dug to 2½ metres depth in the fosse, but almost certainly had not reached the bottom. The

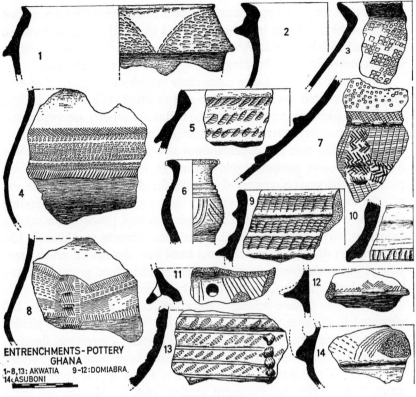

ENTRENCHMENTS - POTTERY
GHANA
1-8,13: AKWATIA   9-12:DOMIABRA.
14:ASUBONI

FIG. 109

fosse was interrupted at gates which formed part of the original plan.

The upper levels within these entrenchments are usually eroded, as happens in a modern forest village, and have practically no habitation-earth; but there is often an accumulation at the sides and against the banks. Only test excavations have been carried out. One would suspect from the size and number of sites that they were not completely built up, but contained gardens to be under protection against attack. They cannot have been defensible against a sustained siege, but would be a useful protection against raiders.

They normally yield archaic and heavily ornamented pottery, which seems to date to pre-European times. From some there are only scraps; all the sherds from Kokobin are small and give little idea of the appearance of the vessels. I have illustrated a selection from three of the large entrenchments in the Birim Valley [fig. 109]. There are usually a few celts, which were probably still in occasional use; grindstones; a few poor microliths; and sometimes evidence of iron-smelting, as at Kokobin Domiabra and

Abodum. At some entrenchments have been found microliths which look mesoneolithic, and may have been exposed by the Iron Age occupation and mixed with later finds. Absence of large-scale methodical excavation has prevented us from drawing up a full repertoire of artefacts.

From Domiabra are said to come three cylindrical beads of glass-frit, made of imported beads ground up and re-fused; also beads with eye and flower patterns, probably Venetian. But the reports are vague, and there is no certainty that these beads are not more recent drops.

It is possible that the concentration of entrenchments in Akim was due to extensive medieval gold-mining in the Birim Valley (above, p. 60). In the gravels, reworked recently for diamonds, large numbers of celts and other late medieval and early modern objects (including apparently worked brass) have been found. A kwe, probably for mining (above, p. 203), came from within the entrenchment at Akwatia. The construction of these entrenchments must have demanded much man-power; but in the forest, once clearings are made, food grows itself and requires little attention, mainly from the women.

To the same culture belongs a trench at Nkara, which cuts off a hill surrounded on three sides by a loop of the Tano River.[168] It yielded heavily-ornamented, incised and stamped pottery, a terracotta figurine, celts, quartz flakes and iron-slag. There may have been gold working also in the Tano gravels, and a kwe was found in the river not far away.[169] A hilltop entrenchment is mentioned at Mensakrom about 25 kilometres north of Sunyani; but no details are recorded.[170]

Entrenchments near Agboville (Ivory Coast), which have yielded finely-ornamented sherds, celts and iron-slag, are probably associated with this culture of southern Ghana.[171]

I regard these fortified entrenchments and hilltop sites as proto-Akan. The pottery and general culture in all of them seems to be similar, and their distribution [fig. 104] roughly corresponds with modern Akan settlement. It does not follow that entrenchments in other areas are of the same date. There are one or two in remote parts of the Ivory Coast. At Kitari on Oti, in an area of relict tribes far outside Akan penetration, a large triple-ringed entrenchment has recently been excavated; it seems to be not older than the seventeenth century. There are fortified enclosures of unknown date in Togo.[172]

Sites with early pottery, which may well be medieval, are known around Achimota, Legon and Tema; but no proper study has been undertaken of this material, which does not seem uniform and may be the work of more than one tribe and over a long period. These sites do

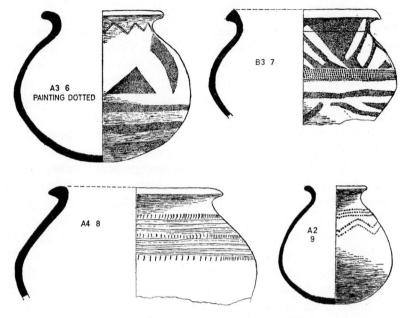

FIG. 110 Pottery, Vume Dugame, Ghana

from Davies O., 1961 (3), p. 39

not yield European goods, which should have been arriving in the Accra area before A.D. 1600. The remains are unlike those from the Akan area, and of modern tribes both Ga and Krobo elements may be represented, perhaps also others. The collection of finely-decorated pottery from Vume Dugame on the lower Volta, including painted pieces, found with a little iron and one ring of copper,[173] is unlikely to be later than A.D. 1600 and may be considerably older [fig. 110].

Apart from the entrenchments, a comparatively small number of sites in southern Ghana can be identified as medieval, compared with more recent periods. This may be partly due to difficulty of exploration, especially in the forest where humus accumulates quickly. Sites with habitations of wood and not clay would leave little trace. The large middens found in parts of southern Ghana (Akwapim, Ashanti)[174] do not seem to have started to accumulate before the sixteenth or seventeenth century. Ntereso, for instance, could never have been discovered but for the activities of road-men. At the same time, there probably was an explosion of population in the sixteenth and seventeenth centuries. This, perhaps, was initiated by gold-prospectors moving southward through Kong and Bondoukou.[175] The clearance and settlement of the forest received further stimulus when the Portuguese arrived; for now the forest was close to the main lines of communication and trade and not on the fringe of the empires in the Niger Valley. The rapid introduction by the Portuguese of new food crops greatly encouraged settlement and increase of population. Recent detailed exploration of the Volta Valley near Kete Krachi has indicated very few medieval sites, but a large number probably of the seventeenth century.

Nor have we a great deal of evidence for medieval settlement in northern Ghana, and it was principally along the navigable rivers. Tightly decorated pottery which is probably medieval has been found on the Black Volta at New Buipe and to a larger extent further upstream at Burufu, Yagha, Wessa, Poura, Boromo and other sites. Here again it may have been the gold-prospectors who led the way. There are gold-mines at Poura, while Wessa and Burufu are not far from the Lobi workings, and Buipe lies on one of the main southward routes to Ashanti. Not sufficient of this pottery has yet been collected or studied for it to be worth illustrating. On the White Volta Daboya is an ancient town, and much of the pottery scattered on both banks is highly ornamented and is likely to be medieval. A stratified section is urgently required, because of the long period of occupation. Daboya's wealth lay in its salt springs.[176] Salt would hardly penetrate from the Sahara so far south; and it could be brought from the coast only when the routes through the forest and up the rivers were opened. Daboya, like Buipe, lies on the main route from Wagadugu to Kumasi.

Elsewhere a very few large mounds are known which yield apparently medieval pottery, for instance Bung, south of Tamale. They would certainly repay excavation, and it might then be possible to date them. Some of the larger tribes, like the Dagomba, had traditionally arrived during the Middle Ages; and they must have had their settlements. There were probably also many relict tribes with cultures hardly advanced beyond the neolithic. Some of the neolithic sites I have described could be as late as the Middle Ages, the Tong Hills (above, p. 214), sites in the Morago valley,[177] and so on.

Among the Lobi, who were an unusually unfriendly tribe in southern Upper Volta, are many fortified settlements with walls built of laterite blocks and clay.[178] They contain one or more houses. They are mainly concentrated around Gaoua, and extend just across the Ivory Coast border towards Bouna. Small excavations have yielded fairly recent material, iron weapons, bones, maize-impressed pottery, and some finely worked copper ornaments which must have formed part of a treasure.

But tradition is unanimous that these fortifications are not the work of the ancestors of the present Lobi, who came from east of the Black Volta about 1800. Their distribution corresponds with an important goldfield, which is believed to have been discovered in the later Middle Ages, when prospectors were exploring southward from the middle Niger. It lies somewhat to the east of the main route into Ashanti, which passed through Kong. Pits have been sunk to a depth of up to 20 m. through laterite, and are usually about 60 cms. in diameter. They must be the work of skilled miners, probably trained in Wangara.

The stone foundations of large rectangular or U-shaped buildings have been found farther to the south-west near Niakaramadougou (northern Ivory Coast). Nothing is known about their date and purpose. Some pottery found with them is heavily ornamented in medieval style. They are traditionally said to have been built by Whites, i.e. perhaps by Saharans. The site may have lain on the road from Kong to the south.

Similar foundations are reported by Toucet at Tondi Koiré (south-west Niger; I.F.A.N. Dakar N 59–59). On the site were collected sherds with walking grooves, comb-impressions, probably millet-cob impressions and deep jabs; also bracelets of copper and twisted iron, such as are not uncommon in northern Ghana. This culture is unlike anything discovered elsewhere, and its date is uncertain; if a glass bead found belongs to the site, it must be later than A.D. 1500.

Similar material, of apparently comparable date, has just been published from Mengao, north-east of Ouahigouya in northern Upper Volta.

Little is known about the tombs and sanctuaries of the central savannah and forest region. A very few stone circles are reported, one at Tanéka Beri (Cer. Djougou, Dahomey),[179] two in north-western Ghana, whose identity is uncertain, as they seem to be no more than rings of small, loose laterite-blocks which the Geological Survey may have imagined as circles. Standing stones are reported at Farendé (Togo),[180] and sculptured perhaps in the form of phalli on Ewlito Mountain near Palimé (Togo).[181]

Mounds which appear to be graves are known in a very few places in southern Ghana;[182] very small cairns were heaped on the graves at Sekondi (below, pp. 310–2). There is a description of the grave of a Muslim saint near Sawla,[183] with a number of mounds inside a stone enclosure. Cord-impressed pottery and bones were excavated from grave-mounds on the Kolodio River above Bui;[184] they may not be of great antiquity.

The usual type of chief's grave in south-eastern Mali, Upper Volta and parts of northern Ghana was an underground vault approached by a

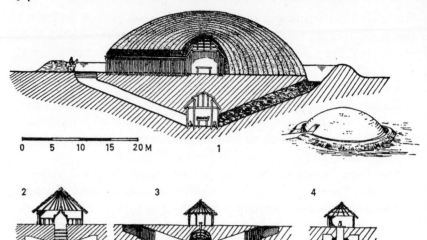

0   5   10   15   20 M   1

2   3   4

FIG. 111 Underground tombs in the northern Sudanic region:

1. Reconstruction of tumulus near the bend of the R. Niger
2. Grave of Gurma prince near Wagadugu, Upper Volta
3. Bini grave near Mopti, Mali
4. Cruciform grave, Bussa, Nigeria

from L. Frobenius, Das Unbekannte Afrika, *p. 122*

vertical or sloping shaft through the block-laterite. These are very difficult to find or to hear of. Frobenius sketches a number of them [fig.
111].[185] They are described independently near Bougouni.[186] The
chamber seems usually to have been roofed with a light structure of
perishable material. Near the Niger Frobenius says that there was a
room for offerings above the shaft, covered by a tumulus. This account
is suggestive of an Egyptian mastaba. Such tombs are probably pre-
Islamic, because they occur as far south as Dagomba. I have heard of
one at Tamale.

The sinking of shafts through the lateritic crust has been mentioned
for gold-mining in Lobi territory. It is also suggestive of the bilegas or
underground cisterns, which are common in northern Ghana [pl. 41].
There are somewhat similar cisterns in the emirate of Fika, south of
Potiskum (Nigeria).[187] Shafts were sunk through the lateritic crust,
which usually is not more than one metre thick, and the cistern hollowed
out of the soft shale below. They were sited in little hollows which would
catch run-off during heavy rain, and water was stored in them through
most of the dry season. It must have become particularly foul. Very few
are now open; but they can be traced by slight depressions. The modern

population knows neither how to dig nor to clean them. They are still in use at the important Gonja settlement of Butie; one is rather broken down.

I do not believe that these underground cisterns are an African invention. They are suggestive of cisterns in the Near East and as far north as Constantinople. I therefore consider that they were introduced by the Arabs. Some of those now in use may not be more than a century or two old. But their commonness in the iron-smelting area around Yeji, often away from modern villages, suggests connection with this industry, which goes back to the sixteenth century and perhaps earlier. So one suspects that these cisterns are a further contribution of the prospectors, who came south from the middle Niger to Ghana in the later part of the Middle Ages.

Iron Age Rock Art in the Savannah

It has been observed in Europe that, with the transition from the palaeolithic to the neolithic, representational art became extremely formalized, figures which had previously been naturalistic became almost unrecognizable, and there appear what seem to be purely symbolic geometrical figures which presumably had some meaning for their makers but are totally unrealistic.

This change may partly be due to a change of outlook. The European and African hunter in a palaeolithic stage of economy had to represent a real recognizable animal in order to get control of it. Frobenius never tired of recounting how some pygmies made a drawing of an animal in the dust before going out to hunt it. The painter of neolithic cattle in the Sahara equally had to represent real cattle, because it was believed that there was a magical connection between the cow and the painting. Human figures were always liable to be more stylized, because they were accessories which the artist did not desire to get into his control. It was only when Late Predynastic kings of Egypt began to practise imperialism and domination over their fellow men, that their enemies had to be represented in exact realistic detail and undergoing thoroughly realistic chastisement. On Bushman paintings human figures are far less realistic than animals; only a few salient points, their sex, their weapons, required emphasis. As humanity developed, the belief in direct magical connection between representation and object weakened. The later animals in the Sahara not only pick up mannerisms but become thoroughly formalized, like the camels which look like complex patterns in wire.

It may also be true that loss of naturalism was partly due to representations in media where naturalism would be hard to execute. Much late

Saharan drawing is suggestive of textiles, an art which had been greatly developed in the Near East and was probably encouraged in the Sahara by the Arabs.

Moreover, the stabilization of societies led to formal and repeated rituals, especially for the gravest crises of life, initiation and death. Where such rituals used representational art, its frequent repetition would produce a shorthand. It is only one stage farther to writing. Shorthand symbols are practically ideograms, though they do not quite indicate grammar; and from ideograms higher civilizations have rapidly developed syllabaries.

The first detailed publication of a large collection of symbolical rock engravings in Africa was from the shelter of Kiantapo (Katanga).[188] Some of the motifs are recognizable, extremely stylized men, animals and sexual organs. Others seem to be complex but meaningless patterns and mere squiggles; but to judge from observers who have watched Australians, they may have been mnemonics for a complex mythology. In the same publication Mortelmans describes other stylized engravings and paintings in the Katanga; some years later he was able to report similar designs in the Lower Congo,[189] some of which he interpreted as inspired by Christian evangelization.

The principal group of stylized art in West Africa is the painted caves in the Mandingo Mountains near Bamako. Best known is the cave at Point G, Bamako, whence I have reproduced a small selection of the paintings [fig. 112].[190] There is another a few kilometres away, up the Oueyanko Valley [pl. 1]. Thirteen other caves are recorded with stylized paintings.[191] They are all believed to be fairly recent and perhaps to be used for ritual up to the present time. Stylized paintings are made today as part of the initiation-ritual in the Mandara Mountains (north-eastern Nigeria),[192] probably in a festival to renew the masks.

The preservation of even recent rock paintings in open shelters is impossible save under fairly arid conditions, so none are known south of the line Bauchi–Pusiga–Bamako. This line trends northward with the isohyets. Whether painting was ever attempted south of this line we do not know.

There are some fairly modern stylized engravings from far north. Formalized animals and other designs have been found engraved on granite domes at Kourki (south-western Niger)[193] and Aribinda (Upper Volta).[194] Apparently similar engravings are reported from Djebel Méla (Ubangui-Chari).[195] The engravings from the northern Ivory Coast are more or less geometrical and symbolic.[196] On Agu Mountain (Togo)

BAMAKO,
CAVE AT
POINT G

FIG. 112 Cave-paintings, Bamako Point G

from Szumowski, Proceedings 2 Panafrican
Congress, *p. 672*

there is said to be a representation of a divine hand by several converging rock grooves (perhaps natural).[197]

Two engravings are known on rocks which are flooded. They appear to be associated with fishing magic. At Bamako-Sotuba is a quite realistic fish.[198] In the Volta gorge at Akosombo a pecked ring round a natural hollow was found on a vertical cliff 9 m. below normal water-level [pl. 40]. The rock had presumably been faulted downwards in recent times. The cup-and-ring symbol is known in Europe and is believed to be sexual.

Three caves are known in northern Ashanti with engravings which seem to be mere scrawls. It is probable that all were used in initiation rites, and possible that each engraved line was made by one initiate. This might account for the meaningless jumbles. At Forikrom there is a remarkable rock amphitheatre with two entrances and several windows [pl. 42–43]. In small caves in its walls, difficult of access, are groups of incised lines which represent nothing natural; each group may have belonged to a family, whose initiates over several generations added to it. Passing through the amphitheatre one reaches a small shelter, on the floor of which are incised many broad arrows [pl. 44] and an oware-board. At Bosumcheche, on the floor and roof of a small cave through a rock-stack is an oware-board and a number of incised lines and designs of broad arrows and what look like spear-heads [pl. 45]. They may well represent male and female sexual organs. Shaw published rock engravings from a cave at Kwamang.[168] There appears to be there a much wider repertory of designs than in the other Ashanti caves, and some are fairly naturalistic, including a hand, a beetle, a spear, a bow and arrow, and perhaps the sun and a house. Others seem to be geometrical.

We have no idea how old this Iron Age rock art is, and we know very few sites. The actual figures may be fairly recent. But I am convinced that they reflect traditions and rituals which go back at least to the Middle Ages, so they can reasonably be described as part of the Iron Age civilization of the southern savannah and forest.

NOTES

1. E.g. in the northern Cameroons, Hinderling, *Stahl und Eisen* lxxv (1955), p. 1263.
2. Sayce, *Soc. Biblical Archaeology Proc.* (1911), p. 96; id., *Liverpool Annals of Archaeology and Anthropology* iv (1912), p. 53; Wainwright, *Sudan Notes and Records* xxvi (1945), p. 65.
3. Wainwright, *Jour. Egyptian Archaeology* xxv (1949), p. 170.
4. *Reise in Aegypten* II ii, pp. 286 ff., quoted not very accurately by Beck, *Geschichte des Eisens* I, pp. 98–102.
5. Mauny R., 1952 (1), p. 574.
6. Huard, *IFAN* 22B (1960), p. 134.
7. vii, ch. 69.
8. Picard, *Académie des Inscriptions C.R.* (1958), p. 44.
9. Herodotus iv, ch. 183 4.
10. von Luschan, *Zeitschrift für Ethnologie* xli (1909), p. 22.
11. Lhote, *Encyclopédie mensuelle d'Outremer* iii (1952), p. 269.
12. Mauny R., 1963.
13. There are traces of continuous process among the Tschede in Teleki who practise continuous tapping of the slag, see Hinderling, *l. c.* (note 1).
14. Hupfeld, *Mitteilungen von Forschungsreisenden und Gelehrten aus den deutschen Schutzgebieten* xii (1899), p. 175.
15. For distribution of high furnaces in West Africa, see Klusemann, *Anthropologische Gesellschaft in Wien Mitt.* liv (1924), p. 120; for description and illustration of some in West Africa, see Francis–Boeuf, *CEHSAOF* xx (1937), p. 403.

    The following are unpublished descriptions from north-western Ghana. Cooper (*GSFNB* 15/4/1927) records furnaces at Busie, five feet high and one foot across at the top, tapering slightly downwards (150 x 30 cms.). Each stood within a smithy which also housed the pot-bellows, apparently of wood and supported on a stem of convenient height for the blower. The tuyere-pipe was three feet long (90 cms.), made of loam mixed with straw and cow-dung and baked hard; it might last a year. It was let into the wall of the furnace. The ore was gritty yellow pisoliths, fluxed with soft dark pisoliths. They were crushed with a heavy iron hammer, and then with small quartz balls. The furnace was charged two-thirds full with charcoal, then with one calabash of broken ore and two of charcoal. Ore and charcoal would be added down the shaft as the charge sank. Slag was tapped during smelting, and at the end the furnace was opened and a bloom of about ten pounds (5 kgs.) was taken out. Outside the smithy was an open hearth for hammering the bloom. These I have seen in 1958 at Billaw. They are now used for fashioning tools of imported iron, the local smelting having been abandoned since the last war. They consist of a bowl-hearth sunk into the floor, over the edge of which plays the tuyere, attached to a pipe from the pot-bellows. Bellows and pipe are set into a mound of clay above the floor.

16. Desplagnes, *Anthropologie* xiv (1903), p. 153; Mauny R., 1961 (1), p. 315.
17. Dixey, *Mining Magazine* xxiii (1920), p. 213.
18. Bellamy, *Iron and Steel Institute Jour.* lxvi (1904), p. 99.
19. For general bibliography of iron-working in Africa, see de Heinzelin, *Acad. royale des Sciences coloniales Bull. des Séances* N.S. v (1959), p. 694.
20. Found on the surface and well above the microlithic level at Achimota Cricket-pitch, see Davies O., 1961 (3), paper 2.
21. de Coutenson, *Cahiers d'Etudes africaines* v (1961), p. 12; perhaps later, see Altheim and Stiehl, *Forschungen und Fortschritte* xxxvii (1963), p. 53.
22. See Altheim and Stiehl, *Klio* xxxix (1961), p. 234.
23. See Cary and Warmington, *Ancient Explorers*, ch. VIII.
24. Hirschberg, *Wiener völkerkundliche Mitteilungen* iii (1955), p. 94.
25. Strabo xviii, p. 820.
26. See Monneret de Villard, *La Nubia Romana*.
27. Philostratus, *Vita Apollonii* vi, ch. 2. As this text transfers to this market the tale of silent barter which belongs to West Africa, the whole account is under suspicion.
28. Seneca, *Quaestiones naturales* VI, ch. 8 3–4.
29. A very few Egyptian objects from south of the equator may have been carried south long after their date of manufacture; see Mauny R., 1952 (1), p. 548.
30. Fairbridge, *Kush* xi (1963), p. 96; Butzer, *Saeculum* viii (1957), p. 359.
31. ii, ch. 32 5.
32. iv, ch. 181–5.
33. Carpenter, *American Journal of Archaeology* lx (1956), p. 231.
34. See Grove and Pullan, in Howell and Bourlière, *African Ecology and Human Evolution*, p. 237; above p. 248.
35. Mauny R., 1947 (1); Mauny R., 1952 (3), with map; Lhote, *IFAN* 19B (1957), p. 617.
36. Lhote H., 1953.

37. Lhote, *Les Touaregs du Hoggar*, p. 63.
38. Mauny, *Bull. de Correspondance saharienne* ii (1948), p. 9.
39. Mauny R., 1952 (1), p. 550.
40. Lhote, *LAPE* 9–10 (1961–2), p. 131.
41. See ch. 1, note 15, above p. 26.
42. Diodorus xx, ch. 10 5; Lhote H., 1953.
43. Strabo xvii, p. 828.
44. Huard and Massip, *SPF* lx (1963), p. 475, fig. 4 23; Huard, *IFAN* 22B (1960), p. 134.
45. Espérandieu, *Soc. de Zootechnie d'Algérie Bull.* ii (1954), p. 23; Gruet, *LAPE* 6–7 (1958–9), p. 79; Alimen, *La Station rupestre de Marhouma (IRS Mémoires* I); Perret, *Cahiers Charles de Foucauld* x (1948), p. 81.
46. Murray, *Inst. Fouad I du Désert Bull.* II i (1952), p. 105; Zeuner, *History of Domestic Animals*, pp. 350–2.
47. Walz, *Deutsche morgenländische Gesellschaft Zs.* 101 (1951), p. 29 and 104 (1954), p. 47; id., *Cong. int. des Sciences anthropologiques et ethnologiques* iv (1952), p. 190.
48. *Bellum Africum*, ch. 68 4.
49. Demougeot, *Annales* xv (1960), p. 208.
50. See Courtois, *Les Vandales et l'Afrique*, especially pp. 98–104.
51. Ammian xxviii, ch. 6 5.
52. Huard, *Encyclopédie mensuelle d'Outremer* v (1955), p. 366.
53. Mauny R., 1947 (2). I cannot accept guessed identifications of places as far south as the savannah in e.g. Berthelot, *L'Afrique saharienne*.
54. iv, ch. 195–6.
55. Pliny, *Natural History* v, ch. 5 36; Pace *et al.*, *Monumenti antichi* xli (1951), p. 150.
56. Lhote, *Revue africaine* xcviii (1954), p. 41; Desanges, *ibid.*, 101 (1957), p. 5.
57. Gsell, *Académie des Inscriptions Mémoires* 43 (1933) i, p. 149.
58. Roman glass probably of the third century A.D. has been found in a cemetery near Ghat.
59. There were Roman buildings and imports at Djerma, but perhaps there was no military occupation.
60. Lhote, *l. c.* (note 56) lists six finds from the Sahara; see Mauny, *CIAO* IV ii (1951), p. 53. I do not accept the cameo found on the beach at Konakry (Mauny, *NA* 89 (1961), p. 11), which seems to be a modern drop of a piece of recent workmanship.
61. Reygasse, *Monuments funéraires préislamiques de l'Afrique du Nord*, p. 88; Gautier, *Geographical Review* xxiv (1934), p. 439.
62. Mauny R., 1952 (1) and 1961 (1), pp. 293–306.
63. Cp. Gautier, *Les Siècles obscurs du Maghreb*.
64. Reygasse, *l. c.* (note 61); see Monod, *Soc. española de Antropologia A.M.* xxiii (1948), p.12.
65. Schiffers, *NA* 60 (1953), p. 104.
66. Benoit *et al.*, *Con. int. d'Anthropologie et d'Archéologie préhistoriques* (1931), p. 218.

67. *Radiocarbon* vi (1964), p. 242.
68. Dalloni, 'Mission au Tibesti', pp. 208–16 (*Acad. des Sciences Mém.* lxii (1935)); Desio, *Il Tibesti Nord-orientale*; Fuchs, *Archiv für Völkerkunde* xii (1957), p. 122.
69. Bailloud in Pearce, *Iron in Africa*, pp. 26–27.
70. Flamand and Laquière, *SAP* V x (1909), p. 180; see list of sculptured stones in Balout, *Bull. de Liaison saharienne* xxxiii (1959), p. 15.
71. Lhote, *II Panafrican Congress* p. 725.
72. I.F.A.N. Dakar N 54–103.
73. Desio, *l. c.* (note 68), pl. XXVIII.
74. iv, ch. 42.
75. iv, ch. 43.
76. The identification in ps.–Scylax with Cap Cantin seems to be due to confusion.
77. Germain, *Hespéris* xliv (1957), p. 205.
78. Cp. Pliny, *Natural History* v, ch. 1 9–10 and vi, ch. 36–37 201–5. Juba is almost certainly one of the main sources of Ptolemy, see Mauny R., 1947 (2).
79. See Sallust, *Histories*, fr. 1 61.
80. Desjacques and Koeberlé, *Hespéris* xlii (1955), p. 193; Jodin, *Bull. d'Archéologie marocaine* ii (1957), p. 9. Cintas' chronology in 'Contribution à l'étude de l'expansion carthaginoise au Maroc' (*Inst. des Hautes Etudes marocaines*, 56) is open to criticism, and his dating of the red-glaze ware from Mogador is not accepted by Tarradell (*Hespéris–Tamuda* I ii (1960), p. 235), who considers that it is not later than 500 B.C.
81. Like the romantic account in Carcopino, *Le Maroc antique*.
82. Luquet, *Bull. d'Archéologie marocaine* v (1964), p. 117.
83. Euzennat, *Bull. d'Archéologie marocaine* ii (1957), p. 41; Camps, 'Massinissa' (*Libyca Archéologie–Epigraphie* viii).
84. See Tarradell, *Tamuda* iii (1955), p. 100.
85. Frézoul, *Bull. d'Archéologie marocaine* ii (1957), p. 65.
86. Mauny R., 1961 (1), pp. 428–30.
87. See diagram, Fagg B., 1956, p. 211, fig. 8.
88. Fagg B., 1959 (1) and (2).
89. From Ninkada River, Pitt-Rivers Museum VI 10 and V 115.
90. Barendsen, Deavey and Gralenski, *Science* 126 (1957), p. 908.
91. Fagg, *Nature* 205 (9/1/1965), p. 212.
92. Fagg B., 1959 (2) (fig. 8) considers that a terracotta from Ire near Ife has reminiscences of the Nok style.
93. Fagg, *III Panafrican Congress* p. 306; Sassoon, *Man* lx (1960), no. 70.
94. Davies, *Man* lix (1959), no. 116.
95. Fagg, *Historical Soc. Nigeria Jour.* i (1956), p. 27.
96. Conant, *New York Acad. of Sciences Trans.* xxiii (1960), p. 155.
97. Palausi, *RGD* v (1955), p. 217.
98. Furon R., 1929.
99. Cp. Siossat, *CEHSAOF* xx (1937), p. 336.

W

100. Scarisbrick and Carter, *Ghana Notes and Queries* i (1961), p. 4.
101. See Mauny R., 1961 (1), pp. 293–306.
102. The recorded evidence is very patchy and unsatisfactory, so it is impossible to map these mounds without a proper survey.
103. Szumowski, *IFAN* 19B (1957), p. 224.
104. Szumowski, *l. c.* p. 250; id., *NA* 64 (1954), p. 102; I.F.A.N. Bamako So 52–31.
105. I.F.A.N. Dakar Se 54–52 and 54–55.
106. Thomassey P. and Mauny R., 1956; id., *IFAN* xiii (1951), p. 438; Bonnel de Mézières, *Acad. des Inscriptions Mém.* (1920), p. 227.
107. Cp. the radiocarbon date for the excavations, Sa–77, 740 ± 120 B.P. (*Radiocarbon* vi (1964), p. 243).
108. Desplagnes, *Géographie* xiii (1906), p. 83; Maes, *CEHSAOF* (1924), p. 31; Clérisse, *Cong. int. d'Archéologie et d'Anthropologie préhistoriques* xv (1931), p. 273.
109. de Gironcourt, *Géographie* xxviii (1913), p. 296.
110. Furon, *Ass. française pour l'avancement des Sciences C.R.* lv (1931), p. 302; Szumowski, *NA* 75 (1957), p. 66 and 77 (1958), p. 1.
111. Chudeau, *Anthropologie* xxi (1910), p. 663.
112. Mauny, *Tropiques* 441 (1961), p. 19; I.F.A.N. Dakar M 62–44.
113. I.F.A.N. Dakar So 55–36.
114. Mauny, *NA* 103 (1964), p. 72.
115. Szumowski, *NA* 70 (1956), p. 36.
116. Szumowski, *NA* 64 (1954), p. 102 and 67 (1955), p. 65.
117. I.F.A.N. Bamako So 52–42.
118. Desplagnes, *Anthropologie* xiv (1903), p. 151.
119. Szumowski, *SAfr* xxxi (1961), p. 97.
120. I.F.A.N. Bamako So 54–23.
121. I.F.A.N. Dakar So 47–42.
122. Mauny, *NA* 62 (1954), p. 33; I.F.A.N. Dakar N 49–277.
123. Mauny in Hugot H. J. ed., 1962, p. 299, pl. IV–V.
124. Mauny R., 1961 (1), p. 489.
125. Camps, *CPF* xv (1956), p. 334.
126. Some of the best pots are illustrated in Mauny R., 1961 (1), p. 351.
127. Monod, in *Afrikanistische Studien* (Deutsche Akad. d. Wissenschaften, Inst. f. Orientforschung, publ. 26).
128. Monod, *NA* 20 (1943), p. 10, 37 (1948), p. 23 and 43 (1949), cover.
129. Vieillard, *IFAN* ii (1940), p. 347.
130. Mauny, *NA* 43 (1949), p. 70; Szumowski, *NA* 70 (1956), p. 33.
131. Masson–Detourbet, *NA* 60 (1953), p. 100.
132. Szumowski, *NA* 67 (1955), p. 69.
133. Ligers, *Revue archéologique* (1961), i, p. 203.
134. Desplagnes, *Le Plateau central nigérien*, pp. 57–66; id., *Géographie* xiii (1906), p. 81; Desplagnes L., 1951; Mauny R., 1961 (1), p. 96.
135. Avinen, *NA* 13, p. 4.
136. Mauny *IFAN* xiii (1951), p. 840; Mauny R., 1961 (1), pp. 112–14, figs. 63 and 70, and pp. 498–9.

137. I.F.A.N. Dakar So 51–141.
138. *NA* 9 (1941), p. 9.
139. Joire J., 1955; Joire, *Man* xliii (1943), no. 34; Mauny, *NA* 43 (1949), p. 72.
140. The finds are not well illustrated; so it has not been considered worth while to copy more than two of the illustrations. The rest can be consulted in the excavation report.
141. E.g. inland near Mbaké; Clos–Arceduc, *NA* 95 (1962), p. 88.
142. Bonnel de Mézières, *Acad. des Inscriptions Mém.* xiii (1923), pp. 265–73.
143. *IFAN* ix (1947), p. 214; *NA* 2 (1939), p. 26 and 3 (1939), p. 33.
144. Joire J., 1955, fig. VII 1–5.
145. Corre, *Revue d'Ethnographie* ii (1883), p. 18; Lafont, *CEHSAOF* xxi (1938), p. 385; Monod, *NA* 4 (1939), p. 11; Bessac, *NA* 57 (1953), p. 1; Mauny R., 1961 (1), pp. 157–62.
146. I.F.A.N. Dakar Se 42-12.
147. Fairbridge, in *Physics and Chemistry of the Earth* iv, p. 171.
148. Corbeil R., 1951, p. 412.
149. Mauny R., 1951.
150. Jouenne P., 1930; Jouenne, *CEHSAOF* i (1916), p. 27; id., *ibid.*, ii (1917), p. 311; id., *ibid.*, iii (1918), p. 57; Hamy, *Acad. des Inscriptions C.R.* (1904), p. 560; Duchemin, *Anthropologie* xvi (1905), p. 634; id., *SAP* V vii (1906), p. 25; Mauny, *NA* 73 (1957), p. 1; Mauny R., 1961 (1), pp. 164–72; Carroll, *Geographical Journal* xii (1898), p. 522; Todd, *Man* iii (1903), no. 93; Parker, *R. Anthropological Inst. Jour.* liii (1923), p. 207.
151. The most easterly is Kotiari at 13° 26′ W. There are tumuli at Gamon south of this, and a degenerate circle at Niokolo–Koba.
152. Teixeira da Mota, *Guiné Portuguesa* i, p. 128.
153. Mauny R., 1961 (1), p. 160.
154. Davies, *V Panafrican Congress* (in press).
155. Gaussen, *SPF* lix (1962), p. 98.
156. See Davies O., 1964 (2), fig. 118.
157. Cp. Dunglas, *NA* 26 (1945), p. 15.
158. Wild R. P., 1934; Wild, *Gold Coast Review* v, p. 150; Nunoo, *Man* 48 (1948), no. 90.
159. Pitt–Rivers Museum IX 496; Ghana Museum 53/141.
160. Wild, *Gold Coast Review* v, p. 180; id., *Teachers' Journal* (1934–5); id., *Man* xxxv (1935), no. 145.
161. Wild R. P., 1934; Wild, *Gold Coast Review* v, p. 1.
162. See Shaw, *R. Anthropological Inst. Jour.* lxxv (1945), p. 45.
163. Kitson, *GSFNB* (14/6/1917).
164. Shaw C. T., 1944.
165. *ARGS* (1930–1), p. 8; (1931–2), p. 16; (1934–5), p. 14; (1935–6), p. 34. Braunholtz H. J., 1936.
166. Davies O., 1961 (3), paper 3, pp. 24–25.
167. Plan in id., *ibid.*, p. 18.
168. Shaw C. T., 1945, p. 494.

169. Pitt–Rivers Museum X 20.
170. Cooper, *GSFNB* (25/1/1927).
171. *NA* 10 (1941), p. 23; Mauny R., 1961 (1), p. 176.
172. Mauny R., 1961 (1), p. 183; Haselberger, *NA* 88 (1960), p. 112.
173. Davies O., 1961 (3), paper 5.
174. Cp. Shaw, *Excavation at Dawu*.
175. Wilks, *The Northern Factor in Ashanti History*, paper 1.
176. *ARGS* (1916); Junner, *GSFNB* (27/3/1937).
177. Davies O., 1964 (2), p. 248.
178. Labouret H., 1931; Labouret, *Revue d'Ethnologie et de Traditions populaires* (1920), p. 177; Delafosse, *Anthropologie* xiii (1902), p. 778; Mauny, *NA* 73 (1957), p. 19.
179. Haselberger, *NA* 88 (1960), p. 112.
180. Mauny, *NA* 75 (1957), p. 73 and 79 (1958), p. 65.
181. *NA* 5 (1940), p. 2; *NA* 15 (1942), p. 5.
182. Particularly at Besedruasi on the confluence of the River Pra and Ofin. which contained a pot and incinerated bones.
183. *GSFNB* (3/4/1916).
184. *ARGS* (1937–8), p. 27.
185. *Und Afrika sprach* i, pl. opp. p. 24; *Das unbekannte Afrika*, p. 122.
186. Francis–Boeuf, *CEHSAOF* xx (1937), p. 413.
187. Reynolds, *Man* xxx (1930), no. 156.
188. Breuil and Mortelmans, *Musée r. du Congo belge, Ann. in 8° Préhistoire*, vol. I.
189. Mortelmans and Monteyne, *IV Panafrican Congress* ii, p. 457.
190. Szumowski, *II Panafrican Congress* p. 673; id., *NA* 58 (1953), p. 35; Lafitte, *La Nature* (9/7/1910), p. 85; Furon R., 1932.
191. de Zeltner, *CRAS* 150 (1910), p. 1461; id., *Anthropologie* xxii (1911), p. 1; Vuillet, *CEHSAOF* (1924), p. 735; Griaule M., 1934; Sommier, *NA* 47 (1950), p. 68; Jaeger, *NA* 60 (1953), p. 97; Dars, *NA* 68 (1955), p. 99.
192. Vaughan, *Man* lxii (1962), no. 83.
193. Rouch, *IFAN* xi (1949), p. 340.
194. Rouch, *Etudes voltaïques* ii (1961), p. 61.
195. Bruel, *Recherches congolaises* xxiii (1937), p. 181.
196. Classens, *NA* 49 (1951), p. 1 and 52 (1951), p. 98.
197. Schwanold, *Zeitschrift für Ethnologie* xlv (1913), p. 970.
198. Szumowski, *SPF* lii (1955), p. 651.

CHAPTER SIX

The Europeans Arrive

It is entirely to the Portuguese that belongs the credit for opening up the sea-ways of West Africa. Suggestions that they had been preceded by sailors from France are due to misunderstood and probably forged tradition.[1] There is no reliable positive evidence that Moors and Arabs navigated the Atlantic, though culture-contacts make it probable that there was occasional communication between southern Morocco and the Canary Islands. It is unlikely that the Arabs carried out coasting voyages; all their activity was from the interior to the coast and in special cases to offshore islands.

Fishermen and explorers from the Peninsula had since well before A.D. 1400 been attracted down the Moroccan coast and to the Canary Islands. The stumbling block for further advance was Cape Bojador, because the regular winds and surge make it almost impossible for coasting vessels to round the line of its reefs on the return northward voyage. Mauny is probably right to maintain that no boat had ever returned if it passed this cape. In 1433 Prince Henry dispatched Gil Eanes to round the cape. The first year he failed; in 1434 he succeeded and returned, presumably with the brilliant idea of standing far out to sea to avoid the Canaries Current, and tacking back eastwards a long way to the north, normally via the Azores. This became the regular route for Portuguese vessels sailing the African coast and beyond.

After a few years delay, due to internal political events, Prince Henry began to encourage further exploration. By 1444 the Portuguese were past the desert at Cap Vert. They then met opposition from Africans who practised navigation in the Rivières du Sud, and they probably did not reach Port. Guinea before 1456. They spent time exploring the River Gambia and the sources of gold in the interior. In 1471 they were at the mouth of the River Pra in Ghana, where they found gold, and in 1474 at Cap Caterina in Gaboon. In 1482 Diego Cão reached the River Congo, and in 1485–6 Cape Cross. In 1488 Bartolemeu Dias rounded the

Cape. By 1498 the Portuguese were in India, the goal of their exploration and the source of the merchandise which medieval Europe insis-
tently demanded.[2]

The Portuguese were not a numerous people, and they had a vast
new world before them. They could pick and choose. They were not
interested in developing natural resources. They built two castles on the
Gold Coast, Elmina and Axim, because gold was already being produced
there and they could obtain it easily by barter. The rest of West Africa
they avoided, except the islands which were easily settled and protected.
They had no inkling of the fabulous wealth of diamonds which lay
beneath six metres of dunes along the South-west African coast. To
them West Africa must have been particularly uninviting, either desert
or impenetrable swamps and forests, with a few savage and quarrelsome
little villages. The cities, civilization and commerce of East Africa must
have appealed more, and beyond was the ancient land of India.

The Portuguese were not solely interested in material gain. The early
explorers had a strong missionary vein, which they had inherited from
Henry the Navigator. They were not colonists; but they earnestly
desired to spread the Christian faith, and to build up a Christian
community of states which would isolate and subject the Muslim
community from which they had long suffered. They were in earnest
in their search for Prester John. In West Africa the only region which
really interested them was the organized kingdom of the Congo,
whither they could spread Christianity. There was little to be done
with the small pagan chieftaincies of Guinea.

The Cultures of Nigeria

By A.D. 1500 many Nigerian states had attained a high level of civilization and artistic achievement, and had learnt to stabilize by religious
and cultural tradition their powerful political societies. Western Europe
was at this date no more advanced, as it was rebuilding its political
structure after the anarchy of decaying feudalism; but Western Europe
had the technological background which encouraged rapid progress as
soon as political order was secured, while in Africa technology was
static, and African states were reduced to the defensive against European penetration.

Ife is still an important political centre, and artistic production
certainly continued until swamped by imported industrial products in
very recent times.[3] Its most remarkable products, the brass portrait-
heads [pl. 37], are almost certainly pre-Portuguese and unaffected by

European influence; their curious alloy (copper-lead-zinc)[4] may be derived from Muslim lands but not from Western Europe; they are not of tin-bronze, though the small percentage of tin in one or two indicates the use of a little bronze scrap. Accurate dates have not yet been obtained from Ife. It is thought likely that its most magnificent work belongs to approximately the fourteenth century. There must, however, have been a period of development, which has not been clearly identified at Ife itself. At Eshure have been found stone carvings considered to be more archaic than those at Ife,[5] at Ire a terracotta transitional between the Nok and Ife styles.[6]

Ife was an important centre. In the neighbourhood are works of art in stone[7] and terracotta,[8] closely resembling those from Ife. Terracotta heads with low foreheads from Ilesha, 30 kms. to the east, are of a style otherwise unknown among the Yoruba and perhaps of late date.[9]

At present only small excavations have been carried out at Old Oyo, 60 kms. north of Ilorin.[10] The site is promising, but its great antiquity and its artistic importance remain to be demonstrated. Between Ife and Old Oyo lies Esie with its stone figures.[11] Old Oyo is not very far from the River Niger, near which from around Jebba there are brass figures.[12]

South-east of Ife lies the extremely important political and artistic centre of Benin. Benin may have learnt brass-casting from Ife in pre-Portuguese days [pl. 35]; traditionally it was a pupil of Ife. Its proximity to the sea and accessibility via the delta waterways enabled the Portuguese to establish contact with it before the end of the fifteenth century,[13] and Benin brass plaques represent Portuguese soldiers. Its artistic traditions were vigorously maintained until it was sacked by the British. Many works of art were looted at the time of the sack;[14] their distribution into European museums has given to the world a more extensive knowledge of the sculpture of Benin than of the rest of southern Nigeria. Excavations were started at Benin,[15] but have not been properly published. The city has not received as much attention from archaeologists as Ife.

The Ife–Benin schools of brass-work seem to be the oldest in the West African forest. There is at present no evidence for fine metal-work in the Volta Valley and Ashanti in pre-Portuguese times, though a few pieces survive from the craftsmanship of the kingdoms of the middle Niger. It has been suggested that the brass-work of the Lobi (upper Volta) and the Dan (Liberia) is associated with Ife–Benin;[16] Benin statues apparently reached the Ivory Coast by trade.[17] This scattered distribution across the fairly coherent stylistic block in Ghana and upper Volta needs confirmation by widespread excavation and not merely by personal aesthetic judgement. Like many features of Nigerian cultures, some motifs and shapes of Benin art are reminiscent of the Nile Valley, from Saite to Coptic. But the eclecticism and lack of chronological coherence of these similarities make it difficult to assume direct contact from the Nile Valley to West Africa at one or more defined periods. There is the same difficulty in the neolithic. Contacts between the Nile Valley and the southern Sahara and savannah fail to indicate one definite route, source or date.

Exploration has been carried out on Fernando Po.[18] Many sites have yielded pottery and stone objects which are generally described as neolithic, without criteria of absolute date. Some of the pottery is reminiscent of medieval and even of post-Portuguese styles on the mainland; but there are no close resemblances to the maritime culture of Sekondi (below, pp. 310–12). Fernando Po was at an early date occupied and partly colonized by the Portuguese. It is unfortunate that sites have not been found to illustrate the introduction of European influences and the transition from an African to a partially colonial culture.

Coastal Cultures West of Nigeria

Most of the monumental art of Dahomey and Togo appears to be recent. The older coastal sites, perhaps as old as the sixteenth century, are cemeteries which have been plundered in search of cylindrical beads of blue glass, which are nowadays prized,[19] while stone beads are little estimated in the forest and coastlands. Similar beads were excavated at Afré-Boka near Toumodi (Ivory Coast).[20] Glass beads can hardly have reached this country except on European ships. Much has been written about the Aggrey beads of Ghana. It is most likely that they are early imported glass beads, many probably from Venice. Haevernick[21] considers that patterned polychrome beads, the so-called Zanaga-beads,[22] were Aggrey beads. These are undoubtedly Venetian, but in the eighteenth century were copied at Amsterdam.[23] Aggrey beads are described in early sources as blue,[24] so the blue cane-glass beads found in Dahomey may belong to this class. There are local names for many different types of old beads. But the Aggrey bead cannot be defined exactly, and may have been a composite trade-term for many types of imported bead.

Many sites are known along the coast of Ghana with abundant, heavily decorated pottery. There has been little excavation, however; and from surface collections it is usually impossible to decide whether a site was contemporary with the arrival of the Portuguese. From the later seventeenth century European imports become common, carried in Dutch and other North European ships. Glazed sherds, glass and fragments of European pipes survive well and are easily recognizable; native pipes indicate tobacco, which also was imported. It has, however, been difficult to identify Portuguese imports, though they would undoubtedly turn up in proper excavations. Old beads, which must have come in in quantity, are avidly collected by local people, so would seldom be lying on the surface. Arms are unlikely to have been lost. Brass bowls, which seem to have been a valuable import, would either be reused as raw material or hoarded, the only one thought to be Portuguese is from Nikki (Dahomey),[25] though others, not dated and perhaps as late as the eighteenth century, have been found at sites in Ghana. Manilas or neck-rings, another form in which brass was imported, are found in seventeenth-century association.[26] They were among the earliest trade goods carried by the Portuguese, if one accepts the emendation of the Latin text of Diogo Gomes.[27] Thus Portuguese imports are more likely to be lying unstratified in stool-treasures than on habitation-sites in association with everyday rubbish.

A good many sites with abundant, highly decorated pottery have been found on the Accra Plains, especially along the coast round Tema. There is at present no good evidence that they were occupied at the time of the arrival of the Portuguese. Some which have been partly excavated or carefully examined, are later than the fifteenth century, like Dewu Asaman,[28] Adwuku in the Shai Hills[29] and Ladoku near Dawhwenya.[30] Other sites are likely to be pre-Portuguese, perhaps surviving until Portuguese times. Although the pottery has not been analysed, the four or more Iron Age sites at Tema, not far from one another, are unlikely to be contemporary, and what seems to be the oldest, near the railway opposite Greenwich Rock, has yielded small weathered sherds with little decoration, similar to sherds found on several sites at Legon at some depth below the surface, and dating far back in the Middle Ages. Elaborately decorated pottery has recently turned up at Bator on the lower Volta. Vume Dugame, a few kilometres downstream, I have claimed as medieval [above, p. 291; fig. 110].[31] But the collection was made by an amateur and it is impossible to re-examine and control the site, so one cannot say if there are Portuguese objects. The place lies at the head of the Volta delta, accessible to fair-sized boats up-river, where the marshes contract and there must have been a crossing at all times. One would expect a site of Portuguese date to be located in the immediate neighbourhood, whether it was directly visited by Portuguese vessels or not.

The sites marked on early maps and mentioned in early records[32] on the Fanti coast between the Rivers Volta and Pra have not with certainty been identified, and important collections of pottery have not yet been made, which could belong to the fifteenth or sixteenth centuries. At Befikrom a mound of uncertain date was excavated,[33] and there are several other sites around Mankesim. European imports have not been found in them, so they are probably older than 1650, and may be pre-Portuguese.

Excavations were carried out at a village and cemetery at Sekondi.[34] The pottery and culture have been identified at two other sites on the coast, and there are connections with the medieval hilltop site of Nsuta (above, ch. 5, n. 158), which is undoubtedly an older foundation. The pottery is unlike the flamboyant Fanti-ware. It is thin and well made [fig. 113], the shapes are simple, almost entirely round-bottomed jars, a few bowls or lids. Ornament consists of fine incisions, especially walking grooves and comb and concentric arcs, of markedly archaic appearance, save that it is usually confined to the shoulder. Large greenstone pebbles were imported to manufacture celts and rubbing-stones. These must have come from Cape Three Points, where greenstone outcrops on the cliffs and there are many pebbles among the shingle. The distribution suggests a culture closely bound to the coast, and probably much occupied in coastal navigation, though the numerous molluscs found on the site come from the shore or from lagoons and are not associated with fish-bones, to indicate dependence on off-shore fishing.

The houses of the village were very small shelters, on platforms levelled on the hillside. More interesting were the graves, with their well defined and distinctive rites. Some of the corpses had been mutilated by decapitation, and in some graves were only skulls. The bodies were buried seated or lying on the side, fairly tightly flexed, and were covered by small cairns. In each grave was one or two pots and a celt in mint condition. One or more stone beads, mostly cylindrical of pinkish quartz, were attached to the heads, and strings of shell beads were placed round the necks. There was no metal in the graves, nor was it found in those houses which were explored.

Sekondi must overlap the arrival of the Portuguese, though it is not mentioned in their records.[35] It has yielded two stones with mortar adhering, which had almost certainly been brought from a Portuguese

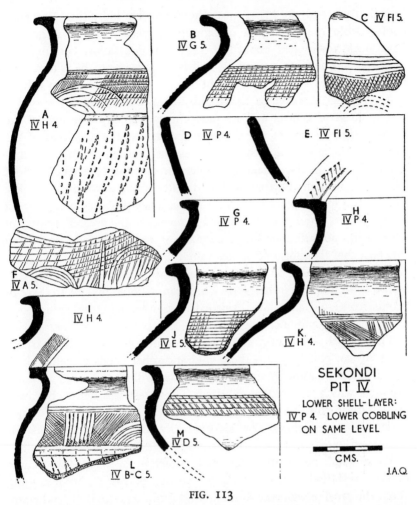

FIG. 113

building. A sherd from a low level had been impressed with a double ring with scorings, which looks as if made with a European medallion of Bellarmine type. The site lies between the harbour and the Dutch Fort Orange, which so far as is known had no Portuguese predecessor. It is tempting to suggest that it was brought to an end by the builders of the castle, who could not tolerate the threat to their communications with Sekondi Bay. But the very scanty traces of European goods and the absence of real imports, except in the top level which was disturbed in laying out the castle garden, suggest that the people of Sekondi were ejected or emigrated by at least A.D. 1500. The inviting and sheltered Sekondi Bay would hardly have been neglected by Portuguese mariners, though they had no major post there. Objects indicating European contact were found only in one group of graves, so the village may have been abandoned about A.D. 1471, but one family continued to bury there. The most interesting find is what seems to be a terracotta banana, perhaps a curiosity brought on one of Vasco da Gama's ships, as the banana is native to India and not to West Africa.

The coast of central and western Ghana, directly fronting on the gold-bearing regions of the southern forest, was the only part of the Gulf of Guinea in which the Portuguese established fortified trading-posts, Elmina at the village of 'Duas Partes'[36] in 1482, Axim about 1508.[37] In 1471 the Portuguese found gold coming down the River Pra to Shama, the first place named La Mina. They probably established a fortified post, which was abandoned in favour of the greater security of Elmina and not refounded for nearly a century. It may have been from this post that the mortared stones were removed to Sekondi. The great era of castle-building on the Gold Coast was the seventeenth and eighteenth centuries, when the North European nations, anxious to share in profits from gold and slaves, rivalled each other by establishing posts at every village and anchorage.

The central Gold Coast was much more inviting than other parts of West Africa. Not only was there gold and other goods of value, there was a fair population anxious to trade and willing to search for local products which the traders required. The forest was dense, but high ground came down to the coast, which was not cut off from the interior by lagoons and swamps. The coast is rocky, and offered headlands for secure settlement and bays for anchorage.

The Sekondi-people must have had contacts as far west at Cape Three Points. Fresh finds may reveal them even west of this; we know nothing about the pre-Portuguese culture around Axim. Duarte Pacheco Pereira speaks of the state of Anda, which apparently did not reach Takoradi, so cannot belong to the Sekondi-people. To the west it may have reached Axim, and it drew gold from a mine somewhere up-country, perhaps from Kanyankaw, in which the Portuguese were interested later, when they founded Fort Duma, some way up the River Ankobra.[38]

West of the River Ankobra swamps begin, and there is practically no evidence for sites of any period before the River Tano. In Krinjabo, around the Aby Lagoon in eastern Ivory Coast, are numerous cemeteries with terracottas of a distinctive style, faces tilted backwards and tall ringed necks [pl. 46].[39] Similar statuettes were recovered from a cemetery at Manso behind Sekondi;[40] there may be others around

Enchi and Axim, but they have never been seen by scholars. A group of stone figures in everyday occupations is described, but not illustrated, from a shrine on an island in the lower Tano near Kansakrom.[41] Many of the Krinjabo statuettes have reached the Musée de l'Homme and the museum at Abidjan; but there are no proper indications of their distribution, and habitation-sites associated have not been discovered and probably not looked for. The date of the Krinjabo-culture is therefore uncertain. It is suggested that it was flourishing in the sixteenth century, so may be in part contemporary with the arrival of the Portuguese.

Cultures of the Forest and its Northern Margin

I have described some medieval sites of the forest of Ghana, on hilltops and surrounded by large entrenchments [figs. 104, 108]. The only objects that they have so far yielded are elaborately decorated pots [figs. 105–7, 109]. It is likely that towards the end of the fifteenth century there was a more advanced culture, especially in Ashanti, and that a whole chapter of West African civilization remains to be unearthed. For by this time traders from the north were penetrating the forest in search of gold, and they almost certainly brought ideas and goods to the chiefs of the gold-working regions. But exploration and excavation have been difficult in Ashanti; so we do not at present recognize there any sites which undoubtedly belong to the fifteenth and sixteenth centuries. Especially, there has been no opportunity of watching the large recent development of Kumasi, where the late neolithic settlement is unlikely to have come to an end and the region to have been swallowed into the encroaching forest in the early Iron Age.

There is, however, a collection of pottery and terracottas from Ahinsan, south of Bekwai [pl. 48]. It has not yet been possible to publish this material in detail, but a short report appeared some years ago.[42] The pottery is not medieval but markedly proto-Ashanti. A date, probably in the seventeenth or end of the sixteenth century, is provided by a handful of beads of whitish glass-paste with irregular Indian-red stripes bordered by blue. These were apparently the only imported objects; no sherds of European china or other material were found in the excavation, though admittedly this did not cover more than a fraction of the site.

The site was almost certainly a dump of ritual objects. Many of the pottery types were ritual, with symbolic decoration in high relief or in the round on the rims. There were also terracotta spoons, which are still used in ritual; these turned up also at Ntereso. The terracottas seem to be ritual and are traditionally said to represent the spirits of the dead.

It is believed that the place was used for funerary ceremonies, a 'place of pots' as described in the Fomena area,[43] and not the actual place of inhumation.

The terracottas are highly sophisticated, conforming rigidly to a small number of types but showing marked originality by individual artists. Though the date of the collection is fairly late, it is difficult to believe that terracotta-making had not had a long history in Ashanti and other parts of the forest. There are from Ntereso scraps of terracotta figures, probably applied to pottery. Fragments from Befikrom may be older than Ahinsan, and Krinjabo is claimed to be early, though none of the terracottas of this group are stratified. Those of some regions, like Kwahu and Asin, seem later than Ahinsan and derived from it. From these arguments it seems almost certain that terracotta sites of the fifteenth century remain to be discovered in what later became Ashanti; and terracotta-making may well have had prototypes in wood. Stone sculpture, known in western Nigeria, has not been found in the forests of Ghana, where unweathered stone is rare. In Nigeria it would appear to have been developed at an early date only at wealthy courts and sanctuaries.

Brass-casting in Ashanti is not known to be older than the eighteenth century. The elaborately decorated pots and the proverb-weights seem to belong to the great period of gold-working, encouraged by European traders on the coast; most of the brass was imported from Europe. Hefel[16] considers that the Ashanti brasswork-style is linked with a group extending north-west to the bend of the Niger, where the floruit was in the pre-Islamic Middle Ages; but evidence of so early a brass industry in Ashanti is lacking.

On the northern edge of the forest of Ghana, there flourished in central Gonja probably in the fifteenth to seventeenth centuries an interesting culture, especially between the Black and White Volta. This land, now a poverty-stricken wilderness, waterless for half the year and suffering from soil erosion [see pl. 11], was thickly populated. There are numerous hut-mounds along the few tracks which it has been possible to follow; the total number throughout this inaccessible region must be large. Water was stored in bilegas or rock-cut cisterns [pl. 41; above, p. 294], a technique derived from Muslim lands to the north.

The most interesting finds from many mounds are fine-polished yellow or red pots, often painted with linear designs in red or mauve [figs. 114–15].[44] This ware appears derived from the painted pottery of the Niger bend and Koumbi Saleh (above, p. 261), and the technique

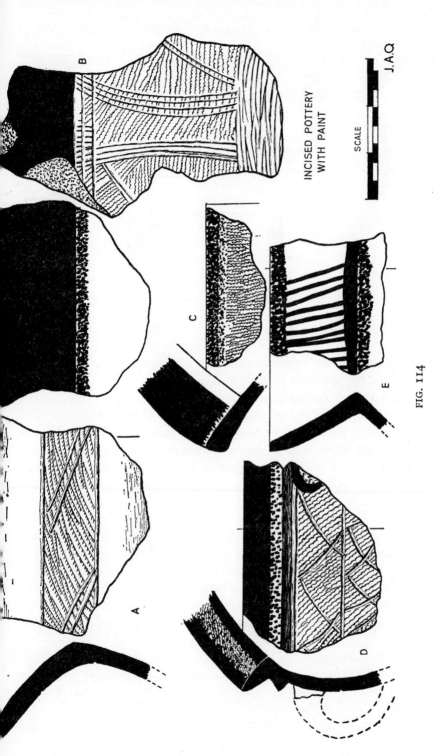

INCISED POTTERY
WITH PAINT

SCALE

J.A.Q

B

C

E

A

D

FIG. 114

from Davies O., 1965 (1), fig. 2; from Kadelso R. H.

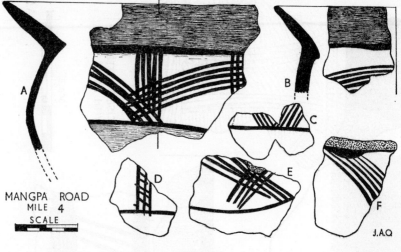

FIG. 115

from Davies O., 1965 (1), fig. 3

was brought south either by the Gonjas or by other immigrants, who are likely to have been mainly Muslim.

An exact date cannot be given for the painted pottery of Gonja. A few pieces have been found on outlying sites on the Oti and down the Volta, especially in the land of the Krachis and as far south as Akroso Beposo, in contexts which seem to be early-modern (sixteenth to seventeenth centuries). In Gonja painted pottery hardly ever appears on tower-mounds, though there was a little at Butie; this would put it earlier than the eighteenth century. It is not common on small low hut-mounds, many of which may be later than 1700, and it is most frequent on fairly small, steep-sided conical mounds. We know nothing of the structures that these contained. Of the two most prolific, that near Kadelso Rest-house has been the victim of bulldozers; while a smaller one at Mile 4 on the Mangpa road served as a landmark for the road-builders, who cut straight through it. European imports have not been found with painted pottery; but as far north as Gonja this would be a poor criterion of date.

From Kissi territory, in central F. Guinea at the back of Sierra Leone, are many statuettes in soft stone and terracotta [pl. 47].[45] The stone pieces are mostly carved with a hammer-adze, a technique more suited to wood than to stone.

Their date is uncertain, perhaps as old as the sixteenth century. They are always found buried, and are not claimed as their work by the present people. One from Massakourou seems to be a copy of a sculpture at Ife; another, with four human heads, of a work from Benin. Another represents a Portuguese crossbowman, again probably copied from Benin.

Outlying sculptures, such as a stone cylinder with human figure from Boundiali (western Ivory Coast), may belong to the Kissi province. The Kissi sculptures are related to the Mande school in steatite, found especially near Sherbro (Sierra Leone), which again are not closely dated.[46]

The picture I have given of West African medieval and early-modern culture and art is extremely disjointed. Doubtless there were centres of population, separated by wide tracts of forest or bush, in which nothing was made because practically no one lived there. At the same time, the extremely patchy nature of our exploration is well brought out; much remains to be found, even perhaps important cultural centres if they are earlier than current oral tradition, and much of this is either lost in the bush or intentionally concealed. The archaeologist is always being confronted with refusals to show what he wants or with blank denials of the existence of things which are undoubtedly there. Peasant superstition is seldom overcome by modern development, because the enlightened African turns his back on his village. In Nigeria only are they beginning to learn the value of their cultural past. Finally, most of the art of earlier centuries in the forest was in wood. This rots, and when the artists' tradition goes, nothing survives.

Cultures of the Savannah

The adventures of the Portuguese on the coast of West Africa had little impact on the cultures of the interior, whose communications were mainly oriented north and east. The Portuguese penetrated up the River Gambia as far as the limit of navigation at Cantor (approximately the present frontier of Gambia),[47] whence there was communication to the gold-placers of the upper Falémé on the northern slopes of Fouta Djalon, and so to the cities of the Niger Valley, especially to Koukia the Songhai capital. It had not been difficult for the empires on the Niger to open routes from the gold districts which they controlled, north of the forest to the sea. There had been traded cotton and silk and some gold, perhaps in exchange for dried oysters, which were a major product of the Rivières du Sud. Iron rods with branches ending in human and animal figures, found in several places in P. Guinea and believed to be royal symbols, were perhaps derived from ancient Mali;[48]

x

one, with a horseman, resembles the staff of the Kpembewura of Gonja, which also may owe its inspiration to the Niger Valley.

It does not, however, appear that the Portuguese were able to establish close contacts up the River Gambia, or to tap the fabulous goldfields by the backdoor. There were probably too many middlemen, and control by the Sudanic empires was too strict. So when the Portuguese discovered their own goldfields in Ghana, and could open direct communication with the producers through Elmina and other posts, they lost interest in the River Gambia. Not long after, they realized the wider and more profitable horizons of the Indian Ocean.

The Sudanic empires thus continued their own historical development without reference to Christian interlopers along the coast. Farther to the east, there has been much recent exploration of the enigmatic Sao culture, centred in a number of town sites around Fort Lamy on the south side of Lake Chad.[49] Sao sites extend as far west as Yo in northeastern Nigeria.[50] and eastward not farther than the eastern edge of the Chari Valley (just over 15° E), apart from one or two sites on Lake Fittri.[51] Traditionally the culture started about the tenth century A.D., and the Sao confederation was broken up and subdued when the Kanuri arrived in the late sixteenth century; but sites like Makari continued to exist and have yielded tobacco-pipes and imported glass beads. Several periods have been distinguished in the architecture and the finds; the oldest settlements are believed to have been unwalled.

The Sao culture is remarkable for its highly decorated impressed pottery and its exceedingly ugly terracottas. It has also yielded a few fine ornaments and animal figurines of copper or an alloy. We do not know if they were made locally; the metal was probably imported from the north. There does not seem close connection with other West African cultures, possibly in sculpture with Nok. At the sanctuary of Tago four flattened terracotta spheres with marked equator had been placed round the central statue. Similar spheres were found at Kadelso with painted pottery and at Damongo (Gonja) (association not recorded); it is impossible to tell whether there is any true association, and the date of both finds is uncertain. The Sao spheres are believed to belong to the second stage of Sao culture, which covers the later Middle Ages down to the sixteenth century or later. An interesting shrine has recently been reported at Bout-al-Kabir near Fort Lamy, with many Sao terracotta heads and statues resting in bowls.[52]

The Kanuri, who conquered and weakened the Sao culture, are perhaps to be connected with the buildings and enclosures of plano-

convex bricks found to the north and north-east of Lake Chad. These
cannot be dated archaeologically; on historical and traditional grounds
they are thought to be earlier, but not much earlier, than the seventeenth
century.[53] There are outliers as far north as Ain Galakka near Faya[54]
and in Tibesti.[55] There is an important example at Garoumélé on the
western shore of Lake Chad,[56] which may have been a temporary
capital of Kanem; also one or two in north-eastern Nigeria.[57]

The weakening of the Sao is typical of what was happening in many
parts of the northern savannah in the fifteenth and sixteenth centuries.
Quite independently of Portuguese exploration of the coast, or at best a
backwash of attacks in the Peninsula and Morocco, Islam was spreading
southward in West Africa and overthrowing older pagan societies. It
was a puritanical Islam, anxious to destroy much of the sensuousness
of animist Africa. Its influence reached patchily to the border of the
forest. When we know more in detail of the archaeology of the northern
regions, we may see that this new Islam was as revolutionary on the old
African culture as the importation of European trade goods to the coast.

Epilogue: The Impact of the Europeans on West Africa

The Portuguese were the first to build fortified trading-posts in West
Africa. Ultimately these became bases whence European powers could
dominate the interior. But for a long time the weakness of their garrisons and the frightful sanitary conditions made control of these
castles precarious; they were no more than depots for goods imported
and exported, and from the seventeenth century a protection for the
several trading nations against each other. For the wealth of West
African trade led to a scramble between European states to share in it.

Colonialism was hardly in the minds of the early explorers. They had
no desire to settle in West Africa, there were pleasanter lands where
younger sons could carve out estates and live like lords. Trade was
valuable, especially to merchants at home who drew profits and did not
face the hardships. At the same time, traders of the first two centuries
probably gave to the Africans more than they got. At first they took
gold, ivory and other local products, not of great value to men struggling
to keep alive; and they introduced more advanced techniques of gold-
mining, probably vein-mining in addition to placers, to encourage
production. Then came the horrors of the slave-trade; but this was
slowly organized, and Africans and Arabs deserve as much blame for
the slave-trade throughout Africa as do Europeans, who at least made
the first move to suppress it. The Portuguese introduced many things

to the backward coastlands to make life easier for the natives, crops from the New World and the Far East which were suited to the forest and promoted growth of population, metal, cloth and so on; later also luxuries which were less necessary for life, tobacco, alcohol, fire-arms, pretty European pottery and all sorts of gewgaws. But if it had not been for European navigators, Africa would have remained introvert, the impassable and unhealthy coastal forests would have still been backward and underpopulated, and life would have been centred on a decadent Islam in the interior. As it happened, the old cultural regions of the Niger Valley and the Sahara remained backward, and the development of modern West Africa has been from the coast inward, so that the outlook of civilized Africans is towards the ocean and the wide world.

<h1 style="text-align:center">NOTES</h1>

1. Mauny, *IFAN* xii (1950), p. 122.
2. The chronicle of the Portuguese discoveries has been constructed from dated maps and charts and from accounts written not much later, especially Diogo Gomes (ed. Monod, Mauny and Duval, *Centro de Estudos da Guiné portuguesa*, no. 21) and Duarte Pacheco Pereira (ed. Mauny, *ibid.*, no. 19). It is set out in detail in many historical works; I have given only an outline, as it lies outside the scope of this work.
3. For the first excavations see Frobenius, *Und Afrika sprach*, especially vol. i, ch. xv, pp. 319–46. For modern accounts of the site and of recent excavations see Willett, *Journal of African History* i (1960), p. 231; Fagg and Willett, *IV Panafrican Congress* ii, p. 357; id., *Odu* viii (1960), p. 21.
4. Barker, *Man* lxv (1965), no. 8.
5. Willett and Dempster, *Man* lxii (1962), no. 1.
6. Fagg, *Historical Society of Nigeria Jour.* i (1959), p. 288, fig. 8.
7. Allison, *Man* lxiv (1964), no. 131.
8. Allison, *Man* lxiii (1963), no. 194; *Présence africaine* 10–11, pl. 24.
9. Willett, *Odu* viii (1960), p. 5.
10. Willett, *Man* lix (1959), no. 135; id., *Historical Society of Nigeria Jour.* II i (1960), p. 59.
11. Fagg, *Man* lix (1959), no. 60.
12. Walker, *Man* xxxiv (1934), no. 193; cp. also the drummer of bronze or brass from Giragi Island; *Nigerian Dept. of Antiquities, Report* (1960–1), p. 39.
13. Cp. Eustache de la Fosse, in *Revue hispanique* iv (1897), p. 174.
14. See Read and Dalton, *R. Anthropological Institute Jour.* xxvii (1898), p. 362.
15. Goodwin, *Historical Society of Nigeria Jour.* i (1957), p. 65.
16. Hefel, *Wiener Beiträge zur Kulturgeschichte und Linguistik* v (1943), p. 1.
17. Knops, *Soc. belge d'Anthropologie Bull.* lxviii (1957), p. 83.

18. Martin del Molino, *Secuencia cultural en el neolitico de Fernando Po;* id., *Tipologia de la Ceramica de Fernando Po*; and a good many recent articles in *Guinea Española*. Of late date, SR–18, 1270 ± 100
19. Mauny R., 1961 (1), p. 179.
20. Delafosse, *Anthropologie* xi (1900), p. 677.
21. *Jb. des römisch-germanischen Museums in Mainz* viii (1961), p. 121.
22. Fourneau, *IFAN* xiv (1952), p. 956 and xvi (1954), p. 1.
23. van der Sleen, *Man* lxiii (1963), no. 219.
24. Mauny, *Historical Society of Nigeria Journal* i (1958), p. 219.
25. Dunglas, *NA* 26 (1945), p. 15.
26. E.g. at Adiopodoume (Ivory Coast), see Aké–Assi and Bouton–Martin, *NA* 89 (1961), p. 4. Some figures from Ahinsan seem to carry manilas.
27. See note 2 above. The Latin reads 'mouilia', which seems to have no meaning.
28. Shaw, *Excavation at Dawu*; the O.S. spelling is as written here.
29. Ozanne, *Ghana Notes and Queries* vii (1965), p. 4.
30. Ozanne, *ibid.*, p. 6, and *West African Archaeological News-Letter* i (1964), p. 8. Both Adwuku and Ladoku may have been on sites of earlier villages, but their latest and most prosperous phases seem to be in the sixteenth and seventeenth centuries.
31. Davies O., 1961 (3), paper 5.
32. E.g. Duarte Pacheco Pereira (1506-8), ed. Mauny pp. 127-9, describes three villages between Elmina and Cabo das Redes, which is probably Dampa Mt., west of Accra; these may be Anomabu Apam and Winneba. Mankesim was important, but being some miles inland may not have been known to the cartographers. Torto west of Elmina may be Komenda.
33. By R. B. Nunoo, unpublished.
34. Preliminary report, Davies O., 1961 (4).
35. The one recorded site between Cape Three Points and the River Pra is Alalaia, which may have been on any of the sheltered bays on this indented coast.
36. Pina's chronicle in Blake, *Europeans in West Africa* i, p. 70. This name was given by the Portuguese, because when they arrived the village was on both sides of the river-mouth.
37. Lawrence, *Trade-castles and Forts of West Africa*, p. 229.
38. Exact site unknown, probably not far from Aniben; see Crow, *Nigerian Field* xxi (1956), p. 52.
39. Holas, *Acta Tropica* viii (1951), p. 1; id., *NA* 53 (1952), pp. 18 and 55 (1952), p. 94.
40. Kerr, *Man* xxiv (1924), no. 27. The terracottas in Nzima are probably unimpressive and fairly modern figures, of which one or two are published by Grottanelli, *Man* lxi (1961), no. 1; they seem unconnected with the Krinjabo group, which must be several centuries old.
41. Paton, *Worship of the Tano Fetish*; Wild, R. Anthropological Institute *Jour.* lxvii (1937), p. 69.
42. Davies, *South African Journal of Science* lii (1956), p. 147.
43. Wild and Braunholtz, *Man* xxxiv (1934), nos. 1–2.

44. Davies O., 1965 (1).
45. Noel, *Anthropologie* xxiv (1913), p. 422; Delafosse, *Revue d'Ethnographie et de Sociologie* v (1914), p. 143; Itier, *CEHSAOF* ix (1926), p. 126; Paulme, *SAP* IX iii (1942), p. 38; id., *Marco Polo* xx (1956), p. 43; Jérémine, *SAfr* xv (1945), p. 3; Knops, *Société r. belge d'Anthropologie et de Préhistoire* lxviii (1957), p. 83.
46. Rütimeyer, *Int. Archiv für Ethnographie* xiv (1901), p. 195 and xviii (1908), p. 167; Joyce, *Man* v (1905), no. 57 and ix (1909), no. 40; Addison, *Man* xxiii (1923), no. 109; Thomas, *Man* xxiv (1924), no. 11.
47. Diogo Gomes, ed. Monod, Mauny and Duval, p. 36.
48. Teixeira da Mota, *Boletim cultural da Guiné portuguesa* lix (1960), p. 625.
49. Wulsin, *Harvard African Studies* x, p. 19; Monod, *La Terre et la Vie* ii (1932), p. 239; Pales, *SAfr* vii (1937), p. 125; Vallois, *Revue anthropologique* xlviii (1938), nos. 10–12; Seliquer, *SAP* IX ii (1941), p. 112; id., *IFAN* vii (1945), p. 191; Lebeuf, *Muséum d'Histoire naturelle de Paris Bull.* II xiv (1942), p. 100; id., *Zaire* iii (1947), p. 543; id., *Archéologie tchadienne*; id., *IV Panafrican Congress* ii, p. 427; id., *Objets et Mondes* ii (1962), p. 135; Griaule and Lebeuf, *SAfr* xviii (1948), p. 2 and xxi (1951), p. 1; Lebeuf and Masson–Detourbet, *La Civilisation du Tchad*; Hartweg, *SAfr* xii (1942), p. 1; Hamelin, *Tribus* 2–3 (1952–3), p. 379.
50. Migeod, *R. African Society Jour.* xxiii (1923–4), p. 19.
51. Lebeuf and Masson–Detourbet, *Préhistoire* xi (1950), p. 143.
52. Courtin, *SPF C.R.* (1965), p. C.
53. Lebeuf, *IV Panafrican Congress* ii, p. 437.
54. Hugot, *LAPE* viii (1960), p. 334; Huard and Bacquié, *IFAN* 26B (1964), p. 16.
55. Seliquer, *SAP* IX ii (1941), p. 112.
56. Binet, *NA* 53 (1952), p. 1.
57. Bivar and Shinnie, *Journal of African History* iii (1962), p. 1.

SELECT BIBLIOGRAPHY

This is intended to be a select bibliography of the most important works on West Africa, strictly within the topographical and chronological limits of this book. Many other works are referred to in the notes to each chapter, but are not included here, as they are not primarily concerned with West Africa before A.D. 1500 or are considered of lesser importance. In particular, there is much material in a number of periodicals, but it is possible to list here only a few articles. The student should go right through the more important periodicals:

CEHSAOF *Comité d'Etudes historiques et scientifiques de l'A.O.F.*
GJS   *Ghana Journal of Science*
          Historical Society of Ghana, Journal
          Historical Society of Nigeria, Journal
IFAN   *Institut français d'Afrique noire, Bulletin*
          the local *I.F.A.N. Etudes*
IRS   *Institut de Recherches sahariennes, Travaux*
LAPE   *Libyca, Anthropologie—Archéologie préhistoriques*
NA   *Notes africaines*
SAfr   *Société des Africanistes, Journal*
SPF   *Société préhistorique française, Bulletin and Comptes rendus:*

also the proceedings of the following conferences:
CIAO   *Conférence int. des Africanistes de l'Ouest*
CISPP   *Congrès int. des Sciences préhistoriques et protohistoriques*
          Panafrican Congress on Prehistory

BERNARD E. A., 1962: 'Théorie astronomique des pluviaux et inter-pluviaux du Quaternaire africain'; *Académie royale des Sciences d'Outremer, Cl. des Sciences naturelles et médicales, Mémoires in 8°*, N.S. xii, fasc. 1.

BESSAC H., 1955: 'Nouvelles découvertes de paléolithique évolué au Moyen et Bas-Sénégal'; *NA* 65, pp. 1–5.

BIBERSON P., 1961 (1): 'Le cadre paléogéographique de la Préhistoire du Maroc atlantique'; *Publications du Service des Antiquités du Maroc* 16.

BIBERSON P., 1961 (2): 'Le paléolithique inférieur du Maroc atlantique'; *Publications du Service des Antiquités du Maroc* 17.

BOETTGER C. R., 1958: *'Die Haustiere Afrikas'*.

BOULE M. and VALLOIS H., 1932: 'L'homme fossile d'Asselar'; *Archives de l'Institut de Paléontologie humaine, Mémoires* 9.

BRAUNHOLTZ H. J., 1936: 'Archaeology in the Gold Coast'; *Antiquity* x, pp. 469–74.

BRIGAUD F., 1960: 'Connaissance du Sénégal, Géologie'; *ESén* ix, pt. 1.

BRÜCKNER W., 1955: 'The mantle-rock (Laterite) of the Gold Coast and its origin'; *Geologische Rundschau* xliii, pp. 307–27.

BUTZER K. W., 1957: 'Late glacial and post-glacial climatic variation in the Near East'; *Erdkunde* xi, pp. 21–35.

BUTZER K. W., 1958: 'Quaternary Stratigraphy and Climate in the Near East'; *Bonner geographische Abhandlungen* 24.

BUTZER K. W., 1958–9: 'Studien zum vor- und frühgeschichtlichen Landschaftswandel der Sahara'; *Akademie der Wissenschaften in Mainz, Abhandlungen der mathematisch-naturwissenschaftlichen Klasse* (1958), no. 1 and (1959), no. 2.

CARTER P. L. and P. J., 1965: 'Rock-paintings from Northern Ghana'; *Historical Society of Ghana Transactions* vii, pp. 1–3.

CORBEIL R., MAUNY R. and CHARBONNIER J., 1948: 'Préhistoire et Protohistoire de la presqu'île du Cap-Vert et de l'extrême ouest sénégalais'; *IFAN* x, pp. 378–460.

CORBEIL R., 1951: 'Les récentes découvertes au Cap-Vert concernant le paléolithique'; *IFAN* xiii, pp. 386–437.

CREAC'H P., 1945: 'Quelques nouveaux sites et nouvelles industries préhistoriques d'A.O.F.'; *CIAO* I ii, pp. 397–430.

DAGAN T., 1956: 'Le site préhistorique de Tiemassas'; *IFAN* 18B, pp. 432–61.

DAVIES O., 1956: 'The raised beaches of the Gold Coast and their associated archaeological material'; *Quaternaria* iii, pp. 91–93.

DAVIES O., 1957: 'The old stone-age between the Volta and the Niger'; *IFAN* 19B, pp. 592–616.

DAVIES O., 1958: 'The late middle stone-age industry in Guinea'; *CISPP* v, pp. 230–5.

DAVIES O., 1959 (1): 'The Distribution of old stone-age material in Guinea'; *IFAN* 21B, pp. 102–8.

DAVIES O., 1959 (2): 'Neolithic Cultures of Ghana'; *IV Panafrican Congress* ii, pp. 291–302.

DAVIES O., 1960: 'Galets perforés du Ghana et des pays voisins'; *NA* 86, pp. 37–39.

DAVIES O., 1961 (1): 'Geological and archaeological evidence for the Late Quaternary climatic sequence in West Africa'; *GJS* i, pp. 69–73.

DAVIES O., 1961 (2): 'Sites du paléolithique moyen à Bamako'; *NA* 89, pp. 5–10.

DAVIES O., 1961 (3): *Archaeology in Ghana.*

DAVIES O., 1961 (4): 'Native cultures in the Gold Coast at the time of the Portuguese discoveries'; *Congresso int. de História dos Descobrimentos* (Lisbon, 1961) iii, pp. 97–109.

DAVIES O., 1964 (1): 'Archaeological Exploration in the Volta Basin'; *Ghana Geographical Association Bulletin*, pp. 28–33.

DAVIES O., 1964 (2): *The Quaternary in the Coastlands of Guinea.*

DAVIES O., 1965 (1): 'Gonja painted pottery'; *Historical Society of Ghana Transactions* vii, pp. 5–11.

DAVIES O., 1965 (2): 'The old and middle palaeolithic in West Africa'; *Rivista di Scienze preistoriche* xix, pp. 1–21.

DELCROIX R. and VAUFREY R., 1939–40: 'Le Toumbien de Guinée française'; *Anthropologie* xlix, pp. 265–312.

DESPLAGNES L., 1951: 'Fouilles du Tumulus d'El Oualedji'; *IFAN* xiii, pp. 1159–73.

FAGG B., 1956: 'An outline of the stone age of the Plateau Minesfield'; *CIAO* iii, pp. 203–22.

FAGG B., 1959 (1): 'The Nok terracottas in West African art-history'; *IV Panafrican Congress* ii, pp. 445–50.

FAGG B., 1959 (2): 'The Nok culture in prehistory'; *Historical Society of Nigeria Journal* i, pp. 288–93.

FROBENIUS L. and BREUIL H., 1930: 'L'Afrique'; *Cahiers d'Art* 8–9.

FURON R., 1929: 'L'ancien delta du Niger'; *RGPGD* ii, pp. 265–74.

FURON R., 1932: 'Notes sur le préhistorique soudanais'; *La Terre et la Vie* ii, pp. 601–9.

GALLAY A., 1964: 'Peintures rupestres recentes du Bassin du Niger' *SAfr* xxxiv, pp. 123–39.

GRIAULE M., 1934: 'Peintures rupestres du Soudan français'; *Revue de Synthèse* vii, pp. 187–8.

HOLAS B. and MAUNY R., 1953: 'Nouvelles fouilles à l'abri sous roche de Blandè; *IFAN* xv, pp. 1605–18.

HUE E., 1912: 'L'age de la pierre au Fouta Djalon'; *SPF Mémoires* ii, pp. 196–263.

HUGOT H. J. ed., 1962: *Missions Berliet Ténéré-Tchad, Documents scientifiques.*

HUGOT H. J., 1963: 'Recherches préhistoriques dans l'Ahaggar nord-occidentale'; *Centre de Recherches anthropologiques préhistoriques et éthnographiques en Algérie, Mémoires* I.

JOIRE J., 1952: 'La Préhistoire de Guinée française'; *CIAO* II iv, pp. 297–373.

JOIRE J., 1955: 'Découvertes archéologiques dans la région de Rao'; *IFAN* 17B, pp. 249–333.

JOUBERT G. and VAUFREY R., 1946: 'La néolithique du Ténéré'; *Anthropologie* 50, pp. 325–30.

JOUENNE P., 1930: 'Les monuments mégalithiques du Sénégal'; *CEHSAOF* xiii, pp. 309–99.

LABOURET H., 1931: 'Les Tribus du rameau Lobi'; *Paris, Institut d'Ethnologie Travaux.*

LHOTE H., 1953: 'Le cheval et le chameau dans les peintures et gravures rupestres du Sahara'; *IFAN* xv, pp. 1138–1228.

MAIGNIEN R., 1958: 'Le cuirassement des sols en Guinée'; *Service de la Carte géologique d'Alsace et de Lorraine, Mémoires* 16.

MAUNY R., 1947 (1): 'Une route préhistorique à travers le Sahara occidental'; *IFAN* ix, pp. 341–57.

MAUNY R., 1947 (2): 'L'Ouest africain chez Ptolemée'; *CIAO* II i, pp. 241–94.

MAUNY R., 1949: 'Sur la préhistoire de la presqu'île du Cap Vert'; *ESén* i, pp. 239–51.

MAUNY R., 1951: 'Poteries néolithiques du Cap Vert'; *IFAN* xiii, pp. 155–67.

MAUNY R., 1952 (1): 'Essai sur l'histoire des métaux en Afrique occidentale'; *IFAN* xiv, pp. 545–93.

MAUNY R., 1952 (2): 'Les gisements néolithiques de Karkarichinkat'; *II Panafrican Congress* pp. 616–29.

MAUNY R., 1952 (3): 'Autour de la répartition des chars rupestres du Nord-ouest africain'; *II Panafrican Congress* pp. 741–6.

MAUNY R., 1954 (1): 'Notes sur deux pièces néolithiques de Guinée française'; *NA* 61, pp. 1–2.

MAUNY R., 1954 (2): 'Gravures peintures et inscriptions rupestres de l'Ouest africain'; *IFAN Initiations africaines* xi.

MAUNY R., 1955: 'Contribution à l'étude du Paléolithique de Mauritanie'; *II Panafrican Congress* pp. 461–76.

MAUNY R., 1956: 'La grande "faune éthiopienne" du Nord-ouest africain'; *IFAN* 18A, pp. 246–79.

MAUNY R., 1961 (1): 'Tableau géographique de l'Ouest africain au moyen age'; *IFAN Mémoires* 61.

MAUNY R., 1961 (2): 'Catalogue des restes osseux humains préhistoriques trouvés dans l'Ouest africain'; *IFAN* 23B, pp. 388–410.

MAUNY R., 1963: 'Poteries engobées et peintes de tradition nilotique de la région de Koro Toro (Tchad)'; *IFAN* 25B, pp. 39–46.

MONOD T., and MAUNY R., 1955: 'Découverte de nouveaux instruments en os dans l'Ouest africain'; *III Panafrican Congress* pp. 242–7.

MONOD T., 1964: 'The Late Tertiary and Pleistocene in the Sahara and adjacent southerly regions'; in F. C. Howell and F. Bourlière *African Ecology and Human Evolution*, pp. 117–229.

OKIY G. E. O., 1962: 'Indigenous Nigerian food-plants'; *WASA* vi, pp. 117–22.

PORTERES R., CLARK J. D., BAKER H. G., MORGAN W. B., ALLISON P. A., STANTON W. R. and KIRK W., 1962: Third Conference on African History and Archaeology, papers on the History of Food Crops; *Journal of African History* iii, pp. 195–267.

RICHARD Comm., 1955: 'Contribution à l'étude de la stratigraphie du quaternaire de la presqu'île du Cap Vert'; *SPF* lii, pp. 80–88.

ROUCH J., 1953: 'Contribution à l'histoire du Songhay'; *IFAN Mémoires* 29, pp. 137–259.

SHAW C. T., 1944: 'Excavations at Bosumpra Cave, Abetifi'; *Prehistoric Society Proceedings* x, pp. 1–67.

SHAW C. T., 1945: 'Prehistory and Archaeology in the Gold Coast'; *CIAO* I ii, pp. 467–99.

SZUMOWSKI G., 1956: 'Fouilles de l'abri sous roche de Kourounkorokale'; *IFAN* 18B, pp. 462–508.

THOMASSEY P. and MAUNY R., 1956: 'Campagne de Fouilles de 1950 à Koumbi Saleh'; *IFAN* 18B, pp. 117–40.

TRICART J., 1957: 'Aspects et problèmes géomorphologiques du littoral occidental de la Côte d'Ivoire'; *IFAN* 19A, pp. 1–20.

VAUFREY R., 1947: 'Le néolithique para-toumbien'; *Revue scientifique* (1947), pp. 205–32.

WILD R. P., 1934: 'Stone age pottery from the Gold Coast and Ashanti'; *Royal Anthropological Institute Journal* lxiv, pp. 203–15.

LIST OF PLATES

1. Painted cave, Oueyanko valley near Bamako, Mali
2. Equatorial forest from the hilltop-site of Ntirikurom, SW. Ghana
3. Hilltop-site of Akroso Beposo, Togoland, marked by a patch of forest in wooded savannah; seventeenth century
4. Gallery-forest in savannah, on River Dayi, Angeta, Togoland
5. Gorge of River Niger, Jebba, Nigeria
6. Grassy swamp without bushes in the Volta valley near the mouth of the River Sheribong, probably marking a fossil lagoon of the period of the Low Terrace
7. Coast at Axim, Ghana
8. Apam Promontory, Ghana, showing marine abrasion-platforms
   Top of hill at 60 metres
   A. Shoulder at 55 metres, probably Beach I
   B. Shoulder at 33 metres, with similar level to right (not visible), perhaps Beach II
   C. Lower promontory with trading-castle, at 23 metres, probably Beach III
9. Savannah of the Accra Plains near margin of the forest, Kotoku, Ghana
10. Highland savannah, Bokkus, Northern Nigeria
11. Thorn-bush savannah on the inner silt-terrace of the Black Volta, Buipe, Ghana
12. Partly cleared forest with thick secondary undergrowth, Agame Beme, Togoland
13. Slope from River Ayensu, Okitsiu, Ghana, with rejuvenation-point of the 9-metre terrace (Low Terrace) in background
14. Hohoe, Ghana, 12-metre gravel of River Dayi (Low Terrace). Above the gravel is a Sangoan piece near the top of the laterite
15. Sand-dunes on southern edge of the Sahara, Mauritania, Draa Malichigdame
   Photo kindly supplied by I.F.A.N., Dakar; photo Mauny
16. Pebbles of Beach III, at about 23 m. S.L., Senya Beraku, Ghana
17. Edubia, Ghana; gravel of Middle Terrace and overlying deposits
18. Gravel of High Terrace of White Volta, Yapei, about 25 m. above low water, capped by massive block-laterite. The gravel contained many rolled pebble-tools

38. Tomb with masonry pillars, Koumbi Saleh
   Photo by courtesy of I.F.A.N., Dakar

39. Entrenchment-ditch, Kokobin, Ghana. The black filling is surrounded by a broken white line for clarity.
   From Davies O., 1961 (3)

40. Cup and ring engraving on cliff on site of Akosombo Dam, Ghana, at 9 m. below normal low water. The cup may be natural, but the ring is artificially engraved round it

41. Bilega (rock-cut cistern), Butie, Ghana

42–43. Forikrom Rocks, Ghana; ceremonial amphitheatre with small caves in which are geometric rock-engravings

44. Forikrom, Ghana; small cave with rock-engravings beyond the amphitheatre

45. Bosumcheche, Ghana; cave with geometric rock-engravings

46. Krinjabo statuette, Ivory Coast
   Reproduced by permission of author from Holas, Arts de la Côte d'Ivoire, publ. Centre des Sciences humaines, Abidjan.

47 Kissi statuette, F. Guinea
   Photo supplied by Musée de l'Homme, Paris

48. Terracotta from site of funeral ceremonies, Ahinsan, Ashanti, Ghana; seventeenth century

49. Sudanic type of mosque, Mandare, Northern Ghana

50. Gold pectoral, Rao, Senegal
   From Man xliii (1943), no. 34, pl. C, by permission of the Royal Anthropological Institute

TOPOGRAPHICAL INDEX

Places within Africa

NOTE. The spelling of African names on modern British maps is fairly uniform, though there is a possibility that variations will be made by independent governments. That on French maps is much less uniform. For sheets issued I have followed the spelling of the recent 1:200,000 map of French West Africa; but for areas where the sheets of this series are not published, I have had to follow older maps whose spelling is often erratic, or the reports of field-workers whose spelling may be even more erratic. I have lately come across a few French sheets at 1:1,000,000, also recently issued. The canons of spelling of this series do not conform to those of the 1:200,000, and I have decided not to use its orthography at all.

It has not been possible to obtain the exact location of every place. Where a location has been possible within half a degree, the map-coordinates are given roughly, preceded by *c*. Where even this accuracy has been unobtainable, the region as well as the territory has been given.

Reference is to pages. A reference of the form 84n72 is to a note on the page. A number preceded by F is a figure, by P a plate.

ABBREVIATIONS OF AFRICAN TERRITORIES
MENTIONED

Al	Algeria	Gb	Gaboon	Rh	Rhodesia
An	Angola	Gh	Ghana	SA	South Africa
Ca	Cameroons	HV	Upper Volta	Se	Senegal
Cn	Canary Islands	IC	Ivory Coast	SL	Sierra Leone
Co	Congo	Ke	Kenya	SS	Spanish Sahara
CV	Cape Verd	Lb	Liberia	Su	Sudan
	Islands	Li	Libya	SW	South-West
Da	Dahomey	Ma	Mauritania		Africa
Eg	Egypt	Ml	Mali	Ta	Tanzania
Et	Ethiopia	Mo	Morocco	Tc	Tchad
FC	Congo (ex-	Mz	Mozambique	To	Togo
	French)	Ni	Nigeria	Tu	Tunis
FG	Guinea (ex-	Nr	Niger	UC	Ubangui-Chari
	French)	PG	Portuguese	Ug	Uganda
Ga	Gambia		Guinea	Za	Zambia

PLACE AND LAND	COORDINATES	REFERENCES
Abalessa: Al	22°53'N 4°50'E	249–50, 255
Abengourou: IC	6°42'N 3°27'W	P29
Abetifi: Gh	6°40'N 0°45'W	3, 187, 217, 287
Abezou: Nr	20°30'N 8°20'E	F46 3
Abidjan: IC	5°19'N 4°01'W	46
Abka: Su	21°50'N 31°12'E	80, 152
Aboadi: Gh	4°58'N 1°38'W	46
Abodum: Gh	6°10'N 0°49'W	288, 290
Abra: Gh	4°54'N 2°03'W	F55 12
Abubiasi: Gh	5°34'N 0°15'W	39, 46
Abuchen: Gh	5°51'N 0°39'W	53, F17 7
Accra: Gh	5°32'N 0°12'W	7, 39, 46, 53, 291, F25 3
Accra, Bishop's School: Gh	5°32'N 0°12'W	73
Accra Golfcourse: Gh	5°32'N 0°12'W	135
Accra Plains: Gh	c 6°N 0°W	5–7, 20, 117, 133, 135–6, 194, 208, 210, 217, 309
Achakar: Mo	35°46'N 5°57'W	174
Achegour: Nr	19°10'N 11°54'E	F61 5
Achimota: Gh	5°37'N 0°13'W	290
Achimota cricket-pitch: Gh	5°37'N 0°13'W	136, 212, 243, 299n20
Achimota, 12 The Follies: Gh	5°37'N 0°13'W	F68
Achimota, 7 Forest Site: Gh	5°37'N 0°13'W	F69 1
Achimota, Legon Road: Gh	5°38'N 0°13'W	F25 1
Adafer: Ma	c 19°N 9°W	232n150
Adiembra: Gh	6°14'N 2°14'W	72
Adiopodoume: IC	5°20'N 4°08'W	321n26
Adrar: Ma	20°–22°N 11°–14°W	177
Adrar Bous, lake-deposit: Nr	20°18'N 9°02'E	79
Adrar Bous, mountain-sites: Nr	20°20'N 9°03'E	80, 100, 156, 160, F40
Adrar Madet: Nr	18°40'N 10°25'E	170, 252, 279, F41
Adrar Zeline: Nr	19°50'N 8°03'E	F46 5
Adwuku, iron-age site: Gh	5°52'N 0°03'E	309, 321n30
Adwuku, mesolithic site: Gh	5°53'N 0°04'E	185–7, F52
Afram Plains: Gh	c 6°30'N 0°W	8, 108
Afrê–Boka: IC	6°45'N 5°02'W	308
Agadem: Nr	16°50'N 13°11'E	79
Agades: Nr	17°00'N 7°58'E	160, 266
Agadir: Mo	30°30'N 9°40'W	253
Agame Beme: Gh	6°50'N 0°15'E	P12
Agaouat: Nr	c 18°30'N 7°40'E	F46 4
Agboville: IC	5°55'N 4°15'W	290
Agisymba	—	248
Agona: Gh	4°54'N 1°58'W	287
Agoreke: Gh	6°40'N 0°09'E	56, 66, 138, F34

PL. 1 Painted cave, Oueyanko valley near Bamako, Mali

PL. 2 Equatorial forest from the hilltop-site of Ntirikurom, SW. Ghana

PL. 3 Hilltop-site of Akroso Beposo, Togoland, marked by a patch of forest in wooded savannah; seventeenth century

PL. 4 Gallery-forest in savannah, on River Dayi, Angeta, Togoland

PL. 5 Gorge of River Niger, Jebba, Nigeria

PL. 6 Grassy swamp without bushes in the Volta valley near the mouth of the
River Sheribong, probably marking a fossil lagoon of the period of the Low
Terrace; cp. Low Terrace in fig. 2

PL. 7 Coast at Axim, Ghana

↓B   ↓A

C→

PL. 8 Apam Promontory, Ghana, showing marine abrasion-platforms

Top of hill at 60 metres
A Shoulder at 55 metres, probably Beach I
B Shoulder at 33 metres, with similar level to right (not visible), perhaps Beach II
C Lower promontory with trading-castle, at 23 metres, probably Beach III

PL. 9 Savannah of the Accra Plains near margin of the forest, Kotoku, Ghana

PL. 10 Highland savannah, Bokkus, Northern Nigeria

PL. 11 Thorn-bush savannah on the inner silt-terrace of the Black Volta, Buipe, Ghana

PL. 12 Partly cleared forest with thick secondary undergrowth, Agame Beme, Togoland

PL. 13 Slope from River Ayensu, Okitsiu, Ghana, with rejuvenation-point of the 9-metre terrace (Low Terrace) in background

PL. 14 Hohoe, Ghana, 12-metre gravel of River Dayi (Low Terrace). Above the gravel is a Sangoan piece near the top of the laterite

PL. 15 Sand-dunes on southern edge of the Sahara, Mauritania, Draa Malichigdame.

PL. 16 Pebbles of Beach III, at about 23 metres S.L., Senya Beraku, Ghana

PL. 17 Edubia, Ghana; gravel of Middle Terrace and overlying deposits, see p. 72

PL. 18 Gravel of High Terrace of White Volta, Yapei, about 25 metres above low water, capped by massive block-laterite. The gravel contained many rolled pebble-tools

PL. 19 Oda, Ghana; gravel of Low Terrace of River Birim at 9 metres

PL. 20 Basal gravel of River Birim, Kibi, Ghana, overlain by silt-terrace

PL. 21 Lateritized basal gravel of White Volta, Lungbunga, Ghana. The gravel contains rolled pieces of Guinea Aterian

PL. 22 Cliff eroded into inner silt-terrace, Limbisi, Ghana. The topmost five metres are white silts, with a few quartz microliths on top. Below are sandbanks and soft sands and muds with organic remains

PL. 23 Limbisi, mud not far above low water, containing layer of compressed leaves and twigs

PL. 24 Limbisi, current-bedded sands below peaty mud

PL. 25 Gravel of Low Terrace, Fétékro, Ivory Coast

PL. 26 Hohoe, stone-line carrying Middle Stone Age flakes near
surface of laterite

PL. 27 Pebbles of Beach IV, Asokro-chona, Ghana, covered with a crust in which lay unrolled Sangoan tools (from above, so that the beach-exposure resembles a wall on the slope of the railway-cutting)

PL. 28 Kuradaso, Ghana; M.S.A. flake (marked by top of ruler) on consolidated lateritic rubble

PL. 29 Abengourou, Ivory Coast, in forest; stones mixed with the soil without a defined stone-line

PL. 30 Angeta, block-laterite overlying the gravel of the Low Terrace and the slope from the Middle Terrace

PL. 31 Akayao, Ghana; artefact on lateritic rubble

PL. 32 Jigbe, Sangoan pick in stone-line near surface of gritty sand

PL. 33 Patakro, stone-line with microliths, marking the Post-pluvial III surface

PL. 34 Section at Little Legon on the edge of a small filled gulley

A Basal rubble which should carry Sangoan
B Stone-line of M.S.A. surface (marked by spectacle-case)
C Line of rolled lateritic nodules with microlithic flakes (marked by ruler)
D Iron Age sherds (level eroded on section at this point)

PL. 35 Terracotta head,
Benin, of same style as
the earliest bronze heads

PL. 36 Terracotta head,
Jemaa, of style of the
Nok-culture

PL. 37 Fragmentary terracotta head from shrine of Olokun Walode, Ife, probably XIII–XV centuries

PL. 38 Tomb with masonry pillars, Koumbi Saleh

PL. 39 Entrenchment-ditch, Kokobin, Ghana. The black filling is surrounded by a broken white line for clarity

PL. 40 Cup and ring engraving on cliff on site of Akosombo Dam, Ghana, at 9 metres below normal low water. The cup may be natural, but the ring is artificially engraved round it

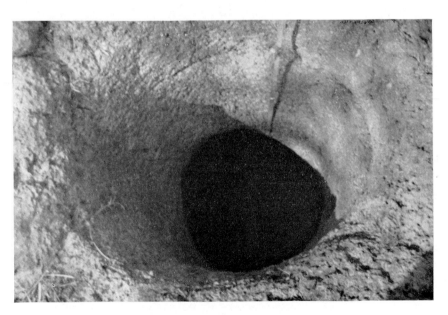

PL. 41 Bilega (rock-cut cistern), Butie, Ghana

PL. 42–43 Forikrom Rocks, Ghana; ceremonial amphitheatre with small caves
in which are geometric rock-engravings

PL. 44 Forikrom, Ghana; small cave with rock-engravings beyond the amphitheatre

PL. 45 Bosumcheche, Ghana; cave with geometric rock-engravings

PL. 46 Krinjabo statuette, Ivory Coast

PL. 47 Kissi statuette, F. Guinea

PL. 48 Terracotta from site of funeral ceremonies, Ahinsan, Ashanti, Ghana; seventeenth century

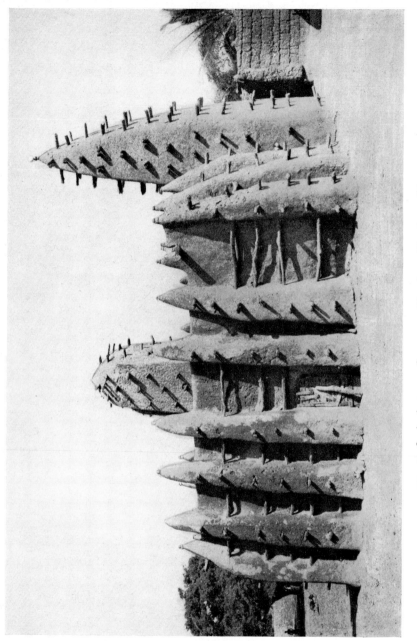

PL. 49 Sudanic type of mosque, Mandare, Northern Ghana

PL. 50 Gold pectoral, Rao, Senegal

* Perhaps misprint for Anefok, 19°07'N 8°15'E

SUBJECT INDEX

including places outside Africa